CANNED GOODS
as
Caviar

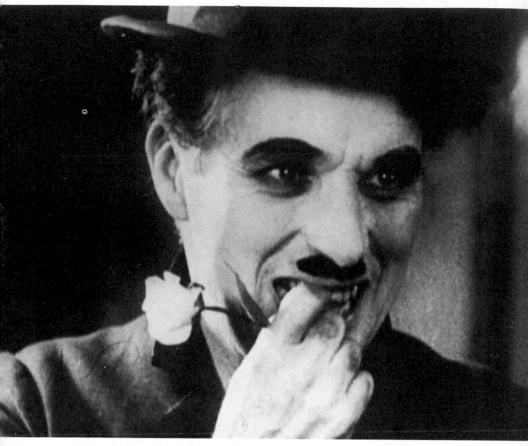

The final close-up. Charles Chaplin. (*City Lights,* United Artists, 1931. The Museum of Modern Art/Film Stills Archive.)

CANNED GOODS as Caviar

American
Film Comedy of the
1930s

Gerald Weales

The University of Chicago Press
Chicago and London

GERALD WEALES is professor of English at the University of Pennsylvania. He is the author of numerous books on drama, a novel, and two children's books. His theater reviews appear regularly in *Commonweal*.

The University of Chicago Press, Chicago 60637
The University of Chicago Press, Ltd., London
© 1985 by Gerald Weales
All rights reserved. Published 1985
Printed in the United States of America
94   93   92   91   90   89   88   87   86   85   54321

Library of Congress Cataloging in Publication Data

Weales, Gerald Clifford, 1925–
    Canned goods as caviar.

    Bibliography: p.
    Includes index.
    1. Comedy films—United States—History and
criticism.   I. Title.
PN1995.9.C55.W4   1985   791.43′09′0917   84-28132
ISBN 0-226-87663-2
ISBN 0-226-87664-0 (pbk.)

For
NORA
who prefers
I Know Where I'm Going

"What you say is rather profound, and probably erroneous."
—the doctor in *Heart of Darkness*

Contents

Acknowledgments

I want to thank the John Simon Guggenheim Memorial Foundation for a grant that allowed me to finish this book; the Rockefeller Foundation for a stay at the Bellagio Study and Conference Center, where I wrote the first drafts of chapters 2 and 3; the Corporation of Yaddo for a visit during which I did a first version of chapter 1;

for access to films I needed to see, Charles Silver and the Museum of Modern Art Department of Film; Emily Sieger and the Motion Picture Division of the Library of Congress; the UCLA Film Archives; Peter Van De Kamp and his fine Chaplin collection; the George Eastman House;

for help in my research, the University of Pennsylvania Library, particularly Jane Bryan and her colleagues in Reference and Mary Jackson and the Interlibrary Loan staff; the New York Public Library Performing Arts Research Center at Lincoln Center; the Free Library of Philadelphia;

The Pennsylvania Gazette, which printed versions of chapters 1 and 2;

and all the people who helped me by giving me information and misinformation, by lending me books and material, by providing hospitable shelter while I was writing or doing research: Val Almendarez (of the Academy of Motion Picture Arts and Sciences), Joseph Blotner, John Bright, Jon Cohen, Mary Corliss, Alice R. Cotten (of the University of North Carolina Library), Malcolm Cowley, Ernest, Alex, Blaise and Columbus Dupuy, Andrew Feinberg, Stephen Goff, Glynne Hiller, Anne Hopkins, John and Janice Kuhn, Nora Magid, Rose

Magid, James B. Meriwether, Bruce Montgomery, Robert J. Nelson, Jim Parish, David Raksin, Anick Scouten, Joe and Joan Silverman, Robert Lewis Shayon, Anthony Slide, André von Gronicka, Meg Walters, Mary L. Weales, Gertrude Zahler. I owe anyone whose name I have inadvertently left off this list a box of popcorn for his next trip to the movies.

Introduction

"Cinema appreciation seems a little far-fetched for a product that is distributed like canned goods. It must be rather like going to school to learn the aesthetic differences between a Pontiac and an Oldsmobile." The speaker was William A. Wellman; the year was 1939; the occasion was an answer to the question "Why Teach Cinema?" The director's doubts are understandable (scholars of batting averages are created spontaneously, not trained), but he must have known, even in 1939, that the aesthetics of differentiation among automobiles was a major concern of curbside America. So was cinema appreciation, although those of us gathered over milk shakes to dissect or exclaim over *Beau Geste* (the latest Wellman film, although we would have called it the latest Gary Cooper movie) would never have used so snarky a phrase. That belonged to the schools where movies were just beginning to be taken seriously and, too often, taken out of the contexts in which they were created and shown.

Now that film courses are an expected part of the curriculum of schools at every level, from grade school to university, Wellman's remarks have an ancient-history sound about them, self-deprecation as false prophecy. Yet the "canned goods" concept of the American commercial film has affected much of the critical writing on the subject. Given the assembly-line production methods of the old studio system, it is difficult to pinpoint the artist whose presence would presumably turn consumer goods into art. "With rare exceptions," Josef von Sternberg wrote, "the making of a motion picture is considered to be a collective enterprise guided by an individual who needs to know no more about the ultimate product than that he has an unalterable conviction that his belief will be rewarded with fame and fortune." Sternberg's quarrels with that "collective enterprise" were international, but his sentence does highlight the perennial Hollywood question, which was never "Is it art?" but "Will it sell?" In the last twenty years, some critics have circumvented that fact of Hollywood life by separating certain figures—directors usually—from their working situation and, on the assumption that they had either complete control of their movies or personalities strong enough to dominate the collective work, have treated single films as part of a total *oeuvre*. There is value in such studies, but there are dangers as well. As in the literary equivalent of such an approach, the individual works are often made to fit a generalized aesthetic and ideational concept of the artist, and the particular film is judged not on its own strengths or weaknesses but on how closely it conforms to the preconceived pattern.

The more pervasive critical approach to American movies embraces rather than tries to escape the "canned goods" aspect of the subject. The movie, like any other popular art, is obviously a reflection of the culture which produced it and which enjoys it. For that reason, films can be examined as artifacts that illustrate American attitudes toward women, blacks, doctors, teachers, artists, capitalists, radicals—name your preoccupation. At their best, such studies can illuminate the movies as well as the overt subject to which the borrowed film images contribute. For the most part, however, whether the approach is objective (count the women and clock the results) or subjective (find the women who prove the attitudinal assumptions of the collector), the final result is likely to be a catalogue, however elegantly presented, in which the great number of movies cited make extended consideration of the films impossible.

Other approaches—the thematic, the generic—have their built-in limitations (the square peg–round hole dilemma), but if I continue to tick off the shortcomings of one critical method after another, readers may begin to suspect that I have a system of my own to peddle. I do not. Occasionally in the pages that follow, I will sound like a reluctant auteurist or an unwilling sociologist, I will talk about theme or genre, I will look at a single frame with the intensity but without the vocabulary of the structuralist. I am a methodology pack rat, an unrepentant eclecticist. The closest I come to a system is a suspicion of systems.

What I have done in this book is to choose—not exactly at random— twelve American comedies of the 1930s, and I have tried to let the films themselves dictate my approach in each case. Although all twelve of the movies can still be—frequently are—watched with pleasure, I do not treat them as timeless art works. I see them as products of the decade in which they were made, which means that I sometimes discuss politics, social assumptions, contemporary trivia which are not immediately obvious nor of particular interest to audiences which, fifty years later, still find the comedies funny. I also accept that they were put together through the "collective enterprise" that Sternberg deplored, which means that, although I sometimes suggest a dominant figure, I focus on any of the contributors—directors, writers, performers, and sometimes producers, composers, cameramen, editors—who seem to have had a visible hand in the final product. Although I often give my attention to technique, in nontechnical language, I share the assumption of Luis Buñuel that "There are qualities in a film that can be of more interest than technique." The original impulse toward the book was simply a desire to look closely and to discuss at length and without preconceptions a number of films that I admire—to treat Wellman's "canned goods" as caviar.

CAVEAT LECTOR I. I went to the Honolulu Academy of Arts one evening in 1981 to see *Best Boy* (1979), Ira Wohl's impressive documentary about a retarded man learning to care for himself outside the confines of his protective family. The audience was not the usual one at film showings, filled as it was with professionals more interested in the subject than the medium, but I was startled when a young man, looking at a brochure for a coming series on MGM, could not recognize John Garfield. After I had identified the actor, he pointed elsewhere on the page and asked, "And who's this woman?" It was Greta Garbo. And he was not joking.

His question stayed in my mind as I wrote or rewrote paragraphs on actors like Dewey Robinson and Fritz Feld, performers whom many regular moviegoers of the time knew as faces, not names. "I do not see that there is any other way to discuss most movies except in terms of personalities," Pare Lorentz wrote in 1930. Although his remark was simply a lead-in to an attack on Garbo in *Anna Christie*, the sentence contains a truth about the films of that decade. The texture of 1930s American movies—particularly comedies like those discussed in this book—depends heavily on the performers, the character people even more than the stars. The critical legitimacy of my concern with supporting players like Robinson and Feld can hardly be denied, but in going through my presentational paces I risk sounding like a movie buff. Ugly word—it always suggests waxing floors to me. The line between the buff and the scholar is a fine one, but it lies somewhere in that gray area in which the buff resents any intrusion of significance into his enthusiasm and in which the scholar suspects the buff of amassing vast amounts of information as a way of disguising an essentially trivial approach to his material. Since I use both buffs and scholars in this book (let the people I quote choose their own labels), I turn my back on buffdom not for its triviality but because it is awash with nostalgia. A consideration of any popular art can become an occasion to return to one's youth, one's childhood, or if the critic is too young to someone else's youth and childhood, a golden age more gratifying than the present. Although my fondness for the films I discuss and my affection for the men and women who played in them will be obvious to anyone who reads this book, my concern—here, at least—is for the films and the performers, not for the boy who spent so many hours in the Auditorium, the Vaudette and the Lyric in Connersville, Indiana. At this point, I should quote someone impressive like the Nobel-winning poet Odysseus Elytis ("I wish nostalgia had a body so that I could push it out of the window!"), but it is more appropriate to turn to Groucho Marx: "I'm allergic to nostalgia."

CAVEAT LECTOR II. Once years ago, I met Rosalind Ivan at a party in New York. She seemed to have some of the dottiness of the characters she often played and none of the malevolence of her nagging wife in *The Suspect* (1944). She had recently finished her scenes in *Ivy* (1947), a thriller starring Joan Fontaine, and she was so entranced with the fragments in which she appeared, she said, that she marched right out to the library to get the Marie Belloc Lowndes novel on which the film was based so that she could find out how the story ended. An exemplary anecdote. Character actors usually knew nothing about a movie other than their often very brief scenes, and they were frequently shooting more than one film at once, even working in several studios at the same time. Writers whose names appear together in the credits often worked alone, sometimes never even saw one another. Directors usually disappeared after the final take, leaving the movie to the good offices of the film editor, the producer, and the distribution mavens. One of the remarkable things about the films discussed in this book—given this bits-and-pieces approach to art—is that they are such finished works. My appreciation of that quality in the pictures is so strong that I may occasionally sound as though the many collaborators on a movie were collaborators in fact and not piece-workers. Purists deplore art by committee, but these films are art and the committees never even met as a whole.

CAVEAT LECTOR III. "Like everyone," James Stewart said in his autobiography, "I am sometimes tempted by wishful thinking to embroider the facts." He was recalling his changing reactions to the compliments on his ability as a skier that he received after the release of *The Mortal Storm* (1940). No skier at all, he at first admitted the fact, giving credit to the man who filled in for him in the escape scene. Later, he modestly shared the praise with his double. Finally, he simply basked in his presumed skill.

Stewart's story, which is really Pete Martin's story since this was an "as told to" autobiography, is a nicely designed illustration of the becoming self-mockery that is part of the actor's charm. It is also a diversionary tactic which in its straightforward way keeps us from questioning too carefully the anecdotes, the facts, the remembered remarks that fill the rest of the pages. Since one of the things I try to do in the chapters that follow is to define the special quality of the figures I discuss, I use a great many quotations by or about the people in question, which means that I deal in fiction. Literary scholars who make use of memoirs, letters, diaries are used to this practice, but my sources present some special problems.

The show-business biography, whether auto- or not, is probably no more untrustworthy than the more temperate accounts of politicians, business leaders, writers, and artists. "Memory, my dear Cecily, is the diary that we all carry about with us," said Miss Prism in *The Importance of Being Earnest*, and her charge answered, "Yes, but it usually chronicles the things that have never happened, and couldn't possibly have happened." Imperfect memory is regularly cozened by perfectly understandable desires to make oneself more admirable, more interesting, less culpable, less self-absorbed. The lives of show-business worthies, whether of the genteel turn-of-the-century notes-from-the-green-room variety or the current scandalous confession, tend to be either biographies patched together from the reminiscences of the subject and his friends/colleagues/enemies, or autobiographies, written by an acknowledged ghost whose sense of the marketability of the manuscript haunts its authenticity. "Do you want it accurate or in the stores?" Ferris Mack is supposed to have asked Dinah Shore. There are exceptions, but for the most part these works consist of anecdotes, told and retold in endless variations; conversations repeated verbatim years after they were held and by people who often cannot put down the easily verifiable dates of films and the correct spelling of names; and the most jazzily inept prose this side of self-help manuals.

Interviews are only as trustworthy as the interviewers. Now that we have the tape recorder, we have a better chance of getting the real statement, word for word, but even these are subject to the intrusions of the transcriber and the editor. Contemporary interviews are often valuable indications of the way a performer or director was perceived in his own time, but if you believe the lines that newspapers put into the mouths of Mae West and W. C. Fields, you probably also believe the story of King Alfred and the burned cakes. Reporters, as anyone who has ever been interviewed will tell you, are largely incapable of and indifferent to the correct transcription of remarks. That occupational deficiency was heightened in the 1930s by the emphasis on the news story as story (the legacy of *The Front Page*) and by the special talents of feature writers who dealt with screen personalities and who saw their columns as a branch of the entertainment industry. Add, too, that many newspapers simply printed material that came directly from the publicity offices of the studios, including imaginary interviews full of neatly turned phrases that never sullied the lips of the star quoted. As for the fan magazines, those treasure houses of a Hollywood life that had only a minimal connection with the real world in which the filmmakers lived, they provide some of the most useful quotations in the book. Read them for their truth, not their accuracy.

Here ends the warning on the label. Open the can and sample the caviar.

1

CITY LIGHTS

· 1931 ·

He mentions things in my pictures
that I never remembered putting there.
—Charles Chaplin,
My Trip Abroad

When *City Lights* opened in London in 1931, the reviewer on *The Spectator* complained about "the thinness of the story" which he found "too ordinary, in the hackneyed American manner, complete to grey-haired mammy in the background." An English reviewer might fail to understand that Florence Lee's stock grandmother could not be a "mammy" in any American sense of the word, but he should certainly have recognized that the story is hackneyed in a good old English way. After the fashion of *Jim: A Romance of Cockayne*, for instance. Back in 1903, Charlie Chaplin, then fourteen, had played a "cheeky, honest, loyal, self-reliant, philosophic" newsboy in the premiere of the H. A. Saintsbury melodrama. His description of the play in *My Autobiography* turns up so many similarities to *City Lights*—the flower girl heroine, the sickness that precipitates the crisis, the hero falsely accused of a crime—that one might suspect his memory (after all he thought the play was called *Jim, the Romance of a Cockney*) if contemporary reviews did not confirm his sense of the plot.

Chaplin's unembarrassed attraction to sentimental melodrama (*The Kid*, 1921; *The Circus*, 1928) might justify *The Spectator*'s attack on *City Lights* if the film were only the story of the poor little blind girl and how she grew. As far back as 1922, in an article in the *Ladies' Home Journal*, Chaplin said[1] that "Most of the people who make pictures . . . make the mistake of wanting too much plot," and he went on to speak of "a slim structure or a sequence of scenes" which became his excuse for "action

------

The newsboy retrieves the tramp's cane. Robert Parrish, Charles Chaplin. (*City Lights*, United Artists, 1931. The Museum of Modern Art/Film Stills Archive.)

and business which will entertain the audience apart from the story that is to be developed." On the surface this passage might seem to give aid and comfort to those Chaplin critics who persist in seeing his films as a string of discrete units, of sequences—whether gag or schmaltz—which carry their own aesthetic value apart from the film as a whole. Chaplin's sentimental melodrama, then, or Chaplin's inspired clowning. The *Journal* piece was written after *The Kid*, however, and surely the most casual or the most critical viewer of that film recognizes that it conveys some quality—an emotion, an idea—more sophisticated than either its saccharine story or its marvelous comic bits. I read the *Journal* passage as a variation on a remark about Chaplin that Meyerhold made in 1936, "The plot of a particular picture did not interest him as much as its associations, the sidepaths along which the spectator might go to find the true meaning of the film." By 1922— certainly by 1931—Chaplin had learned to use the corny old plots that he loved with a dexterity that approached his mastery of his hat and his cane, just as he had come to see that his gags lost none of their power to provoke laughter by being put in the service of a theme or a dramatic action more complex than a borrowed melodrama plot.

In "The Chaplin Buncombe," George Jean Nathan's famous attack on the comedian as a good clown gone wrong, the critic correctly traces Chaplin's sentimental roots, but he stays on the surface of *City Lights* when he describes the "thematic thread of pathos" as "blindness which imagines it beholds beauty and, with the return of vision, finds to its own and another's heartache only the commonplace and the sadly ugly." Nathan's rather grand sentence is accurate after its fashion, but it does put the flower girl center stage (screen) and that misplaces the important emphasis in the film. Chaplin made that point—at least by implication—to young Alistair Cooke, who had come to Hollywood in 1934 to help Chaplin write a script on Napoleon for a film that would never be made. In *Six Men*, Cooke, who has either good notes or a phenomenal memory, recalls Chaplin's advising him to find a small incident to fix each of the characters around Napoleon: "They stay the same. You know them every time they appear. This is no different from the characters who surround 'the little fellow'. *He's* the one we develop." There are three leading characters in *City Lights*—the tramp, the flower girl, the millionaire—but there is only one protagonist. The millionaire varies his attitude toward the tramp according to his degree of sobriety, but he undergoes no recognizable change; he simply disappears from the film after the tramp runs off with the money, his plot having served its comedic and thematic purpose. The flower girl is cured of her blindness, actually and, in the last scene, metaphorically, but her final, "Yes, I can see now" would contain only the pathetic irony Nathan found in it if it were simply the culmination of her story. That last scene is the necessary conclusion to the central action of the film—as the final close-up is the perfect visual coda—because *City Lights*, like all the Chaplin films that preceded it, is about the tramp and what befell him. "*He's* the one we develop."

City Lights is the most complex, the most painful treatment of a theme that emerged early in Chaplin's work and became a major preoccupation of his 1920s films—the physical and psychological consequences of any attachment to another creature, to a dog (*A Dog's Life*, 1918), a child (*The Kid*) or a damsel in distress (from *The Tramp*, 1915, to *Limelight*, 1952). In one sense, this is simply standard comic practice, the placing of the farceur in a situation which creates its particular set of obstacles ("all my pictures are built around the idea of getting me into trouble," Chaplin wrote in 1918), but the development of the tramp character over the years increased the sense of risk whenever Charlie was forced to make room for another person within his self-sufficient world. In a marvelous scene in *The Kid*, having failed to dump the child in the irate woman's baby carriage, he sits on the curb, stares at the sewer grate, lifts it tentatively and hesitates just long enough for the audience to feel the black comedy beat of horror in the joke; then he shrugs, closes the grate, and begins the process of transformation from the tramp dandy we first saw strolling the alley to the exhausted figure who, having failed to find the stolen child, moves with the familiar Chaplin walk, but slowed now as though the character were crippled with pain. This is no place for a catalogue of the Chaplin films, but consider how in *A Dog's Life* the tramp is chased by a pack of dogs for Scraps's sake, menaced by thugs for Edna's; how in *The Pilgrim* (1923), he must confront his old prison mate to protect Edna; how in *The Gold Rush* (1925), he fights Jack and almost loses his pants for Georgia; how in *The Circus* he shares the abuse from Merna's father. Most of these films finally gloss over the pain that necessarily accompanies connection by providing happy endings or, in *The Circus*, a final gesture that suggests a restoration of the original figure. Only *The Pilgrim* is an exception. As it ends, the tramp races along the border, one foot in Mexico, one in the States, menaced by gunshot on one side, the promise of jail on the other. This broadly comic finish suggests, at a considerable distance, the ambiguity in the famous final close-up in *City Lights*.

There is an ominous note sounding through the paragraph above, a hint that the tramp figure, suffering (however comically) for others, may be on the point of apotheosis. I want to close my ears to that sound, protect myself from the siren call that might lead me the way of the French critics. Some of the best criticism of *City Lights* has been written by Pierre Leprohon, but he finds "a sort of divine power" in Charlot and sees him as the savior of both the girl and the millionaire: "And because he is like a god according to the messianic principle, he must lose his life to save it." Guy Perol is even more specific: "It is by love that Charlot, carelessly free, saves a man and a woman by losing himself, as Christ—let us venture the parallel—saved mankind by dying on the cross." Filmmakers are no more invulnerable to Christ figures than playwrights and poets are (see the discussion of *Mr. Deeds Goes to Town*, chap. 7, pp. 182–83), but I resist Chaplin's tramp in that role because what he undergoes in *City Lights* seems to me preeminently human. The film is not about a pantomime Jesus. It is about me. And you. Or at least about a tramp who embodies the contradictory impulses toward and away from community that seem to plague us all. The best approach to *City Lights* is through its protagonist; the necessary first question asks, who is this man.

There are a host of critics who assume that the tramp in *City Lights*, like all the manifestations of Charlie, is Charles Chaplin, the filmmaker who cannot stop talking about himself. "The story of The Kid is in reality a chapter from the life of Charles Spencer Chaplin," writes Carlyle R. Robinson, who was Chaplin's publicity man from 1917 to 1931. "I have Charlie's own word for this." Presumably he means that Charlie, at seven, was torn away from his mum and sent to the poorhouse. Anyone who favors the simplistic biographical approach of Robinson will remember that Chaplin began work on *City Lights* as early as 1928, the year his mother died, the year following the ugly divorce from Lita Grey. There are spiritual and financial pains enough in these two events to school the tramp in the dangers of attachment. The more sophisticated biographical critics go not for the specific events in Chaplin's life but for a generalized motivational line, as Gilbert Seldes does when he reduces *The Gold Rush* and *The Circus* to revelatory one-liners: "the story of a man who found wealth and missed happiness"; "the story of a clown who was funny until he was told he was funny." Waldo Frank, whom Chaplin called "the first to write seriously about me," develops an elaborate work–life analogy in his 1929 *Scribner's* piece which finds that "The theme of the Chaplin picture is Chaplin himself, in relation (opposition) to the world." Parker Tyler, in full flight in *Chaplin: Last of the Clowns*, mixes psychology, symbolism, literary-theatrical allusion, and elegant writing to find "the epos, or essentially biographic pattern, in the comic history of Charlie, the tramp hero," and uses *City Lights* to illustrate the conflict within Chaplin between the child-poet (the tramp) and the power figure (the millionaire). Artists inevitably use themselves and all their friends and relations; their thematic preoccupations obviously reflect their offstage lives. There is, then, more biography than theology in *City Lights*, but I am wary of this critical method even though playing with psychobiography can lead to amusing essays (else what's a Parker Tyler for) and the visible tension between a creator and his work provides a useful starting point for any understanding of the creative process. If I were writing a biography of Chaplin, I would certainly turn to *City Lights* for clues to the comedian's state of mind and heart between 1928 and 1931. My concern here is *City Lights* for its own sake—or for the viewer's—and that means that I must look elsewhere to find the tramp.

Chaplin's tramp had been a familiar figure since 1914, long before his narrow shoulders had to carry the burden of mythical allusion and spiritual/social significance. There is a passage in *My Autobiography*, a marvelous piece of retrospective fakery, in which Chaplin puts on his famous costume for the first time and a character emerges on the spot. "You know this fellow is many-sided," he has himself explaining to Mack Sennett, "a tramp, a gentleman, a poet, a dreamer, a lonely fellow, always hopeful of romance and adventure." Sennett somehow failed to remember it that way. In *The King of Comedy* he retells (through Chester Conklin) the more persistent and more popular account of the invention of the costume, the one in which it was pieced together from the wardrobe of other Keystone comics—Fatty Arbuckle's pants, Ford Sterling's shoes. This story has no greater claim on truth than Chaplin's memory, but it has the virtue of allowing the tramp to be born in a comic context from which he can gradually emerge into the inimitable figure he became. The standard practice in histories of Chaplin's work is to trace that emergence film by film, detecting the exact point where a new element was added, as Theodore Huff does in *Charlie Chaplin* when he says, here he introduced *satire*, here *pathos*, here *fantasy*, here *irony*. Chaplin's growing sophistication in the use of his tramp figure upset some critics who suspected him of being seduced by concepts; Robert E. Sherwood, who was later to turn into a Broadway-serious playwright himself, is an example of this group in his complaint that *The Gold Rush* showed that Chaplin had "listened too much to the depressing advice of those professional highbrows who are always urging him to play 'Hamlet.'" Convince an inspired practitioner that he is an artist—so goes the conventional wisdom—and he will hang himself from an easel; that was apparently what happened to Harry Langdon. But Chaplin was no Langdon. It is true that he was celebrated by artists early in his career—by Yvan Goll in *Chaplinade* (1920), by Hart Crane in "Chaplinesque" (1921), by Léger, who designed an animated Charlot to introduce *Le Ballet Mécanique* (1924)—and that he was lectured by critics like Stark Young (see his 1922 "Dear Mr. Chaplin" column), but the comedian was never the simple funnyman whom admirers like Sherwood wanted to protect. As early as 1915, he was discussing his comic method in the pages of *The Theatre*, and through Harry C. Carr, who contributed a four-part interview-biography to *Photoplay*, he indicated his awareness of what has become a commonplace of Chaplin criticism—that pathos first entered the canon in *The Tramp*. Accident may have had much to do with the birth of Charlie, but his development was clearly a conscious process for Chaplin.

The protagonist of *City Lights* is, then, an established mask, but it is one that had already been decorated with fifteen years of critical graffiti when the film appeared, and there have been fifty years of evocations of Pucks and Pans and Pierrots since then. The trick is to sort through the detritus of little fellows and immortal tramps, of clown princes and kings of tragedy,[2] and find the image that best suits a particular film. For *City Lights*, I turn to Winston Churchill, who was not thinking of that film at all when he placed Chaplin's tramp in the tradition of the "American hobo" who "was not so much an outcast from society as a rebel against it. . . . He hated the routine of regular employment and loved the changes and chances of the road." It was probably Chaplin's recognition of the strength of the hobo impulse in his tramp that explains his attraction to Jim Tully, who worked for him briefly in the mid-1920s. "Two beggars, Jim," Chaplin is supposed to have said by way of greeting, a reference to Tully's *Beggars of Life* (1924), an account of his own hobo adventures which reflects a degree of romanticism, cruelty, and chicanery not beyond Chaplin's tramp. The most persistent note in Tully's book is one of separation, the hobo's conscious desire not to be tied to place or job or other person. It is a familiar note in Chaplin's films as well. That final shot of the tramp alone—lonely, perhaps, but free at last—is so celebrated that lovers of that image conveniently forget all the happy endings. Not an ending in *City Lights*, but a beginning.

If *City Lights* is to be the story of a free man's becoming prisoner to his best impulses toward others (he said, reducing the film to a Seldes one-liner), the character's separation needs to be established as the film commences. Since that quality is already familiar in Chaplin's tramp (visually in the wonderfully dismissive back-kick with which he disposes of unwanted cigarette butts, crumpled paper, any prop that might become an embarrassing attachment), the job is already half done when the character appears. Even so, it was Chaplin's customary practice to reestablish the figure with each film, to provide a brief scene—sometimes no more than a gesture—in which the audience is reminded or, if necessary, told for the first time just what kind of fellow this tramp is. In *The Kid*, for instance, the introduction takes place through the insouciance of the opening stroll, the rapidity with which Charlie regains his aplomb in the face of flying garbage, the elegance with which he pulls off his fingerless gloves, the delicacy with which he chooses a butt from his sardine-can cigarette case. Chaplin is much more deliberate in *City Lights*; he uses the first three sequences to define the character. If an audience were to respond to the pain as well as the joy of his instant infatuation with the blind girl, they would have to understand what he had to lose through the encounter.

The Spectator reviewer with whom this chapter began found the opening scene, one of the few things he liked in the film, "a deadly stroke of pure satire." The sequence has always appealed to those who see Chaplin as the archetypal little man facing the Establishment. The speeches catch the perfect note of civic foolishness. By substituting a kazoo for the human voice,[3] Chaplin indicates what anyone who has half listened to a presidential address knows, that official oratory is a matter of rhythm and intonation, not content. The pomposity of the occasion is emphasized by the physical presence of the dignitaries, particularly that of Henry Bergman, whose bulk had been one of Chaplin's best props since 1916. As the oration ends ("To the people of the city we donate this Monument: 'Peace and Prosperity'"), the unveiling reveals that one of the people has actually accepted the donation, that the tramp lies sleeping in the lap of the female central figure, and official benevolence turns into official outrage. Commentators like Jean Mitry, for whom the statue shows "capitalist power represented in an absurd allegory," have always made much of the monument itself. A piece of conventional public sculpture, somewhat in the fashion of Paul Manship, it can serve as a symbol, but for me it has always been less a representative statue than a practicable one: a lap to lie in, a sword to hang on, a hand to sit on, another hand to provide a monumental nose-thumb. Satirical the scene is, but not purely so, and the statue becomes the prop that shifts the focus from satire in which the emphasis is on others to character presentation in which the tramp is the center of attention. The scene makes a mockery of the platitudes of public occasion, but its real business is to establish the tramp not simply as outside that world, but comfortably outside it, willing to use what is has to offer, but unwilling to be sucked in by its demands, not so much defying it as dismissing it.

This is clear from our first sight of the tramp. We (the camera) stand with the crowd, looking past the official party at the tiny figure in the lap of the giant statue, his black costume sullying the purity of all that whiteness. In *My Autobiography*, Chaplin describes a scene in *Skating*

(I assume he is remembering *The Rink* [1916], by the title of the Karno sketch which was one of its sources) in which, having dumped a great many people, Charlie moves to the rear of the rink, "becoming a very small figure in the background . . . funnier than he would have been in a close-up." That shot was not in *The Rink* the last time I saw it, which does not mean that it is not in some copies of the film, but even if the shot existed only in Chaplin's imagination that would not invalidate the effectiveness of the bit he describes. The joke depends on keeping all eyes on a tiny point in a large field, the comic fly in an expanse of ointment. If one wanted to hang on tightly to the social satire in the scene, I suppose much could be made of the little man caught in the cold embrace of bigness, but there is no menace in the scene—simply a perverse sense of the tramp's being at home. This becomes obvious as a new camera setup, closer in, lets us focus on the man and the statue. We get his awakening—the scratch, the stretch, the ritual of private behavior. As he becomes aware of his onscreen audience, he works to extricate himself from the situation, a fumbling performance in which he tips his hat indiscriminately to the shouting humans and the inanimate figures. "I entered and stumbled over the foot of a lady," he says in *My Autobiography*, describing the celebrated hotel-lobby routine with which he is supposed first to have won the approbation of his Keystone colleagues. "I turned and raised my hat apologetically, then turned and stumbled over a cuspidor, then turned and raised my hat to the cuspidor." An old Chaplin speciality, the gesture takes on new strength in *City Lights*. The tramp conveys not traditional comic confusion, but something like self-absorption. Even his very correct response to the national anthem feeds the image of his separateness. The maneuver that presses the statue's thumb to the tramp's nose, an echo of a gesture that goes back to Keystone days (see the nose-thumbing stills in Denis Gifford's *Chaplin*), may be a comment by Chaplin, but it is an accident to the tramp. There is no need of so overt a response to the officials; for them, there is desecration in his presence, malevolence in the time he takes to remove himself. The tramp goes, not in panic and trailing no clouds of regret.

In the next sequence the tramp confronts the teasing newsboys and holds his own. That their taunts have little effect on him is clear in the way he dismisses them with a snap of his fingers, having first grandly removed the finger of his glove to get the proper resonance. Although it is obvious that the tramp is a man who is not having any of the newsboys' nonsense, the scene is less important for its own sake than as a contrast to the one at the end of the film. Just out of prison, completely defeated, he again meets the boys. The best that he can do is make a tentative admonitory gesture when he is attacked with a peashooter. One of the boys grabs at the shirttail sticking through a hole in his pants, tearing off a piece of it, and, although he snatches back the rag, touching it to his nose, tucking it into his handkerchief pocket, the lassitude in his reactions makes him a butt as he certainly was not in the early scene. He has become a comic figure to the flower girl, who can now see. The Chaplin critics whom I have read on *City Lights* understandably focus in this scene on the tramp, but there is another element in it that I find attractive. I may be reading something into the newsboys that is not there, but I sense in them a feeling of disappointment at having lost their spirited antagonist of the first scene. This may reflect my own response to what the tramp has become, but it is also a hangover from the scene in which the boys witness his arrest. Their excitement is plainly pro-tramp (or at least anti-policeman) and, when the tramp drops his cane during the encounter, the boy (Robert Parrish) who snatched the cane in the first scene now picks it up and hands it back to him. The newsboys are among the few characters in the film who become something other than props, and one of their functions is surely to testify to the tramp as outsider, a target but an admirable one.

In the third introductory sequence, the tramp, as connoisseur, stops outside a shopwindow to examine the statue of a nude woman. As he steps back and forth, ostensibly in search of the perfect perspective, a freight elevator rises and descends, managing to be flush with the sidewalk whenever his foot comes down on what, seconds before, had been a gaping hole. A typical teaser gag, fondling the audience's expectation of disaster, it would have ended, had it been played conventionally, with the clown's plunging out of sight. In *Behind the Screen* (1916), with relentless predictability, one member of the cast after another falls through the stage trap. Here, however, the tramp simply steps on the elevator as it starts to go down, and then scrambles to safety and another familiar gag. Now the irate citizen, the tramp threatens the worker until, as the elevator rises, he realizes that the man towers above him and quickly makes his getaway. The tramp here is essentially the same man we have seen in the two earlier sequences, but this is also a transitional scene, a hint of what is to come. The tramp becomes preoccupied with a woman who, being a statue, is blind; and, unaware that he is courting danger, he almost comes to a bad end. *Almost* is the imperative word in that sentence, for at this point the tramp is still a free man.

Before I introduce the tramp to his flower girl, let me stop to say a few words about the opposition he faces in the film. He has already confronted the angry officials, the newsboys, the tall worker, and he will eventually face an unbeatable opponent in the boxing ring, but *confrontation* is hardly the word. There is no villain in this movie, no one like Black Larsen in *The Gold Rush* or the proprietor in *The Circus*. Even the dispossessing landlord who threatens the flower girl and her grandmother is not a mustachioed figure in a black cape (although this is a variation on the who'll-pay-the-rent melodrama) but an eviction notice signed "M. B. Mint." The nearest approximation of a human villain is the millionaire's disapproving butler, who regularly ejects the tramp when the newly sober millionaire no longer recognizes his buddy; but compare Alan Garcia's butler to his circus proprietor and you can see how villainy in *City Lights* has been reduced to impersonality.

This was certainly not true of the earlier Chaplin films. Siegfried Kracauer, writing in 1960, said that the sermon in *The Pilgrim* "highlights a major theme of the Tramp films," an idea that Chaplin had long ago made explicit. In 1922, a few months before *The Pilgrim* was released, Chaplin looked back at *Easy Street* (1917) and wrote, "The triumph of the mite over the mighty was sure to be sympathetic. It is the old idea of the underdog, or of David and Goliath." Even earlier—in *Behind the Screen*—he had given the names David and Goliath to himself and Eric Campbell. By 1931, however, Goliath had become so amorphous that the tramp could not find where to aim his stone. So Richard Dana Skinner suggested in his review of *City Lights* when he described the tramp as "the modern equivalent of David and sling shot matched against the giant of organized society, of wealth and of the cruelty of indifference." You can take on an abstraction like wealth only by finding a suitable surrogate butt; by—say—dropping ice cream down a rich woman's dress, as Charlie does in *The Adventurer* (1917). One might try to pump social significance into some of the incidents in the nightclub sequence or the one in which the millionaire throws the party that Jean Mitry calls "an orgiastic eruption, a frenzy, a waste of all the material pleasures that wealth can offer to those who possess it." Although these scenes provide a necessary contrast to the quiet ones between the tramp and the girl and, although the plot hinges on the girl's poverty, accusatory eloquence like Mitry's (the phrase sounds even grander in French) cannot mask the fact that the film does not pit the tramp against society but depicts the consequences of his reluctant attempt to join it. This being the case, it is probably useful to consider the city in *City Lights*.

According to the pressbook prepared for the 1931 release of the film, the setting is "any large city, throughout the world." It is, of course, no city at all. It is not used, as the city is in *Easy Street, A Dog's Life, The Kid,* to suggest an environment. It exists either as a playing area for the performers or as an indiscriminate busyness outside the action. The pedestrians, animated images of impersonality, move as though timed by a metronome and both their speed and their mechanical quality set apart the unhurried tramp, the staggering millionaire, the tranquil flower girl. In the art appreciation scene the people in the background, on the other side of the street, walk more slowly than elsewhere in the film, but the contrast remains because the tramp moves up and back, either vertically or obliquely, while the crowd cuts a clean horizontal. The peopled city, then, is simply a moving backdrop.

Nor do the physical settings contribute to the dramatic action. They serve as prop—as in the opening fun with the statue—or as a frame in which the changing psychological state of the protagonist can be displayed. Take, as an example, the three scenes played against the arch that leads into the courtyard off which the flower girl lives. When the tramp brings her home in the millionaire's limousine, the arch frames the storybook arrival; the tramp, handing her through the arch, attempts an elegance to match that of the car. Later, when he comes to find out why she is missing from her customary corner, he passes through casually; the arch, no longer triumphal, is simply an entrance. Later still, after his escape from the millionaire's house with the money, he edges nervously along the side of the arch like someone out of *The Informer*. The arch itself, the house, the neighborhood, the city have not made the changes in the tramp; the changes in him have defined the arch in each instance. To present the physical and human city this way may suggest Skinner's "cruelty of indifference," but if the tramp is the hobo whom I see at the beginning of the film, he is neither victim nor challenger of society. He wears his own protective coat of indifference. His difficulty begins when he lets the blind girl inside that coat.

To get to the flower girl, the tramp has first to skirt a policeman on a motorcycle, a maneuver that has less to do with his civic transgressions in the first scene than with all those years of Charlie on the run. A specific evocation, but also a general one. "Mr. Antrobus is a very fine man . . ." says Sabina in *The Skin of Our Teeth*. "Of course, every muscle goes tight every time he passes a policeman." The millionaire, as well as the tramp, seems to want to avoid the cop in the foiled suicide scene. In any case, pushed by plot, tradition, or a standard human impulse, the tramp escapes through a parked car only to be trapped by the lovely girl (Virginia Cherrill) who offers him a flower. Chaplin used a similar routine in *The Idle Class* (1921). There, also with a cop in chase, the tramp steps through the limousine and is mistaken for one of the guests at a posh costume ball. One certainly does not need to have seen *The Idle Class* to comprehend the blind girl's mis-understanding in *City Lights*, but a memory of the earlier film adds a slightly sardonic note to the tramp's mask within mask, particularly when his later encounter with the millionaire puts him, however peripherally, in the other, the non-hobo idle class. The sound of the car door is her only key to the man in front of her and, when his chance encounter with the millionaire gives him the means to play the part—the money and the automobile—he becomes the person she imagines. The tramp's manner before the nude statue hints at dandyism before he ever sees the girl; and his reaction to the proffered flower, before he knows the girl is blind, is a flirtatious who—me gesture which suggests the urbanity that will follow. He becomes a charming, hand-kissing cavalier. There is an echo here of all those early shorts in which he played the swell for girls who ignored or rejected him—were blind to his charms, so to speak—but in *City Lights* the flower girl's blindness makes him acceptable.

Theodore Huff said of Virginia Cherrill as the flower girl that "all she brought to the part was good looks and near-sightedness," which made it possible for her to look blind as well as pretty. There must have been something beyond that, however, because she manages to sug-gest substance enough to give force to the final scene. For the most part, however, the character is pure stereotype. The scene in which she goes home to her neat, clean, melodrama-poor lodgings and, in rapid succession, turns on the victrola, waters her flowers, and talks to the caged bird is so saccharine that it might almost be parody. Her grandmother is conventionally be-spectacled, be-shawled. The girl, who certainly needs a melodrama hero, is faced with both eviction and a sudden illness (shades of *The Kid*), which seems rather beside the point in a plot in which the hero's primary business is to find a way to cure her blindness. None of this is to be taken seriously, I assume. The stock crises are simply excuses for the tramp to be pulled more and more deeply into the girl's life. The reality of the film lies not in the hokey plot devices, but in the scenes between the tramp and the girl, the growing relationship which is so beautifully, so solidly grounded on illusion.

The girl's imaginary admirer floats comfortably on the surface of the relationship; it is the tramp, who just happens to embody him, who sinks in it. The jobs that he takes to help her out and the jail that he faces for her sake, are the strongest examples of the changes worked on the unencumbered, self-sufficient fellow we met as the film began. There are early comic indications of the dangers in human attachment, one of which comes when he first meets the girl, before he has any idea that he will find occasion to court her. After their initial encounter, when the sound of the car makes her think he has driven away, he settles down, entranced, simply to admire her. She makes her way to a fountain, rinses out a container, and then throws the water over him. "The slapstick is perfect," Gilbert Seldes said in his review of the film, "but it rises legitimately out of the pathos of the girl's blindness." An appropriate gag, then, with its own internal logic, it serves both to undercut the sentimentality of the scene and to give a first hint of the film's serious theme. A similar slapstick promise of what is to come can be found in the scene following immediately on his taking her home in the limousine. A cat on a windowsill, established as they arrive, knocks a flowerpot on his head, but he is so delighted with the girl that he shrugs off any hurt and climbs up to peep in her window. Caught by the janitor (Henry Bergman again), he manages to tip the barrel on which he is standing and to get away as the water splashes the fat man. However prophetic, the scene is a broadly funny one, just right for the happy occasion. It becomes more effective in retrospect as a contrast to the later courtyard scene after the tramp overhears the doctor discussing her illness. He withdraws to the bottom of the stairs where he sits, an isolated figure in the right-hand lower corner of the frame. The set, filled with frenetic business in the earlier scene, is now emptied of everything, including hope, and a proper pathetic note is struck. The falling flowerpot has belatedly left its mark.

The scene which best shows how deeply and dangerously the tramp has become attached to the girl is the one in which he comes to comfort her in convalescence. His delight in his new role as breadwinner and her pleasure in his presence give the scene a warmth that transcends the comic detail—the byplay with the cauliflower, for instance. Chaplin had toyed with keeping house in the parody happy ending of *A Dog's Life* and in the improvised arrangements in *The Kid* (and would touch both those bases again in *Modern Times* [1936]), but this scene in *City Lights* sounds a genuine note of domesticity and does it primarily through the interplay of the two characters. To bring the scene to culmination Chaplin falls back on an image which has long been used—sentimentally or satirically (in reams of cartoons and comic strips for instance)—to represent two people bound to one another. The girl asks the tramp to hold her yarn as she winds it, but his joy turns to consternation as he realizes that she has somehow caught a loose thread and is slowly unraveling his long underwear. He cautiously shifts from one side to another so that she will not feel a catch which might lead to revelation, embarrassment. When that device proves too slow to match the steady rhythm of her winding, he feverishly pulls the thread from the front of his shirt and feeds it into her hands. His face wears an expression which seems to be asking that his idyllic dream not be shattered even though it contains a heavy dollop of nightmare. The yarn, as Jean Mitry says, "seems to emerge from Charlot's entrails." It is in this scene, necessarily, that the tramp tells the girl about the doctor who might be able to restore her sight and responds to her "Then I'll be able to see you" with a look which suggests how much he has to lose from the gift he wants to give her.

It is from the millionaire (Harry Myers) that the tramp hopes to get the money for the girl's operation—and does get it but in not quite the way he first intended. The millionaire, however, is much more than a plot device. He provides the tramp with a relationship analogous to the one he has with the flower girl—an opportunity to play at friendship as he plays at love. The tramp encounters the millionaire shortly after his first meeting with the girl when, mooning over the flower she gave him, he wanders onto the bridge where the other man is attempting to commit suicide. In the ensuing rescue scene it is the tramp, the incipient savior, who must be saved (his dunking gives him a chance to do the comic leg-shake that Charlie imitators so love). The drunken millionaire embraces the tramp as a friend and, as long as he is drunk, continues to see him in that role. Anyone who knows Bertolt Brecht's *Herr Puntila and His Man Matti*, in which the playwright borrowed Chaplin's device and gave it overt political significance, may attempt to read social satire into the fact that the millionaire rejects the tramp when he is sober. If it is there, however, it is little more than a whispered recognition that rich men are traditionally villains in popular culture; as Chaplin said back in 1918, "nine tenths of the people in the world are poor, and secretly resent the wealth of the other tenth." It is more important, for *City Lights* as a unified work, that the millionaire's drunkenness be accepted as the equivalent of the flower girl's blindness, a mechanism for transforming the tramp into walking wish-fulfillment. Whether he is suicidal or flamboyantly jolly, the millionaire in his cups suggests a vulnerability that needs someone to hold onto. He regularly receives the tramp with a hearty embrace, even kisses him on the mouth, and the tramp has a way of stroking the millionaire as though to assure him that his friend is still there. The stroke is also a kind of testing touch by which the tramp convinces himself that the millionaire is real. I do not want to elevate this gesture into some sense of deep commitment on the tramp's part, for the distinction between the millionaire and the flower girl is that the tramp's relationship to the former, however frenetic, remains essentially casual.

Some of the French critics (as in the Chaplin-Christ comparison from Guy Perol quoted early in this chapter) suggest that the tramp saves the millionaire, gives him a desire to live, as he saves the girl, gives her sight, and sacrifices himself in the process. Certainly that loop in the rope that catches him and lets the millionaire's stone pull him into the river has some of the effect of the misdirected water, the falling flowerpot. Still, the millionaire remains unsaved in either a metaphorical or a dramatic sense. In his last scene, sober, he fails to recognize the tramp, forgets that he has provided for the operation, forces the tramp to grab the money and run. It is not the millionaire, drunk or sober, saved or unsaved, on whom we really focus in this relationship. It is the tramp who demands our attention. He is conscious of the role he plays, whether with the millionaire or the girl, but there is no indication of pain with the rich man; he might be the tramp of the opening scene, nestling in the lap of luxury as he does in the lap of the statue. His independence is obvious in the shake of his shoulders when he stands, back to camera, trying to face down the butler who is barring him from the mansion. It is neatly reemphasized in two brief bits. In one, as a mock millionaire, he rides in the borrowed limousine, tracking a man with a cigar, and then leaps from the car to elbow another bum away from the discarded butt. In the other, thrown out by the butler, he stops long enough to pick up a banana which, as Theodore Huff sees it, "he nonchalantly peels as he stalks off in unperturbed dignity." For me, the tramp strolls rather than stalks, and it is not the peeling but the first bite of the banana that effectively cuts any suggestion of a real tie between tramp and millionaire.

When the film was first released, most reviewers talked about it not in terms of unity or theme—matters for critics with more time and space—but as a collection of comic scenes; even those who had doubts about the movie would stop to indicate which bits—the boxing match, the eating of the paper streamers as spaghetti, the swallowed whistle—most appealed to them. Sid Silverman in *Variety* praised the "cigar bit between Harry Myers and Chaplin" as "the only original piece of business" in the film. More than forty years later, Walter Kerr, having just sat through scores of movies to write *The Silent Clowns,* said "the film may seem a summary of all the gags that silent film was preparing itself to abandon." Kerr is particularly adept at finding in *City Lights* situations that had already been used by Buster Keaton or Harry Langdon, by Max Linder or by the early Chaplin himself, but in so doing Kerr is simply building on the customary critical practice of finding the sources of the boxing sequence in *The Knockout* (1914) and *The Champion* (1915), or of the nightclub scene in *The Rounders* (1914) and *A Night Out* (1915). Any explanation for the repeated use of gags must begin with the fact that they are, as Chaplin said in 1924, "those good old tricks that have always proved successful." In *City Lights* there are two very obvious substitution gags. One occurs when the tramp, now a street sweeper, stops for lunch and accidentally puts a bar of soap in place of a wedge of cheese in a fellow worker's sandwich, and the other in the party scene, when he mistakes a bald head for a cream pudding. The second of these—essentially a visual joke—recalls the gag in *The Pilgrim* in which the tramp ices the derby, and the first suggests the one in *The Strong Man* (1926), in which Harry Langdon, suffering from a cold, accidentally rubs Limburger cheese on his chest to the predictable distress of those around him. The gags work in *City Lights* partly because they are venerable and partly because they end so neatly, the one with curses that turn into soap bubbles, the other with the tramp's haughty dismissal of the real pudding when it is offered.

In some cases, as I suggested in the discussion of the tramp's escape through the limousine, echoes of an earlier gag can add resonance to its use in *City Lights*. This can be seen whenever Chaplin employs one of the tramp's familiar signatures—the tip of the hat, the flick of the cane. There are internal echoes as well as those carried from past films into the present one. Consider the hesitation gesture that Chaplin so often uses when his character gets his hands on money. In *The Floor-walker* (1916), for instance, when Charlie realizes that he has a satchel full of money, he goes into a demonic dance during which he kicks away a roll of bills, recovers it, whips off a single to hand to Eric Campbell, only to snatch it back and put it in the satchel. In *City Lights*, when the millionaire gives the tramp money to buy all the girl's flowers, he takes a bill, hesitates, takes a second one, starts to leave, seems about to return, finally goes. Hardly flamboyant after the fashion of *The Floorwalker*, the restrained bit in *City Lights* shares with the earlier gag an understanding that human fingers are generally reluctant to let go of cash. The value of the gag in *City Lights* is that it is later echoed in situations in which the tone of the device changes. When he buys the flowers, he gives the girl the first bill, refuses the change and, then, impulsively thrusts the second bill into her hand. Later, when he brings the money for her operation, he withholds a bill almost instinctively and, when she kisses his hands in thanks, he has to let the last bill go. In these two instances, the hesitation gag, already established within the film, takes on a touch of pathos and an obvious thematic relevance.

Although there is something fascinating about the attempt to trace a gag back to its source, it is finally more interesting in the way it has been transformed for a particular film. The fights in *The Knockout* and *The Champion* are so different from the boxing match in *City Lights* that they seem to me only vague ancestors of the later sequence. For one thing, realism of a sort invaded the gags. In *City Lights*, Chaplin bases a naughty expectations joke on what a man cannot do wearing boxing gloves, where in *The Knockout* Sennett lets Fatty Arbuckle run amuck, firing pistols with his boxing gloves still on. More important, a sense of artistic unity infected the gags. With a film as sophisticated as *City Lights* the impulse is to make everything fit the grand design. One might even make a case for the substitution gags as exercises in illusion, comic counterpoint for the flower girl's imaginary lover. I hesitate to go that far, and then I watch the tramp, drunk in the nightclub, attempt to save the apache dancer from her partner and I cannot avoid the parallel between that brief incident and the film as a whole. Since the most extended comic sequences have their own internal build, gag growing out of gag, there is no reason for every laugh-provoking gesture to be given extracomic significance. Still, it is worth taking a second, nonlaughing look at those scenes in which the millionaire takes the tramp out to play (the nightclub, the party) and those in which the tramp takes a job for the girl's sake (the street-cleaning bit, the boxing match).

Much of the comic invention in the scenes with the millionaire seems to exist for its own sake, but the scenes as a whole convey a sense of frantic gaiety which underlines the fact that the friendship of the two men is only a figment of a drunk's imagination. This would be enough to give the scenes aesthetic value beyond their immediate comic effect, but I am intrigued by the comments of Muriel Brenner, who examined "the Choreography in Chaplin Films" as part of "A Study of the Structure of Dance Comedy." Describing the incident of the swallowed whistle, she says, "The violent staccato, hiccup movements that at first overpower his entire body, gradually diminish to lingering sustained actions—devoid of energy." She also explains how the musical beat, in the nightclub scene, takes possession of the tramp, pulling him into a dance that ends in "a frenzied climax—where he loses all resemblance to a self-motivated human being. When the tension finally snaps, the mesmeric jazz demon leaves behind an inanimate mass, giving a decisive conclusion to this parody on rhythm as a life-giving force." This last is a rather grand way of saying that he whirls a woman and then a waiter and finally falls stiffly backward in drunken collapse, and the former statement ignores that the last whistle is accompanied by a pack of dogs. Still, the rhythms she overdescribes are appropriate to Chaplin's most sustained bits in the two sequences. Given her special subject, Brenner does not follow the implications of her remarks into the film as a whole, but her deflationary images reflect what the tramp is undergoing in the central dramatic action of the film.

The boxing and the street-cleaning sequences are overtly connected with the decline of the tramp from free spirit to responsible citizen. Alexander Bakshy called the first of these "the desperate venture of our hero into the business of prize fighting," a phrase that emphasizes that for the tramp boxing is a job, not a sport. He gets into it in the first place on the understanding that he will split the purse by throwing the fight, but when his opponent runs away, he is faced with a genuine contest—still another example of the way the film plays with the uncertain nature of illusion. This episode, the longest in the film, is divided into two sections—the preparations and the match itself. Incidental jokes about boxing gloves and rabbit's feet aside, the first of these shows the tramp abasing himself in a way that would have been impossible to the man we saw at the beginning of the film. His flirtatious attempt to show how harmless he is, which his opponent (Hank Mann) takes as a homosexual advance, suggests nothing so much as the placating behavior with which animals assure the pack leader that they are not challenging his position. In the match itself, the tramp puts up a marvelous defensive fight, ducking to safety behind the tall referee, popping out to take a poke at his opponent. The maneuvers are so beautifully executed that this is a scene critics usually point to when they want to praise Chaplin as the dancer W.C. Fields once snarlingly called him ("The son of a bitch is a ballet dancer"), but part of the effect depends on the presence of Hank Mann and his total lack of expression. The appeal of the scene is further enhanced by the echoes from Chaplin's past, not so much the early boxing films as all those fear-aggression situations in which Charlie attacks from hiding to deliver a kick and then races away before retaliation is possible. These echoes are deceptive, however. They set up the expectation of victory, and the film demands that the tramp be knocked out.

By comparison, the street-sweeping scene is very slight, most of it devoted not to the job itself but to the lunch break. It is really a one-joke affair in which the tramp, having reluctantly faced up to a single helping of horse apples, turns away from a herd of the creatures only to meet an elephant. "A world in which the poor are good for nothing but to clean up after others," laments Jean Mitry, but the juxtaposition of the two work sequences suggests something much less elegant but more forceful. Give up your independence and you may end up either shoveling shit or having it knocked out of you.

The gags come to an end; the film moves toward that finish which, in James Agee's famous phrase, "is enough to shrivel the heart." There is one last echo. Just before he enters the prison, the tramp discards his cigarette with his dismissive backward kick—a regeneration gesture with no content. When the tramp comes out of prison he is totally defeated. In *My Trip Abroad*, Chaplin revisits his old neighborhood and describes a blind derelict he "used to see as a child of five. . . . He is the personification of poverty at its worst, sunk in that inertia that comes of lost hope." For almost twenty years, Chaplin's tramp denied that kind of inertia, but at the end of *City Lights* he is overcome by just such hopelessness. He moves much more slowly, a dragging gait that we have had a glimpse of earlier in the helpless moment between the boxing match and the last meeting with the millionaire. He has become more ragged and he has lost the cane which Chaplin once called the tramp's "attempt at dignity," Parker Tyler his "magic wand." We do not need to play sexual symbology with the poor man's walking stick to recognize in his pathetic figure a loss of manhood. How could the flower girl be expected to find her prince charming in this failure clown? The impossibility is emphasized in the scene just before the tramp's final appearance, in which the girl—cured now of her blindness—sits in the flower shop waiting for her savior to reveal himself. She looks with longing at a young man so conventionally beautiful that he has to be an ironic joke, a cardboard lover who could not possibly be mistaken for the very human tramp. His final encounter with the newsboys catches her eye, awakens her sympathy. Her act of charity—the flower she offers to replace the tattered one he picks up from the gutter—becomes an act of revelation as the touch of her hand tells her who he is. "Yes, I can see now," she answers his question. The camera stays on her face just long enough to suggest the meaning of that line for the girl. Then, it turns to his last terrible close-up in which those eyes, that smile mirror rejection even as they bless her discovery which lets him slip the illusionary bonds and accept the pain of reality.

And is that all? That tale of loss, diminution, decay? I think not. Parker Tyler saw *City Lights* "as a sort of last-ditch stand of the Bohemian Poet that was the Tramp's spiritual nucleus." And so it is. Call him "Bohemian Poet" or "the child aristocrat" (another Tyler label) or "American hobo" or simply "the Tramp," he disappears after *City Lights*. That fellow in *Modern Times* wearing his costume is a worker who becomes unemployed, which is hardly the same as the free spirit who rejects being tied down; and surely no one would mistake the barber in *The Great Dictator* (1940) for the tramp. *City Lights* is not only a losing battle, but a necessary one. A man can remain a self-sufficient outsider only by rejecting any connection to place, to occupation, to another human being. The tramp struggled to get out of his safety glass through most of the 1920s, but Chaplin saved him from the implications of his act by sheltering him with happy endings or wry romantic ones. I use negative terms to describe the tramp's progress through *City Lights* because there is some small corner in all of us that is forever fugitive. Yet the tramp's failure in *City Lights* has more substance than all his earlier victories. "He is capable of loving, of working, of suffering," Pierre Leprohon said. "He accepts life."

What better loss could one wish for a comic hero?

Notes

1. In this chapter I am pretending that Charles Chaplin really speaks through every essay and book that carries his byline, although we know that he used ghost writers in a number of instances. In *Charlie Chaplin* (New York, Arno Press, 1972, p. 4), Theodore Huff assigns "What People Laugh At" (*American Magazine* [November 1918]) to Rob Wagner, the schoolteacher turned publicity man whom Chaplin in *My Autobiography* (New York, Pocket Books, 1966, p. 229) calls a "friend of mine . . . a portrait painter and writer." Huff (p. 147) also describes how *My Trip Abroad* (New York, Harper, 1922) was dictated by Chaplin to Monta Bell, the *Washington Post* reporter who worked for the comedian in the early 1920s and then became a successful director in his own right; in the bibliography in *Chaplin* (Garden City, N.Y., Doubleday, 1974, p. 126), Denis Gifford lists Bell as coauthor. In his *Charlie Chaplin* (Garden City, N.Y., Doubleday, 1978, p. 90), John McCabe assumes that Rose Wilder Lane, who later published biographies of Henry Ford and Herbert Hoover, wrote *Charlie Chaplin's Own Story* (Indianapolis, Bobbs-Merrill, 1916) and that Chaplin never even read galleys on the book. In *A Dozen and One* (Hollywood, Murray & Gee, 1943, pp. 14, 39, 21–22), Jim Tully, who worked for Chaplin the mid-1920s, says that he was hired "to write articles with Chaplin's name attached." He calls Chaplin an "inarticulate" man with "an ambition to write" and describes an attempt to compose an article of his own which ended in "A few paragraphs of misspelled words." One does not have to go as far as Tully (whose acrimonious separation from the Chaplin organization may have colored his memory) to accept the fact of ghosts in Chaplin's pages. Still, the comedian must have given his blessing to some stage of all his presumed writings; so it seems as fair as it is convenient to assign ideas and quotations to the titular author.

2. In *Six Men* (New York, Knopf, 1977, p. 33), Alistair Cooke has Chaplin, speaking in 1934, call his tramp "the little fellow." Certainly by 1942, when *The Gold Rush* was re-released with a spoken narrative, Chaplin was so attached to the label that he substituted it for "The Lone Prospector" to describe the hero of the film. All these names refer to book titles: Peter Cotes and Thelma Niklaus, *The Little Fellow, The Life*

and *Work of Charles Spencer Chaplin* (New York, Philosophical Library, 1951); R. J. Minney, *Chaplin, The Immortal Tramp* (London, George Newnes, 1954); Kalton C. Lahue and Samuel Gill, *Clown Princes and Court Jesters* (South Brunswick, N.J., Barnes, 1970); Gerith von Ulm, *Charlie Chaplin, King of Tragedy* (Caldwell, Idaho, Caxton Printers, 1940).

3. In an earlier version of this chapter ("Blind Devotion," *Pennsylvania Gazette*, 78 [March 1980], 17), I called the source of the "voices" a saxophone, following the lead of one of the publicity articles in the 1931 pressbook. In a letter (May 4, 1980), David Raksin, who worked with Chaplin on the music for *Modern Times* (1936), told me that it was a kazoo which provided the voice of the mayor and "in a higher tessitura" that of the woman civic leader. Jean Mitry (*Tout Chaplin*, Paris, Cinema Club-Seghers, 1972, p. 299) says the instrument is a *"trompette bouchée,"* but he gives no authoritative source for the muted trumpet that he hears. I have chosen to go along with Raksin, who added, "And I'd bet just about anything that the kazoo track was made by Chaplin himself; it is the kind of thing he would have trusted to no one else."

2

SHE DONE HIM WRONG

· 1933 ·

While Eadie (Jean Harlow) tries to trap a millionaire in *The Girl from Missouri*, her comic friend Kitty (Patsy Kelly) keeps a ready eye out for muscular big men. Kitty dismisses Eadie's advice about men and economics, saying in Kelly's tough-broad voice, "I'm just an old-fashioned home girl—like Mae West." It is tempting to find complexities in the joke, if only because one of Kitty's conquests is a lifeguard played by Nat Pendleton, whose biceps Mae West fondles admiringly in *I'm No Angel* and because West often seemed to equate muscularity with sexuality, a tendency which reached ludicrous apotheosis in her muscle-man nightclub act in 1954. Tempting, but unnecessary. Kitty's remark is a simple laugh line, hinged on nothing specific, depending on a generalized comic reference. By 1934, when *The Girl from Missouri* was released, Mae West's name had become a household word. The success of *She Done Him Wrong* and *I'm No Angel* the year before had not only established her as a movie star, but had given America a new comic tag, a name which in any vaguely sexual context would get a laugh. Boys in the street and men in smoking cars knew this as surely as script writers, such as *Missouri*'s Anita Loos.

To reduce Mae West to a gag line is a little like forgetting that Peoria, another perennial comic name, is an Illinois city of more than a hundred thousand. In 1934, jokes aside, Mae West was an extremely skillful performer with almost thirty years of experience in show business. "She has studied the stage, studied audiences, studied herself,"

Mae West and prey. Cary Grant. Unused swan bed in the background. (*She Done Him Wrong*, Paramount, 1933. The Museum of Modern Art/Film Stills Archive.)

Sam M'Kee wrote in 1922 in a review of her act at the Palace. "The result is highly gratifying all round." Recalling her arrival in Hollywood, she told a *Los Angeles Times* interviewer in 1934, "When I came here I was a finished product," meaning a perfected one, and that same year, Ruth Biery, in a four-part biography in *Movie Classic*, written with the obvious cooperation of her subject, said, "When Mae West says she thinks only of herself, again she is speaking of the impersonal—the public institution that she has built of herself to entertain others." That institution was to take on mythic proportions, as Stark Young predicted in 1933. His somewhat amorphous fascination with the actress in his 1928 review of *Diamond Lil* had taken a recognizably Youngian shape by the time he got around to *I'm No Angel*: "Miss West has created a sort of Lillian Russell-gay-nineties-bad-good-diamond-girl myth or figure, heightened and typified, that is becoming as distinct as Charlie. If she keeps it up a few years longer it will be only a character, like Harlequin or Columbina in the old *commedia dell'arte*."

By 1943, when she made *The Heat's On*, the last, sad remnant of her Hollywood career (I am assuming that *Myra Breckenridge* [1970] and *Sextette* [1977] are simply accidents of her old age), Mae West's Columbina was not only larger than life; she was larger than art. Fitzroy Davis, remembering his difficulties with the script, quotes West, "We can't have 'Her' do something like that. . . . The audience will look down on 'Her,'" and he adds, "In time, I got accustomed to Miss West using the third person when she referred to herself or, rather, when she referred to the Mae West character." In *Goodness Had Nothing to Do with It*, the autobiography which she wrote[1] in 1959, a mock modest celebration of her own importance, there are ample indications of a professional at work, calculating the effect of light, costume, gesture, word, but the creation gets more space than the creator and, finally, like the malevolent ventriloquist's dummy in *Dead of Night* (1945), the creation consumes the creator. "Diamond Lil is all mine," Mae West told Lucius Beebe when she revived the play in 1948, "I'm she. She's I, and in my modest way I consider her a classic." By 1971, the pronouns had slipped. "I see myself as a classic," she told *Playboy*, but it was clear by this time that image and performer had merged. Charles Chaplin might escape the Tramp, Groucho Marx take off the greasepaint mustache and the frock coat, but Mae West was encased, spiritually at least, in the corsets of Diamond Lil.

There has always been some confusion about both the substance and the appeal of the Mae West image. In the autobiography (particularly in the chapters added to it when it was reprinted in 1970), in the interviews of the 1960s and 1970s, in books like *On Sex, Health and ESP*

(1975), Mae West has been presented—has presented herself—as a kind of missionary of uninhibited sexuality, as an early advocate of sex equality, as a major force in sexual and social change in America. Reporters like Helen Lawrenson and Richard Meryman, who went to her in the 1960s expecting the wit and irony implicit in the heroine of *She Done Him Wrong*, were startled to find how seriously she took herself. Meryman projected two Mae Wests for his *Life* article, one "shrewd, detached, able to spoof everything" (Mae West "A") and the other who "believes completely in those melodramatic plots— that sexiest-woman-in-the-world role—the outrageous overstatement" (Mae West "B"). In late years she took to repeating familiar one-liners ("Sex is an emotion in motion") as though they were antic oracles from the shrine of the goddess, but she interspersed the joking ritual with homilies—on sex, health, and ESP, as the book title says— as dull and pretentious as any self-help manual. This transformation of comedian into guru might be taken simply as the necessary invention of a woman who refused to face her own aging—the shell who could not escape Diane Arbus's camera when the photographer of the grotesque came to record her for *Show*—if it were not that her sense of mission began early in her career. After her first Hollywood success she took to the fan magazines giving advice to girls on how to get, hold, and treat a man—conventional publicity pieces which took on deeper significance because she was packaged as an authority on such matters. The presumed expertise she brought to the readers of movie magazines was given more elegance in other circles. George Davis, who had been a West admirer since her years on the "now vanished two-a-day," complained in a *Vanity Fair* article in 1934 that "our Bright Intellectuals" had got to her, altering her sense of professional self: "But the most offensive claim of the West school is that she stands as the Joan of Arc of Sane Sex Living." There is evidence that she fancied that role before she ever got to Hollywood. When *Parade* printed the somewhat solemn "Sex in the Theatre" in 1929, the editors may have taken the piece as a sophisticated joke, but I suspect Mae West of being serious when she put her name to lines like "For years I have been devoting my career in the theatre to the education of the masses to certain sex truths." The Meryman dual personality seems to have been with West from the beginning, but in her first years in Hollywood she was able to keep her reformer self in proper perspective.

The people who took her seriously all along were the censors, the prigs, the prudes who bought her presentation of sex at face value: the police who closed plays like *Sex* (1926) and *Pleasure Man* (1928); the officials who are supposed to have asked her not to bring her homosexual play, *The Drag* (1927), into New York; the pressure groups that used her early movies as weapons in the fight for a stronger Hollywood code; the outraged minority who got her banned from radio after the broadcast of the innocuous Adam-and-Eve sketch in 1937. It is difficult at this distance to understand how anyone could find West's work dangerous, unless one goes to a level of subversion—implicit in the best film comics—far more basic than the assumption that the sanctity of society is threatened by Mae West as sex exemplar. In that role, she is essentially comic. That was her defense in 1934, when the newly strengthened Production Code was about to bowdlerize *Belle of the Nineties*, the first of the West films to make true believers look back longingly at *She Done Him Wrong* and *I'm No Angel*. In an interview in the *Los Angeles Times*, she compared herself to Chaplin: "He always had a lot of sex in his pictures. . . . He kidded it, and that's exactly what I do." At about the same time, Andre Sennwald, whose *New York Times* article was one of a number of defenses of West's art, said, "To be an earnest believer in the iniquity of Miss West, to be convinced that she is a breeder of licentiousness and an exponent of pornography, is to be unusually blind to her precise qualities as an actress."

As far back as 1913, she was billed as an "Eccentric Comedienne" at Proctor's Fifth Avenue, and Nellie Revell in the *Morning Telegraph* called her "That Cohanesque, Tanguayish president of the female 'nut' club." Revell added, in a phrase the actress would adopt as her own, "it isn't what Miss West does, but the way she does it that assures her a brilliant career on the stage." West would suggest later that she was not consistently comic. "I got laughs in vaudeville and in revues," she told Richard Meryman, "but I was a dramatic star in my first couple of plays." What she was was a kind of phenomenon. Even as late as the production of *Diamond Lil*, the reviewers tended to talk about the play as though it were simply a melodrama, to dismiss it as "trash," as George Jean Nathan did, or to put it up with it for the sake of "my favorite rosebud of the boards," as Charles Brackett called her in the *New Yorker*. It was obviously still not the what but the how of West's doing that made a difference. "I had learned by now," she says in her autobiography, "that I could say almost anything, do almost anything on a stage if I smiled and was properly ironic in delivering my dialogue." She quotes Ashton Stevens's response to *Diamond Lil* when it played Chicago; he was shocked to the point of leaving, when "my own laughter saved me. . . . I saw that the embraces in *Diamond Lil* are much the same funny, fiendish exaggerations that the obscenities are in *The Front Page*. They belong not so much to Sex as to Humor." She increasingly made use of such exaggeration, she later told *Playboy*, "Especially, in movies."

Comedy and sexuality can coexist in a single performer, as Jean Harlow and Marilyn Monroe indicate. With Mae West there is a difference. She was obviously a popular sex figure, as the Mae West jokes indicate, but not in the reverential way that she and her more dedicated admirers falsely remembered in the 1970s. In her review of *She Done Him Wrong*, Regina Crewe talked about West's "hearty, hippy hilarity" and her "honest, open and above-board, cards on the table and nothing concealed in the sleeve brand of bawdiness." Crewe is not talking about sex; woman reviewer though she may be, she is praising the actress as one of the boys. This was the tone of most of the favorable West reviews in the 1930s. There was always something ambiguous about her sex appeal, some uncertainty about its nature and its audience. Reviewing *Klondyke Annie* (1936), as it was spelled in England, Graham Greene assumed that she was the darling of the middle-aged, "that bowler-hatted brigade gathered invisibly like seraphs about her stout matronly figure." Lewis H. Lapham, who reported that "at the age of 71 Miss West still possesses overwhelming sexual force," attempted to place her appeal in terms of the "image of woman . . . toward which all young men strive, groping for it through the dim mists of their adolescence." Lowell Sherman, the director of *She Done Him Wrong*, put the same thing less elegantly when he said of that movie, "it will be the great American wet dream."

In the 1934 *Vanity Fair* piece quoted earlier, George Davis praised West as "the greatest female impersonator of all time," and the same year George Kent, in an ingenious *Photoplay* article called "The Mammy and Daddy of Us All," compared her to Will Rogers, the father figure, and said, "The shape of her body and the shape of her spirit spell MOTHER in letters so large we would have read them and understood them years ago if we all hadn't been led astray by the naughty-naughty act she stages for our delight." Kent recalled seeing *I'm No Angel* at a matinee with an audience full of children who loved West and the movie without understanding the lines. As West later told an interviewer, "I always think of the kiddies." Probably without having read either Davis or Kent, Parker Tyler merged their two aperçus ten years later when he found in Mae West both the accepting mother and the homosexual son. What all these critics seem to be saying is that they enjoy Mae West but that it is the other guy who responds to her erotically. "She gives her public what it wants," said Harold Clurman, reviewing the 1949 revival of *Diamond Lil*; "a glittering facsimile of what it craves and, through laughter, a means of keeping itself free of what it fears. She horses around with sex so that we can have our cake and not eat it." In these lines, Clurman cuts through middle-aged longings and adolescent fantasies, through mock mothering and homosexual identification and gets to the heart of the matter. For me, the most fascinating thing about Mae West as a sex figure is the absence of sex in her films, the strategies by which she keeps her ostensible subject from taking flesh.

When I was in the fourth grade, at the height of Mae West's popularity, one of my fellow students brought to school one day a new toy that titillated the boys in the class. A crude cousin of the talking doll, it was a small wooden box with a string running through it. When one pulled the string, the box said—or we believed that it said—"Come up 'n see me some time." I was too young or too innocent to understand the visual pun, to appreciate the implications of that kind of invitation from a box. Now that the incidental joke seems obvious, I am more fascinated by the toy as accidental symbol. Mae West's invitations seem always to have come from a thing, a machine, an automaton, rather than a person. As Parker Tyler said in one of his periodic reconsiderations of the figure who so fascinated him, "she seems made from a mold, as if her whole body were a layer of simulated flesh about an inch thick, with nothing whatever inside."

After the success of *She Done Him Wrong*, full-form fashions returned, for the moment replacing the flatness of the 1920s, and Mae West signed articles or accepted interviews explaining her part in the resurrection of the curve. In one of these, she told Cecelia Ager that she did not write *Diamond Lil* until her corsetière had designed a workable corset for her. Ager's description of the contraption, at least the one worn in *She Done*, emphasizes the freedom of movement it allowed, but there is a difference between the practicality of an object and the way it is perceived. Although it allows West to perform her justly celebrated walk, she appears to be encased in a covering that is at once advertisement and protection. It is a superstructure that lets her look larger than life. A small woman—"a tiny, fragile figure, like some blonde Dresden shepherdess," Lowell Brentano said—she padded herself heavily, not to make herself sexy but to allow her to be the most imposing figure on stage. She was not Tennessee Williams's Laura in *The Glass Menagerie* slipping on "Gay Deceivers"; she was a Greek actor pulling on cothurni. On screen, of course, the camera could do the job for her, emphasizing her metaphorical size by her placement within a frame. Even so, she held on to the padding and the lifts. Edith Head, who designed the costumes for *She Done Him Wrong*, said at an Academy tribute to Mae West, "I wonder if you know that I'm five feet tall and she was exactly my height. She used to wear enormous shoes, built up almost like a stilt." Abetted by the directors she worked with, she used stage tricks as well as costumes to allow her to loom over the other performers. When Lady Lou first meets Serge (Gilbert Roland) in *She Done Him Wrong*, he is on the stairs, she below, but before she gives him an obvious come-on, they have changed places and she is looking down not only at him but at Rita (Rafaela Ottiano) and Gus (Noah Beery), both of whom have cause to be jealous. In her first scene with Cary Grant, the one in which Lady Lou helps Cummings rescue a man from the police, West stands on the first step, Grant on the floor. Not exactly a queen taking homage, as she seems to be in the scene with Roland, she is at least meeting her very tall leading man eye to eye.

I am aware that there is a certain inconsistency in the paragraph above, that I seem to be talking about West both as artifact and royal personage, but either guise emphasizes her essential untouchability. To some West admirers, those who take Lou's line about men ("It's their game. I play it their way") as a statement of the actress's philosophy, the calculated largeness of her image is part of her aggressive stance in the relations between the sexes. It is true, as she told *Playboy*, that she dominates her pictures. "Everything is written around me, and that includes men." Artistic aggression, however, should not be confused with sexual aggression. Frank S. Nugent reported that an unnamed producer[2] chided Mae West for her misuse of Victor McLaglen in *Klondike Annie*, pointing out that a script could have two leading parts and citing *Romeo and Juliet* as an example. Mae West's answer: "Shakespeare had his style and I have mine." When a star's conventional fear of being upstaged is translated into artistic control of the films or plays in which she appears, there are inevitable aesthetic and ideational consequences. It is possible to read the Mae West oeuvre as an early instance of the liberated woman in action. For me, however, her centrality not only turns her into a monument but unsexes the men in her films. There is an accidentally revealing sentence in *Goodness Had Nothing to Do with It*. In describing her first experience with the occult, she explains that she had always been a materialist, living in "a pleasant world of inanimate objects like money, cars, suites, good reviews, diamonds, clothes, strong lovers."

Mae West had ways of objectifying the men in her movies. The most obvious of these was to cast nondescript actors—conventional pretty boys, strong silent types, dress dummies, society swells, gigolos—as her lovers or would-be lovers. She may not have chosen all the performers in her films but, given the degree of control she had, she must have either accepted or picked actors like Kent Taylor, Roger Pryor, John Miljan, Paul Cavanagh, Phillip Reed, Lyle Talbot, Dick Foran. These are stick figures, not grizzly bears. I borrow the animal image from West herself. The first song she wrote on her own, she says in the autobiography, was "The Cave Girl" in 1915; in a stanza on what the titular girl learned from the animals, one line reads "And a grizzly bear taught me how to hug." In *On Sex*, West recalls a dream she had at thirteen in which she was taken by a "huge, furry brown-black bear." If the possibility of animal sexuality remained with Mae West, she saw to it that it did not touch her film character. Even her celebrated muscle men suggest statues rather than live creatures. Whenever a possibly bearish actor came along, she managed to emasculate him by reducing him to an innocent rube (Randolph Scott in *Go West, Young Man* [1936]) or a comic butt. Victor McLaglen is the best example of the latter. His size and his exterior roughness make him a great bear of a man, as popular usage has it, but he was in danger of becoming a teddy bear on screen. His marvelously expressive face, which collapsed so effectively in *The Informer* (1935), would succumb to mannerism by 1937, when he displayed a gallery of comic and sentimental faces in a largely successful attempt to hold his own with Shirley Temple in *Wee Willie Winkie*. Temple, like West, had a way of erasing the men with whom she appeared. McLaglen was not nearly so successful in *Klondike Annie*. As Ernst Lubitsch said, "Victor McLaglen's part, as she wrote it, was simply that of a stooge." In the early scenes of the film, he has something to do and does it well, but that something is to be a big little boy, full of aw-shucks eagerness in her presence, rather than the adult sexual partner that his role of ship's captain might suggest. By the end of the film even the boy is lost; McLaglen has joined her gallery of stick figures and all that he is given to do—perhaps as consolation for having lost real scenes to play—is stock clumsy bits, running into a post, bumping into a hanging lamp. The only men who ever held their own, artistically, with Mae West were comic character actors, which is why *Every Day's a Holiday* (1938) is so attractive a film and why West purists tend to dismiss it; Edmund Lowe, as the hero, is almost the stuffed exhibit he appeared to be in *Dinner at Eight* (1933), but Charles Winninger, Charles Butterworth, Walter Catlett, Herman Bing, playing with West but not opposite her, do their specialties and retain their comic force.

One of the best brief scenes in *She Done Him Wrong* might serve as an illustration—accidental perhaps—of the Mae West character and her men. When Lou goes up to Sing Sing to visit Chick Clark (Owen Moore), she walks along a corridor lined with cells and as she passes each one she greets the inmate with an appropriate gag. A funny sequence, it makes its verbal point about the range of Lou's intimacies. Visually, it does something else. Lou is wearing a black dress with white sleeves and a hat with long white plume-like decorations, one of which comes down across the right side of her face. This glittering figure—the bright light emphasizes the whiteness of her skin, her plumes, her sleeves—moves, a ministering presence, past a line of adorers, all safely closed away from her. As for the rest of the men in Lou's life, those who actually share space with her, metaphorical bars have to be raised.

The actors who play Cummings, the hero, and Serge—Cary Grant and Gilbert Roland—are potentially much more interesting than most of the wimps that West used in her later films, but they are essentially pretty boys, inanimate objects. This is made clear by the story West tells in *Goodness Had Nothing to Do with It* about how she came to choose Grant for the lead in her film. She saw him walking across the Paramount lot one day, admired his looks, and, told that he had not yet made a picture, said, "If he can talk, I'll take him." The story has had to be revised in later retellings, particularly by Grant biographers who know that *She Done Him Wrong* was his eighth picture and that he had already performed with such Paramount stars as Marlene Dietrich, Nancy Carroll, and Sylvia Sidney. His function in *She Done Him Wrong* is explained in an interview which appeared in *Variety* shortly after the release of *I'm No Angel*, his second film with West. "In her pictures it's the tempo of the acting that counts rather than the sincerity of the characterization," Grant explained. "Her personality is so dominant that everyone with her becomes just a feeder." According to Pauline Kael, West "brought out his passivity," but that is a positive way of stating a negative. At this point in his career, Grant was a long way from the accomplished performer he was to become by the end of the 1930s. His first film, *This Is the Night* (1932), is one of those Paramount comedies with music that aped the successful sophistication of Ernst Lubitsch's *Monte Carlo* (1930) and *One Hour with You* (1932). *Night* is imaginative in its use of sound and has first-rate comic performances from Charles Ruggles and Roland Young; yet, Grant, who would eventually hold his own with these performers—*Bringing Up Baby* (1938), *Topper* (1937)—gives little indication of the comedian he would become. In part, his stiffness is a requirement of the role, the stuffy husband who is almost cuckolded by Gerald (Young). He is asked to look doubtful, assured, stern, depending on the circumstances of the plot, but Grant's expressions are free-floating indicators since neither the script nor the actor creates a character to which they may be attached. It is only in our first glimpse of Grant's Stepan as he comes singing along the hall that we get a hint of the latent charm of the performer. For the most part, he tends to be awkward whenever he is asked to be more than a well-dressed presence, not only in *Night*, but in other pre-*She Done* films like *Blonde Venus* (1932) and *Hot Saturday* (1932). It is possible that no one could speak convincingly a line like

"It's no use my trying to kid you or myself—I'm crazy about you," but the emotionless clip-clip-clip of Grant's delivery in *Blonde Venus* only emphasizes its fatuousness. In the autobiography he published in *Ladies' Home Journal* Grant describes Josef von Sternberg's struggles with him on the *Blonde Venus* set. "He bemoaned, berated and beseeched me to relax, but it was years before I could move at ease before a camera." It was this rigidity and his undeniable good looks which made him a proper partner for Mae West's smoldering ice unmaiden.

Gilbert Roland had been a screen lover since his early twenties— Armand to Norma Talmadge's Camille, for instance, in the Fred Niblo silent (1927). Yet Alfonso Pinto, in a sketch of Roland's career in *Films in Review*, says of some his first English talkies, "he played nothing more than the slick foreigner required in such pictures as Clara Bow's *Call Her Savage* [1932], Constance Bennett's *Our Betters* [1933] and Mae West's *She Done Him Wrong*." This is certainly true of the West film. Roland does little more than kiss her hand, speak with a kind of oily politeness which is supposed to be provocative, and pose prettily between Lou and Russian Rita, the last hors d'oeuvre caught between two hungry guests. In contrast to Roland and Grant are the rough diamonds who play the rough diamond-givers. The decision to make Dan Flynn (David Landau) no more than a variant of Gus Jordan, to make look-alikes of the man who wants to keep Lou and the man who does keep her, reduces Landau to an imitation at best, an animated costume more often.

Noah Beery, as Jordan, is much more interesting, and so is Owen Moore, as Chick Clark. Both of them endanger the sanctity of West's performance—Beery by threatening to become a character, Moore by performing in a style that is out of place in this movie. In the novel version of *Diamond Lil*—called *She Done Him Wrong* in some of the postfilm printings—Gus Jordan is presented as an aging man who seems to want Lil as much to sustain his image, big man on the Bowery, as for the sex she provides. There is the hint of that characterization in the movie. In the scene in which Gus needs to have Lou assure him that she cares nothing for Serge, Beery, who after all has a usable face compared to the handsome masks of Grant and Roland, almost lets reality break in, but the scene is too brief to allow more than a suggestion. Interruption is the structural principle of a film with so many plots that its central dramatic line looks like a cat's cradle.

The subversiveness of Owen Moore in *She Done Him Wrong* grows out of a performing style that separates him from the rest of the cast, the star included. He eats his speeches, pushing them down rather than out, and he slurs the edges of his words in an accent that I would call Irish drunk if propriety did not forbid and if I were not afraid I was being influenced too greatly by what I know of the actor's life.[3] He uses his hands excessively and articulates them oddly, from the wrist not the knuckles. He often has a single finger extended, not to point or to emphasize, but as though it were a wagging tail on the helplessly flapping hand. These mannerisms, running amuck in *As You Desire Me* (1932), seem simply ludicrous—in a film that already exceeds the ludicrousness content one has come to expect of the weaker Greta Garbo movies. However inappropriate to Tony, the articulate artist of *As You Desire Me*, Moore's idiosyncrasies serve the incipient hysteric in Chick Clark. Student audiences with which I have seen the West film often laugh at Moore, but it is not the kind of laughter elicited by West's lines. I suspect it grows from the disquieting possibility of real anguish in so unlikely a context. Physically and verbally, Moore is like shattered glass, jagged ends with which the West deliberation fits uncomfortably. Their scenes together are played on a psychological split screen.

Dewey Robinson is the strongest male performer in the film. A large, stocky man with a very heavy head and an oddly gentle face marked with dark eyebrows and the shadow of a beard, he is more than a physical presence. He knows how to read lines, even when his Spider is conveying subservience to West's Lou, in a way that insists on his place on the screen. There is a very brief scene in *Blonde Venus* in which, as the owner/cashier of a hashhouse, he refuses charity to the heroine on the skids; he carries himself and speaks his few lines with such authority that Marlene Dietrich's scene with him stays in my mind much more clearly than the more emotional passages with Herbert Marshall or Cary Grant. Robinson has a much larger role in *She Done Him Wrong*, and his flashy suit and bowler hat emphasize his physicality. Finally, however, he works with West as the gifted comedians do in *Every Day's a Holiday*. Although Spider adores Lou ("I'd do anything for you," he says at one point, and he does dispose of Rita's body), there is never the presumption of sexual connection between them as there is with all the other men in the script. His role is a little like that of Pearl (Louise Beavers), Lou's black maid; the loyalty of both characters testifies to Lou's essential goodness. The scene in which she undresses while talking to Spider is a comic teasing scene, but there is never a possibility that he will violate the screen behind which she disrobes. In *Sextette*, more than forty years later, the agent as loyal servitor (Dom DeLuise) finally declares his love by singing to a cardboard cutout of the star. Seen narrowly, that image may stand for the Spider-Lou relationship, but it might well be a metaphor for sex in all the West films.

Jon Tuska reports that "the most tempestuous love scenes" in *I'm*

No Angel were filmed with only one lover at a time on the set. First Mae West, then Cary Grant would take her/his place and purr at the camera lens. Masturbatory acting is commonplace in the movies, particularly when close-ups are called for, but Tuska's conjuration seems particularly appropriate as an image of the familiar West presentation of sex without contact. Not that the principals have any "tempestuous love scenes" to play. In one scene, Jack Clayton (Grant) kisses Tira (West) on top the head as she plays the piano, and he later gets to kiss her, mouth to mouth, but in a very genteel way. The only suggestions of sex are in the clinches between Tira and The Chump (William B. Davidson), but, as one would expect in a West movie, they are interrupted before any implicit promises are kept. Stark Young, after seeing *Angel*, primly congratulated West on her restraint, contrasting her to those film actresses who "manifest a revolting abandon of all reticence." After looking at a film like *Belle of the Nineties*, particularly the scene in which Ruby and Tiger Kid (Roger Pryor) come together, one suspects that West's reticence is actually a fear that an embrace might cause her facade to flake off.

On the page, as a novelist, West goes in for a kind of genteel pornography with a metaphorical splendor which suggests *Diamond Lil* as an unlikely influence on Ernest Hemingway (the earth-moving sleeping-bag scene in *For Whom the Bell Tolls*) and Tennessee Williams (Stanley's "colored lights" in *A Streetcar Named Desire*). Lil and Pablo (the Serge of the film) get together in the novel and, since he is a Latin lover and Mae West is not an author to disturb popular fables, he performs superbly:

> She felt herself swept from her feet, and presently the
> world became a place of exploding stars and bursting suns.
> Every nerve throbbed with a pleasure that was a refine-
> ment of pain. And then suddenly the soul hung suspended
> in sublimity.

The scene somewhat confuses me both practically (she undresses after she "had been his") and generically. The chapter title, "Touch and Go," suggests that we might take the whole thing as an elaborate joke, but I am afraid that it was Richard Meryman's Mae West "B" who wrote this prose. The novel was written after the play was performed, and the author presumably had an opportunity to fill in the blanks that stage presentation necessarily left empty. The script, at least the incomplete version I read in the Library of Congress, calls for a number of passionate kisses and Ashton Stevens used the plural in his review when he spoke of "kisses such as never were kissed on any stage before." Yet, Francis R. Bellamy, finding the play fakily naughty, reported,

> There's just one kiss in the play, and nobody seduces any-
> body, at least so far as we could observe, and the best that
> is produced in the way of gilded sin is a large gilt swan
> bed, imported, we are told, from Paris by the very bad sa-
> loon owner for the delectation of his very bad mistress.

When *Diamond Lil* becomes *She Done Him Wrong*, the swan bed is seen only in fragments and moderation becomes a matter of principle. "There's only one kiss," West told an interviewer, "only one in the whole picture. . . . But in a play, one of my plays, they expect hot love scenes all the time." At this distance, stage productions being ephemeral, it is impossible to mediate between West's proclaimed wickedness and Bellamy's remembered innocence, but the film is still here to testify to West's discretion. At one point, Lou lets Dan Flynn put his arm around her and she leans on his shoulder, but without ever joining him on the love seat; at another, she sits on the arm of Gus's chair, puts her arm around his shoulder and lightly strokes his hair. Chick, newly escaped from prison, kneels and puts his arms around her, an act of adoration rather than sexual love. Serge, who usually is consigned to hand-kissing, gets to embrace Lou when he gives her a diamond, but his kiss is aborted, his lips just touching the edge of her mouth; and Rita interrupts. Lou and Cummings share the "only one kiss" for the ritual happy ending. These few tentative touches consti-tute the film's only concessions to physicality, but the gauge for measuring the film's sexuality quotient is the love scene, if that is what it is, between Cummings and Lou in her boudoir. She is in negligee, her hair down, her shoulders bare, but she is still trapped in a body binder. Cummings has come to ask her about the missing Sally (Rochelle Hudson), whom Gus and his fellow white slavers have spirited away, but he stays on to discuss her "cold" diamonds and to suggest that she has the warmth, the soul that they lack. West gives no indication of such warmth, just as Grant cannot "loosen up, unbend" even if Cummings wants to accept Lou's invitation to do so. At the door, she stops him from leaving; when he tries to kiss her, she counters the pass and lets him out, and only then, with him safely out of the room, does she mutter, "It won't be long now." The scene by the door which is supposed to be an instance of Lou's seductive powers in full tide is, in fact, almost a still life. The characters face one another, and the camera, looking from the side, flattens them like silhouettes, framing only the tops of their bodies and thus cutting off Mae West's most expressive feature, her hips. West fanciers like to quote Lou's line to Cummings, "You can be had," as an example of the emancipated stance of the character/performer/author. Looking at those two polished artifacts facing one another, one realizes that it can't happen here. The genuinely revolutionary joke in Mae West's comedy is that she is a sex figure who renders sex implausible.

The "unregenerate Thaises of the Tenderloin that Miss West loves to play—and plays so grandly—move in a world that has little or no relation to life." John Mason Brown may be wrong about regeneration—West's Thaises always manage a semblance of it—but his otherwise accurate comment helps explain the Mae West character's need for a properly artificial setting. There may have been moments of incidental splendor in many of her movies—her singing of "I'm an Occidental Woman in an Oriental Mood for Love" in *Klondike Annie* is surely one of the finest—but *She Done Him Wrong* remains the best display case for her wares. After her success in a featured role in *Night after Night* (1932), she insisted that her first starring role be Diamond Lil, renamed Lou presumably to free Paramount of the taint of naughtiness attached to the original. John Bright, one of the authors of the screenplay, has said of *Diamond Lil*, "La West believed it was a work of high art. . . . My own view—shared by the producer, Le Baron, a very civilized fellow—was that the play was a creaky, dated and absurd drama which Bwy audiences laughed *at* rather than *with*—while they were enjoying the ribald personality of the star." This is about as neat a description of *Lil* and its popularity as one could hope to find in a single sentence, but the implication—that the play could or should be improved for the screen—is false. "She contrived her plays much as The Flying Codonas contrive their trapezes," George Davis said in *Vanity Fair*. "In them she didn't act: *she did an act*." To make *Diamond Lil* more believable, even more workable in terms of 1930s Hollywood melodrama, would have been to take away West's safety net.

Although one can sympathize with Bright in his struggles with the star over the screenplay—he was eventually fired from the movie—he seems an odd choice to be repairing West's trapeze. He and Kubec Glasmon turned up at Warner Brothers in 1931 with a story called "Beer and Blood," which, as *The Public Enemy*, not only made a star of James Cagney but placed Glasmon and Bright among the most talked-about writers in Hollywood. They were mentioned so often during 1932 that the studio publicity office seems to hover over the news items whispering, this is the way to package a successful new team. "They are the only American realists developed almost entirely by the talkies," John S. Cohen, Jr., wrote in early 1932, and at midyear, reporting their signing a new contract with Warners,[4] the *Los Angeles Times* called them "young writers of realistic drama." At this distance, a film like *The Public Enemy* takes on a fantasy quality of its own, partly because it helped to create the stock characters of Hollywood gangster films; but the texture of that movie—or of a less celebrated one like *Blonde Crazy* (1931)—is realistic in comparison to *She Done Him Wrong*, which, whatever Bright brought to it, remains pretty much *Diamond Lil*. "I wrote all the dialogue, every word of it; and it was my story," West told an interviewer. "That fellow Bright and somebody else fixed up the continuity, because I didn't know all about that." The nameless "somebody else" was Harvey Thew (he also had a hand in *The Public Enemy*), who was brought in, as Bright said, "for what Hwd calls euphemistically a 'polish job.'" It is not necessary to buy at face value West's modest assessment of her own contribution to see that while she thought she was defending her "high art" she was instinctively protecting the proper setting for her kind of comedy.

Lowell Sherman, who once told an interviewer that "Consistent virtue on the screen, dear, is the very skim-milk of monotony," may seem a better choice for director for Mae West than John Bright does as writer. In *Goodness Had Nothing to Do with It*, West explained her difficulties with Archie Mayo, "an excellent picture director," on *Night after Night* because "alas, he had no background of real theatre" and hence did not know how to deal with her as performer. (In the 1933 interview in which she annexed the Bright-Thew credits, she explained how much she had learned from Mayo.) Sherman was "a former actor, a leading man of the legitimate stage, and a very amusing man, with a good sense of theatre," she said in *Goodness*, and, for that reason, she implied, she chose him as director. It seems likely, however, that her producer did the choosing. William LeBaron, then at RKO, had hired Sherman as a director in 1930 and, beginning with *Lawful Larceny*, the film version of one of his Broadway hits (1922), Sherman directed and, although West thought him a "former actor,"[5] usually starred in a number of well-received movies—reason enough for LeBaron, now back at Paramount, to bring Sherman along. On the basis of the Sherman films I know—*Morning Glory* (1933) and *Born to Be Bad* (1934), as well as *She Done*—he is a director who makes minimal use of the special qualities of film. In *Morning Glory*, there are some extremely effective close-ups of Katharine Hepburn, but Sherman is given to medium shots, groupings of two, three, sometimes more, almost always with a theatrical emphasis. Although the anthology of Bowery scenes that opens *She Done* and Eva's long, loving approach to the theater at the beginning of *Morning Glory* indicate that Sherman understands cinematic effects, his best quality as a director is that he appreciates the peculiar talents of his actors, helping to bring one of her most touching performances from the young Hepburn, standing aside to let Mae West strut her stuff. He could do little for Loretta Young and Cary Grant in *Born to Be Bad*, however, for he, like his performers, seems trapped in Ralph Graves's soapy screenplay. At most, he could set up an interesting, if largely meaningless, scene like the frame within a frame in which Letty (Young) and Fuzzy (Henry Travers) struggle through an expositional heart-to-heart talk while the camera watches their mirror images. Yet, he occasionally frames a shot that is so startlingly right—one that catches the emotional moment, the sense of character, the quality of the film as a whole—that he suggests a level of directorial inventiveness beyond his customary work.

In *Morning Glory* there is a scene in which Louis Easton, the producer (Adolphe Menjou), feeling guilty for having spent the night with Eva, leaves Joseph Sheridan (Douglas Fairbanks, Jr.), the playwright whose attraction to the girl is more sentimental, to face Eva, to get rid of her, to pay her off. For the briefest instant, Sheridan stands screen right, his hand on the bannister, ready to go upstairs, while Easton, on the far left, is struggling into his coat to make a hasty exit. The two men, turned away from one another, almost a full screen between them, are divided by more than space; yet, they are held together personally, professionally, within the frame. The film is a conventional story about the theater, honest in its sentimentality, disquieting in its doubts about the standard clichés, and in this moment, this frame, Sherman catches the complexity behind the film's obviousness and does so, for once, without the richness of Hepburn's presence. There is a similar and, of course, very different frame in *She Done Him Wrong*. In a confrontation between Gus Jordan and Dan Flynn, they meet belly to belly, their checked vests touching like curves. Anyone who has seen David Landau as the gambler in *Horse Feathers* (1932) or the hunger marcher in *Gabriel over the White House* (1933) knows that the actor is not a heavy man, but he hooks his thumbs in the armholes of his vest and somehow suggests that he is Noah Beery's size. The juxtaposition of these two half-moons makes a point about the similarity of the characters and their desire for Lou. A photograph of *Diamond Lil* in Jon Tuska's *The Films of Mae West* suggests that the visual comparison may have been Mae West's idea, but Sherman keeps the frame a cartoon, a proper image of the essential artificiality of the whole movie.

On insufficient evidence, I would guess that Sherman is a much more impressive director than his lack of reputation suggests (he is virtually unknown today) and that his best quality is his ability to understand the nature of the material with which he works. Certainly, *She Done Him Wrong* is stagey, tackily so since the movie was obviously produced on the cheap, appropriately so since *Diamond Lil*—its comic centerpiece aside—belongs to the kind of popular drama that Mae West must have played when, as a child, she trouped in Hal Clarendon's stock company. "I thought melodrama and nostalgia would please everyone," she says in the autobiography, recalling the creation of *Lil*. For West, however, melodrama is less a generic form than a catchall for familiar plots. *She Done Him Wrong* is the story of the diamond-hard Lou softened by the love of a good man. . . . is the story of the master detective, the Hawk (Dan Flynn's "He's the slickest bird in the business" is one of my favorite lines in the film), who disguises himself as a Bowery missionary to trap the crooks. . . . is the story of Chick, the imprisoned lover who breaks out to wreak revenge on Lou for being unfaithful to him. . . . is the story of Gus Jordan and Dan Flynn and their struggle for control of the Bowery and possession of Lou. . . . is the story of Sally, the betrayed maiden, who barely escapes being carried off by white slavers. . . . is the story of Russian Rita, whose jealousy finally kills her. It is all these things and none of them since it is peculiarly without suspense or the exacerbated emotions of old-fashioned melodrama. Rafaela Ottiano is the only performer in the film who plays melodrama, and she does so stylishly. In the scene in which Rita offers to help Sally, Ottiano rolls her eyes discreetly, lets the edge of her tongue play hungrily along her teeth and lips, so that the audience will know she is up to no good. Her performance is in complete contrast to Mae West's. Lou is at the center or on the fringe of all these plots, but they become static in her presence, painted back-drops against which the performer stands out. West's undulating walk, her appraising stare, her insinuating mutter remain essentially the same regardless of context. The unreality of melodrama becomes the more unreal in being robbed of its generic devices, of its urgency, of its audience-corrupting rhythm.

The fragmented plots are like ruins around which the audience keeps peering in search of the resident nymph. Knowing this, West delayed her appearance in *Diamond Lil* until well into the play—page thirteen of the typescript I read. "She has built up an entrance for herself such as Roman emperors are supposed to have enjoyed," John Mason Brown said in his review. In the film, the delayed entrance is even more elaborate. Before we see Lou, resplendent in her carriage, we get not only the introduction to Jordan's saloon and the chief characters, and the first exposition of the many plots, but the opening anthology of period songs and scenes which sets the essential inno-cence of the script: "When You and I Were Young, Maggie" . . . a horse-drawn trolley . . . "The Bowery" . . . an organ grinder and his monkey performing before a cluster of people . . . bicycles . . . "Daisy,

Daisy" . . . a street cleaner who sees a horse, sighs, and begins to sweep (see *City Lights*) . . . a street peddler being eyed by a policeman . . . two young women arm-in-arm . . . swinging doors . . . a street band . . . "Ach Du Lieber Augustin." In the novel, the description of Suicide Hall, Gus's place, with "the bleared eyes and bloated faces of habitual drunkards . . . the bruised, swollen faces of rowdies and gangsters, killers, drug addicts," is a great deal uglier than anything that appears in the film. Murder, white slavery, prostitution, all manner of crime and corruption are subsumed under nostalgia in the movie, as the opening sequence makes clear. The Bowery, chosen as the proper sinful setting for Lou and her underworld friends, had long since been sentimentalized in popular theater. Back in 1891 when the Bowery was presumably flourishing at its wickedest, Percy Gaunt and Charles H. Hoyt had written "The Bowery" for Hoyt's *A Trip to Chinatown*. "They did such things and they said such things," says the written prologue to *She Done Him Wrong*, echoing the Gaunt-Hoyt song, but the things they do in the movie, as I suggested above, are never more than shadow plays, and the things they say are not even as blunt as those in Raoul Walsh's *The Bowery* (1933), which was obviously made to cash in on the commercial success of *She Done Him Wrong*.

It is hardly happenstance that Darryl F. Zanuck and Joseph Schenck launched their new company, Twentieth Century, with a comedy about the Bowery less than nine months after *She Done Him Wrong* appeared, a movie about Chuck Connors and Steve Brodie eight months after Mae West told an interviewer that they were good movie material. The interesting thing about *The Bowery* is that, before it succumbs to the horseplay of Wallace Beery and George Raft, the saccharinity of Beery and Jackie Cooper, it is far rougher and raunchier than *She Done Him Wrong*. Pert Kelton's "Every Inch a Sailor" manages as many overtones as Mae West's "A Guy What Takes His Time," although Kelton never caresses her song as West does. It must have amused Wallace Beery to be on a Bowery so much coarser than the one his brother Noah inhabited, and sometimes his grossness—blowing his nose on his hand for instance—seems a comment on the refinement of *She Done Him Wrong*. In at least one instance Raoul Walsh seems to offer a gloss on Lowell Sherman. In *She Done*, a man lightly punches a girl who is too entranced with a terrible tenor, singing "Silver Threads among the Gold"; in *The Bowery*, a woman breaks a bottle across the face of a man who smiles too obviously at Kelton as she performs. Elsewhere, Beery blackjacks a drunk woman who tries to sweet-talk him, and we see the waiter drag her out with one hand as he balances a tray of beers with the other. The amiable vulgarity of *The*

Bowery probably goes beyond that of *She Done Him Wrong* because it followed and built on the audience receptivity that the West movie had uncovered. In part, however, the difference between the two lies in the concept of the Bowery. For all the flippancy and exaggeration of the Raft-Beery movie, it seems to accept the Bowery as a place, a neighborhood, a historical fact. For Mae West, it is a state of mind transformed into a stage set, a place for Lou to proclaim herself "One of the finest women ever walked the streets" without ever having to put the verbal image to the test.

The last scene of *She Done Him Wrong* has always been troublesome. When all of the malefactors still alive have been rounded up, Cummings (the Hawk) arrests Lou and, in a tender scene in a carriage, sentences her to life with him. "That engagement ring ought to be a laugh," complained the *New Yorker*, "but in the picture it isn't." Later admirers, clinging to Lou's reaction to the tiny diamond, have decided that it is a laugh. The scene is preposterous, as are most scenes in the film, but it is unnecessary either to explain it or to explain it away. Mae West—at least Meryman's Mae West "B"—may have believed in the hokey plots she regularly mutilated, but, whether by art or accident, she chose settings and plots that would not allow reality to impinge on her image. She is not a philosopher, a moralist, a parodist, a satirist. She is, as Richard Schickel once said, a "great grotesque." A sexless sex goddess, she is the avatar of sex in the head. Her best lines—like those of Groucho Marx and W. C. Fields—are widely quoted and misquoted, usually in an approximation of her own suggestive delivery, and by people who—quite rightly—remember her in fragments, not in films. She was a remarkable comedian who built a comic persona just right for her limited but undeniable abilities. It escaped the performing context and, as celebrated comic personae tend to, found its way into the popular imagination where—as the opening paragraph of this chapter suggests—it diffused into a generalized joke about sex. When the actress, the creator tried to take the image into real life, it became a dybbuk that made her pathetic rather than funny, as even the most sympathetic interviews of the 1960s and 1970s indicate. It is a moot question whether *She Done Him Wrong* is a classic or an eccentric art object, like *The Spanish Tragedy* or an art deco orange juice stand. As an admirer of Kyd and kitsch, I lean toward the second designation. In any case, *She Done Him Wrong* is the best available example of Mae West, the performer; the purist presentation of Mae West, the image. It is tempting to puff up that image with significance, but so many people have fallen victim to that temptation that I will take refuge in Huey Long's remark—surely as appropriate to Mae West as it was to the man who spoke it—"Just say I'm *sui generis*, and let it go at that."

Notes

1. The problem of Mae West as author is much more complex than
that of Charles Chaplin. There are nine playscripts in the Library of
Congress files by or presumed to be by Mae West, covering the years
from 1921 to 1930, from the one-act *The Ruby Ring* to *Frisco Kate*, the
play on which *Klondike Annie* (1936) was based. These include *Diamond
Lil*, of which the authorship has always been in doubt. Jack Linder,
who produced the play originally, said in 1933, "It was not Miss West's
play, nor was it written by Miss West. My brother, Mark Linder, wrote
a play called 'Chatham Square' and it was revised by Miss West and
Miss Greta Willard" (quoted by Thornton Delehanty, *New York Post*,
February 15, 1933, p. 12). When Mark Linder died in 1950, the *New York
Times* obituary (November 11, 1950, p. 15) recalled the old controversy,
"Mr. Linder was never established as the author, although his widow
. . . said yesterday, 'of course he wrote it.'" According to West's own
version of the matter, in *Goodness Had Nothing to Do with It* (Englewood
Cliffs, N.J., Prentice-Hall, 1959, p. 108), she found *Chatham Square*
"tired in construction, banal in plotting, characterless" (descriptions
which sound like variations on the critics' comments on her own
melodramas) and went on to write her own play with the Bowery
setting. Still, she gave him credit ("Suggested by Mark Linder") and a
part in the play. *Chatham Square* was copyrighted in 1928, the year of
Diamond Lil, but there is no script in the Library of Congress; so no real
comparison can be made. Beginning with *I'm No Angel*, West was
given screenplay credit on all her films through *My Little Chickadee*
(1940), in which W.C. Fields shares the credit; newspapers and magazines during the decade were sprinkled with articles on her presumed
authorial skills. Shortly after the release of *She Done Him Wrong*, she
told an interviewer (Charles Parker Hammond, "She's No Angel,"
New York Post, February 18, 1933, sec. 3, p. 5) that she was responsible
for everything in her scripts—ideas, construction, dialogue—and that
she had a distinctive style, "just as Eugene O'Neill's style is easy to
identify." For a tongue-in-cheek article called "Literary Lil" (*Picture
Play*, 39 [September 1939], 62), Malcolm H. Oettinger talked to West
about her writing habits; she dictates, she explained, "Then my sec'at-
ary would piece the different parts together and arrange chapters and
things." Most of her films testify to someone's sure sense of the kind of
line that fits the Mae West character and to a fondness for the creakiest
kind of melodrama, and her well-known distaste for writers assigned
to her suggests that she was that someone. "Wish I could find some
writer who understands me," she told George Daws (*New York World-
Telegram*, August 9, 1934, p. 3). "But I can't, and so I have to do two

jobs." I think that it is safe to say that, in her plays and screenplays at least, she is, if not sole author, a very persistent rewriter. On her other works, she seems to have received the kind of help conventionally sought by celebrity writers. *Pleasure Man,* the novel version of her 1928 play, published by Dell in 1975, was written with "the kind assistance of Lawrence Lee," and at the beginning of *Goodness,* West thanks Stephen Longstreet "for his editorial assistance." The autobiography (pp. 140–42) makes clear that Howard Merling joined the road company of *Diamond Lil* primarily to work with her on the book that became *Babe Gordon* (1930) and, renamed after a contest for a new title, *The Constant Sinner* (1931). Of the many articles that appeared under her name, some were obviously ghosted. Robert Lewis Shayon, who was an editor of the short-lived *Parade,* told me (telephone conversation, October 9, 1980) that he wrote "Sex in the Theatre," which she signed for the first number of that magazine (1 [September 1929], 12–13, 32) and the article she did for *Liberty* ("Ten Days and Five Hundred Dollars," 4[August 20, 1927], 53–56) after her ten-day jail term when the police closed her first play, *Sex* (1926), is so uncharacteristic in tone that another hand may be suspected. As in the Chaplin chapter, I will assume that anything her name is on is hers.

2. Presumably Ernst Lubitsch. Lubitsch became production head at Paramount in early 1935, replacing Emanuel Cohen, an executive who pretty much let West have her own way. At the time, Lubitsch praised West, but managed to color his compliments with "she is not a director's star. . . . Her films are vehicles built around her and I, personally, cannot make a good picture unless I am dealing with someone more pliable" (quoted by James Robert Parish, *The Paramount Pretties,* New Rochelle, N.Y., Arlington House, 1972, p. 311). A year later, Lubitsch was removed as production chief, and an Associated Press story (*New York Post,* February 25, 1936, p. 2) implied that West was instrumental in his replacement by "her old friend" William LeBaron. She had known LeBaron since 1911, when she appeared in *A La Broadway,* a revue for which he did the book and lyrics, and he had served as producer for her films. A second AP story, (*Post,* same page), datelined Chicago, where Lubitsch was interviewed on his way to New York and Europe, quoted his reaction to the charges of West's manager, Jim Timony, " 'Try to push her around, did I?' he grinned. 'She's much too heavy.' " In interviews in New York (*New York Times,* March 1, 1936, sec. 9, p. 5) and London (Campbell Dixon, "Mae Goes West," *London Telegraph,* May 18, 1936, p. 7), Lubitsch continued to snipe at her, using Victor McLaglen as his weapon. Despite Timony's "Well, in the end she pushed him around," (*New York Post,* February 25, 1936, p. 2) West's own influence with the real powers at Paramount seems ques-

tionable. It was in 1936 that she left Paramount to form Major Pictures Corporation with Emanuel Cohen. In her autobiography (*Goodness*, p. 190) she indicates that her departure had much to do with her differences with Lubitsch, whom she describes as "in some ways a gifted man, but in the opinion of many, arrogant, narrow and already slipping." A comparison of the post-1936 films of West and of Lubitsch suggests that the slip was on the other foot.

3. Moore is largely forgotten in the history of film, except as the drunken husband whom Mary Pickford had to buy off so that she could marry Douglas Fairbanks. Moore began his career early in the century with D. W. Griffith and worked regularly all during the silent era, playing not only with Pickford, but with stars like Dorothy Gish, Blanche Sweet, Elsie Janis, Fritzi Scheff. Myron Selznick advertised him in 1919 as "A Man in Man's Size Plays" (unidentified clip, Owen Moore file, NYPL-PARC; see also, *Morning Telegraph*, July 13, 1919, sec. 5, pt. 1, p. 11). He made the transition to the talkies and appeared in one or more films every year until *She Done Him Wrong*. He made just one film after that, *A Star Is Born* (1937). Somewhat ironically, given his own reputation as a drinker, he played the director who hates to deal with the alcoholic Norman Maine (Fredric March).

4. Bright said in a letter to me (July 30, 1980) that he offended Darryl F. Zanuck, then production chief at Warners, who bought up his contract, and that Bright's agent, Myron Selznick, to prove that Zanuck was wrong when he said Bright would never again work in the industry, immediately got him the job on *She Done Him Wrong*. That explains why half of Warner's highly touted team turned up at Paramount shortly after signing a new contract on the home lot.

5. His skill as a performer can be seen in his good-natured drunk and would-be lecher in Frank Capra's *Ladies of Leisure* (1930); he succeeds somehow in convincing the audience that he is less desirable than the wooden hero of Ralph Graves.

3

DUCK SOUP

· 1933 ·

The carrot seeds you gave me didn't grow.
Did you plant them?
No.
Then I can't understand why they didn't grow. What did
you do with them?
I ate them.
Out of curiosity?
No, out of a bowl.

If you could insinuate a stage Italian accent and a merciless pun or two
into these lines, they might pass for an exchange between Groucho
and Chico Marx. It is their kind of logic, but it is also the stock in trade
of the men who spoke the lines—Joe Cook, whom W. C. Fields once
called "Biggest of the nut headliners," and his chief stooge, Tom
Howard. The passage comes from *Rain or Shine* (1930), the movie
without music that Frank Capra made from Cook's successful Broadway musical (1928). The Cook/Marx logic sometimes invaded Hollywood production decisions. The film also featured Cook's other
stooge, Dave Chasen—"the little man with the wild hair and the wild
gesture," as Marian Spitzer called him—given mostly to silent physical
bits which, despite the differences in kind and quality, indicate that he
and Harpo Marx had roots in the same witless vaudeville character.
   I let Joe Cook open my chapter on *Duck Soup* to emphasize the

The Marx Brothers pose as heroes of Freedonia. Chico, Zeppo, Groucho, Harpo. (*Duck
Soup*, Paramount, 1933. The Museum of Modern Art/Film Stills Archive.)

American context in which the Marx Brothers developed. Some admirers of the Marxes invoke words like *surrealism* and *dadaism* to describe their work, a usage that is as misleading in fact as it is complimentary in intention. The practice has an impressive history. Antonin Artaud was probably the first person to describe the work of the Marx Brothers as surrealistic in his celebration of *Animal Crackers* (1930) and *Monkey Business* (1931) in the *Nouvelle Revue Française* on January 1, 1932. Later that year, reviewing *Horse Feathers* (1932) for *The New Statesman and Nation*, Francis Birrell wondered condescendingly about the popularity of the comedians ("But presumably *surréalisme* has a direct appeal to the majority, which I should never have expected"), and Philippe Soupault, one of the founders of surrealism, praised the same film in *L'Europe Nouvelle*. Soupault, however, did not use the label, perhaps because for him—having broken with the movement out of distaste for the codification that had set in—it had a specific meaning inappropriate to the Marx Brothers. Unless one wants to work as Artaud does, positing "a distinct poetic state of mind" that is then defined in terms of the disintegrative elements in the films, the French movements seem too programmatic to describe the Marx Brothers and their movies. "I don't think the word art, which happens to be my son's name, has ever come up in my thoughts or my conversations," Groucho said in 1970. "We were trying to be funny, and we were getting very good money for it." His ingenuousness need not be taken at face value, but the sentence implies, correctly I think, that the Marx Brothers movies had more to do with popular taste and prejudices than with intellectual theories about the restrictive nature of society, psychology, language. That *Duck Soup* reminded Pierre Bost of *Ubu Roi* and that Salvador Dali embraced the Marxes as surrealists do less to define the Marxes in European terms than to recognize the cross-cultural similarities in antirealistic art.

Birrell, uncomfortable with the juxtaposition of popularity and *surréalisme*, turned to English sources and found the analogues he wanted in Edward Lear and Lewis Carroll. If he had not been so relentlessly high-toned, he might have rummaged around the English music hall and come up with useful comparisons—say the Fred Karno sketches that schooled Charlie Chaplin and Stan Laurel for the world at large. The Carroll connection had already been made in *Photoplay*, in which Sara Hamilton invoked *Alice in Wonderland* in a standard fan-magazine personality piece called "The Nuttiest Quartette in the World." If Lewis Carroll and Morrie Ryskind are brothers under the skin, as Groucho suggested in the interview in which he disowned art, it is not because *Animal Crackers*, the Ryskind script he had in mind, is very like *Alice*, but because all nonsense writing—particularly the kind that implies a deeper level of sense—bears a family resemblance.

Twentieth-century France and nineteenth-century England may have produced works distantly related to that of the Marxes, but the clearest likenesses, as my opening paragraph shows, can be found at home—not only among vaudeville comics but in American silent film comedy which flourished on the kind of destructiveness and aggression that the Marxes carried from vaudeville to Broadway to sound film. So, too, the literary genre closest in spirit and style to the Marx Brothers is an American one. It was William Troy, in his dismissive review of *Duck Soup*, who first commented on the connection between the Marxes and "the whole 'crazy-fool' humor of the post-war epoch," but it was Alva Johnston, writing in 1936, who gave point to the comparison: "They were influenced also by the lunatic school of writers. They became followers of Stephen Leacock, Donald Ogden Stewart, Robert Benchley and others in the war to free the human mind from the domination of reason and judgment."[1] Influences are more difficult to document than Johnston's statement suggests, but similarities abound. There is a chapter in Stewart's *Mr and Mrs Haddock Abroad* (1924) in which Mr Haddock comes down to breakfast and the waiter, as one line suggests another, becomes a barber, a prosecuting attorney, the defense attorney, and a politician making a nominating speech; what begins as a breakfast turns into Haddock's acceptance of the presidential nomination to the enthusiastic response of the multitude. This kind of identity shift is used routinely by Groucho and his writers although the shifts come more quickly in the films, often within a line or two. An example is the balcony scene between Groucho and Lucille (Thelma Todd) in *Monkey Business* in which he imitates a tomcat and then, touching a number of parody bases, is a youth calling for madder music, an officer off to the front, a lover who wants to take her away "from all this." It is virtually impossible to identify who wrote what in any of the Marx movies, but one of the scriptwriters on *Monkey Business* was S. J. Perelman, who has "crazy humor" connections of his own. None of the credited writers on *Duck Soup*—Bert Kalmar, Harry Ruby, Arthur Sheekman, Nat Perrin—are identified with the "crazy humor" group, yet a speech like the first assault by Rufus T. Firefly (Groucho) on Mrs. Teasdale (Margaret Dumont) uses an associational technique worthy of the best of the *New Yorker* non-sequitur fantasists, Stewart and Frank Sullivan. When Mrs. Teasdale says, "I feel you are the most able statesman in all Freedonia," Firefly answers, "Well, that covers a lot of ground." Then in an intricately constructed speech, empty of meaning, full of simulated emotive content, he skips from idea to idea, from word to word:

Say, you cover a lot of ground yourself. You'd better beat it. I hear they're going to tear you down and put up an

office building where you're standing. You can leave in a
taxi. If you can't leave in a taxi you can leave in a huff. If
that's too soon, you can leave in a minute and a huff.

The comparison of 1930s movies with 1920s humor inevitably suggests that one is the source of the other, but it is more useful to think in
terms of a shared intellectual and social climate in which lunacy, verbal
and physical, could flourish. After all, 1924 was the year in which the
Marx Brothers moved from vaudeville to Broadway in *I'll Say She Is* and
became the quadripartite toast of New York; in which Donald Ogden
Stewart wrote *Mr and Mrs Haddock Abroad*, which fifty years later he
would call "something more resembling *Alice in Wonderland* or the
Marx Brothers" than his earlier work. The year before, Robert Benchley had turned professional performer, taking "The Treasurer's Report" into Irving Berlin's *The Music Box Revue*, and the year after, the
New Yorker was born. The interchange between the theater and the
humor magazines was casual, expected. Donald Ogden Stewart wrote
for Joe Cook (*Fine and Dandy*, 1930); Groucho Marx wrote for the *New
Yorker* and *College Humor*.[2]

Comic writers and performers moved to Hollywood in the 1930s,
and in the first years of that decade irrationality still flourished. The
studios, faced with the talkies, scooped up Broadway actors of all
kinds, the comedians prominent among them. The Marx Brothers
were among the first, shooting *The Cocoanuts* (1929) at Paramount's
Astoria studios while they were still playing *Animal Crackers* (1928) on
stage. Although transplanted comedians worked all over Hollywood—Jimmy Durante at MGM, Bert Wheeler and Robert Woolsey at
RKO, Eddie Cantor for Samuel Goldwyn—and although Francis Birrell
could put Cantor's *Palmy Days* (1931) among the "*surréaliste* pictures"
and rate it above the Marx Brothers films, Paramount is the studio
which seemed most open to the outrageous. Groucho Marx liked to tell
the story—in *Groucho and Me*, for instance—of his difficulties with
conventional moviemakers who did not want him to use his painted
mustache or talk directly to the audience. There may have been an
executive at Astoria who firmly believed in the verisimilitude of film,
but a look at the Paramount comedies of the early 1930s suggests that
the studio had no hard rules about the use of the medium and that it
sheltered a great many artists with an inclination for the inventively
artificial. Besides the Marx Brothers, it brought in comedians such as
Mae West, W. C. Fields, and George Burns and Gracie Allen, the
queen of the non sequitur. It was the studio that produced an all-star
Alice in Wonderland (1933), an homage to Tenniel as well as to Carroll,
which, being an act of reverence, was more solemn than it should have

been. Even so, it remains appealing for its cameo performances—Gary Cooper's White Knight is one of the best—and it stands as an affirmation of an antirealistic bias at Paramount.

It is Herman Mankiewicz who is generally taken as Paramount's resident lunacy sage. He came to Hollywood in 1926, a pioneer breaking ground for the horde of New York writers who would follow in the next decade. He is now being transformed into myth, an embodiment of the wicked wit and the self-destructiveness that marked the Eastern intellectuals who mistook emigration for exile. He served as producer on *Monkey Business, Horse Feathers,* and *Million Dollar Legs* (1932), for which he sometimes claimed his brother Joseph's writing credit—a film with not so accidental similarities to *Duck Soup*—and was acting in the same capacity for *Soup* when he was fired, first from the movie, then from Paramount. Richard Corliss, in *Talking Pictures*, lists him as uncredited contributor to the scripts of *Monkey Business, Horse Feathers,* and *Legs*, and Pauline Kael says "surely there is a comic spirit that links" *Soup* and *Legs* and assumes that Mankiewicz is "a key linking figure." In *The Groucho Phile*, Groucho Marx dismissed Mankiewicz as "an irritating drunk who didn't give a hang about the movie project," a comment that may reflect the irascibility apparent in so many of the books and interviews of the comedian's old age or a defensive reaction to the post-Kael tendency to inflate Mankiewicz's contributions to the Marx movies. Still, in *Groucho and Me*, seventeen years before *The Groucho Phile*, twelve years before Kael's "Raising Kane," Groucho has an acidulous portrait of Mankiewicz, presented pseudonymously since the early book is almost genteel in its circumspection. Nat Perrin testifies to Mankiewicz's influence on *Monkey Business* and his ability to use a well-placed word or two to shape the direction of a script.

Since apportioning credit in any Hollywood film is as thankless as assigning lines in an Elizabethan collaboration, this apparent digression on Mankiewicz may seem at once arcane and unrewarding. Yet, Mankiewicz is a figure who, even in his casual attitude toward his job, suggests an atmosphere at Paramount in which the Marx Brothers would be at home. "The Marxes were extremely glad to see me," Mankiewicz wrote to his wife after *Horse Feathers* was finished. "They insist I'm crazy and that they wouldn't think of doing a picture without me." If that craziness, the "comic spirit" Kael speaks of, can be detached from the individual and extended to the environment, the special quality of the early Paramount sound comedies becomes clearer. Perhaps it can best be illustrated by looking beyond those comedians who, like the Marxes, came from vaudeville and Broadway, beyond a writer like Mankiewicz, whose New York roots were in the newspaper-theater world represented by George S. Kaufman, his old boss on the *New York Times* and the author, with Morrie Ryskind, of the Marxes' Broadway hits, *The Cocoanuts* and *Animal Crackers*. The Ernst Lubitsch touch is rather far removed from the Marx bludgeon, but a look at *One Hour with You* (1932) indicates an amused indifference to realism as marked as that in any of the Marx Brothers films. Maurice Chevalier, as Andre, has long discussions with the audience and at the end, when Andre and Colette (Jeanette MacDonald) become reconciled, they both speak directly to the camera, to the folks out front; it is Groucho's asides turned into shared confidences. Much of the dialogue is in rhymed couplets which can modulate easily into song. There are exchanges that might have come from the crazy humorists. At one point, Adolph (Charles Ruggles), dressed as Romeo, learns that Colette's party is not a costume ball. He rings for his butler—played by Charles Coleman, a master of Hollywood domestic gravity—and demands to know why he was misinformed about the nature of the party. A hesitation beat, and then the butler leans a little forward, still the immense dignity but now a politely sly smile, "I did so want to see you in tights." This is the Paramount where the title song of *One Hour with You* could become the Klopstokian love song "Woof Bloogle Gik" in *Million Dollar Legs*. The Paramount where the Marx Brothers could become Artaudian surrealists, hunters of the snark, animated crazy humorists, themselves.

The Marx Brothers who came to Paramount had been more than twenty years in the making. "I believe all comedians arrive by trial and error," Groucho Marx says in *Groucho and Me*, and he insists that all comedians begin by stealing material. Louis Calhern, the superb Trentino of *Duck Soup*, once told a *Saturday Evening Post* reporter that in his youth he and John Bartels played vaudeville in a pirated Weber and Fields act. "In time," Groucho went on to say, if the comic "was any good, he would emerge from the routine character he had started with and evolve into a distinct personality of his own. This had been my experience and also that of my brothers." Although the Marx memories of their vaudeville days are sometimes contradictory, it is clear that Groucho's trademarks—the walk, the cigar, the mustache, the frock coat—were established before *I'll Say She Is* brought the brothers to Broadway. Hector Arce assumed that they were adopted when Groucho was playing an old man, teacher to a gaggle of Marxes and others, in the tabloid shows the brothers developed, with the help of their uncle Al Shean, for vaudeville before World War I; yet, the photographs, the cartoons, the advertisements for *Fun in Hi Skule, Mr. Green's Reception,* and *Home Again,* reproduced in *The Groucho Phile,* show Groucho with a naked upper lip. According to Arthur Marx, his father's fast-talking style also goes back to the school act when "he was never sure whether his material was any good or not, so he decided that if he talked very rapidly, there would be less chance of the audience getting bored." That is an attractive story—neophyte comedian turns uncertainty into a virtue—and perhaps a true one, but for the Groucho we know on film the interplay between joke and delivery is so inevitable, the voice so assured, that hesitancy seems never to have been a possibility. If Firefly's speech quoted earlier in this chapter were spoken with some deliberation the associative devices would uncouple and the speech collapse into useless fragments.

Personality, in the context of comic performance, goes beyond the surface details of costume, voice, movement and suggests a character, however unreal, for whom there is a definite social and psychological identity. Groucho plays the confidence man in quest of money, sex, power. Yet, he has the Marxian equivalent of the motiveless malignity with which Coleridge saddled Iago; he is a case of motiveless manipulation. He woos the Margaret Dumont character or flirts with the Thelma Todd character, but it is the immediate encounter rather than the potential marriage or sex that interests him. The plot may demand that he win a football game or a war, but he is without goals, all drive and no destination. "But I don't think Groucho ever gave any serious thoughts to whether a line would interfere with the flow of the story," Nat Perrin said. "If it was a good bit of business or a funny line I'm certain it would have been in, no matter, what damage it did to the rest of the scene." To worry about story rather than line is to risk writing *Dimples* (1936), which Perrin and Arthur Sheekman did, instead of *Duck Soup*. It may have been the performer's desire for a laugh at any cost that dictated the Groucho character's constant shredding of situation, as Perrin suggests, but, whether accidental or deliberate, that practice is the most imaginative thing about the Groucho of the Paramount films. The sentimentalization of the Marxes, which began with Irving Thalberg's insistence on plot in *A Night at the Opera* (1935), tended to focus Groucho's aggressions too narrowly. There are still funny lines and marvelous scenes (the classic stateroom debacle in *Opera*), but the old exuberance, a little hampered by plot in *Opera* and *A Day at the Races* (1937), turns into a kind of desperation by the end of the decade. The verbal destruction that the Groucho character committed in the early films might be likened to the physical havoc in Charlie Chaplin's *The Rink* (1916). You cannot use body count to prove victory; it lies in the exhilaration of the twists and turns of language, as in the grace of Chaplin on skates.

Perhaps because the Groucho insults come so rapidly and so indiscriminately, he is usually thought of as the most aggressive member of the team. This reputation was increased with the success of his radio and television show, *You Bet Your Life*, in the 1950s and with its recurrent popularity in reruns in the 1970s, and with the indulgent reports of the acidulous offstage remarks of the man rather than the character. The venomous old man, the quizmaster, and the Groucho character from the films run together in the eyes of his fans, and they imagine his quips as scalps hanging from his belt. This is a misleading view of Groucho among the Marx Brothers. Alongside Margaret Dumont or Edwin Maxwell (the secretary of war in *Duck Soup*) or Harry Woods (the presumably tough gangster of *Monkey Business*), Groucho is a relentless aggressive force, but he is regularly overrun by his brothers. If we can believe S. J. Perelman's memory of *Home Again*, the vaudeville act that he saw as a boy in 1916, Groucho, as a father, was beset by a needling son, played by Gummo (then the fourth Marx Brother), and a wife, "a scraggy termagant in a feather boa." This sounds more like a W. C. Fields sketch than the image of Groucho Marx on the attack. In the films Groucho is regularly engulfed by Chico and Harpo. In the later films—the tootsie-frootsie scene in *A Day at the Races* or the train-boarding scene in *At the Circus* (1939)—Chico bests Groucho so relentlessly that the latter's defensive jokes become a kind of self-mockery. From the beginning, however, when Chico and Harpo close in on him at the hotel desk in *The Cocoanuts*, he is helpless because their brands of irrationality are even stronger than his. The scene that best illustrates this in *Duck Soup*, another desk scene, is the one in which first Chicolini (Chico) and then Pinky (Harpo) keep Firefly from answering his own phone, assure the caller that he is not in. "I wonder whatever became of me," Firefly says. "I should have been back here a long time ago."

Chico's identification tag—his piano aside—is his accent and his use of puns so outrageous that Groucho's "minute and a huff" seems restrained. Dialect comedians were rampant in vaudeville. Uncle Al Shean had his celebrated act with Ed Gallagher. Groucho began as a German dialect comedian, "doing 'Dutch,'" as Sime Silverman put it, and switched to a Yiddish accent—or so the story goes—on the day the Lusitania was sunk. Gummo did "a passable Hebrew" in the school act, according to Sime's review; played "a Jew comedian," as both Gummo and Groucho put it in *The Marx Bros. Scrapbook*. Chico had already developed his Italian dialect, doing a vaudeville double with Arthur Gordon, before he joined the family act in 1912. His was the accent that stayed. Although Willie the Wop, his character's name in *The Cocoanuts* on stage, was sanitized for the movie version, Hollywood in the 1930s was full of dialect comedians, doing mock Italian, German, Swedish, Spanish, Greek, Chinese, American black: Henry

Armetta, Luis Alberni, Herman Bing, Sig Rumann, Fritz Feld, El Brendel, Chris-Pin Martin, Billy Gilbert, Willie Fong, Stepin Fetchit. Sometimes, as with Billy Gilbert's Greek, the comedian turned it on or off on demand; more often, as with Bing's German and Brendel's Swedish, it became the performer's career. The joke about Chico's dialect is that it was never meant to approximate the real thing. Compare his reiterated "'at 'sa good" or his very elaborate puns with the more conventional Italian dialect turn of Henry Armetta (they are both in *The Big Store* [1941]), and the deliberate fakery of Chico becomes obvious. "What is it has a trunk, but no key, weighs two thousand pounds and lives in a circus?" asks Chicolini in the trial scene in *Duck Soup*. "That's irrelevant," snaps the prosecutor (Charles B. Middleton), and Chicolini, "A relephant! Hey, that's the answer."[3] The most fascinating thing about Chico's speech is not the dialect itself, but the way it fills space pointlessly. I am not thinking here of the non-sequitur content of the lines, but of the way he uses sentences, fragments, phrases, single words, particularly in the scenes with Harpo, to build a kind of cradle around the purely visual business. That same quality, given a forward thrust, becomes a pushiness that allows Chico to force his way into any situation. *Time*, in the cover story it did on the Marxes back in 1932, defined Chico "by a certain irrelevant vehemence which makes it seem that he is chagrined by something but has forgotten what it is." Chico's speech may never have been very Italian, but it became Chico even more clearly than Groucho's became Groucho or Harpo's silence became Harpo.

In *Harpo Speaks!* Harpo has a story to explain how he acquired each of his props, each of his specialties: the gookie, the pop-eyed, puff-cheeked stare he had had since childhood; the red wig which became blond for the movies; the horn; the raincoat with the bottomless pockets; the girl-chasing routine. And the harp.[4] And the silence. When Al Shean wrote *Home Again* for his nephews, so the familiar story goes, he wrote so few lines for Harpo that he suggested that the young man play silently. According to Harpo, he tried to improvise his own lines until a reviewer in Champaign-Urbana praised his pantomime and added, "Unfortunately, the effect is spoiled when he speaks." From then on, he played silently. Walter Kerr has pointed out that Harpo is not strictly a pantomimist since so many of his most effective bits depend on verbal cues from Chico, Groucho, or another performer. What the silence allowed Harpo to do was to develop the dim-witted boy, the Patsy Brannigan ("a standard character of the time," said Groucho) he had been playing since the school act began, into a kind of transcendent fool for whom there are no social taboos. By 1961, when the *New York Times Magazine* ran a photographic essay,

"Harpo in Toyland," Harpo had turned into a gentle and fey creature far removed from the character whom Percy Hammond called "the most animal of the 'Animal Crackers.'" Those admirers who like to think of Harpo as childlike should remember the children in *Monkey Business* who take such delight when Harpo and Gibson (Tom Kennedy) invade the Punch and Judy show and Harpo is stuck with a pin, hit with a paddle, throttled. The scariest scene in any of the Marx Brothers films is in *Horse Feathers* when the camera looks away from Professor Wagstaff's desk to pick up the dogcatcher (Harpo) shoveling books into the fireplace, a look of demented glee on his face. Harpo's innocent clown, most obvious in his reveries with his harp, has always been balanced (and in the early films, overbalanced) by the demonic clown. It is this aspect of Harpo that has most contributed to the reputation of the Marx Brothers as an all-purpose demolition crew.

Zeppo is the odd man out, the straight man who was never happy in the act. As early as 1929, before their first film, Zeppo told an interviewer for *Theatre Magazine* that he was going to retire as soon as *Animal Crackers* closed. In 1931, when Groucho, Chico, and Harpo, with Louis Sorin and Margaret Dumont, made two appearances in Heywood Broun's *Shoot the Works!* to help shore up that foundering revue, the *New York Times* reported that Groucho made "a sly curtain speech in which he expressed gratification that the three brothers could get along without the fourth." It is characteristic of Zeppo's reputation that even those who worked with him are unclear about what he did. Morrie Ryskind said that he and Kaufman "would try to throw a line to Zeppo if we had a situation," but that "Zeppo was involved with the love story and nobody cared a lot about the love stories." In fact, the love stories in the Kaufman-Ryskind shows, *The Cocoanuts* and *Animal Crackers*, were played by juveniles other than Zeppo. He did court the college widow (Thelma Todd) in *Horse Feathers*, as did all the brothers, but his only conventional juvenile role was in *Monkey Business*. According to Joe Adamson, Bert Kalmar and Harry Ruby "created a romance between Zeppo and Raquel Torres" in *Duck Soup*, but Leo McCarey, the director, "went ahead without it." Never really the juvenile, then, Zeppo was something more than the "peerlessly cheesy improvement on the traditional straightman," that James Agee called him. "He was a character of no importance. He was a lousy actor and he got out as soon as he could." So Groucho said with the gracefulness that colored so many of his remarks during the 1970s, but when Richard J. Anobile tried to follow up his dismissive comment in *The Marx Bros. Scrapbook*, Groucho began to defend his brother, "I had a couple of great scenes with Zeppo." And so he did. The quality that Zeppo had, which presumed substitutes like Allan Jones, Kenny

Baker, and Tony Martin could never approximate, grew out of his being a Marx brother. "We're four of the three musketeers," they sang in *Animal Crackers*, in the celebrated song which unfortunately never made it into the film version of that show. In key scenes in the films, for instance the musical extravaganza and the war sequences that end *Duck Soup*, the four of them play so effectively as a unit that one says "they sang" unselfconsciously, knowing full well that Harpo did not actually sing. Zeppo, even when he stood around simply looking well-scrubbed, conveyed a sense of acceptance, of willingness not to be surprised that contributed to the benign and malignant unreality of the Marxian enterprise.

Duck Soup was the fifth of the Marx Brothers movies, the last and best of the films they did for Paramount. They began by transferring their stage pieces—*The Cocoanuts* and *Animal Crackers*—to the screen, and then they had to have vehicles built for them, settings in which they could erupt (an ocean liner in *Monkey Business*, a campus in *Horse Feathers*), popular forms that they could parody and eviscerate (the gangster film in *Monkey Business*, the college musical in *Horse Feathers*). According to Hector Arce, they were next to confront Ruritarian operetta in something called *Oo La La* with Ernst Lubitsch, the old master of the genre, to direct them. The opening of *Duck Soup*, a stock shot of a picturesque European village, suggests that that idea may have materialized, but all that Lubitsch gave to the Marx film is the name Sylvania—where Jeanette MacDonald reigned in *The Love Parade* (1929)—for the country that declares war on Freedonia. There were so many mythical kingdoms in Hollywood in the early 1930s (Will Rogers was American envoy to still another Sylvania in *Ambassador Bill* [1931]) that Lewis Milestone's *The Front Page* (1931) could phrase its opening mock apology, "This story is laid in a Mythical Kingdom." Although one might make a case for a connection between the Chicago of Ben Hecht and Charles MacArthur and the Marxes' Freedonia, the latter was more likely to remind contemporary audiences of the El Dorania of *Cracked Nuts* (1931), where Wheeler and Woolsey vie for power, or the Klopstokia of *Million Dollar Legs*, of which W. C. Fields is president.

Although there is a qualitative difference between the work of Wheeler and Woolsey and that of the Marx Brothers (Mordaunt Hall, reviewing *So This Is Africa!* in 1933, said, "With the clever twisted humor of the Marx brothers, this production would have been much more effective"), it seems less than an accident that *Duck Soup* was originally called *Cracked Ice*. There was a casual exchange of personnel between the Wheeler and Woolsey movies and the Paramount comedies. Edward Cline directed *Cracked Nuts*, went to Paramount for

Million Dollar Legs, was back with Wheeler and Woolsey again in *So This Is Africa!* Among the writers, both Herman Mankiewicz (*Girl Crazy*) and S. J. Perelman (*Hold 'Em Jail*) wrote for Wheeler and Woolsey in 1932, but Joseph L. Mankiewicz is a more interesting case. He and Henry Myers wrote both *Million Dollar Legs* and *Diplomaniacs* (1933). When Mankiewicz was skirmishing with Paramount in late 1932 over his signing with RKO, the legal department demanded to see his original story for *Diplomaniacs* to be certain that he had not used anything from the *Cracked Ice* script that was to become *Duck Soup.* Since *Diplomaniacs* was released months before *Duck Soup* (RKO ground out Wheeler and Woolsey shows like sausages—and with more filler than meat), the influences, if any, might run the other way. It is possible that the blackface musical number in which Wheeler and Woolsey lead the delegates to the peace conference in "Are You Ready for Judgment Day?" suggested the off-to-war number in *Duck Soup,* but the presentation is so static in *Diplomaniacs* that the Marx Brothers film transforms any possible borrowing into something completely new.

Actors, too, passed back and forth between Paramount and RKO. Ben Turpin was in both *Cracked Nuts* and *Million Dollar Legs,* and Hugh Herbert and Teddy Hart, members of the plotting cabinet in *Legs,* took their conspiratorial talents to *Diplomaniacs,* Herbert as a very unlikely Chinaman. Raquel Torres had her trial by Wheeler and Woolsey (*So This Is Africa!*) before she came to *Duck Soup,* and Edgar Kennedy went from presiding over the peace conference in *Diplomaniacs* to running a lemonade stand in Freedonia. More important for *Duck Soup* is Louis Calhern, the chief spy for the munitions men in *Diplomaniacs.* He had a reputation in the 1920s for playing elegant scoundrels on Broadway. "Louis Calhern works with well-tailored statuesqueness and disdain," Gilbert Gabriel said of his performance in *A Distant Drum* (1928). In Hollywood in the early 1930s, when suavity was still often a characteristic of gang leaders (Paul Lukas in *City Streets* [1931]), Calhern played mostly criminals until he was introduced to nonsense comedy in *Diplomaniacs,* in which one of the jokes is at the expense of his own screen image. We first see him contemplating himself with some admiration. "I must look my best tonight," he says. "There's dirty work afoot. I've conspiring to do." His minuscule valet (Teddy Hart) assures him that he can "conspire freely in that suit." Despite this promising introduction, the film scarcely makes the best use of Calhern. Still, his initiation in *Diplomaniacs* presumably prepared him for *Duck Soup,* in which his "well-tailored statuesqueness" was to make him a perfect foil for the Marx Brothers.

The film most often compared to *Duck Soup* today, thanks to the Herman Mankiewicz connection, is *Million Dollar Legs*. In only one of the 1933 reviews that I have seen—the one in the *New York Post*—is *Legs* mentioned at all. Comic spirit aside, *Duck Soup* may have borrowed a few details from the earlier Paramount film, but they were much transformed in the process. The spy joke in *Legs*—Ben Turpin's cross-eyes staring from one hiding place after another—may have suggested the enlisting of Chicolini and Pinky as spies for Sylvania. The influence on the distaff side is more obvious, although less fruitful. Glamorous female spies were all over Hollywood at this time. On Paramount's home lot, for instance, Marlene Dietrich played X-27 in *Dishonored* (1931), but it was Greta Garbo, as the protagonist of *Mata Hari* (1932), who had a direct effect on *Million Dollar Legs*, an indirect one on *Duck Soup*. Garbo was the immediate target of the Lyda Roberti character in *Legs*. She was not only called Mata Machree ("the woman no man can resist"), but she had a terrible Swedish dialect ("I bane fond of yumpers") superimposed on the performer's own German-Polish accent. Vera Marcal in *Duck Soup* presumably derives from the same sources. She is identified as a dancer, which suggests that a musical number may once have been intended for her, but about all that Raquel Torres gets to do in the role is wear slinky gowns, whisper conspiratorially, and in the sequence at Mrs. Teasdale's clutch a dressing gown across her discreetly provocative bosom.

A resemblance might also be seen between Fields's first routine and the one that Groucho performs just before the final confrontation between Firefly and Trentino, although the styles of the two comedians are so different that it may not be immediately apparent that these are the same joke. Fields's president is dictating a message to an eminent military personage, the opening of which he keeps rewording to make the greeting less cordial, ending finally with "Dear Corporal." Firefly, having been persuaded to meet Trentino once more in the cause of peace, imagines Trentino's rebuffing his gestures of friendship, his anger so escalating as he invents the scene that he slaps Trentino when he arrives. The resemblances between *Duck Soup* and *Million Dollar Legs* are almost as tenuous as those between *Soup* and the Wheeler and Woolsey films. They reflect a shared access to comic material and method, a community attraction to certain ideas, and a genuine expectation that movie audiences are ready to laugh even at such ugly subjects as corrupt governments, failed diplomacy, and the possibility of war.

If only for the sake of Fields, Roberti, and a primly erotic love-at-first-sight scene in which Migg (Jack Oakie) and Angela (Susan Fleming) brush off one another after having knocked each other down, I remain fond of *Million Dollar Legs*. Still, it lacks the staying power of *Duck Soup*. There is no comic center in *Legs*; Paramount was still using Fields—as in *International House* (1933)—as though a movie were a vaudeville bill. Although *Soup* is also composed of self-contained fragments and it has even less plot than *Legs* does, it is clearly designed as a Marx Brothers movie. One of the obvious reasons is that the script was put together by old Marx hands. Bert Kalmar and Harry Ruby, songwriters turned scenarists, had first worked with the Marxes when they wrote the music for *Animal Crackers* on Broadway and had rejoined them in Hollywood to contribute both the songs and the screenplay (with Perelman and Will B. Johnstone) to *Horse Feathers*. Arthur Sheekman and Nat Perrin had worked on *Monkey Business* and the radio show, *Flywheel, Shyster and Flywheel* (1932–33), and Sheekman is said to have helped Groucho with his humor book, *Beds* (1930). In the case of Kalmar and Ruby, it is easy to identify one of their significant contributions to the film. Although Groucho once said, "Not to listen to Ruby is a liberal education," Kalmar and Ruby understood how to concoct an elaborate musical number which would introduce the Groucho character to the film: "Hooray for Captain Spaulding" in *Animal Crackers*; the presentation of Professor Wagstaff as the new president of Huxley College in *Horse Feathers*; "His Excellency Is Due" in *Duck Soup*. "Dr. Hackenbush," the number they wrote for *A Day at the Races*, was never filmed, but it became almost as well known as the other songs because, as George Seaton said of Groucho in 1971, "He'll sing it at the drop of a hat!"

"Dr. Hackenbush" was to turn into a representative Groucho Marx song, but it is the musical numbers *in situ* that are impressive. The one in *Duck Soup* resembles both the earlier ones; it uses the hesitation device of "Captain Spaulding" and the definitional technique of *Horse Feathers*. In *Animal Crackers*, Hives (Robert Greig) leads the other butlers in an expectation song about "one of those men," but it is followed not by the Captain's entrance, but by that of Roscoe W. Chandler (Louis Sorin). Then the entire chorus lines up to welcome the celebrity in a passage that ends, "At last, the Captain has arrived," although it is Jamison (Zeppo) who comes in. Then a second lead-in brings the Captain, who sings, "Hello, I Must Be Going." In *Duck Soup*, Bob (Zeppo) and Mrs. Teasdale lead the chorus in "Hail, hail, Freedonia!" to welcome Rufus T. Firefly, the new leader; trumpeters play fanfares, guards stand with swords uplifted, ballet dancers scatter flowers and kneel in homage. Everyone stares expectantly up the steps, as fanfare after fanfare hails an entrance that does not take place. Firefly slides down a fireman's pole and comes on from the rear, taking his place alongside the guards, his cigar held out with their swords. The audience, knowing this kind of music, waits with the reception guests for the scene to build to a climax, but the joke demands that the situation simply peter out. To keep the audience from responding viscerally rather than intellectually to the flattening effect of the gag, the script gives Mrs. Teasdale a monumental understatement: "We've been expecting you." After a few minutes of typical Groucho dialogue, in which Firefly manages to insult or disconcert Mrs. Teasdale, Trentino, and Vera Marcal, he presents his program for the nation in song. This is the equivalent of "Whatever It Is, I'm Against It," in *Horse Feathers*, the one a philosophy of education, the other of government. Firefly seems to be promising a regime that will be both repressive and permissive, but the number itself is less biting than the one in *Horse Feathers*. It is most successful as an occasion for the turns Groucho gets between verses—a sailor's hornpipe, a "Yankee Doodle" fife bit, snatches of familiar songs—which provide a taste of the musical mosaic that will be used more impressively in "The Country's Going to War" number at the end of the film.

The visual superiority of the *Duck Soup* number to the one in *Horse Feathers* and the greater control of the frustrated-expectation device compared to its use in *Animal Crackers*, suggests that Kalmar, Ruby, and Groucho had special assistance. And so they did. Although Norman McLeod, who did *Monkey Business* and *Horse Feathers*, is a more accomplished director of comedy than he is usually credited with being, Leo McCarey is clearly the best director who ever worked with the Marxes. Groucho would remember him years later as "the only first class director we ever had." As for McCarey, he tended to dismiss the wild comedies he directed in the 1930s—*Duck Soup*, *The Milky Way* (1936), even *The Kid from Spain* (1932), although he was proud of the *corrida* scene in the last. He was much more willing to talk about his early years (1923–29) with Hal Roach, when he worked as supervisor, director, or writer on many of the Laurel and Hardy and Charley Chase shorts. It is conceivable that the Leo McCarey who could say of *Going My Way* (1944) and *The Bells of St. Mary's* (1945) that "one might say that they alone constitute almost my whole career" would not want to dwell on *Duck Soup*. Looking through eyes other than McCarey's, however, I see *Duck Soup* as one of his best films.

Much has been written on the Laurel and Hardy elements that Leo McCarey presumably brought to *Duck Soup*. *We Faw Down*, which McCarey directed in 1928, is one of the many movies in which Laurel and Hardy do the hat-switching routine—in which each momentarily gets the wrong derby—that is used so superbly in *Duck Soup*. A three-headed switch, involving Harpo, Chico, and Edgar Kennedy, it is born in accident but fed by Harpo's cheerful malevolence and Chico's complicity; a Laurel and Hardy motif swells to a Marx major theme. The doorbell sequence in which Chicolini and Pinky try to get into Mrs. Teasdale's house, a routine in which first one, then the other, finally both, end up outside, is obviously an extension of the scene in *Early to Bed* (1928), in which a tipsy Hardy tricks Laurel by ringing the bell, hiding, and then running inside and shutting Laurel out. The tendency, once one begins to think of the Laurel and Hardy films, is to multiply the borrowings, as Charles Silver did so ingeniously in his 1973 *Film Comment* piece on McCarey. I suspect that the bathtub scene in which Harpo, bugle blowing, rises out of the tub from under a startled Edgar Kennedy has less to do with the peekaboo nude scene of Max Davidson in *Call of the Cuckoo* (1927) than it does with the bit in *Monkey Business* in which first a woman, then a grinning Harpo, finally a third battered passenger rise from a deck chair. When I see Pinky and his horse in bed together, I do not think of *Angora Love* (1929), in which the goat that adopts Laurel and Hardy never goes to bed with them, but of the scene in *Animal Crackers* in which Mrs. Whitehead (Margaret Irving) sweet talks the Professor (Harpo); she asks him if there isn't someone he loves and he pulls out a picture and kisses it. A horse, of course. Actually, the fact of the animal is just a distraction in the *Duck Soup* scene, since what it provides is a standard exploded-expectation joke. Pinky, in his Paul Revere role, interrupts his midnight ride when a girl signals him from a window. The camera moves from Pinky's discarded boots to the girl's slippers to the horse's shoes; then it goes to the bedroom where, despite the juxtaposition of boots and slippers, the girl lies alone and Pinky and the horse share a bed.

Whatever the Laurel and Hardy echoes in these two sequences, there is one bit which seems to have been borrowed from another of Hal Roach's comedians and doctored to fit the Harpo character. Although Harpo's raincoat is celebrated as a catchall for the most unlikely props (the cup of hot coffee the dogcatcher gives to the panhandler in *Horse Feathers*), when Pinky pulls out a blowtorch to light the cigars in the scene in Trentino's office, I am reminded of the one lovely touch of fantasy in *Innocent Husbands*, the charming farce that McCarey directed for Roach in 1925; to light the cigar of the house detective (Lucien Littlefield), Charley Chase pulls first one, then a second lighted match out of his coat pocket, and the film moves casually across that piece of fine nonsense back again to the quasi-realistic level at which McCarey and Chase have been working. There is one other joke with its roots firmly in silent comedy, although whether it was inspired by McCarey and Roach I do not know. This is the running gag in which Pinky, as Firefly's driver, takes off on the motorcycle, leaving his excellency sitting in the sidecar.[5] In one of the early imaginative variations on that gag, in *Big Moments from Little Pictures* (1924), Will Rogers, doing a Ford Sterling parody, commandeers a car only to have the driver roar off, leaving the back end of the car still sitting. In *Duck Soup*, the joke is played, then repeated, and finally topped when Firefly insists on mounting the motorcycle, and Pinky drives off in the sidecar.

The most important sequences in *Duck Soup* that can be said to have come from Laurel and Hardy are the quarrel scene, of which the switched-hat joke is a part, in which Chicolini (as peanut vendor rather than spy or minister of war, his other offices) and Pinky fight with the lemonade vendor (Kennedy); and the reprise, in which only Pinky and the lemonade vendor take part. The presence of Kennedy has much to do with the Laurel and Hardy feel of the scene, for he, too, is an old Hal Roach hand, having both directed and acted with the comic team. In *Two Tars* (1928), that superb essay in anarchy, he plays the driver behind Laurel and Hardy, whose argument with them spreads through the whole line of cars, leaving a trail of destruction, an automobile graveyard. The sequence in *Duck Soup* is not in that societal hysteria vein. It is modeled on a quieter—if just as lethal—confrontation of which the one in *Big Business* (1929) is the finest example. In it, mild annoyance escalates until Laurel and Hardy dismantle James Finlayson's house while he tears their car apart. Each movement is studied, premeditated, and although Finlayson seethes with anger, he, like the more coolly calculating Laurel and Hardy, stops to register each indignity before making his own move; the result is a rhythm so deliberate, so stately even, that mayhem becomes almost a dance. The battle of the vendors in *Duck Soup* is played at that rhythm. Even though McCarey may have left the Roach studio before *Big Business* was filmed, I assume that the director, so familiar with the Laurel and Hardy pace, and Kennedy, an actor famous for his "slow burn," were largely responsible for the speed of the scenes. The first one begins with a fight between Chico and Harpo, the usual encounter in which Chico spars protectively while Harpo goes under his guard and kicks him in the pants. When Kennedy intrudes, he becomes the target. While Chico explains relentlessly, illustrating his remarks with an occasional kick in the pants, Harpo harasses Kennedy by getting his hand in Kennedy's pocket, his leg—in the characteristic Harpo manner—hanging from Kennedy's hand; by bumping him with his horn; by using his scissors, a new Harpo prop that becomes a running joke in the movie; by implementing the hat routine which is topped by the burning of Kennedy's bowler. In this case, familiar Marx elements are modulated into the borrowed rhythm. The second scene is more directly on the *Big Business* model. Kennedy takes a bag of peanuts and when Harpo, tending the stand for Chico, holds out his hand for payment, Kennedy spreads mustard across it. Harpo wipes the mustard on Kennedy's sash, cuts off the soiled end, and throws it away. They continue to give *Tit for Tat* (as a 1935 Laurel and Hardy movie was called) until Kennedy turns over the peanut stand and Harpo splashes, barefoot, in his opponent's lemonade.

Chico and Harpo have played slow aggression scenes before—the one in *Monkey Business*, for instance, in which they cut off the officer's grand mustache a "snoop" at a time. Characteristically, they work at a brisker pace, and *Duck Soup* is blessed with a fine example, the scene in which Chicolini and Pinky, spies for Sylvania, report to Trentino. A comparison of this scene with the Kennedy sequences might best begin with a look at the two foils. Louis Calhern and Kennedy have size in common—height, not bulk, since Calhern is imperially slim— and both of them loom over Chico and Harpo. Kennedy is a participant, however, very much a part of the aggressive pattern of his scenes. Calhern has a similar active role in Trentino's scenes with Firefly although, fox to Kennedy's lumbering bear, he plays it differently. He uses his hauteur as a rapier, trading insults with Groucho; that Groucho is invulnerable does not invalidate his stance. In fact, his role as provoker in the first of the slapping scenes (on the word "upstart," Firefly, who has reacted to neither "swine" nor "worm," hits Trentino) provides an offscreen antagonist useful but not necessary to Firefly's self-fueling anger which brings on the war.

Consistency of character is hardly essential to a Marx movie, so the Trentino of the Firefly scenes—the character implicit in the film's whisper of a plot—gives way to an elegant straight man, the male equivalent of the greatest of the Marx foils, Margaret Dumont. As Mrs. Teasdale here—as all the other *grandes dames* she played—Dumont moves through the Marxian world as though courtesy and reason were possible. Similarly, Calhern is a figure of rectitude and dignity who responds to the irrationality and violence of Chico and Harpo with none of Kennedy's volcanic fury. The most his Trentino expresses is exasperation that they are not getting on with important business; his reiterated *gentlemen* is so ludicrous in this context that one marvels at Calhern's ability to repeat it always with a proper sense of correctness and an apparent expectation that the chaos around him will resolve itself into a workable agenda. He is allowed to show distress at the very end of the sequence, when Chico and Harpo, cheerful as ever, depart, leaving him with his coattails cut off, a newspaper pasted to the seat of his pants, and his fingers in a mousetrap, but for most of the scene he is a barely animated prop. He towers above Chico and Harpo, a maypole attacked by wasps. These amiable insects bring to the scene a ragbag of old and new tricks, the best being an imaginative reworking of a bit from *The Cocoanuts*. In the earlier movie, in the scene at the hotel desk, Harpo begins to throw the pens like darts and Groucho rings the bell and starts to tout the game. The variation here is more complex. Trentino, still treating his spies as spies, asks to see Firefly's record. Harpo pulls a phonograph record from under his coat and hands it to Calhern who, with a "No, no!" throws it over his shoulder. Harpo whips out a pistol and fires, breaking the record as though it were a clay pigeon, as Chico hits the bell on the desk and hands him a cigar. At the same time, he slams the humidor shut on Calhern's fingers. A beautifully conceived and executed moment, it is a testimony not only to the skill of Chico, Harpo, and Calhern, but—when one remembers the primitive version in *The Cocoanuts*—to the talent of McCarey. I assume that the director not only brought the Laurel and Hardy rhythm to the Kennedy sequences, but helped to sharpen the details, to point up the movement in this very Marxian scene.

McCarey was also responsible, as Groucho willingly admitted, for the celebrated mirror scene, an uncharacteristically lyric moment for a Marx movie. Despite the obvious care with which the scene is composed, it communicates a sense of gleeful spontaneity seldom achieved on film; it seems to blossom out of the performers, so much so that one has to stop and remember that this, too, is one of the film's borrowings. *Variety* called it "the old Schwartz Bros. mirror routine," a familiar vaudeville act, and English and French reviewers remembered it "on the music-halls," "*sur les pistes*." Charlie Chaplin did a variation of it in *The Floorwalker* (1916) and Max Linder in *Seven Years' Bad Luck* (1921), but neither of these film versions is as intricate, as extended, as oddly touching as the McCarey/Marx variation. The scene in *Duck Soup* takes place when Chicolini and Pinky, in search of Freedonia's war plans, both disguise themselves as Firefly, who is running around Mrs. Teasdale's house in nightshirt and nightcap, an animated illustration from *Beds*. After a particularly violent scene of Harpo's, in which Pinky is trying to silence a radio that will not quit playing, he sees Firefly, who has come to investigate, and runs into a large mirror which conveniently shatters, leaving the empty frame. Pinky must then play Firefly's mirror image. Firefly, suspicious, hopes to catch Pinky out, but the character's motivation is of no importance here, for both he and Pinky give way to Groucho and counter-Groucho (Harpo), who play a game so intoxicating that Groucho can retrieve a hat Harpo has dropped, hand it back to him through the mirror frame and go on as though the illusion has not been violated. Groucho stops, starts, crawls, prances, skips, bends down, wiggles his backside, dances the

Charleston, and Harpo is a simultaneous playback of his every gesture, every movement. Almost every movement; at one point—the
first of the anti-illusionary jokes within the illusionary frame—Harpo
fails to spin around when Groucho does, but when Groucho comes to
rest, arms lightly outstretched in the half bow with which dancers
often finish, Harpo has struck the mirror image of the pose. The
dropped hat comes late in the routine. Earlier, they circle one another,
passing through the frame and returning to their original positions. At
this point, Groucho is carrying a white hat hidden behind his back,
Harpo a black top hat. Groucho sees Harpo's hat and silently laughs in
anticipation of his exposure, but when Harpo claps an identical white
hat on his head just as Groucho does, the joke is not really on Groucho;
it is on the audience which has retained some sense of the presumed
original motivation for the whole sequence, long after the performers
have disappeared into the routine. How can we know the dancer from
the dance? The routine ends, the communion is broken when a third
Groucho (Chico) steps into the frame. It is Firefly, not Groucho, who
grabs Chicolini, and the film moves on to Chicolini's trial, a more
familiar kind of Marx comedy.

By using McCarey here, Kalmar and Ruby there, the particular
qualities of the Marxes elsewhere, I have been talking about *Duck Soup*
as though it were simply a collection of bits—which, in a sense, it is.
There are scenes, routines, gags that I have not dealt with, and it
would be possible to extend this catalogue for pages. Yet *Duck Soup*, as
I have suggested from time to time, is more of a piece than any of the
other Marx Brothers movies. In part, that may reflect some sense of
aesthetic order that McCarey was able to impose on Marxian chaos.
More important, that chaos found a setting that was congenial rather
than antagonistic, and the result is a film which fully utilizes the
demonic energy of the Marxes.

In the late 1940s, when I used to haunt those long-gone theaters that
John Hollander memorialized in his poem "Movie-Going," I discovered the early Marx Brothers movies which I had not seen as a
child. While I was working on this chapter, I went back in search of a
half-remembered sentence to the master's thesis I wrote on Sean
O'Casey in 1950. I had said of *The Silver Tassie*, "It puts O'Casey in
distinguished company ranging from Euripides in *The Trojan Women* to
the Marx Brothers in *Duck Soup*." The sentence was in part a joke, an
intentional touch of antiacademic cheekiness—which I am sure now
Oscar Campbell recognized and, unruffled, let stand—but it was also a
testimony to a movie which had affected me, in its way, with almost
the intensity of my first exposure to Euripides. Looking back at the

sentence thirty years later, I suspect that I was instinctively right, that *Duck Soup* belongs among the great pacifist statements, but that its strength does not lie in its apparent directness, that it is not an open attack on war as both *The Silver Tassie* and *The Trojan Women* are.

It is customary these days to emphasize that directness, to celebrate the Marx Brothers as satirists, to see *Duck Soup* as an attack on government (the cabinet-meeting scene), on power (Groucho as Firefly), on diplomacy (the Calhern-Groucho scenes), on the legal system (Chicolini's trial), on war (the mobilization and war scenes). If it is the "virulent political satire" that André Hodeir called it, it seems almost to have become that without the help of the people who made it. Joe Adamson quotes Harry Ruby: "We wrote shows and movies for only one purpose. Entertainment. That is all there was to it!" And Arthur Sheekman: "Comedy is best when you upset stuffy people or notions, but that doesn't mean that you start out with social criticism." In 1970, Groucho told the interviewers from *Take One* that the Marx Brothers films "were about something. . . . We were trying to be funny, but we didn't know that we were satirizing the current conditions. It came as a great surprise to us." When Richard J. Anobile, who seems to have a deep commitment to protecting the Marx Brothers from their intellectual critics, asked of *Duck Soup* "did you have any intent other than to make a funny and entertaining movie?" Groucho answered, "No, but it turned out to be a satire on war and I attribute that to McCarey." Although Joe Adamson quotes McCarey as saying, "it kidded dictators," the director's few remarks on the film in the *Cahiers du Cinéma* interview give no indication of satirical intention. Perhaps Nat Perrin gets closest to what really happened when he says, "It is possible that whatever satire is there kind of crept into it because that was the way the men involved thought."

It is somewhat difficult to take this retrospective naiveté at face value. Pacifism and political satire were abroad in the land in the 1920s and 1930s, and writers closely allied with the Marx Brothers were neither immune to the ideas nor reluctant to turn their hands to the genre. According to Maxwell Anderson, Laurence Stallings was at work with Herman Mankiewicz on a musical "about the war" before Anderson and Stallings wrote *What Price Glory?* (1924). This war musical never materialized, but *Strike Up the Band* tried out and then closed in 1927, presumably because George S. Kaufman's antiwar sentiments led him to a harsher book than audiences were ready to accept. Morrie Ryskind, whose pacifist sympathies helped shape Kaufman's own attitudes on the subject, rewrote the show for the 1930 production and, although it was a success, neither he nor Kaufman was happy with the softer version. They went on to write *Of Thee I Sing* (1931), again with the Gershwins. The show may seem somewhat pallid fifty years after the event, but it is a bona-fide political satire with a Pulitzer Prize to prove it. Certainly, the Marxes must have recognized the intention of the show when, in their abortive attempt to set up their own company in 1933, they negotiated to have the musical turned into a film script for them. Even earlier, they had considered a Howard Dietz sketch which, from his description of it in his autobiography, was "a war act" with a great many similarities to *Duck Soup*. Someone involved with the film must have noticed that Hollywood was full of implicit and explicit pacifist films during the early 1930s, of which Ernst Lubitsch's *Broken Lullaby* (1932), from Paramount's own lot, is one of the most outspoken.

Some of the initial reactions recognized *Duck Soup* as a satire, often suggesting nothing more serious than that the lines and sketches were comments on other show-business genres or the more obvious societal fads and foibles. Thus a number of the reviews saw the movie only as "a mythical kingdom burlesque," as *Variety* put it. Variations on that phrase appeared so often that I suspect a publicity release at work in reviewing circles although no evidence of it appears in the Paramount pressbook. Most of the reviewers went beyond the idea of a genre burlesque to suspect or to assert the presence of political criticism, whether, like John S. Cohen, Jr., in the *New York Sun*, they thought it did not work, or, with Philip K. Scheuer in the *Los Angeles Times*, they proclaimed it "inspired satire." The strongest statement of the latter position is to be found in *Les Annales politiques et littéraires*, in which Pierre Bost wrote:

> *Duck Soup*, a crazy film, is, at the same time, a vigorous sa-
> tire in which one sees politics, ministers, war, a dictator,
> diplomats come alive through the strokes of caricature,
> which demonstrates once more that the Americans have, in
> this matter of the cinema, which today is the literature of
> the people, a freedom that we have lost.

Despite Bost's elegant compliment to American comedy, I find myself drawn to the doubters, of whom Richard Watts, Jr., and William Troy are the most articulate. Watts, an admirer of the Marxes, in a generally favorable review, compared *Duck Soup* to the new Kaufman-Ryskind musical, *Let 'Em Eat Cake*, and found that in both cases the "American experts at satirical farce are not at their best when mocking the frailties of dictatorship. Perhaps they are not bitter enough. Possibly they strive too definitely to retain their good disposition." The transformation of *Strike Up the Band* mentioned above indicates a tendency in popular American theater (and in the movies) to protect the property at the expense of potentially disturbing ideas. The bitterness that Watts misses could be introduced into a show only by moving the presumed satirical object, as presented, closer to the reality it represents. This could endanger the work by violating the safety limits implied by the words "musical comedy" or, in the case of *Duck Soup*, by calling the unreal world of the Marxes into doubt. Groucho, defending his painted-on mustache in *Groucho and Me*, said, "The audience doesn' believe us, anyhow." According to one report, the agitator (Leonid Kinskey), who has only a few lines in *Duck Soup*, was originally to make "a fervent oration" to the Freedonia poor (Trentino is trying to incite a revolution), but Kinskey did it so well that the scene had to be cut as too "realistic." Think what would happen to *Duck Soup* if realism crept in and the attack of Chicolini and Pinky on Trentino had to be seen as happening to a real person.

Even if the Marxes, as satirists, could be rescued from Watts's charges that they remain too likable, they would be tripped up by the unsympathetic William Troy's insistence that "the essence of Marxian humor is its pointlessness." One of the virtues of crazy humor becomes a liability in satire, in which one expects, if not an alternative system at least a recognizable point of view toward the satirized objects. With the Marx Brothers, as with George S. Kaufman, one gets the wisecrack as satire, the unanchored funny line often with an immediate social or political reference. In *The Cocoanuts*, in lines written by Kaufman, spoken by Groucho, Mr. Hammer convinces the striking bellboys that they do not want to be wage slaves and that it is wages that make wage slaves. This is simply clever word-play; it implies no attitude toward trade unionism, capitalism, or even hotel managment. The Marx Brothers movies may be said to comment on the Florida land boom (*The Cocoanuts*), fashionable celebrities (*Animal Crackers*), ocean travel (*Monkey Business*), but they satirize these subjects only as *New Yorker* cartoons do, lightly, echoing the popular consensus, and, since the Marx comic method will not allow a sustained focus on any one thing, without even the aesthetic (hence intentional) wholeness of the cartoons. When Groucho, as Professor Wagstaff in *Horse Feathers*, says, "We're neglecting football for education," his remark is a neat reverse platitude, but he is no more satirical than Dick Powell in *Varsity Show* (1937), when he sings, "We're working our way thru college / To get a lot of knowledge / That we'll probably never ever use again." This playfulness continues into *Duck Soup*, where the context is potentially more serious. Let me illustrate with a passage that is a particular favorite of those Marx admirers who like to stress the satire in the film. Firefly takes up a machine gun and begins to fire, crying out happily, "Look at 'em run . . . They're fleeing like rats." He is so engrossed that he at first does not hear Bob, "But your Excellency, you're shooting your own men." When he finally understands, he offers Bob a banknote with "Here's five dollars. Keep it under your hat. Never mind. I'll keep it under my hat." Which he does. The ugliness of the incident is milked away by a familiar crazy-humor device. Assume that it is a satirical comment on war, in which, since all "rats" look alike, destruction of one's own fellow soldiers is a far too common event. Assume further, that it is a satirical comment on what, since the days of *Duck Soup*, has come to be called, official coverup. But Firefly's offer of bribery disintegrates as the referent for *it* shifts from the event to the five-dollar bill and the meaning of "keep it under your hat" from the metaphorical to the literal. André Hodeir may find "the whole history of corruption . . . in this single exchange," but I find a typical Groucho speech in which the words rather than the content provide the joke. Satire, in *Duck Soup*, as in the other Marx movies, functions rather like Captain Spaulding, singing "Hello, I Must Be Going."

In questioning the efficacy—even the existence—of satire in these films, I do not deny that they contain a great many random funny lines, comments on society which could provide suitable epigraphs for sociological treatises. And I certainly do not assume—in the case of *Duck Soup*, at least—that the Marx Brothers made only knockabout comedy. To get to the seriousness at the heart of the hilarity in *Duck Soup*, one must turn from the social meaning of individual lines to the essential quality of the Marx Brothers, the demonic element that made Artaud want to embrace them. "They are nihilists—these Marx boys," Brooks Atkinson said in his review of *Animal Crackers* on Broadway. Charlie Chaplin muttered, "Nothing but anarchists." The unreality of the Marxes and their world, which makes it difficult to take their specific social comments seriously, becomes a vehicle for a deeper reality, the energy they generate in their collective endeavor to deflate, destroy, defuse, defenestrate everything around them and in their guiltless joy in the process. The audience, laughing with them, taps into that energy. There lies the truly subversive element in the Marx comedy.

Philosophically, psychologically, this energy cannot be kept within bounds. Artistically . . . well, that is another, a moot question. From their first film, the Marx Brothers and their fellow creators—perhaps unconsciously—seem to have been trying to find ways to channel the energy—not to dilute it, but to bring it to climax, to make an aesthetic whole of these vaudevillian fragments. Conventional plot fails to do the trick in *The Cocoanuts* and *Animal Crackers*. To find the missing jewels in one, the missing painting in the other, and to bring the young lovers together in both, may bring the films to a close, but they have precious little to do with the Marxian destructive force. With *Monkey Business* and *Horse Feathers*, the experiments are more productive. Someone on these films decided that they needed smash finishes, big, crazy scenes that could tower over the rest of the movie. So we get the struggle in the barn in *Monkey Business* ("a hymn to anarchy and wholehearted revolt," Artaud called it) and the lunatic football game in *Horse Feathers*. Yet, these do not grow out of the films; they are attached to them, like luxury cabooses. In *Duck Soup*, for the first time (and the last), the Marxes have a structure that both contains and releases their malevolent energy. The end of *Duck Soup* is a genuine conclusion—to the film if not to the Marx drive toward demolition. The ending is an extended one, beginning with Firefly's slap and Trentino's response, "This means war!" His words, changed to "Then it's war!" become a slogan, a warcry, a fanfare, and the film segues into the gigantic musical number in which the four brothers and the assembled Freedonians sing their way to the battlefield. The musical jokes—Cab Calloway's "hi-de-ho," the spiritual ("All God's chillun got guns"), the banjo strumming—are funny perhaps, but they are more important for the emotional quick-change they provide, the note of hysteria that runs through the whole number, parodying patriotic calls to arms and at the same time retaining their emotional quality. The war itself is a shambles, a collection of war jokes. Some of them are very imaginative: Firefly's changes of costume which suggest that this war is all American wars; the call for help that brings stock footage of speeding fire engines, motorcycles, marathon runners, swimmers, monkeys, elephants, porpoises. Some are potentially bitter: Firefly's shooting his own men. Most are typical crazy humor: "I'm sick of messages from the front. Don't we ever get any messages from the side?" The war ends with the capture of Trentino and, as Mrs. Teasdale sings to their victory, the four brothers begin to pelt her with fruit while "Hail, Hail Freedonia" swells from the offscreen orchestra and the film comes to its conclusion.

The ending is not so outrageous as the one in *Horse Feathers*, in which Groucho, Chico, and Harpo all marry Thelma Todd's college widow and jump on her at once, but it is more effective because the force that was stirred up by the musical mobilization and carried with such urgency through the war scenes simply keeps on going—past such mundane matters as apparent victory. The destructive energy does not choose sides. It has been fed all through the film—by the Groucho-Calhern scenes, the Chico-Harpo-Kennedy routines, the Chico-Harpo-Calhern confrontation, Harpo's attack on the radio. It has been fed, too, by the mirror scene which, with its gaiety and grace may seem at odds with these varieties of pointless violence. It is not simply a gentle rest in the chaos, like the harp solo in other films; it is the benign side of the demonic, shattering, oh so lovingly, the concept of identity. In the earlier films, the Marxes have had antagonistic relationships with their settings and their subject matters. In *Duck Soup*, there is an alliance. War is the natural setting for meaningless destructiveness. The film has a shape, a movement, a texture that none of the other films has because it has accepted the evil implicit in what we have so often celebrated in the Marxes. The film is more than simply funny because these are our heroes and we see them—or at least sense them—for what they are. Harpo once said, "We're a sort of safety valve through which people can blow off steam. People all have inhibitions and hate them. We just ignore them." His remarks have a cozy sound to them—the Marxes as therapy. But they are a dangerous drug. By identifying with them, we accept that part of ourselves which insists that there are no boundaries, no limitations, no restrictions. Liberation. Exultation. But where are these Pied Pipers leading us? There are hints in the earlier films, sudden frissons in the laughter. The shot of Harpo tossing books into the fireplace in *Horse Feathers* is an example. To deal with the sense of disquiet I feel when I see that scene, I can conjure Hitler or talk solemnly about anti-intellectualism in America, but those are explanations that only explain away. I suspect that those critics who insist on *Duck Soup* as satire are embarked on a similar operation, trying to retain the Marxes in their heroic mold. I know that I am upset by the book-burning scene because I have a long-standing allegiance with Harpo and those are my hands with his on the shovel. The uneasiness under the laughter in *Duck Soup* comes from the fact that I now recognize the darkest elements in the admirable energy of the Marxes, and I still hang onto them, whispering, through my laughter, *mes semblables, mes frères*.

Notes

1. Johnston's description suggests something more formal than the shared impulse toward outrageousness that marked the comic writers who filled the pages of *Judge*, *College Humor*, *The New Yorker*, and *Vanity Fair* in the 1920s. The serious underside of their deliberate foolishness, most obvious in the work of Benchley, was personal rather than the product of an ideology, either social or aesthetic, even though there were tentative connections with the French avant-garde I have just disowned for the Marxes. For instance, Ring Lardner's "I Gaspiri (The

Upholsterers)," one of the lasting triumphs of "crazy humor," was not only performed at a 1923 Authors' League banquet by Benchley, Stewart, and Marc Connelly, but it was published the next year in Ben Hecht's *Chicago Literary Times* (1 [February 15, 1924], 3), that halfway house between art and games. From there, Stewart steered it to *The Transatlantic Review* (2 [1924], 103–4), in which Lardner and the temporarily expatriated Stewart shared space with Paul Valéry, Gertrude Stein, and Jean Cocteau; Lardner's play elicited this comment from the editors: "how very much better dadas the American dadas, who do not know they are dadas, unless, of course, Mr. Seldes has told them, are than the French and Roumanians who know it so well." Troy's "crazy-fool" designation stems presumably from the book by that title that Stewart published in 1925.

2. Oddly enough, most of Marx's written work—other than his unidentifiable contributions to the musicals and movies in which he appeared—are in comic genres other than the "crazy humor" which approximates his performance style. The Va and Vi exchanges which he contributed to the *New Yorker* under his own name, Julius H. Marx, are standard joke dialogues like the ones used in *Judge* and *College Humor*; for instance, "Vaudeville Talk" (1 [June 20, 1925], 14) is a collection of predictable marriage gags. Perhaps the predictability is the joke, the piece a comment on vaudeville rather than marriage, but I think not. Later pieces signed Groucho Marx (with the production of *The Cocoanuts* [December 8, 1925], the nicknames of the brothers became their professional names) were often variations on the standard *New Yorker* casual, the familiar essay which brought a mixture of anecdote, undigested comic line, and wry rumination to a single subject. "Press Agents I Have Known" (*New Yorker* 5 [March 9, 1929], 52–55) is such a piece, and so, in its autobiographical way, is "My Poor Wife!" (*Collier's* 86 [December 20, 1930], 15, 59); the latter should be interesting to Marx biographers because the situation it treats as a recurring comic contretemps, the dilemma of the comedian's wife forced to rehear his stories, was—or so Arthur Marx suggests in *Life with Groucho* (New York, Simon and Schuster, 1954, p. 239)—one of the causes of his parents' divorce. *Beds* (New York, Farrar & Rinehart, 1930) and *Many Happy Returns* (New York, Simon and Schuster, 1942)—both written with the unbilled help of Arthur Sheekman, according to Hector Arce's *Groucho* (New York, Putnam's, 1979, pp. 169, 272)—are book-length variations of the single-subject article, although the first manages some non sequiturs and the latter the kind of nonsense writing that income-tax jokes seem to generate. The scripts that Marx did with Norman Krasna—the screenplay *The King and the Chorus Girl* (1937) and the play *Time for Elizabeth* (1948)—are

conventional comedies. The chapters in *Memoirs of a Mangy Lover* (New York, Bernard Geis, 1963), in which the Groucho character is usually the victim, are throwbacks to the kind of *New Yorker* piece about the little man beset which E. B. White, James Thurber, and Robert Benchley did much better. *Groucho and Me* (New York, Bernard Geis, 1959)—"a long list of semi-fabrications" (p. 13)—mixes a little autobiography and too much sermonizing with both the single-subject comic essay and the little-man anecdote. It is dedicated to the "Six Masters Without Whose Wise and Witty Words My Life Would Have Been Even Duller": Robert Benchley, George S. Kaufman, Ring Lardner, S. J. Perelman, James Thurber, E. B. White. A rare example of Groucho Marx's offscreen use of "crazy humor" is the non-sequitur biography of Bert Kalmar and Harry Ruby that he contributed to *The Kalmar-Ruby Song Book* (New York, Random House, 1936); it begins, "While still in their teens, Kalmar and Ruby were born in a firehouse in Pelham, New York" (p. 17).

3. In *The View from the Sixties* (New York, McKay, 1966, pp. 99–100), George Oppenheimer, one of the writers on *Flywheel, Shyster and Flywheel*, the radio show that Groucho and Chico did in 1932–33, gives the elephant-irrelevant pun as one of his favorites from the show. He credits Groucho and Arthur Sheekman with having invented it. The recycling of comic material was standard practice—W. C. Fields was probably the champion among the comedians—so it was natural for Groucho and Sheekman to move the pun from the legal comedy of the radio show to the trial scene of *Duck Soup*. According to Joe Adamson, in *Groucho, Harpo, Chico and Sometimes Zeppo* (New York, Pocket Books, 1976, p. 222), Chico's Saturday-Shadowday pun also moved from the radio show to the film. A more elaborate example of the reuse of material is the scene in *Monkey Business* in which each of the brothers—Harpo with a gramophone strapped to his back—does an imitation of Maurice Chevalier in an attempt to get through immigration. This is a variation of a theatrical agency sketch that they used in *I'll Say She Is* on Broadway but that went back at least as far as *On the Mezzanine Floor* (1921). At various times, they imitated Chaplin, Gallager and Shean, and Joe Frisco, depending presumably on how recognizable the subject was to a particular audience. When the Marx Brothers came to Hollywood in 1931, Paramount filmed the sketch from *I'll Say She Is* to use as a promotional short; it can be seen in the television special *The Marx Brothers in a Nut Shell* (1982). Chevalier is the subject here, as he is in *Monkey Business*, probably not simply because the audience knew him, but because he was another Paramount star and the ways of publicity offices are far from mysterious.

4. Harpo's harp, like Chico's piano, lies outside a discussion of

Duck Soup, the one film which dispensed with those specialities. "He was always sitting down, playing the goddamn harp," Groucho told Charlotte Chandler (*Hello, I Must Be Going*, Garden City, N.Y., Doubleday, 1978, p. 258). "And I hated the harp. I always walked out of the theatre when the harp came on." Groucho's distaste for his brothers' music, often emphasized in interviews late in his life, may have been genuine. It was certainly part of the act. Harpo, in an article called "My Brother Groucho" (*Coronet*, 29 [February 1951], 133–34), a lightly disguised plug for *You Bet Your Life*, tells how, as he played more and more softly during a performance of *The Cocoanuts*, Groucho called out, "Softer! I can still hear you!" He often talked across Chico's piano, but the bluntest comment comes in *Horse Feathers*. As Chico begins to play, Professor Wagstaff (Groucho) starts to leave, only to be held back by Jennings (David Landau). Groucho steps forward and speaks directly into the camera—the performer now, not the character—"I've got to stay here, there's no reason why you folks shouldn't go out in the lobby until this thing blows over." Harpo and Chico often got better notices than Groucho did in their vaudeville days and the favorable reviews usually praised the music. (See, for instance, *Sime., Variety*, February 24, 1912, p. 17; Marjorie C. Driscoll, *San Francisco Chronicle*, March 24, 1920, p. 7.) Their specialties remained popular in the films, and they might even be given aesthetic relevance by suggesting that to stop pandemonium for a harp solo only to begin it again is itself an act of crazy humor. I confess that, for me, one of the pleasures of *Duck Soup* is the absence of the piano and the harp.

5. Longevity note on the gag. In 1949, Howard Hawks used it in *I Was a Male War Bride*, in which Ann Sheridan, as the American WAC, drives the motorcycle that leaves Cary Grant, as the French officer, stranded in the sidecar. There was such a note of insipid desperation about that film—as though Hawks knew how inferior it was to his great comedies, *Twentieth Century* (1934), *Bringing Up Baby* (1938), and *His Girl Friday* (1940)—that he also turned to Laurel and Hardy, borrowing from *Habeas Corpus* (1928) the gag in which Hardy, lost, laboriously climbs the post only to find that the presumed helpful sign says WET PAINT. Grant does the climbing for Hawks.

4

★ It's a Gift ★

· 1934 ·

"Le Comique le plus comique des Comiques"
—theater poster, Olympia,
Paris, c. 1904

It is said that once, in Columbus or Toledo,[1] W. C. Fields, scheduled to follow immediately after the Marx Brothers on a vaudeville bill, invented an injury and left town. "The only act I could never follow," Fields said. The story may be as legendary as its details are amorphous, but it contains an essential truth about the difference between the two acts. A few years ago, when I was teaching a course in film comedy, I showed *It's a Gift* the week after we had seen and discussed *Duck Soup* (1933), and some of the more vocal Marx admirers complained that Fields was not funny, that the jokes went on too long. Contrariwise, Kenneth Tynan, reporting on a revival of *Gift* and *Monkey Business* (1931), said that "the Fields section of the audience took [the Marx Brothers] in glacial silence." For the true believers on both sides it may be a matter of comic superiority for their hero, but as both Fields and Groucho Marx tell the story, it is simply a conflict of styles. "His tempo was adagio," *Time* neatly summed up Fields, and heaven knows the Marxes were allegro. Back in 1936, Clifton Fadiman wrote a perceptive comparison of the comedians:

> His is the comedy of careful understatement; that of
> the Marxes, of prodigal overstatement. . . . Even in
> his juggling act Mr. Fields seems to move slowly;
> the Marx gestures are rapid, explosive, extravagantly

Gag publicity still, not in the film. Tammany Young, Charles Sellon, W. C. Fields. (*It's a Gift*, Paramount, 1934. The Museum of Modern Art/Film Stills Archive.)

> unnecessary. . . . As philosophers, Mr. Fields would
> be a Stoic, the Marxes Anarchists.

What Fields and the Marxes had in common was that all of them (I keep wanting to say, both of them) brought to the screen the very different personalities that they had developed in vaudeville and on Broadway, and that their films were collections of sketches, routines, comic identifiers that were far more important than the plots that pretended to give a frame to the material. Even when Fields was doing a part in a non-Fields movie, he imposed his recognizable comic mannerisms on the character he played. For instance, in *Mrs. Wiggs of the Cabbage Patch* (1934), when Mr. Stubbins comes courting Miss Hazy (ZaSu Pitts), it is Fields who climbs through the barbed wire fence to get to her house. He gets trapped on the wire and then tangled in a rope tied to a fencepost; his cane gets caught, he loses his hat, and he is assaulted by a kite that a boy is trying to get off the ground. This physical business has less to do with Alice Hegan Rice's Mr. Stubbins (in *Lovey Mary* rather than *Mrs. Wiggs*) than it does with Fields's inheritance from his youthful self, the comic juggler who was already a popular vaudeville performer when Rice published the two "Cabbage Patch" books (1901, 1903). Even Micawber manages to get his hat caught on the end of his cane in *David Copperfield* (1935), although Fields plays that character straight—or as straight as a Dickens character can be played. The comedian's precarious attachment to his hat and cane—to any prop for that matter—is part of the detail that adheres to his personality, like his sotto voce mutter and his startled reaction to unexpected presences. These become routines within routines, comic business that gives resonance to longer sketches that he played variants on all through his career. His golf act, first presented in *The Ziegfeld Follies of 1918*, was filmed in *So's Your Old Man* (1926), in which his pantomime is so good that one can almost hear the sounds that annoy him, in *You're Telling Me* (1934), and in *The Big Broadcast of 1938*. His billiard routine, which became part of his vaudeville act early in the century, is an excuse for his first film, *Pool Sharks* (1915), a welcome digression in *Six of a Kind* (1934), and his contribution to the all-star revue, *Follow the Boys* (1944), one of his last movies.

"If you have got a good gag, milk it until the blood runs out," Carlotta Monti quotes the protagonist of *W. C. Fields & Me.* Although Monti's book hardly inspires faith in the authenticity of her quotations, this one is an appropriate description of both the way Fields performed his sketches, moving through them with great deliberation, and the way in which he worked and reworked material. Since two of the sequences in *It's a Gift* derive from sketches first used in *The Comic*

Supplement (1925), a Ziegfeld revue that never made it to New York, and since J. P. McEvoy is the only writer listed in the program of that show, it is perhaps appropriate to indicate that Fields, who was belligerently protective of his own work, was sometimes said to have reworked material or ideas that were not his own. According to Gene Fowler in *Minutes of the Last Meeting*, Gregory La Cava set out to persuade Fields not to sue a seedy nightclub comic, partly because "Fields stole this routine himself thirty years ago." La Cava—and he was one of Fields's closest friends, the director of two of his silent films—was even more emphatic in the line attributed to him by Robert Lewis Taylor in his biography of Fields: "He would steal any act he could get away with, but if somebody tried to borrow something from him, he went crazy." Back in 1912, annoyed that another performer was using a curtain call he considered his own—"walking off the stage as the curtain rises and walking on as it descends"—Fields took an advertisement in *Variety* staking his prior claim. In 1920, in a letter on copyright to an unidentified friend, he explained that he had forced Ned Wayburn, the Ziegfeld regular who staged the 1918 *Follies*, to stop billing himself as coauthor with Fields of "A Game of Golf."

An intrepid defender of comic property, then, but not always, not everyone's. "W. C. stole Harrigan's make-up and tricks when he first started," Joe Laurie, Jr., says in *Vaudeville*, and Douglas Gilbert, who admits in *American Vaudeville* that Harrigan, "The Tramp Juggler" (Fields even used the name), "was not in a class with Fields," describes an act using "old plug hats, broken cigar boxes," and depending on planned accidents for effect. As though these similarities were not enough, there is contemporary confirmation in a joking letter (November 19, 1904) from another vaudevillian, O. K. Sato, who kidded Fields for once having armed himself against possible attack from Harrigan, "the man whom you had so many looks at before they ever let you onto a stage." Sime Silverman, the founder of *Variety*, who liked to chronicle "borrowings," said in his reviews of the 1918 and the 1920 *Follies* that both "A Game of Golf" and "The Family Ford" owed something to successful sketches of Harry Tate, the English comic, although he thought the squeaky shoes of the caddy in the golf routine in the 1918 show may have come from an act that Cecil Dean had done the season before at the Century. Harry Tate did a "Billiards," too, but Robert Lewis Taylor thinks Fields's idea in this case came from "a Professor Devereaux," who "performed with trick billiard devices" and who "Fields now understood vaguely," had retired before Fields put his act together. Faced with "a stupid baseball sketch" in *George White's Scandals of 1922*, Alexander Woollcott defended Fields after his fashion: "The program accuses him of having written this little interlude, but that is libellous. Mr. Fields will hardly admit having written the story, which is the climax of the sketch—for it has been circulating in this town these many weary years."

Despite Fields's occasional cries of outrage, casual pilfering of characters, situations, lines was standard practice in vaudeville, as it was in films. The McEvoy-Fields connection is somewhat more complex. Although "Alley Scene" and "Picnic Scene" in the typescript of *The Comic Supplement* have a few things that lasted as late as *It's a Gift*, they are at most skeletons of the sketches that Fields was to develop; in any case, the Library of Congress has a version of the former, called "The Sleeping Porch," which Fields submitted for copyright in 1925. After the collapse of *Supplement* early that year, Fields and Ray Dooley, who played the brat in the sketches, went into the spring edition of the *Follies* carrying with them these sketches and "Drug Store," which is listed in the program for the Washington presentation of *Supplement* but is not in the McEvoy typescript. Given Fields's fondness for tested material, it is hardly surprising that the three sketches should become the basis for *It's the Old Army Game* (1926), the first of the Paramount silents in which he was unmistakably the center of attention. McEvoy is credited with the story on which the screenplay was based, and Fields gets no writing credit at all. But, then, he never got such credit on his silent films, even when—as with the golf sequence in *So's Your Old Man*—the material was verifiably his.

The *New York Times*, in its unsigned review of *Allez-Oop* (1927), said, "It is the weakness of Mr. McEvoy that he is more fertile in idea than adept in the execution thereof." For Fields admirers that may explain how the embryonic "Picnic Scene" of the typescript became the remarkable picnic sequence in *It's a Gift*. Yet McEvoy's *The Potters* (1923)—which Fields made as a silent in 1927—is an adroitly made play, and the Fields sketches on paper—those in the Library of Congress and those in *W. C. Fields by Himself*—are unbelievably crude without the presence of the comedian whose smallest gesture might give them substance. Fields had a knack for reading the most pedestrian line as though it were richly funny. McEvoy and Fields shared certain social and aesthetic ideas. Although McEvoy was not as venomous in his presentation of the Potters as Fields was of the families in *It's a Gift*, *The Man on the Flying Trapeze* (1935), and *The Bank Dick* (1940), Pa Potter (played on stage by Donald Meek) is clearly a role that could be tailored to Fields's talents.[2] Both Fields and McEvoy were fascinated by the minutiae of middle-class family life, the clichés of speech and behavior. Heywood Broun, in his foreword to *The Potters*, called McEvoy "a realist" and a "stout-hearted truth-teller," who emphasized the ugliness, the frustration of life, and such a description might well fit Fields—particularly the Fields of the family comedies. Broun's "realist," however, is not an aesthetic category, just as Fadiman's "understatement," in the comparison between Fields and the Marxes quoted at the beginning of this chapter, has more to do with Fields's performing style than with total context. *The Potters* is set up like a series of revue sketches (most of McEvoy's theater work was on revues), and the Fields settings, even when they have reportorial accuracy—the bathroom in *Gift*, the breakfast tables in most of the family films—never try to disguise their artificiality. There were frequent reviewers' laments during the early 1930s, complaints that Paramount imposed cheap production values on Fields; the pseudonymous Argus of *The Literary Digest*, for instance, said that *Gift* "looks as tho it had taken two days to make, had cost $100, and had been photographed with one of the early Biograph cameras." Such remarks are valuable as testimonies to the esteem in which Fields was held,[3] but they do rather miss the point. It was the very tattiness of those films (like the unmistakably fake city streets of *City Lights*) that let Fields put his real toads, in Heywood Broun's truth-telling sense, into imaginary gardens—to make the movement from the possible to the preposterous a very natural one. As with setting, so with character. "It is the fact of the types being overdrawn which makes their funny side appeal to our sense of humor," Fields said in an interview back in 1914. "If they were depicted exactly true to type, it would be merely life." It was a show called *The Comic Supplement*, after all, which brought Fields and McEvoy together.

In giving so much attention to J. P. McEvoy, I want neither to rescue him from the obscurity into which he has fallen (although I would like to see a good production of *The Potters*) nor to diminish Fields in any way. Like Joe Laurie, Jr., who called Fields "the greatest American comedy juggler" while he was pointing out the comedian's debt to Harrigan, I want simply to emphasize that Fields, like the Marx Brothers, came out of an identifiable theatrical context. As with most strong performers, Fields made his material, borrowed or invented, peculiarly his own. Whatever sources may have fed into the comic sequences in *It's a Gift*, they are unthinkable now without his presence and his controlling imagination. Yet, the credits remind us that Jack Cunningham's screenplay was based on *The Comic Supplement* by J. P. McEvoy and an original story by Charles Bogle. Cunningham was a journeyman screenwriter who had been in the business since he abandoned newspaper work to go to Hollywood in 1916; that he worked with Fields on *The Old-Fashioned Way* (1934), *Mississippi* (1935), and *The Man on the Flying Trapeze* as well as *Gift* may say less about his talent than his accommodating spirit. After all, Fields kept a firm hand on his own dialogue whenever he could. "I feel that an actor always knows the lines and the argot of his peculiar character," he said in a letter in 1941, "and feels more comfortable in speaking those lines if written by himself." Bogle was Fields, of course, the pseudonym he also used on *Way* and *Trapeze*; the name presumably amused him since a Charlie Bogle turns up as early as 1930, a character in "The Midget Car," one of the sketches in the Library of Congress.

The ubiquitous William LeBaron, who had worked with Fields on his silents in the 1920s, was the producer of *It's a Gift*, and it may have been he—it was almost certainly someone at Paramount other than the star—who chose Norman McLeod as director. McLeod is largely ignored these days, although his best work is seen frequently on campuses and in repertory houses. It is indicative of the obscurity into which he has fallen that Andrew Sarris, confused between two Normans, neither of whom much interests him, assigns *Gift* to Norman Taurog, and even more outrageous—considering that McLeod directed both *Monkey Business* and *Horse Feathers* (1932)—that interviewers who imagine themselves familiar with the Marx Brothers material could hear Groucho Marx say, "Norman McCloud was a good director" or "Then we had Norman McCleod for a director and at least he spoke English." In a casual remark in his Charles Laughton biography, Charles Higham, presumably echoing Elsa Lanchester, dismisses McLeod as a "mediocre director." Even if the present neglect were justified, which I doubt, McLeod seems an obvious choice to do a Fields picture in 1934. McLeod had done one presumably serious picture—*The Miracle Man* (1932), a remake of a Lon Chaney silent—but he was primarily a comedy director and a very successful one. Besides the Marx Brothers, he had directed Charles Ruggles and Mary Boland in *Mama Loves Papa* (1933), the film that turned them into a popular comedy team. He had worked with Jack Oakie in *Touchdown!* (1931), Burns and Allen in *Many Happy Returns* (1934), and almost everyone on the Paramount lot—including Fields—in *Alice in Wonderland* (1933). Since Fields, as Humpty Dumpty in that film, was little more than a familiar disembodied voice inside a giant egg, shot head-on, it was hardly an indication of how McLeod might work with a Fields who had come out of his shell.

In a letter to "friend Bill"[4] in 1943, discussing the possibility of his appearing in the movie *Ziegfeld Follies*, Fields wrote:

> It dawned upon me today that when I was referring to the porch scene, you were referring to the one we did in Florida [for *It's the Old Army Game*]. That really was awful but I

sincerely believe that I had nothing to do with it being photographed the way it was. Norman McLeod was kind enough to let me do my own version of the scene up at the Lasky Ranch for Paramount and that was really a very fine scene.

The key to understanding McLeod as a comedy director may lie in the phrase "let me do my own version." According to Joe Adamson, McLeod's one attempt to interfere with the Marx Brothers' routines in *Monkey Business* was his insistence on reaction shots showing people on screen laughing at Harpo; understandably the footage he took was discarded. Three years and nine movies lay between *Monkey Business* and *It's a Gift*, and the neophyte who worked with the Marxes may have become more certain of himself; even so, what he may have learned was to let experienced comedians find their way. Although McLeod's *Topper* (1937) is one of the celebrated screwball comedies of the period, it is visually unimaginative, despite the trick photography, and is sustained only by the charm of Cary Grant, Roland Young, and Billie Burke (Constance Bennett always seemed too determined when she had to be charming). Unlike the Leo McCarey of *Duck Soup*, McLeod may have been the right director for Fields because he backed off and let the comedian get on with the latest variations of his *Follies* sketches. Still, he may have been actively useful to Fields in the family scenes. McLeod's first Paramount film, codirected with that other Norman, Taurog, was *Finn and Hattie* (1931). Although it is a very dull adaptation of Donald Ogden Stewart's funny *Mr and Mrs Haddock Abroad*, the Haddocks (Leon Errol, ZaSu Pitts, Mitzi Green) may be seen as distantly—very distantly—related to the Bissonettes of *Gift*. More to the point is the mixture of sentiment and comedy that informed *Mama Loves Papa*. Reviewing that film, Andre Sennwald recalled *Skippy* (1931), for which McLeod wrote the screenplay, and praised him for bringing the same "blend of gentle comedy and gentler pathos" to the character Charles Ruggles plays. *Gentle* may seem an unusual adjective to use in the presence of W. C. Fields, but there is an uncharacteristic tender moment toward the end of *Gift* when Bissonette (Fields), sitting amid his desiccated dream of an orange grove, looks sad, beaten; a dog, of all things, comes up and kisses him.[5] Although the fans of the comedian-as-iconoclast tend to forget the fact, Fields often played for sentiment, particularly in the 1930s, but frequently—*Tillie and Gus* (1933) is the obvious example—the sentiment seems intrusive. There are implications to this scene in *Gift* (his wife regularly treats him like a dog), but intellectual nuances aside, the moment is surprisingly touching. I suspect that its effectiveness lies not simply in Fields's ability as an actor, but with the fact that McLeod understood the qualities that might be found in the scene.

"A motion picture is really a high-class job of carpentry," McLeod said in 1946. He was shooting *The Kid from Brooklyn* at the time and was putting down his thoughts on movie musicals, but the metaphor might serve for *It's a Gift* as well. Fields worked rather the way my father did when he set out to build something. He looked around the garage for usable bits of lumber, bought new material only when it was absolutely necessary, and consistently managed to produce finished objects that belied the accidental availability of their parts. The garage of Fields's mind was stacked with the lumber he had collected over the years, in vaudeville and in revues, and whenever he was given a free hand, in the construction of a film or a speech, he rummaged around in search of a sketch or a line that still had wear in it. Unlike my father, he was often more interested in the individual parts, which he kept polishing, than in the totality, but at his best—and *It's a Gift* is Fields at his best—not only did the glue of plot hold the bits together but a varnish, compounded of personality and social perspective, gave the work the glow of art. I will get to the glue and varnish, but for the moment, consider the lumber—at least the bigger pieces, the extended sequences in the film.

It's a Gift* opens with the family comedy, our introduction to the Bissonettes—pronounced Bis-o-nay, as we are often reminded.[6] Fields's family sketches presumably began with the Flivertons of "The Family Ford" in the 1920 *Follies*, continued in other revue sketches and became the heart of his most impressive silent movies—*So's Your Old Man, The Potters, Running Wild* (1927). His Elmer Prettywillie is a bachelor in *It's the Old Army Game*, but he has a surrogate family, a sister (Mary Foy) and a nephew (Mickey Bennett), who give him an opportunity to play family scenes. The Fields family sometimes includes a venomous mother-in-law (*The Man on the Flying Trapeze, The Bank Dick*) and a malevolent brother-in-law (*Trapeze*), but the basic family consists of a long-suffering husband, a complaining wife, an older daughter, and a young child, sometimes a son, sometimes a daughter.

Amelia, Mrs. Bissonette, is played by Kathleen Howard, surely the greatest of the Fields shrews—a high compliment when one remembers the work of Cora Witherspoon in *The Bank Dick*. "As the nagging wife," Andre Sennwald said in the *New York Times*, "Kathleen Howard is so authentic as to make Mr. Fields's sufferings seem cosmic and a little sad despite their basic humor." Howard's voice, a combination of a shout and a whine, cuts through the film like a saw. She can wrap it in vocal cotton wool, when Amelia wants to bandy nastily polite remarks with another woman, but it is never completely hidden. We know it will break out in commands to her son ("Take off those skates, I told you") or more often to her husband. It is at its best in full flight, in an extended aria, and it is here that Howard's training is her strength. She was new to the movies in 1935, having made her debut in *Death Takes a Holiday* the year before. An editor at *Harper's Bazaar* and *Photoplay* and a lecturer on fashion, she had come to those relatively quiet callings after more than twenty years as an opera singer, twelve of them with the Metropolitan. No wonder she could sustain a whine. Given her bearing (she is also the most regally dowdy of the Fields wives), she might have remained the well-dressed aristocrat she played in *Death* and *One More River* (1934) if someone had not had the inspiration to cast her in *You're Telling Me*. There she plays Mrs. Murchison, the society woman who is more Sam Bisbee's antagonist than his wife is. In the early scenes, she does a very good but rather standard snob turn—blunt, mean, dismissive—but as the film goes on her performance gets more impressive. When Princess Marie (Adrienne Ames) arrives in Crystal Springs and, by her presence, elevates the Bisbees to the highest ranks of society, Howard's Mrs. Murchison mixes her hoity-toity manner with a kind of elegant cringing which is much more imaginative than the simple reversal such a situation customarily dictates. Fields must have recognized the quality of Howard's performance here, for she was elevated to the wife role in *Gift* and then in *Trapeze*. She went on to have a fifteen-year career as a character actress and was often very effective—for instance, as the priggish housekeeper in *Ball of Fire* (1941)—but she never again achieved the glory of those performances with Fields.

The grown daughters, whether they are sympathetic to the Fields character or not, tend to be played by innocuous ingenues (Una Merkel in *The Bank Dick* is a happy exception), and Jean Rouverol, as Mildred Bissonette, is clearly one of that company. The quality that makes these performers so forgettable can be put to effective use, however, when, as in *Gift*, the daughter's chief feeling for her father is indifference. Rouverol is the proper partner for Fields in the bathroom scene, our first glimpse of the home life of Harold Bissonette. Mildred taps at the door and her father says, "Well, come on in; I'm only shaving." The *Variety* reviewer, oddly prudish, found this "rather coarse-grained," but to anyone raised in a large family in a one-bathroom house—as a great many moviegoers were in the 1930s—this is a recognition line which roots the comedy that follows in ordinary life. Harold is in front of the medicine cabinet, straight razor in hand, when Mildred marches in and, ignoring him opens the cabinet door. He moves to the side to go on shaving, but by this time she has found the lipstick she wants and closed the door to use the mirror herself. He comes in behind her and, in trying to see around her, is constantly jiggled, bouncing the razor about precariously. She opens the cabinet again, this time to get her comb, and he once more moves to the side only to have her shut the door. He tries again to see around her as she begins to use the comb, hair flipping in his face, finally getting into his mouth. He gives a strangled cry—a bleat, really—as he tries to get it out. Then, giving up on the medicine cabinet, he attempts to see his reflection in the concave bottom of a can of some kind, registers the hopelessness of the endeavor, finally finds a hand mirror. At this point, Mildred—the kind of girl who would take advertisements seriously—is ready for her mouthwash. Gargle. Jump. Gargle. Jump. "If you want me to cut my throat, keep that up," he mutters. Gargle. He finally ties the mirror to the light pull and, as it revolves, tries to use it by turning with it, then by taking quick swipes as it passes. He climbs up on a chair, sitting on the back, and falls off, the razor all the time hovering near his throat. He is lying across the chair, still trying to finish shaving, when Amelia bursts in with "What kind of tomfoolery are you up to now?" Only then does he realize that Mildred has left the room. He promises to be down in "half a tick." Fields and Peggy Hopkins Joyce do a routine in *International House* (1933) in which, unwittingly assigned to the same hotel suite, each prepares for bed, passing unseen between bedroom and bath; they finally discover one another only after each has taken to one of the twin beds. It is neatly performed but completely predictable, a joke about comic timing. By comparison, the shaving scene in *Gift*, which completely depends on timing (and reminds us that Fields was a celebrated juggler), is character comedy which establishes Harold's place in the family and in the film, and elevates a common enough bathroom encounter into a comic ritual of near disaster.

The children in the Fields family were originally played by adult comedians. In the 1921 *Follies*, for instance, Ray Dooley (who had been praised for her "squalling infant" in a skit with Charles Winninger the year before) and Raymond Hitchcock were the children of Fields and Fanny Brice in a subway sketch. The infant in the carriage in *It's an Old Army Game* is plainly not an infant, and an adult Babe Kane played the bad little girl in *The Pharmacist* (1933), one of the Mack Sennett-Fields short films based directly on the Fields sketches. These were exceptions. The realism at the heart of Fields's comedy demanded real children once he turned to film. Barney Raskle, the immense fat boy who played Elmer Finch's stepson in *Running Wild*, is a kind of grotesque, suggesting one direction Fields might have taken in replacing his *Follies* partners, but for the most part the children

Fields used at least looked like ordinary children. Tom Bupp, who plays Norman Bissonette, certainly does. Since Baby LeRoy is also in the film, and his Elwood Dunk is Harold's chief child nemesis, Fields has only a few scenes with Bupp. Norman's presence at the breakfast table allows Fields to use one of his favorite jokes, one that had already served in *Army Game* and *The Pharmacist* and would appear again in *The Bank Dick*. When Norman, after an exchange with his father, wants to know whether or not his father loves him, Harold pulls back his arm as though to swat him and snarls, "Certainly, I love you." Then he mutters to Amelia, "He's not going to tell me I don't love him." Norman helps delay their departure when the family leaves for California later in the film, and he is prominent in the picnic scene. It is here that Amelia insists that Harold share his sandwich with his son, and Harold carefully folds the meat over so that it all lies on one side of the bread, tears the sandwich in half and gives the meatless half to Norman. "Certainly, I love you." The chief joke about Norman is that he always wears those roller skates his mother demands that he remove at the beginning of the film. He has them on in the picnic scene, skating adeptly across the lawn, and he has them on at the end when, gussied up in their new prosperity, all the Bissonettes except Harold climb into the new limousine. Norman does manage to get one skate off in the breakfast scene so that Fields can use it for a pratfall.

A consideration of Fields and that skate tells us a lot about the way the comedian worked. In an article he published in *American Magazine* in 1934, Fields contradicted the "Professors of Humor" who insist that laughter depends on surprise. His example comes from *You're Telling Me*. In that film, Sam Bisbee explains his burglar trap, a chair which catches the intruder and stuns him with a great iron ball. Once the device is demonstrated, as Fields says in his article, "the audience knows what's coming" and anticipates the laugh. In *Gift*, when the "half a tick" has passed and a neatly dressed Harold has come down the stairs, we see him in the hallway. The skate is on the lower right of the frame and he appears to be walking toward it. The audience expects him to fall, but, momentarily distracted, he turns slightly, and the audience relaxes, beginning to suspect that this is a joke about W. C. Fields's not falling down. Then, of course, he steps on the skate as he comes into the room. If this were simply an expectation-fulfilled joke, it would end with the fall, but it modulates quickly from a mechanical joke to a character one. "Get up off the floor," Amelia shouts, and points out that she has just had the skates repaired. The scene goes on to other things, but Fields is a master of the comic echo, and after the meal is well underway, he asks, apropos of nothing being said at that point, about the price of fixing skates.

The breakfast is an occasion to dispense with some of the plot, the impending death of Uncle Bean (when Amelia says he is at death's door, Harold wonders if they will be able to pull him through) and Harold's desire to own an orange grove. It is also a setting for familiar Fields physical business, the substitution gag that in some form figures in all his films; here he drops his cigar in a glass of water and tries to light his boutonniere. Mainly, however, it is an opportunity to see Amelia at her best. She barks out commands—"Don't smoke at the table"; "Don't throw matches on the floor"—and once she latches onto a workable grievance, she rises into the empyrean. She finds it in "I haven't a stitch to my back.'[7] Her emphasis on *stitch* does not have quite the grandeur of her elongation of *maid* in her "I have no maid you know" in the later bedroom nagging scene in which the word is extended as her voice rises, the *maaaid* becoming both keen and war cry. Still *stitch* stands out in the sentence and rightly so since, as she moves from complaint to complaint, it is as though she were sewing all Harold's insufficiencies into a ribbon of regret. Norman is ordered away from the table and Mildred leaves in tears before Amelia's lament really gets underway, and Harold exits while it is in progress. He oozes into the kitchen as her voice continues in the empty room, his "go on, go on" all the assurance she needs that someone is listening. He explains to Mildred, who has a gripe of her own, that the whole family has one thing to learn: "That I . . ." he begins in full voice, throws a tentative glance toward the door to the dining room, and finishes in a whisper, ". . . am the master of this house." In an odd way, as the film illustrates, he is the master; over everyone's protests, he buys the orange grove. In these scenes, however, he is the soul of family comedy—the henpecked husband, the browbeaten father.

From Harold at home to Harold at work. The next extended sequence is in the store. Although Harold Bissonnette runs a grocery, this section of the film derives from Field's sketch, "The Drug Store," which moved from *The Comic Supplement* into the *Follies* and then was used in both *Army Game* and *The Pharmacist*. It is not its details, but its central assumption that the grocery scene in *Gift* borrows from "The Drug Store." The sequence in *Gift* never reaches the fine level of hysteria with which *Army Game* opens, the arrival of the desperate woman—played by the marvelous comedian, Elise Cavanna—who awakens Elmer Prettywillie in the middle of the night to buy a postage stamp. Yet, both films are based on the conception of the merchant as fall guy, the accommodating victim of his customers. And, in *Gift*, of his employees.

Everett Ricks, Harold's helper, is played by Tammany Young, one of the best of the Fields stooges. He had played in films as early as

Checkers (1919) and had appeared on Broadway—he was one of the reporters in *The Front Page* (1928)—but he was largely restricted to small roles. If you are very attentive to *She Done Him Wrong* (1933) and *The Bowery* (1933), you can catch glimpses of Tammany Young on the periphery of the action, as he always seemed to be on stage and on screen. His oddly inexpressive face, his ability to suggest attentive inattention, his strangely aggressive self-effacement, all made him a natural as a Fields foil. He appeared with Fields first in *Six of a Kind*, in which his main task is to listen to Sheriff Hoxley (Fields) explain how he came by the name "Honest John"—he returned a customer's glass eye when he was a bartender in Medicine Hat—as he goes through the pool routine. Young went on to work in *You're Telling Me* (the caddy in the famous golf act), *The Old-Fashioned Way*, *Gift*, *Trapeze*, and *Poppy*, which was released in 1936, the year he died. As Everett, he is primarily a presence, a focus of exasperation for Harold. Whether he does the right thing—opening the door while Harold messes with his key, distracted by a little girl who has a piece of chalk and wonders if he wants to play hopscotch—or the wrong thing, he seems to be at fault. Sent to sweep up, he fails to hear Harold's cries to open the door before blind Mr. Muckle comes crashing through. Returning from delivering Mr. Muckle's gum, he rides his bicycle into the store, into Harold, who is sent flying over the counter. His gravest sin in Harold's eyes is that, for "a ten cent piece," he agrees to watch Elwood, thus turning loose "blood poison," as Harold calls him, to wreck the store.

Baby LeRoy has dwindled over the years to an exemplary figure in one of the anecdotes presumed to prove Fields's status as a child-hating drunk. The comedian's account of spiking the infant actor's bottle, as his use of it in "Alcohol and Me" indicates, was never more than a joke, although it keeps reappearing as a biographical fact. Whatever Baby LeRoy has become in the Fields iconography, in 1934 he was a celebrated infant actor who, being past two, was at the end of his career. He was well under a year old when he made his debut in *A Bedtime Story* (1933), a foolish and flaccid comedy in which a man-about-town (Maurice Chevalier) is domesticated by a baby left in his car. A doting Mordaunt Hall said in his review of the film that Baby LeRoy "comes close to winning the pantomimic laurels," which would not have been difficult, and Andre Sennwald, reviewing *Torch Singer* (1933), the child's second movie, found that the baby "proves definitely in the course of his two or three minutes on the screen that his earlier performance was not done with mirrors." Baby LeRoy is charming in *A Bedtime Story*, but despite the testimony of Hall and Sennwald, he does not really seem to smile, cry, crow on cue; close-ups of the child are cut into sequences which give the impression that he is responding to a line or a song. There are some two-shots, but except for one nose-to-nose with Chevalier, the infant is not at his cinematic best with others; his one action, throwing the watches to break them (a very tiresome gag), is not really his, since one can see Chevalier jostle him ever so lightly so that the watch falls from the unsteady baby's hand. When he first came to Fields in *Tillie and Gus*, his third film, his stock in trade was to be beguilingly cheerful, to perform small tasks as though he understood their significance and to be funny, as babies are funny, by warming the hearts of audience and critics alike. Although he has some naughty tricks in *Tillie and Gus* (pulling the plug of his bath, turning the radio knob so that Gus follows directions for mixing paint that have turned into exercise instructions), he is primarily a gurgling charmer whom the titular reformed tricksters (Alison Skipworth and Fields) have to save from drowning. It was after this essay in saccharinity that Fields realized the potential for malevolence in the angelic child.

In Baby LeRoy's one scene in *The Old-Fashioned Way*, he makes a shambles of the Great McGonigle's dinner, while the sufferer, unwilling to offend the doting mother, can only mutter through his indulgent smile ("How could you hurt a watch by dipping it in molasses?") and wait for the moment when he can plant a kick on the brat's backside. A gratifying instance of poetic justice, like a similar kick in Chaplin's *The Pilgrim* (1923), the scene was celebrated by an anonymous critic in the *New York Times* as "a pure, classic motion that liberated the life-time frustrations of all males everywhere." Harold Bissonette is no Great McGonigle; so there is no liberating moment in *Gift*. But, then, Elwood's actions are not so clearly targeted as Albert's were in the earlier film. It is true that he hits Harold in the elbow with a can of clams ("I hate clams," grumbles the victim), but for the most part he is simply there, immaculate in his little white suit, promising disaster. It comes when he turns on the molasses tap, flooding the store, an event with a pure Bissonette finish. Elwood's mother (Josephine Whittell) storms into the store, accuses Harold of releasing the molasses to get the child's shoes dirty and announces that she will never enter the grocery again. Later, in the sleeping-porch scene, Elwood, who lives above the Bissonettes, drops a bunch of grapes through a hole onto the unsleeping Harold. Then single grapes, one of which goes into his mouth. Finally, an ice pick which sticks in the arm of the swing near his head. This time Harold vows vengeance ("Even a worm will turn"), but when he storms upstairs, weapon in hand, he is confronted by Mrs. Dunk. "Your ice pick," he says, but she ignores all conciliation, complaining that he is feeding the child grapes after having dumped molasses on him.

At the end of the first of the Baby LeRoy scenes, Harold, beset by molasses and an outraged mother, stunned by Everett's explanation for not having stopped the child ("I told him I wouldn't do that"), finally explodes, but it is an explosion that tells a great deal about the way in which Fields used his voice. He simply looks at Everett and says, very softly, "I hate you." It is more powerful than a shout. An even better example of quiet emphasis can be found in one of the plot scenes that interrupts the store sketch, but its effectiveness can best be illustrated by going back to one of the silent films. In *It's the Old Army Game*, Prettywillie refuses to take his nephew with him on one occasion, riding over the boy's tantrum with "No-no-no-no-and NO!" The growing typography was presumably the only way the filmmakers could indicate in titles the hero's determination. The scene in *Gift*, blessed with Fields's voice, turns the device inside out. When Mildred's boyfriend, who sold Harold the worthless orange grove, comes to tell him that he will help get his money back, Harold, suspecting chicanery, orders him out of the store with a marvelous *GO* which works into a diminuendo *go-go-go*. There is a similar string of diminishing *drats*—and a very nice run it is—when Sam Bisbee misses his stop on the train in *You're Telling Me*, but the *go*s of *Gift* are more impressive for they come in a dramatic confrontation in which the downward flow simply washes the well-meaning John out of the scene.

There are many other gags—good and bad—in the grocery sequence. When Harold dresses in a fur coat and hat to go into the freezer, Fields seems to be straining for a joke, but I forgive that weakness when he wraps the meat on his return. The finished package—like the gum he wraps for Mr. Muckle earlier in the scene—is a great, crumpled mass of butcher's paper, unfolding even as he holds it. The extended business with the man who wants ten pounds of cumquats, as he laboriously spells it, becomes a running gag about Harold's unwillingness to admit that he has no cumquats, perhaps does not even know what they are. But these—and even his business with Tammany Young and Baby LeRoy—pale alongside the incredible Mr. Muckle, the blind and deaf customer who wreaks so much havoc in so short a time. Fields had used a blind man as a hazard as early as the 1920 sketch, "The Family Ford," in which the man manages to smash a headlight as he passes, and he presumably intended to reuse the joke in *If I Had a Million* (1932). At least William K. Everson prints a photograph in *The Art of W. C. Fields*, a shot of a blind man, which he describes as a still of an unused part of the Fields–Alison Skipworth contribution to *Million*. The actor in the photograph is somewhat nondescript looking, certainly no Charles Sellon. The wonder of Mr.

Muckle is that Fields's conception, the irrascible old man who stifles any possible audience sympathy, finds a perfect embodiment in Sellon.

A stringy man—almost emaciated in this film—with arms and legs like unanchored wires and a face like a leather tobacco pouch, Charles Sellon lent himself to stereotypical casting—a grouch or a fidget. He had been in the movies since the early 1920s, usually in very small roles, emerging infrequently into real visibility. In *Bright Eyes* (1934), he played one of those curmudgeons that Fox invented for Shirley Temple to enchant, an effective but conventional performance. Much more interesting is his work in *Life Begins at Forty* (1935). He plays a death-obsessed old man, wanting to control his children from the grave, until the country editor (Will Rogers) convinces him to live now, and he turns up, newly dandified, with a striking widow on his arm. In the party sequence, he dances himself into semi-collapse, a bromidic old-man joke if it were not that his buckling knees still retain the roosterish sprightliness with which he begins, and at the end of the brawl that concludes the party he is doing a sparring routine every bit as attractive as the one that a few years later became one of Barry Fitzgerald's identifying mannerisms. An early instance of his remarkable physical comedy, his ability to suggest rigidity despite the performer's obvious agility, can be found in Gregory La Cava's *Feel My Pulse* (1928). In this film he plays Sylvester Zilch, the caretaker of the Manning Sanitarium, who is trying to keep the hypochondriacal owner (Bebe Daniels) from discovering that it has been turned into a rum-runner's base. For the most part, he has nothing to do but express nervousness and a querulousness that is obvious even in a silent film, but he has one very funny extended scene. On showing Miss Manning to her room he there discovers a keg which he must carry to the window and throw out without her seeing it. He moves in a kind of eccentric dance in which first one leg, then another is thrust out as he attempts at once to retain his balance, hide the keg, and give the impression that he is totally involved with the well-being of the woman. Once he has dumped the keg, he moves back across the room in a movement that is part a stumble of exhaustion, part a caper of triumph. Not exactly a one-performance actor, then. Still, Sellon—like Kathleen Howard—never worked better than he did with Fields.

Mr. Muckle is one of Fields's loveliest inventions. Reviewers like Richard Watts, Jr., and Andre Sennwald, apparently a little nervous at having found the sequence so funny, invoked the saintly Chaplin in their insistence that the joke is in no way tasteless; any reader who knows *Gift* only from my words in these pages will have to see for himself to discover why the conventional taboo against the handicapped as comic material is totally irrelevant in Mr. Muckle's case. He comes crashing into the store, snarling that Harold has the door closed again, and when the grocer, who has arrived at the entrance a second too late, touches him gently, he recoils, knocking over a stack of boxes. "Just a little glassware," says Harold. He seats Mr. Muckle and takes his order (a package of gum) and, as he turns to get it, Harold sees a display of light bulbs and adds a "please" to his request that Mr. Muckle stay put. Following the comic logic Fields propounded in his analysis of the burglar trap in *You're Telling Me*, the bulbs have to break, but not all at once. The impatient Mr. Muckle gets up, and the first bulb falls. Inquisitive, he picks one up and when he replaces it, it rolls to the floor. He leans, then, against the display and another bulb falls. Disconcerted now, he waves his cane above the stacked bulbs. Finally, they begin to roll as a group, and a great many of them crash to the floor. Through all this, Harold, who is busily wrapping the gum, tries to soothe him with "dear" ("Mr. Muckle, please, dear") and "honey" as though the endearments—as mechanical as those he uses with his wife—were verbal charms that might defuse this destructive force. Growling that he wants the gum delivered, Mr. Muckle makes his exit, breaking the glass in the other half of the door and repeating his entrance line about its being closed. Harold, attentive still, starts him across the empty street and, just as he steps off the curb, pandemonium breaks loose. From an overhead shot, we watch a perfectly composed Mr. Muckle pass unharmed while a sudden rush of cars and at least three fire engines race past. A startled Harold topples backwards into an ashcan and the scene ends on his attempt to lift himself out with a shovel that he uses as a lever. A very weak ending to a superior comedy scene, this bit reflects the sketch origins of Fields's work, his dependence on a gag that, on stage, could signal the curtain or the blackout. There are too many such finishes in the Fields films, unnecessarily so since both his style and the medium make it possible for comic sequences simply to unravel, leaving threads that can be picked up later. The real finish of the Mr. Muckle joke comes in the departure scene in which the neighbors, including the blind man, gather to see the Bissonettes off to California. As the car finally pulls away, the crowd signals its good-byes; Mr. Muckle stands slightly apart, waving in the wrong direction.

There are a number of other brief comic sequences—the departure, a scene in an auto camp—which are self-contained enough to suggest sketches, but the other two extended ones are the sleeping porch and the picnic. The first of these fills almost two reels of a five-reel movie, a happy imbalance reflected in the original title of the film—*Back Porch*. There is an introduction of sorts, presumably derived from "The

Nagger," a sketch by Gus Weinberg that Fields and Edna Leedom played in the summer edition of the 1925 *Follies*. In the film, Amelia's continuing complaint keeps Harold from sleeping, first on the couch in the parlor, then in his own bed. In consequence, he moves to the porch, where a string of animate and inanimate irritants continue to keep him awake. The setting is the back of a three-story wooden building (wood makes a better sounding board than cement or brick), and the Bissonette porch is the one in the middle, a position that allows him to be assaulted from above or below and tortured by passage up or down. The camera sometimes stands off and looks at the building as a whole, particularly when Fields wants the audience to see the source of a noise that Harold cannot locate; sometimes it focuses on the Bissonette porch alone. It can look up or down, from Harold's perspective, or work in close-up to record provocation or reaction. From whatever perspective, Harold remains the center of the action, and the deliberate speed of the sequence reflects not only Fields's characteristic comic rhythm but Harold's fatigue. First, one chain holding the porch swing begins to pull out of the ceiling and, as soon as Harold tests it and finds it secure, the swing falls, leaving him head down, feet up, still trying to sleep. The milkman rattles his bottles to the third floor and back while Harold calls down for quiet when the man is above, calls up when he is back on the street. The milkman, oddly enough, has delivered a coconut which then proceeds to roll all the way downstairs, even managing to make the turns at landings by smashing into garbage cans. Sometimes it moves in rushes, and then, losing momentum, it hesitates, drops a step, hesitates, drops again, each hit timed to Harold's settling back into his pillow. A man (T. Roy Barnes) comes looking for Carl LaFong, a name he must spell, indicating typography as well as letters (capital-L, small-a, capital-F, etc.), before Harold, spelling it back, says he does not know LaFong; even so, the man comes up to sell him insurance, and Amelia bursts out to want to know why they are telling "ribald stories." After the scene with Baby LeRoy, there is an even better confrontation with the Dunks. The mother on the third floor and the teenage daughter in the street carry on a marvelously banal exchange in full voice about which store the girl should go to, whether she should buy ipecac or syrup of squills, the conversation shot through with a penetrating "I don't care. . . . I don't care, either" that cuts into Harold as the words fly by. There is a squeaking laundry line, a vegetable man calling his wares, a shotgun that goes off, the complete collapse of the swing. The sequence ends, appropriately enough, with a very gentle finish—Harold using a fly swatter almost caressingly—but never an indication of sleep.

In the picnic sequence, the family, heading west, stops for lunch on the lawn of a private estate which they mistake for a public park, but the joke has less to do with ownership than it does with man's habit of fouling any nest that is not strictly his own. As they drive in, the car smashes a statue ("She ran right in front of me"), and from that moment the Bissonettes go through the picnic ritual of defilement. They litter the place with paper, with feathers, with cans, with food (Fields does the mouth-stuffing routine that he used in *The Fatal Glass of Beer* [1933], in which he spews crumbs whenever he tries to speak). Norman turns on the lawn sprinklers, but the family cannot stay to watch their debris turn sodden; they hurry away, over Amelia's protests, when the owners order them out. Earlier versions of the sketch are much more destructive, for the family trashes the mansion and, in *Army Game*, exits by driving through a brick wall. The sequence is more effective in *Gift* because it retains its relation to reality and becomes a comment on the kind of self-absorption that has fueled all the scenes described above. Harold, who has been victimized by his family, by Mr. Muckle, by the Dunks, by the world at large, turns out to be one of the victimizers as well. Fields, as social commentator, could not afford to use his character as a butt only, for that way lies sentimentalization.

Many gags ago, I proposed to discuss the comic sequences in *Gift* as though they were self-contained inheritances from the *Follies*; by now it is clear that the Fields persona is not simply the varnish that gives a gloss to the picture as a whole, but the substance that gives both comic and social point to the individual scenes. The appeal of the Fields character, which is more complex than the performer's undeniable talent as funnyman, can best be understood if we can pry him loose from the offscreen legend, the totem embedded in his biography or pseudo-biography: the battered child who became such a good hater he was elevated to anti-Establishment hero. His hard-scrabble childhood provided Fields with interview material from early in his career, but it was with Alva Johnston's 1938 *Saturday Evening Post* piece that the child really became father of the man, on screen and off: "His comedy is largely autobiographical." Robert Lewis Taylor used this assumption as the organizing principle of *W. C. Fields, His Follies and Fortunes* ten years later and it has now become the reigning cliché of Fields commentary. I would no more deny that there are autobiographical elements in Fields's work than that Charles Chaplin's life is reflected in the Tramp, but it is the fictional creations that interest me here. To pull lines out of context, to juxtapose silly publicity shots with stills from the movies, to pretend that the pathetic alcoholic of Fields's last years is a comic figure, as so many articles and paste-up books do, is to peddle a Fieldsian worldview at the expense of the comedian's art.

Fields is a great American comedian not because he said he liked children "with mustard" or "somebody stole the cork from my lunch," but because he created and embodied Elmer Prettywillie, Sam Bisbee, Elmer Finch, the Great McGonigle, Ambrose Wolfinger, Eustace McGargle, Cuthbert J. Twillie, Larson E. Whipsnade, Egbert Sousè and, above all, Harold Bissonette.

As this list indicates, there are—or appear to be—two different Fields characters—the con man and the harassed everyday citizen. Both presumably have their roots in Fields's juggling act, the former in its setting, the latter in its content. With a routine built on planned mistakes, hairbreadth recoveries, Fields must not only have illustrated his very real juggling skill but conveyed a figure of ineptitude, surviving almost by accident. Heywood Broun once said, "Fields is, as far as I know, the only one who is able to introduce the tragic note in the handling of a dozen cigar boxes." As the juggling act expanded into sketches, then into films, the recalcitrant props grew into an uncontrollable environment. The con man Fields, the circus man who knew that juggling was just an act, might seem more able to cope with resistant reality, but to think so is to confuse mask with matter. The Fields con men, from Professor McGargle in *Poppy* (1923), Fields's only nonrevue success on Broadway, to Cuthbert Twillie in *My Little Chickadee* (1940), have found an orotund voice and a fulsome vocabulary (the target of most Fields imitators) for their contributions to the American tall-tale tradition and have developed duplicitous mannerisms that promise a great deal more trickery than they ever deliver. Alva Johnston says that "the Fields comedy is built to appeal to the dormant larceny and chicanery of audiences." Although audiences do love con men—which helps explain the continued popularity of Odysseus and the bibilical Joseph—the attraction in Fields's case seems to lie with the fact that McGargle and Bissonette are brothers under the skin. The audience may warm to McGonigle's outsmarting the prune of a landlady (Nora Cecil) in *The Old-Fashioned Way*, but it is Fields under attack from Baby LeRoy that remains the memorable scene in the film.

In a paraphrase, intended to express Fields's own ideas, Alva Johnston wrote, "A funny man stops being funny the moment he loses his underdog psychology." There are, of course, two possible responses to the comic loser. One can feel superior to him hence sympathetic toward him, or one can recognize oneself in him. J. B. Priestley found "the secret of his huge and enchanting drollery" in the fact "that he moved, warily in spite of a hastily assumed air of nonchalant confidence, through a world in which even the inanimate objects were hostile, rebellious, menacing, never to be trusted." Since most of us—at least on some days—live in the world Priestley described, self-recognition seems to lie at the heart of Fields's comic appeal. It is not, however, simply a business of loser loves loser, for the Fields character does move, however warily, through that world. His comic mannerisms constitute a kind of survival kit. Take the voice—not the tall-tale voice, but the persistent one. Wilfrid Sheed points out that Fields, like Will Rogers, was a performer who came to words as an afterthought, an addition to a silent act—Fields's juggling, Rogers's rope tricks. As a result, he says, Fields talks "as a man mutters to himself when engaged on an intricate task." It is true that both Fields and Rogers are more often overheard than heard, but Sheed's sensible account of the probable origin of their verbal styles falls short of differentiating between them. Fields seems less like Rogers finally, than like that other master mutterer, Rogers's occasional partner, Stepin Fetchit. Like Fetchit's barely articulate murmur, Fields's very audible asides are used to establish a defensible territory within the jungle of his character's daily life. Bissonette's remark about hating clams provides a mechanism that—momentarily, at least—erases Elwood, Everett, the whole Harold-eating store. As with the voice, so with the physical business, the mesmerizing attention to detail, that adagio tempo *Time* mentioned. Fields, the performer, on behalf of the character he embodies, creates a small area of invulnerability at the center of that social, familial, and personal battlefield on which he struggles and loses. Those ludicrous happy endings to the even more ludicrous plots, those suddenly profitable oil leases, inventions, real-estate holdings, Beefsteak Mines that bring wealth to the Fields bumblers, are never more than jokes. Cash in abundance may temporarily sweeten the voice of Amelia Bissonette, it may free Harold from the domination of the Muckles, it may give him a chance to share a fade-out drink with his friend the dog, but it cannot retroactively erase the truth-telling at the heart of the laughter.

As I write these words, a sudden burst of wind tears through the open window. Finished pages and stacks of notes blow all around the room. "Just a little glassware," I mutter as I crawl around, retrieving the pieces of paper. "I hate clams." And I begin to laugh, sitting in the debris, rescued from exasperation not by the touted hater of bankers and dogs and children, but by a comic genius that knew how to make victory of loss. It's a gift? It's a gift.

Notes

1. It was Columbus when Fields referred to the incident in one of the captions he wrote for *Coronet* in 1943 for an unpublished picture-spread on vaudeville (*W. C. Fields by Himself*, New York, Warner, 1974, p. 562); it was Toledo when Groucho Marx told the story in *The Marx Bros. Scrapbook* (New York, Star Books–W. H. Allen, 1976, p. 34).

2. I say "could be" because there is no way to verify the tailoring unless we take the word of Mordaunt Hall in the *New York Times* (January 23, 1927, sec. 7, p. 7), who was jubilant about Fields's performance. But, then, Hall, who was otherwise a bit suspicious of Fields, really liked movies that looked like plays. The *Potters* is still among the missing Fields films, although enthusiasts need not despair. Fifteen years ago, the only Fields silents known to exist were *Pool Sharks* and *Sally of the Sawdust* (1925), but since then copies of many of the others have been discovered.

3. When Fields was rediscovered in the 1960s and elevated to secular sainthood as an anti-Establishment figure, his new devotees, moved by enthusiasm and ignorance, came to his work as Columbuses, never noticing that several generations of Leif Ericsons had been happily living there. For example, Michael M. Taylor, who in 1971 prepared a new edition of *Fields for President* (New York, Dodd Mead), a tepid attempt at nondramatic comedy first published in 1940, he began his introduction with the conventional placard: "Today W. C. Fields is considered one of the greatest comic geniuses, although during his lifetime he never received such just acclaim" (p. xiii). Fields, like all performers, had his detractors, but the reviews of his work, on stage and on screen, are so full of love and admiration that his greatness seems never to have been in doubt. In 1925, the *New York Times* (March 11, p. 19) called him "one of the supreme comedians of our time"; ten years later, Otis Ferguson labeled him "a natural resource" (*The Film Criticism of Otis Ferguson*, Philadelphia, Temple University Press, 1971, p. 88). Both reviewers were voting with the majority.

4. Presumably Bill Grady. He had been Fields's agent in the 1920s and had gone with him to Florida when *It's the Old Army Game* was shot there. He was now an executive at MGM, which produced *Ziegfeld Follies* (1946). Fields was not in it, but at least one of his old Follies partners (Fanny Brice) was.

5. A still of the scene decorates the cover of the paperback edition of *W. C. Fields by Himself*. A great deal of nonsense has been written about Fields as a dog-hater, based for the most part on jokes, like those in "Alcohol and Me," a tiresome piece he published in *Pic* (12 [October 13, 1942], 32–34), proving the superiority of drink over dogs. The

business with the dog in *Gift* is unusual since dogs, like children, tend to be aggressors in Fields's films. This footnote is not designed, however, to defend dogs against Fields or Fields against dogs. It is a testimony to a dog named Rex, who appeared with Fields in *Running Wild* (1927). In that film, the browbeaten Elmer Finch (Fields), made brave by hypnosis, overcomes all his oppressors, human and animal. In his confrontation with Rex, the dog runs in, barking, ready to harass him as usual, but stops dead, sensing a new Finch. Rex then retreats in a remarkable cringing walk, his belly almost dragging on the floor, his legs bent so that his joints stick out like elbows held akimbo. In this unlikely position, he moves clear across the room to his exit, his escape. Unrelenting dog lovers may think that this sounds demeaning—an insult to dogs everywhere—but to me it is a performance, like those of Fields, which depends on art rather than lovableness. It is a canine thespic triumph.

6. Fields was fond of pronunciation jokes. He used the hard "g" for *gypsy* in *Gift* and for *tragedian* in *The Old-Fashioned Way* and somehow made the studied mispronunciation seem like significant comic invention. There is a whisper of social pretension in the constantly corrected name in *Gift*, but there is more urgency in the same joke in *The Bank Dick*, in which Egbert Sousè, a regular at the Black Pussy Cat Café, has to remind everyone that there is an accent *grave* over the "e".

7. Later, in what is presumably her mourning dress for the departed Uncle Bean, she wears a black gown with very short, slit sleeves that barely cover the shoulders and with a gigantic white bow at the neck, high on the right. As unmistakably 1930s as anything Jean Harlow and Myrna Loy wear in *Libeled Lady* (1936), it is a vision of indiscreet elegance, tastelessly right for Amelia Bissonette.

5

STEAMBOAT ROUND THE BEND

· 1935 ·

"When the legend becomes fact, print the legend."
—Dutton Peabody in
The Man Who Shot Liberty Valance

There's A Vacant Chair For Will Rogers (In Every Home Tonight). This is the title and, without the parentheses, the opening line of the chorus of a song, "Respectfully Dedicated to the Memory of Our Beloved Will Rogers," written by Lou Leaman and Mitchell Parish shortly after the plane crash (August 15, 1935) that killed Rogers and Wiley Post. The song never made its way into the popular consciousness as, say, "The Wreck of the Shenandoah" or "The Death of Floyd Collins" did. That may be because the song is so bad—all treacle, no theatricality—but I suspect that the more important difference between it and the other disaster songs lay with the audience. The public were simply spectators for the destruction of the dirigible, bystanders at the cave-side vigil for the trapped Kentucky boy; the crash near Point Barrow, Alaska, seemed to most people a personal loss.[1] "The restaurant waitress, the street-car conductor, the filling-station attendant," said a *New Republic* editorial, "spoke of his accidental death . . . as though each had lost a dearly loved personal friend." Roger Butterfield, writing on "The Legend of Will Rogers" in 1949, said that visitors to the Will Rogers Memorial in Claremore, Oklahoma, "buttonhole the curators . . . and relate with startling exactitude what they were doing when they heard the news of Rogers' death . . . almost 14 years ago." The reaction of the public was recorded, analyzed and a little falsified, I suspect, by the immediate response of newspapers and magazines, in which the editors and writers had not only to mourn Will Rogers but to explain him.

Doctor John and "that old bull frog." Will Rogers, Irvin S. Cobb. (*Steamboat Round the Bend*, 20th Century Fox, 1935. The Museum of Modern Art/Film Stills Archive.)

Hard on the heels of the obsequies, came the books: P. J. O'Brien's *Will Rogers, Ambassador of Good Will, Prince of Wit and Wisdom* (1935); Jack Lait's *Our Will Rogers* (1935: Homer Croy would use the same title eighteen years later); David Randolph Milsten's *An Appreciation of Will Rogers* (1935); *Folks Say of Will Rogers, A Memorial Anecdotage* (1936), a celebrity-heavy collection of comments put together for the Oklahoma Society of Washington. In part these volumes may indicate a commercial confusion between a hearse and a bandwagon, but they almost certainly reflect as well a general desire to hold onto something that was irrevocably gone. Not that any of the books ever had an audience as vast as the one that Rogers reached as a radio performer, as one of Hollywood's top box-office stars, as a widely syndicated daily and weekly newspaper columnist.

"As soon as he was dead," Butterfield wrote, "almost everyone agreed that Will Rogers was the best-loved American of his time." I do not think that Butterfield intended the double edge that that line has out of context, but it does suggest a process of sentimentalization, almost of deification that followed Rogers's death. "Will Rogers was a humorist who won recognition as a secular saint," William R. Brown said in *Imagemaker*.[2] The transformation in Rogers can be seen in what befell one of his most famous lines: "I never met a man I didn't like." The first use of the phrase, so far as I know, is in a 1926 *Saturday Evening Post* article about his visit to Russia in which he explained that he was sure that he would have got on well with Trotsky had he been allowed to see him. As was customary in Rogers's work, the line reemerged to serve other purposes. Homer Croy, in a rumination on Rogers's fondness for inventing epitaphs for himself, calls attention to the comedian's use of that somewhat special form of epigraphic humor in some postsermon remarks he made in a Boston church in 1930. It is characteristic of the amorphousness of popular quotations that the neat version Croy gives is not the one quoted in the *Boston Globe*, his announced source. The line, in the form quoted above, passed from comment to credo when it was carved in stone at the base of the Jo Davidson statue of Rogers in Claremore. A loving celebration of the homespun philosopher, the sentence somewhat obscures the comedian who could make the joke that W. C. Fields so admired: commenting on a wreck on the New York, New Haven, and Hartford in 1918, Rogers said to the *Follies* audience, "I see the NY, NH & H have started their Spring drive." From all accounts Rogers was open, kind, loving, charitable—admirably so—but even Irvin S. Cobb, who called him "almost the only man I ever knew who went plumb to the top and yet never used the necks of his friends for the rungs of the ladder he climbed on," had misgivings about the famous "never-met" phrase.

"But he neither was sappy nor overly sentimental," Cobb wrote. "He had his favorites and his antipathies and privately he never hesitated to express these judgments in salty language."

Perhaps it was inevitable that the very real public grief at Rogers's death should lead to an idealization of him. There is a tendency to make him too wise as well as too good. The Rogers who emerges in Donald Day's biography sometimes seems to have been the only man in America with the understanding and the concern to solve the country's problems during the 1920s and 1930s. In fact, as with most commentators—comic or not—Rogers had very little influence on governmental policies or business practices. He was a man who made jokes about society and government and, reading through his work today, one discovers that many of his gags were conventional ones depending on the popular concept of the crooked politician and the greedy businessman, that most of them were harmless ("You folks know I never mean anything by the cracks I make on politics"), that a number of them were remarkably prescient, sensible then and now. Yet, it is not Rogers as real political power—which he never was—nor as unheeded prophet—which he sometimes was—that I am concerned with here, but Rogers as a personality with whom so many people could identify. There is ambiguity enough in that. A wealthy celebrity, at ease in the company of millionaires and successful politicians, he seemed to speak for the ordinary man. Butterfield suggested that Rogers's appeal lay in his being "just folks," but he added, in a sentence that denies a widespread tendency to equate Rogers with a nostalgia for old-fashioned virtues:

> In many other ways too he was typically American—in his restlessness, his craving for speed and physical action, his adaptability to new ways of life like the airplane, his openhearted sentimentality, his aversion to intellectual processes, his irreverence toward important people.

The list could have been extended and made more complex by turning some of the items inside out—his distrust of new ways of life, his attraction to important people—but it is clear that Rogers at many points touched the prejudices and attitudes of his fellow Americans. He has been called "Vox Populi in person" and "America's most complete human document," but what his admirers saw on the lecture platform, on stage and screen, and heard on the radio was something a great deal less abstract than a Vox Populi or a document. It was a man called Will Rogers; it was also a work of art who usually—but not in his movie roles—bore the same name.

Andrew Sinclair, in his biography of John Ford, says that the director "had to give Rogers his head, making a virtue out of his star's bumbling and unpolished delivery." He seems unaware that Rogers had spent more than thirty years perfecting that bumble, polishing that unpolish. Yet, of all the comedians discussed in this book, Rogers is the one in whom the performer is most identified with his persona. Jerome Beatty's "But Will Rogers off the stage is no different from Will Rogers on" is a standard comment from a typical theatrical-personality piece. Even Betty Rogers, who emphasized the way her husband practiced his rope tricks in the early years and pored over the newspapers for material later, could say of his delivery on stage that it was "simply the way Will talked, off-stage or on." Surely she did not mean that Rogers, at table, used the almost formal pattern that Richard Henry Little detected when the comedian was still in vaudeville, the *Ziegfeld Follies* still in the future:

> He makes a remark and apparently marks a period by doing some trick with the lasso and the part of the audience that sympathized with his statement applauds madly. Then Mr. Rogers drops another remark that is diametrically opposed to his first statement and starts another section of the audience to great applause. But as this tumult drops down he makes still another comment along the line of his original thought that is a trifle more pertinent than either of the first two and differs widely from them.

Little's description may be too neatly a case of thesis-antithesis-synthesis, but in later years, the lasso gone, Rogers did retain this basic gag structure, the delayed needle. What Betty Rogers presumably had in mind was manner not form, an air of casualness, an indifference to the niceties of grammar, a projected sense of the performer as friend and neighbor.

"I am just an old country boy in a big town trying to get along," Rogers wrote in 1924. "I have been eating Pretty Regular, and the reason I have been is because I have stayed an old country boy." Given the material that Rogers used and his sensitivity to situation and to audience, he must have improvised frequently, presumably working, as do most good ad-libbers, out of a reservoir of possible jokes. In the archives of the Will Rogers Memorial there are some notes reaching back to those days when he was still doing a roping act with a horse and a rider, a list of "Gags For Missing the Horses Nose." The secret of Rogers's comedy lay not in improvisation but in a delivery which made his remarks, prepared or spontaneous, appear to be happy surprises.

The *New Republic* editorial quoted at the beginning of this chapter recalled that one of the editors, visiting Rogers in his *Follies* dressing room, saw several versions of the same joke on a sheet of paper in the comedian's typewriter; later, in the middle of his monologue, "he stopped, chuckled as though a thought suddenly occurred to him at that moment, and repeated the final version of the joke verbatim." A lot of nonsense has been written, some of it by Rogers, about his just being himself on stage, but this preference for the gifted amateur over the careful professional is a manifestation of a popular prejudice against art that belittles when it means to compliment. Betty Rogers was surely correct when she wrote, "His whole career was the development and unfolding of a personality through the various vehicles that seemed to be constantly and almost miraculously presenting themselves," but that development must have been as much nurtural as natural. Lew Ayres, more than forty years after he appeared with Rogers in *State Fair* (1933), recalled that he did not really think of Rogers as an actor then, but that he had come to believe that "The capacity of a man to communicate his personality—and we thought of Will Rogers as a personality—to communicate that to an audience is an art."

As with Mae West, the Marx Brothers, W. C. Fields—personality performers, all—Rogers retained a comic persona through all his films. Reviewers tended to identify Rogers on screen with Rogers in his other entertainment guises; as far back as 1918, the *New York Times*, commenting on *Laughing Bill Hyde*, Rogers's first film, said, "The real Will Rogers is on the reels." Yet I distrust this reviewers' impulse. Although he was clearly Will Rogers, whatever name he carried, whatever plot he followed, he was at war with himself in a way that these other comedians were not. Fields could move his sketches directly from the *Follies* to the screen, but Rogers, the monologist, the columnist, the radio performer, the "Cowboy Philosopher" (as the titles of his first books identify him) could never really do his routine in the movies. His characters occasionally had lines that might have suited that other Rogers—after all, he invented much of his own material—but Rogers the movie personality and Rogers the commentator on the current scene worked from two different and conflicting popular genres.

Although Rogers as humorist is a professional optimist, his writing is shot through with a kind of fatalism, an assumption that things will work out despite attempts to improve them, a belief that human nature is unalterable. E. B. White, in an unsigned *New Yorker* note, once complained that Rogers's "social wisdom consists in repeating that because we have two arms and two legs and look like monkeys, we are always going to act like monkeys." That *New Republic* editorial I keep returning to said that, "Like Twain, he concealed a profound pessimism about ultimate objectives beneath a jester's exterior." This dark strain in the comedian's work may be central to Rogers the man, as I think it is, although it is certainly not the image most Rogers biographers present. Personal or not, however, this gloomy note has always been an important element in popular art and Rogers always had a tapline into popular feelings. James Whitcomb Riley's poetry was not only full of up-and-doers like Little Orphant Annie and the Raggedy Man (look at those adjectives), but it had its share of sentimental and exemplary deaths. George M. Cohan could put into a single show, *Little Johnny Jones* (1904), both "The Yankee Doodle Boy" and "Life's a Funny Proposition After All," in which the sentiments— "With all we've thought, and all we're taught, why all we seem to know is,/We're born, live a while and then we die"—are very like Rogers's response to Will Durant's request for his philosophy: "What all of us know put together dont mean anything. Nothing dont mean anything. We are just here for a spell and pass on. Any man that thinks that Civilization has advanced is an egotist." It is not simply that Rogers reflected and responded to an element in the popular consciousness. His calling presupposed a negative attitude. Political humorists from Bill Nye to Mort Sahl may have envisioned an ideal world, but their trade depended on that vision's never invading the real one. It is the defects of the system which create their jokes, put the bite into their commentary. It was Will Rogers's function to stand off, observe, smile wryly, point an amiably accusing finger, comfort his audience not with solutions but with the laughter that grew out of a shared distrust of society.

In contrast, the Will Rogers character in the movies was never allowed to be simply an observer. The demands of the genre insisted that he be a problem solver. The actions the Rogers character performs—bringing the young lovers together, saving the innocent man from false accusation, unmasking and often winning over the villain, solving a financial dilemma—are the stuff of conventional comedy drama. Nineteenth-century theater-goers would have felt no disorientation had they been transported to the 1930s neighborhood movie house. Even the Rogers character would have been familiar, for it has its roots in all those Yankee characters, those Jonathans that filled the nineteenth-century American stage, those sometimes illiterate natural sages who both mock and embody American virtues. The Rogers character is a comic hero, like Asa Trenchard in Tom Taylor's *Our American Cousin*,[3] and the emphasis is on both elements in that label—the comedy and the heroism. It is difficult for a protagonist, even one as apparently unhurried as Doctor John in *Steamboat Round the Bend*, to be the same Will Rogers as the humorist on the public platform; the observer can only invade the doer's territory when, as I think happens in *Steamboat*, the tone of the work makes the ending both solution and observation. I cannot demonstrate that possibility until I have finished discussing the film. In the meantime, let's see what Will Rogers on the screen borrowed from his other self.

The manner, clearly. The delivery. The suggestion that the character, at least at the vocal level, is all spontaneity. The Rogers mutter, like that of W. C. Fields, sometimes seems to imply that the character is only physically present, but since that character must finally act—unlike the Fields persona, who is usually acted upon—he is more overtly a part of the society in which he operates. Consider the scene in *Steamboat* in which Duke (John McGuire) brings Fleety Belle (Anne Shirley) to Doctor John's boat. His uneasiness about the presence of the girl and, as the scene progresses, his distress at the killing to which Duke confesses are not so much voiced as talked around. Doctor John defines not only his state of mind but his attachment to his nephew, his suspicion of the girl ("She's a swamp gal, ain't she?") while attempting to feed the two of them. "I've got some hot coffee here. I'll get some bacon in a minute," he says, but in the theater the lines come across as a barely audible murmur in which the words *hot coffee* emerge, like a signboard defining an event, his setting a cup of coffee on the table. Since Rogers, the trick roper, like Fields, the juggler, has an uncanny command of his hands, they become an embodiment of Doctor John's uncertainty, the physical equivalent of that ambling and—in this scene—slightly querulous voice. The way he uses the cooking fork, shifting it from hand to hand, and plays with his handkerchief makes props an extension of his physical, his vocal self. Henry King, who directed Rogers in *Lightnin'* (1930) and *State Fair*, once said that "whether he was a good actor, or not, he sure knew how to use props." There is another cooking scene in *Life Begins at Forty* (1935) in which Kenesaw (Rogers), making pancakes and boasting of his skill, quiets the angry Lee (Richard Cromwell), while both voice and gesture seem to be doing something else. In *They Had to See Paris* (1929), when Idy (Irene Rich) insists that Pike (Rogers) take the family to Europe in quest of culture and background, Rogers's physical business—the way he strokes his nose, leans on his hand, wipes his face, pulls off his glasses—lets us know that a reluctant Pike will give in to his wife's demand. Rogers uses many of the same gestures in *Judge Priest* (1934), but for a very different effect; they become indicators of the Judge's relaxed attitude in the scene on the porch between him and his socially pretentious sister-in-law. The rigidity of Brenda Fowler's Caroline alongside Rogers's Judge, slumping in his chair, is a physical image of a conflict of values.

As these scenes indicate, Rogers is able to use his physical and vocal effects—*mannerisms*, if the word be taken positively—to fulfill the immediate emotional needs of a scene. At the same time, the naturalness that the performer conveys makes calculation (i.e., art) seem to have little to do with the success of the scenes. The air of accident that hangs over Rogers's performances was heightened by publicity men, film reporters, and reviewers who got a lot of cheerful lineage out of the disruptions Rogers's improvisatory techniques presumably brought to the set. The biographies are full of anecdotes, and the reminiscences that Bryan B. Sterling elicited from the comedian's Hollywood associates for *The Will Rogers Scrapbook* emphasize the missed cues, the confusion and—this above all—the happy results of letting Rogers have his own way. There is a lot of embroidery in all this, stemming in part from the fact that the source is sometimes Rogers himself or another comic exaggerator like Irvin S. Cobb. Asked if he had read the script of *The Texas Steer* (1927), Rogers is supposed to have answered, "Nope, what's the fun of making pictures if you know how they're goin' to come out." What kind of answer would a professional comedian have been expected to give? Cobb, in a loving column he wrote at the time of Rogers's death, tells how he and Rogers admitted not knowing the story of *Steamboat* when John Ford asked. "Tell you what, John," Cobb's Will Rogers says,

> you sort of generally break the news to us what this sequence is about and I'll think up a line for Cobb to speak, and then Cobb'll think up a line for me to speak, and that way there won't be no ill feelin's or heart burnin's, and the feller that kin remember after it's all over what the plot was about—if there is any plot by then—gets first prize, which will be a kiss on the forehead from Mr. John Ford.

Even an amateur analyst of verbal styles ought to be able to tell a Cobb speech from one that Rogers might have made. When Cobb got around to retelling the story in *Exit Laughing*, the speech disappeared altogether, but the point of the anecdote—that Cobb and Rogers were amusing amateurs—remained. Although John Ford is hardly famous for his accuracy[4] and, in his interview with Sterling, he clearly overstates his part in Rogers's habit of concocting his own lines, I am inclined to accept the version of the Rogers method he described to Peter Bogdanovich:

Some of the lines he'd speak from the script, but most of the time he'd make up his own; he'd stop and let people pick up their cues and then go on; he wouldn't write the lines down, but he'd work it out beforehand and then just get in front of the camera and get the sense of the scene in his own inimitable way.

The Rogers locution, then, but within the context of the scene.[5] Rogers may have ad-libbed on the set of *Steamboat*, but the marvelous mutter I described in the paragraph above belongs to Doctor John.

Although Rogers occasionally did conventional comic bits—the tipsy scene in *They Had to See Paris* in which he dresses in armor, the scene in *Life Begins at Forty* in which Kenesaw and the irascible banker (George Barbier) threaten and avoid one another as though they were Viola and Andrew Aguecheek—he was customarily quiet, ruminative, the comedy rising from personality rather than funny business. His style as a performer was largely responsible for his screen image, but his naturalness was heightened by a tendency to surround him with unnatural actors. I am not thinking of the young lovers in the films—who were often unnatural in their way, too—or of the members of his family in those movies which gave his character a family, but of the other comics who contributed so much to the success of the Rogers movies. This contrast may be particularly obvious in the Rogers films that John Ford directed—*Dr. Bull* (1933), *Judge Priest*, *Steamboat Round the Bend*—for Ford had a taste for "vintage gargoyles," to use Andrew Sarris's phrase. Consider Victor McLaglen in *Wee Willie Winkie* (1937) and a dozen years later in Ford's cavalry pictures—*Fort Apache* (1948), *She Wore a Yellow Ribbon* (1949), *Rio Grande* (1950). *Steamboat* provides an abundance of performers for Will Rogers to play against, five of them in important supporting roles—Irvin S. Cobb, Francis Ford, Eugene Pallette, Berton Churchill, Stepin Fetchit.

Cobb at thirty was "a porky, simian Kentuckian"—so Ward Greene once said—and that odd conjunction of animal adjectives was still viable when Cobb, pushing sixty, played Captain Eli, Doctor John's rival on the river. With his puffed-cheek face and his immense belly (emphasized in one shot in which he lies flat and the camera gives us the stomach pushing skyward), he looks rather like a mature orangutan, surely the porkiest of the simians. Sara Hamilton said in *Photoplay* that Cobb in profile looked like "a roll-top desk" and Doctor John describes Captain Eli as "that old bull frog." These labels are also appropriate. Cobb's film credits go back to the 1920s, but his appearances in silent films were largely guest shots by a well-known writer; in

The Great White Way (1924), for instance, he was one of a large band of columnists and cartoonists on hand to give local color to a melodrama about a boxer. In 1934, he signed with Hal Roach for a series of two-reelers[6] in which he plays a retired steamboat captain, but it is the personality not the character that Roach hoped to sell; Cobb uses his own name and, in "The Ballad of Paducah Jail," he is identified not as Captain Cobb but as the "Internationally Famous Writer." Cobb was not much of an actor, as his later movies show, his repertory of gestures pretty much limited to a carnivorous grin, rolling eyes, and a marvelous O-mouth (used for surprise or exasperation) which the camera liked to catch head-on. I assume that it was not his work with Roach that led to his being cast as Captain Eli, but his friendship with Will Rogers.[7] Captain Eli has little to do in *Steamboat* but hold a drink, play with his cigar, and exchange insults with Doctor John, but his incipient outrage, which is never to be taken seriously, makes a balance to Doctor John's apparent equanimity, and Cobb, as celebrity actor, provides a nice contrast to Rogers in their scenes together.

Francis Ford was one of the performers Sarris mentioned by name when he spoke of "vintage gargoyles." Ford had been a very successful actor and director in silent films, "the only influence *I* ever had, working in pictures," his brother John once said. His career came apart in the 1920s and he spent the rest of his life playing character roles, often very tiny ones, most frequently in his brother's films. During the 1930s he developed a stock character, an old, grizzled, dirty drunk, moist of eye and damp of lip, who became almost as familiar to moviegoers, who probably did not know his name, as Jack Norton's more fastidious souse. He was occasionally used seriously (one of the bums with Fredric March's Norman Maine in the night-court scene in *A Star Is Born*, 1937), but the figure was primarily comic, particularly in his brother's films. As Efe, who has signed on as mate of the decrepit *Claremore Queen* to have access to Doctor John's alcohol-laced Pocahontas Remedies, he has a scene in which he is painting the side of the wheelhouse or the cabin. This time, thanks to a far too eleborate mistake-joke, he drinks turpentine rather than the medicinal tonic, and is galvanized into frenetic action, splashing paint around wildly, swinging clumsily on a rope. At one point he jumps to touch the overhang, as though a single brushstroke had been missed; this bit got a laugh from a student audience I once saw the film with, newcomers to *Steamboat* who were not at all sure it is a comedy. Despite this testimony, the scene never seems quite successful to me. It cries out for sophisticated physical comedy, the kind that Chaplin or Keaton might have provided, but I may be wanting to impose mimetic fantasy on a joke that is only about Efe's cheerful, drunken ineptitude. Neither here nor elsewhere is there any evidence that Ford can or wants to use comic nuance. His walk, his gestures, his bleary stares are all conceived and performed broadly.

"I can't do your kind of humor at all," John Ford is supposed to have said to Howard Hawks. ". . . mine is just pure corn." He presumably intended the term to be descriptive, not disparaging, for he always insisted on the importance of his very obvious comedy in even his most serious movies. Efe's painting scene is one of the best examples of Francis Ford's providing the "pure corn" that his brother liked, almost as impressive as the routine in *Judge Priest*, in which, as the tobacco-chewing juror, he punctuates the remarks of Senator Maydew (Berton Churchill) by scoring one bull's-eye after another even though a court official keeps moving the spittoon farther and farther away. Efe is one of the fattest roles of Francis Ford's last years, although not so substantial as his Joe Bolero in *Drums along the Mohawk* (1939) or his lynching victim in William Wellman's *The Ox-Bow Incident* (1943). His Joe in *Drums* is not only one of the film's funny drunks, but he makes a heroic run for help (Francis's white hair highlighted like a halo by brother John and his cameramen) and dies, an Irish male Saint Joan, spread-eagled on a burning hayrick. Nothing so grand for Efe, although he is one of the unlikely band of heroes who save Duke from hanging, and little for the actor to do beyond his regular *shtik*. Yet it is Ford's broadness that helps set off Will Rogers, as the wedding scene indicates; both Doctor John and Efe are moved to tears, but Rogers lightly touches his eyes while Ford wipes his nose with his folded hat. They can be seen together to best advantage in the early scene in which Doctor John and Efe explore the derelict steamboat. They are like little boys playing at being sailors, but, despite the similar impulse of the characters and the deliberation with which both performers work, their rhythms are dissimilar enough to allow Ford to suggest a kind of random energy, jagged alongside Rogers's smoothness.

Eugene Pallette played more than 1,200 roles in his film career, *Time* said in his obituary, "first as a juvenile lead in the Norma Talmadge era, later as an archetypical funny fatman." His comic cowpoke in *The Virginian* (1929) is given to drink and wild (albeit clean) swearing, but the character is oddly formless. Perhaps it is the newness of talkies, perhaps a deficiency in the script. Certainly, by 1932, he was creating sharply defined portraits in small roles in films as different as *The Half-Naked Truth* and *Shanghai Express*, and by 1935, when he played Sheriff Rufe Jeffers in *Steamboat*, he was the master of whatever character/caricature directors and writers wished to house in his ample body, to voice in his celebrated croak. He always talked as though he had a giant wooden tea strainer lodged somewhere in the neighborhood of his larynx, but he could modulate that unlikely voice, as can be seen in a comparison of his wedding sermon in *Steamboat* with the lightly snarled remarks at the bar in the party at the beginning of *My Man Godfrey* (1936). He was primarily a comedian although, in the year of the *Steamboat*, he played the crude casino owner murdered by his adulterous wife (Bette Davis) in *Bordertown*. Probably his most familiar character is his testy millionaire father in movies like *Godfrey* and *The Lady Eve* (1941); yet, his Friar Tuck (*The Adventures of Robin Hood* [1938]) remains one of the glories of casting to physical type.

His Rufe is a Pollyannish lawman, relentlessly cheerful and friendly even as he leads Duke to the hangman, and the Dudley Nichols–Lamar Trotti script emphasizes the contradictions between man and job by giving him lines completely inappropriate to the context in which they are spoken. As Fleety Belle and Doctor John come back from the courthouse, they meet Rufe outside a wax museum he has just seized from its decamping proprietor; he expatiates on its wonders and invites Fleety Belle, whose beloved has just been found guilty of murder, to "Come on in and see the show, honey; it'll just cheer you right up." Pallette delivers Rufe's lines with a bouncy certainty that makes clear the sheriff's deafness to nuance and implication. The actor may expect the audience to hear contextually, but Rufe knows he always says the right thing. Both writers and performers frequently depend on the laugh that falls between the line delivered and the line received (see Chekhov; for that matter, see Will Rogers), but a device that can be used for comedic complexity is here put in the service of a figure conceived and beautifully played as caricature—another effective juxtaposition with the Will Rogers image.

Berton Churchill had played the blustering antagonist to the Will Rogers hero in *Dr. Bull*, *Judge Priest*, and *The County Chairman* (1935) before, as the New Moses, he became Doctor John's unlikely ally in *Steamboat*. The role of the riverboat evangelist, one of the best of Churchill's film career, is an uncharacteristic one for the comic. Back in 1925, after another atypical role had brought him his first Broadway stardom in *Alias the Deacon*, he described[8] what the trade called "Berton Churchill rôles": "I was always being picked as the domineering, but secretly tender-hearted, father; the gruff but delightful uncle; the elderly husband; the keen banker; the man of big business affairs." He took his "Berton Churchill rôles" with him when he moved into the films in the early 1930s, but what is missing from his catalogue, with its emphasis on relationship and profession, is that the characters were almost always endowed with great pomposity, provided with lines studded with clichés of high rectitude. He was first of all a physical presence, tall, heavy, with a strong face, a commanding head (Mary B.

Mullett called him "handsome")—the perfect image of the public man as hypocrite. When the greedy bank directors meet in *American Madness* (1932), he is the one who catches our eye, although, less bombastic than usual, he is the first of the board to announce his support of Thomas Dickson (Walter Huston). More often, that magnificent container, the Churchill character, houses a supply of righteous indignation, ready to burst out whenever his principles—real or faked—are questioned or endangered. In *Dimples* (1936), aghast that his family and friends are becoming enmeshed with the tatty world of show business, Churchill's Colonel Loring attempts to lead them from the theater when Professor Appleby (Frank Morgan) brings them to a box and forces them to sit through a performance. Trapped between his virtuous contempt for the theater and his adherence to social convention, the colonel cannot simply explode. All that he can manage is an outraged burble, but Churchill was as impressive in that travesty of restraint as he was in full voice. One of the screen's most accomplished blusterers, Churchill could use his talent nastily—his absconding banker in *Stagecoach* (1939) is such a variation on his stock performance—but it was generally a comic characterization. His magnificent voice—*stentorian* is a likely adjective if it can be made to mean not only *loud*, but *deep, resonant, mesmerizing, enveloping*—is his burble released and given its head. Invaluable to his politicians in *The County Chairman* and *Judge Priest*, it follows him off the platform; at the ice-cream social in *Priest*, in casual conversation, while eating, his Senator Maydew sounds as though he were addressing a public meeting. At the beginning of the film, in a comic forecast of the more serious trial to come, the Senator thunders, "He comes from no one knows whence," as though he were calling down destruction on the world rather than simply attempting to pin a chicken theft on Jeff (Stepin Fetchit). It is but a step from the senator to the New Moses, the evangelical rhetoric of the latter growing out of the biblical periods of the politician.

When the *New York Times* reviewed *Alias the Deacon* (called simply *The Deacon* when it first opened), the unidentified critic compared the con-man protagonist with Eustace McGargle in *Poppy* and, since the latter was still playing at the time, Churchill's performance with that of W. C. Fields: "One accordingly continually expected an unction that was not forthcoming and was periodically plunged into disappointment by Mr. Churchill's emergence as an actor rather than as a human being." It may be a little startling, if gratifying, to see Fields praised as the embodiment of dramatic realism, but the actorishness of Churchill sounds exactly right. He is always the performer doing a character rather than the man himself, and as Senator Maydew or the New Moses—actors themselves in the traditional politician-preacher mode—he reaches heights of unreality that help emphasize the special qualities of Will Rogers's Judge Priest and Doctor John.

Reason enough to open *Steamboat*—after some shots to establish the setting—with the contrasting pitches of the New Moses and Doctor John. The New Moses comes first. The usually clean-shaven Churchill wears a long beard, gray streaked with a darker color, which is somehow made more prominent by the high forehead, the whisper of baldness beginning to nibble at the part of his gray hair. Rescued from the conventional dress of his other roles, he is in a white robe, the more ludicrous for a later shot in which we see the robed figure wearing a tall silk hat and smoking a cigar. Preaching temperance, calling men to sign the pledge, using his own terrible past as an example ("raised me from a hog to a man"), the New Moses rolls out the splendid Churchillian tones, touched with the suggestion that inspiration is a kind of madness. This quality gets a little scary during the race sequence at the end of the film when, short of fuel, the *Claremore Queen* must burn the wax-museum figures; the New Moses, working like a man possessed, shouts "Into the fiery furnace," as he tosses in mock human beings. From the New Moses to Doctor John, selling his own brand of salvation, the cure-all with the high alcoholic content. His is a standard medicine-man spiel, but it is not delivered as it might be by an actor— Frank Morgan, say—closer to the stereotype. Will Rogers speaks more formally than he does in most of the picture, but if the mumbles are temporarily put aside, he continues to speak softly, conversationally. When the crowd seems to doubt his assertion that John Smith had to marry Pocahontas to get the recipe, he does a gargle-fumble that segues into assurance that the story is true. At another point, pretending to have no change, he forces a second bottle into a buyer's hand, telling him that it "should hold you" until his return trip. It is not simply the quiet confidence in these transitions that makes Doctor John a plausible panacea peddler; it is the voice of the New Moses still echoing in our ears.

Of the five counter-Rogers performers, I have saved Stepin Fetchit until last because he is a difficult comedian to talk about in what a Berton Churchill character might call "these enlightened times." The Fetchit stereotype—the shiftless nigger—is understandably anathema to contemporary blacks and, insofar as it represented white attitudes toward blacks, was reprehensible in its own time. Critics today— Andrew Sarris in *The John Ford Movie Mystery*, for example—tend to good liberal outrage and a discreet lowering of the eyes in the face of the phenomenon of ethnic comedy; to color blindness (Harry Menig: "Fetchit's outward image is one of the clown of any color"); to the happy discovery that Fetchit was a closet radical. The comedian leaned toward the third of these in his last years, in part as a response to his being sacrificed to the contempt so many people felt for the stereotype to which he had given such flamboyant life. "I was the first Negro militant," he told Joseph McBride in 1971, although never a militant in the 1960s sense of the word. "When people saw me and Will Rogers together like brothers, that said something to them." Donald Bogle reminds us, in *Toms, Coons, Mulattoes, Mammies, & Bucks*, that the white brother in *David Harum* (1934) both received and traded the black one along with the racehorse he cared for.

The difficulty in coming to terms with the Stepin Fetchit character is that both Fetchit and Bogle are right. Bogle says that Fetchit chose the "coon" stereotype because "those lazy, no-account, good-for-nothing, forever-in-hot-water, natural-born-comedians—were loved by everyone." Fetchit was, certainly. Since my attempt to deal with the comedian will reflect all three of the critical attitudes I mentioned above—all of which I deplore to some extent as attempts to remake the past—let me declare my admiration for Fetchit, the performer, in the past and in the present. Black scholars, Alain Locke and Sterling A. Brown, could see in Stepin Fetchit in *Hearts in Dixie* (1929) "instinct itself, a vital projection of the folk manner. . . . the emotional vibrancy of the race." As a boy, taking delight in Fetchit a few years after the 1930 Locke-Brown essay, I never thought of him as representative, never jumped from him to the blacks in my town, none of whom acted that way. There were almost certainly moviegoers who did make such a jump, imprinting Fetchit on the blacks around them, but for me Fetchit was unique. He still is. Watching him now, I am amazed at his skill as a performer, the effects he can get from the smallest gesture, the most incomprehensible mutter; he is light years away from a competent comedian like Willie Best, who made a career of a similar character.

No comedian can find a stereotype to inhabit unless his society creates and condones that stereotype. The stock lazy servant is a great deal older than the presence of either the blacks or the whites in America, yet the shiftless-nigger variation on it does reflect American racist attitudes, casually accepted in the 1930s when Fetchit found his greatest success, still apparent today in most of the antiwelfare platitudes. Yet the stereotype in the Stepin Fetchit movies was never as direct or as blatant as the later attacks on it suggested. Two things worked against so simple a reading (making my childhood response possible, I assume); one has to do with the character's place in the plots of his films, the other with the subversive tone implicit in its presentation. Although no example comes immediately to mind, I am sure that there were films in which Stepin Fetchit was little more than comic window dressing, like a bug-eyed Mantan Moreland doing his fright turn, but in the Will Rogers films, particularly *Judge Priest* and *Steamboat*, he is a central part of the action—a key figure in Priest's manipulation of the jury, one of the rescuers riding to save Duke. One of the good guys, then, and they are always identifiable in Rogers films by an intimacy between them and the Rogers character that transcends the comedy dictated by stereotype—the master-servant jokes in Fetchit's case.

The subversive quality may be a little harder to pinpoint than the plot function, particularly since I am attracted to Michael Dempsey's insistence that all the talk of parody is "rationalization, clever but hopeless." Yet, there were differences in the presentation of the black stereotype in the 1930s that make *parody* very like the proper word. Take a film far removed from the Fetchit comedies, the Bette Davis drama *Jezebel* (1938). It has a particularly nauseous happy-darky view of the Old South with a sterling family retainer named Uncle Cato, a sassy maid for the sassy heroine, a stolidly loyal servant played uncomically by Eddie Anderson, some pickaninny comedy, and a passel of plantation folk that gambol onto the lawn to sing "Let's Raise a Ruckus Tonight," for all the world like refugees from the Harpo Marx parade in *A Day at the Races* (1937). But, there is a scene in which Mrs. Kendrick (Spring Byington) arrives at a party in an open carriage, rapping out commands at her driver—a mummy of a man, wrapped in a coat, buried under a hat—to which he answers "Yowzah," always with the same inflection; a rhythm is created which carries Mrs. Kendrick and her guests to the door when the sound of the knocker brings one more "Yowzah." It is Byington not the character who does a fine double take, turning the whole sequence into a comic comment on the stereotype it is presumably presenting. In a review of *Charlie Chan in Egypt* (1935), Andre Sennwald calls Fetchit "the master of slow motion, who manages as usual to be both hilarious and unintelligible." As the line suggests, Fetchit took the physical and vocal mannerisms of the lazy stereotype and so exaggerated them that movement almost became stasis, communication gibberish. He could move quickly, as his dance in *Hearts in Dixie* shows, and he could speak clearly when the gag called for clarity. In *Steamboat*, when the New Moses is brought aboard the *Claremore Queen* after having been dragged in the river, a single sentence emerges from Jonah's[9] wordless mumble of solicitude, the offer of a "glass of water." His character customarily denied these possibilities. When Dempsey, deploring the way Fetchit was forced to demean himself, says "his extreme submissiveness makes him practically a vegetable," he misses the point. It may be rationalization, but I am convinced that this is the heart of the good Fetchit joke about a very bad American joke. Whether or not I am right, it should be obvious from my emphasis on his particular brand of overstatement that Stepin Fetchit, like the other four performers, helped create the unnatural frame to the natural Rogers protrait—which brings me, I suppose, back to Menig's "clown of any color."

In my presentation of Rogers and his gallery of associates, *Steamboat Round the Bend* has emerged in fragments; let me put the pieces together. Ben Lucien Burman, on whose novel the film was based, recalled in 1973 that Rogers had written him a fan letter when the novel was first published (in 1933, after serialization in *Pictorial Review*) and that John Ford had taken an option on the book. There are period references (a Burman interview with Eileen Creelman, some remarks in *Liberty's* "Vital Statistics" addendum to its review) that suggest that both Rogers and Ford had a prefilming interest in the property, but there is no indication of such in either the Rogers or the Ford biographies. Filmmaking was just one of the many Rogers activities, and he was generally content to get a film shot and out of the way so that he could continue the travels which, more and more, were providing the material for his columns. Although he could refuse a film he did not want to make, his movies usually developed from within the studio. There is no reason to assume that *Steamboat*, his last film, was any different, except that—according to Burman—he particularly liked the result and wanted it released before *In Old Kentucky*, which had been finished earlier. As for Ford, his Fox assignments at this time were seldom labors of love. Dan Ford, in his biography of his grandfather, says that Sol Wurtzel came to John Ford in 1933 and said that he wanted him to be "Will Rogers' director." Since Rogers made films with James Cruze, David Butler, John Blystone, and George Marshall while he was working with Ford on the three films they did together, a special Ford-Rogers connection is hardly acceptable. I assume that Ford was assigned *Steamboat*, as he was later assigned *Wee Willie Winkie*, and that he did the professional job the studio expected of him, the one that had earned him the right to work off the lot when he wanted to.

Although Dudley Nichols had frequently worked with Ford since *Men without Women* (1930) and they were beginning—with *The Lost Patrol* (1934) and *The Informer* (1935)—to gain a reputation as a formidable director-writer team (like Frank Capra and Robert Riskin), *Steamboat* is clearly not one of those projects that either man would remember later when they described their shared writing sessions. For Nichols and for Lamar Trotti, *Steamboat* was presumably just another writing assignment. While the film was being made, Twentieth Century merged with Fox and Darryl F. Zanuck, wielding his new power

as head of the studio, recut what "should have been a great picture,"
Ford told Bogdanovich, "and took all the comedy out." Zanuck, as Mel
Gussow's biography indicates, had a reputation as an editor with an
emphasis on speed, movement, getting on with the story. If his cutting
set the tempo for the end of *Steamboat*, then his was an important
contribution, but Ford (and Nichols) have elsewhere used a leisurely
introduction to character followed by plot-induced acceleration without the help and blessing of Zanuck (*Stagecoach* and *The Hurricane*
[1937]). *Steamboat* is then a Rogers-Ford-Nichols-Trotti-Wurtzel-
Zanuck picture, a real studio product—one of the miracles of the 1930s.
"A bad picture is an accident," Rogers wrote in 1934, "and a good one
is a miracle."

Steamboat follows one of the two standard patterns used in most of
the Rogers talkies.[10] In many of his last films he plays an unattached
male—bachelor or widower—surrogate father to one or both of the
young lovers for whom he is matchmaker; he usually rescues a man
from injustice (the young man in *Life Begins at Forty*, the girl's father in
Judge Priest) and, in the course of the film, achieves something for
himself (winning the horse race in *David Harum*, retaining his
judgeship in *Priest*, his newspaper in *Life*). His movies were customarily based on popular novels or plays, and Burman's *Steamboat Round
the Bend* was—with a few alterations—suitable to this Rogers image.
The Burman theme—the unattainability of the heart's desire—and the
odd note of overreaching in Doctor John were dumped, along with
Miss Robbie, Doctor John's lady friend, whose presence would have
demanded a strong performer to share center screen with Rogers.
Peppmint, the book's loyal black, an old man who dies a sentimental
death, had to be lightened into Jonah for Stepin Fetchit. The filmmakers moved the time from the present to the 1890s, altered a great many
details, added a climactic boat race and ended with a product that
moved Burman to say, "My novel that depended on subtle humor and
satire and character and mood was turned into a farce melodrama."
Not that Burman quite caught the tone of the film, but there is some
justice in his remark. The movie's Doctor John is a bachelor, surrogate
father to his nephew, Duke, and he brings the young lovers together
by saving Duke from hanging; in the course of the rescue, he wins the
boatrace and Captain Eli's *Pride of Paducah*, thus fulfilling his desire for
a steamboat, the aged *Claremore Queen* having been pretty much de-
stroyed while winning.

There have been attempts to deal with *Steamboat* thematically, by
Martin Rubin, who sees it as a John Ford film, and by Peter C. Rollins,
who sees it as a Will Rogers film. Neither reading is quite convincing to
me because both involve the imposition on the picture of conceptions

about Ford's ideas, Rogers's image. If I were going to work thematically, I would begin with the salvational opening—the twin cure-alls of the New Moses and Doctor John—and work through the latter's protecting Fleety Belle from her daddy (Charles B. Middleton) to the last-minute reprieve on the gallows. I would attach this theme to Doctor John's discovery that justice is achieved not through the proper acceptance of the legal system—which finds Duke guilty and whose visual representative is Sheriff Rufe—but through manipulation, skill, commitment, and a good heart, as both the aborted attack on the wax museum and the victory in the race indicate. Salvation through work and—since happy accident plays its part—a little grace. Or to put it in terms of the theatrical genre from which it stems, the good guys win when they are not so good that they fail to make or take advantage of opportunities on the way to victory.

For me, the real quality—the real meaning, perhaps—of *Steamboat* lies in the way it plays with the genre. This can be seen most clearly in the love story and in the glorious ending. In most Rogers films the young lovers and the performers who play them—Anita Louise and Tom Brown in *Judge Priest*, Rochelle Hudson and Richard Cromwell in *Life Begins at Forty*—are stock juveniles. Duke and Fleety Belle are a comic variation. Fleety Belle comes closer to a conventional sentimental relationship in her developing attachment to Doctor John. From his initial distrust of the girl, through a first recognition that she has spunk, to a need to save her from her father, Doctor John grows ever closer to her as they work together to save Duke. Their father-daughter romance culminates in the scene in the pilothouse in which they exchange kisses, momentarily losing control of the wheel; a little silly, a little sticky, the scene is possible only because of the charm of Rogers and Anne Shirley. It has a kind of warmth that is never allowed into the scenes between Shirley and John McGuire.

Commenting on John Ford's uneasiness in dealing with "sensuality, love, passion, sex," Michael Dempsey complains that "Over and over again, he gives us blushing swains and simpering maidens straight out of mid-Victorian valentines." This may be a drawback when the lovers are Maureen O'Hara and John Wayne (*The Quiet Man* [1952]) or O'Hara and Tyrone Power (*The Long Gray Line* [1955]), but the valentine is just right for *Steamboat*—and a comic one at that. Handsome John McGuire plays Duke as a big, dumb boy—a backward Li'l Abner—and Anne Shirley, whenever she gets in his company, becomes a starry-eyed innocent, as though she had overdosed on sweetness while making *Anne of Green Gables* (1934), the film that gave her her new name and began her adult acting career. Their love scene at Duke's jail window is a case in point. Fleety Belle has come to say good-bye—she and Doctor John are taking the wax museum along the river to raise money for an appeal—and Duke, exuding contentment in his present situation, explains to Fleety Belle that he is learning to play the saw. Then, with no irony on his part, he gives a concert—"Home! Sweet Home!"—accompanied by the black prisoners, singing from their segregated cells. After it's over, he says, "You ain't never kissed me yet." Since Duke has carried her away from her swamp home, killed a man to protect her, traveled with her to Doctor John's boat, this is a bit thick even for a combination of Will Rogers and John Ford working in the heyday of the Hollywood censor. Their kiss, through the bars, is a comment on the preposterousness of the whole thing.

Their wedding is even more outrageous. Since Duke's appeal has failed, Fleety Belle will, of course, marry him before he goes to the gallows. The wedding takes place in the jail. The sheriff's daughter, who has inherited his size, is to play the wedding march, and the black prisoners are brought out of segregation to provide a back-up choir. A fat freckled creature—"an uncredited plumpling," as *Liberty* said—Addie May laboriously pounds out the only piece she knows, and the bride makes her entrance to "Listen to the Mocking Bird." (This detail comes from Burman's book, but the tone of the two scenes is quite different.) Rufe, who has laid aside his gun for the family Bible, praises the groom ("There ain't never been a finer man in this here jail") and works his way, with the help of the traditional service, to the fine, final comedy of "till death do us part." Efe cries. Doctor John dabs at his eyes. The choir comes up again behind the nuptial kiss. The scene is funnily gentle in its details, sardonic in total effect.

It is possible—necessary perhaps—both to accept and to laugh at the romance of Duke and Fleety Belle. Such a double response is even more important at the end of the film. As the *Claremore Queen* races toward Baton Rouge, pushed by the need both to win the race and to reach the governor in time to stop the hanging, the movie builds momentum, feeding the expectation and the tension of the audience for all the world as though this were melodrama pure and simple. The steamboat is the cavalry galloping to the besieged wagon train, Tarzan swinging in at the last minute. Yet, the whole thing is frenetically funny as well as exciting. Having at last found the New Moses, the only witness to the killing, Doctor John lassos him (a Rogers joke) and pulls him aboard. Efe, the New Moses, even Jonah, work like men possessed to feed the "fiery furnace" with wood torn from the boat itself, with the wax figures, finally with Efe's hidden supply of Doctor John's cure-all which shoots fire out the smoke stack and carries the boat to victory. Andrew Sinclair suggests that the John Ford silent, *Cameo Kirby* (1923), is an influence on the race in *Steamboat*, but the race is so sketchily presented in the earlier film that that seems unlikely. There are a number of shots of boats on the river, but they are not differentiated from one another; we cannot tell the *Maud* from the *Memphis*, although the plot hangs on which of them wins. The immediate source for the *Steamboat* race—as John Reddington said at the time—is *Tillie and Gus* (1933), in which Gus (W. C. Fields) begins to chop up the boat itself for fuel, but in which the race is won by burning fireworks rather than firewater.

There is no letdown when the race ends. Doctor John and the New Moses sprint to the stand where the governor is waiting to present the silver cup. There is a marvelous bit of pantomime, right out of slapstick comedy. Doctor John is handed the cup, puts it down, gets it back again. This time he hands it to the New Moses, who passes it on to an official who hands it to a third and, this time, when it comes back to Doctor John, he throws it across the crowd to Jonah, who catches it. While this byplay is going on, a band is playing ("There's a Hot Time in the Old Town Tonight") so loudly that no one can be heard. Both Doctor John and Fleety Belle try to signal the band to become silent only to appear to be directing it, and the band continues with renewed vigor. Finally, the governor understands. Just as the rope is going around Duke's neck, a trumpet sounds and a wagon comes tearing into the prison yard, Doctor John at the reins.

For the quiet finish, the *Pride of Paducah* is on the river again, Duke and Fleety Belle together at the wheel. Doctor John sits in the stern, presumably listening "to that old river sing," as he told Captain Eli he wanted to do when he got his own boat. We do not hear the river, however. The transition is too abrupt to still the scream of "Hot Time," to erase the inspired insanity of the rescue. It needs no one to tell us directly—as Mr. Peachum does in *The Threepenny Opera*—that in real life mounted messengers do not come riding in with a pardon. The film does that by teasing the genre it uses so efficiently. In that final shot of Will Rogers—which was indeed the final shot of Will Rogers—the observer merges with the actor, the cynic with the sentimentalist. That is not the river you hear, Doctor John; that is Addie May playing "Listen to the Mocking Bird."

Notes

1. For almost fifty years I have remembered the line as "There's a vacant chair in every home tonight for Will Rogers," which means, I suppose, that at ten I had a better sense of the proper dramatic build of a line than Mitchell Parish did, but then he needed a tonight-bright-

light rhyme to get through the chorus. I remember the song at all—it is mentioned in none of the Rogers biographies—because I was in my song-sheet period at the time. I used to borrow my older sister's song sheet—a once popular publication that printed lyrics to all the new songs—and sing my way right through, fitting all the words to my one tune. My mother was never an admirer of my vocal prowess, but it was only later that I understood why she might be particularly exasperated when for the hundredth time I repeated in my monotone whine, "Our lovable Will has gone over the hill." The unforgettable forgettable Leaman-Parish song was published by Mills Music, Inc., a company that seemed to have a knack for memorializing celebrity deaths. They had published "There's a New Star in Heaven Tonight" for Rudolph Valentino and "They Needed a Song Bird in Heaven (So God Took Caruso Away)." In 1937, after the death of Jean Harlow, they would issue "There's a Platinum Star in Heaven Tonight." The *New York World-Telegram* carried a note on the Harlow song on June 16 (p. 40), just nine days after the actress's death. The speed with which the company responded to the unhappy news, rounded up Nat Simon and Dick Sanford to grind out the Harlow song, got it printed and on the stands suggests that the Mills crowd were the fastest graveside singers in the business. Next only to Emmeline Grangerford in *Huckleberry Finn*, and none of the Mills offerings have the real class of "Ode to Stephen Dowling Bots, Dec'd."

2. Brown's volume is a determined and often fascinating effort to place Rogers on an ideational line that carries the "American Dream" from the colonists through nineteenth-century writers like Emerson, Thoreau, and Whitman. It is particularly interesting in relation to *Steamboat Round the Bend*, for many of the admirers of John Ford see the film's director in a similar context, as Michael Barkum does explicitly in "Notes on the Art of John Ford," his 1962 article for *Film Culture* (no. 25 [Summer 1962], pp. 9–13).

3. Taylor is English, I know, but the play provides one of the best examples of the American type I have in mind. Besides, rescued from oblivion by Laura Keene, who gave it a first performance in New York in 1858, the play is American by adoption. After all, Lincoln was watching it when he was shot.

4. The cinematographer Winton C. Hoch, who worked with Ford on *Three Godfathers* (1948) and *She Wore a Yellow Ribbon* (1949), once said, "Jack Ford, the old buzzard, would never sacrifice a good story for want of a few facts." (Joseph McBride, "Winton Hoch: 'A Damn Good Job,'" *Film Comment*, 15 [November–December 1979], 74)

5. "Lamar Trotti, God rest his soul, he could write closer than anybody for Will," Ford told Sterling (Bryan B. Sterling, *The Will Rogers*

Scrapbook, New York, Grosset & Dunlap, 1976, p. 175). Yet, according to Rochelle Hudson (Reginald Taviner, "On the Set with Will Rogers, As Told by Rochelle Hudson," *Photoplay*, 48 [August 1935], 108), Rogers so "Rogersized" Trotti's "grand script" for *Life Begins at Forty* that every time Trotti came on the set, Rogers would put his hands over his eyes and "yell in a stage whisper to the whole company: 'Jiggers, here comes the *author*. Now, nobody knows nothin', see?'" Trotti not only wrote *Life*, but with Dudley Nichols *Steamboat* and *Judge Priest* as well.

6. The scripts, copyright submissions, are in the Motion Picture Division of the Library of Congress, which also has negative copies of the four films. As I write this, there are no prints available to researchers.

7. The presence of these two old friends was the occasion for one of the inside jokes that Hollywood so liked. In *Mr. Deeds Goes to Town*, for example, the law firm in the original story becomes Cedar, Cedar, Cedar and Budington, presumably in mock honor to the author of that story, Clarence Budington Kelland. Since Kelland was a popular magazine writer, the *Deeds* gag was not as arcane as it seems now. Readers of Rogers and Cobb would have known that the boats of Doctor John (*Claremore Queen*) and Captain Eli (*Pride of Paducah*) were named after the performers' hometowns. Since the plot of *Steamboat* makes it necessary for the *Claremore Queen* to beat the *Pride of Paducah* in the race, Rogers and Cobb would, in ordinary circumstances, have made something of the event in print. The film was released after Rogers's death, and the joke went largely unheralded. The reviewer in the *Kansas City Star* (September 1, 1935, sec. B, p. 8) did comment on the naming of the boats; since the review told again the Rogers-Cobb-Ford story about improvisation on the set of *Steamboat*, using Cobb's obituary piece on Rogers without identifying the source, the remark on the names of the boats may reflect a publicity handout rather than the reviewer's taste for allusion.

8. To Mary B. Mullett. The article ("The World Was His Oyster But It Took 35 Years to Open It!" *American*, 102 [November 1926], 37, 171–76) has a particular charm for Churchill admirers because the actor is given to platitudes about achievement, ambition, and other such predictable virtues that sound as though they belong in the mouth of one of his characters.

9. When Doctor John first meets Jonah, the latter says that his name is David Begat Solomon, "But I changed it to George Lincoln Washington." Peter Bogdanovich uses that name in his John Ford filmography (*John Ford*, Berkeley, University of California Press, 1968, p. 127). Doctor John, who discovers the Fetchit character in the artificial whale

in the wax museum, decides to call him Jonah. The pressbook for *Steamboat* uses that name—and so will I.

10. In the other pattern he plays a husband, usually with a wife obsessed with social and cultural ambitions. *They Had to See Paris*, his first talkie, is the best example. He was still doing this plot as late as *Handy Andy* (1934) and *Doubting Thomas* (1935), which tried to fit George Kelly's *The Torch-Bearers* (1922) to the needs of Will Rogers.

6

Ruggles of Red Gap

· 1935 ·

> *Louka*: You have the soul of
> a servant, Nicola.
> *Nicola*: Yes: thats the secret
> of success in service.
> —*Arms and the Man*

"The clever absurdities in the film," Mordaunt Hall wrote of *A Lady's Profession* (1933), ". . . may cause many to hark back to Harry Leon Wilson's immensely successful novel 'Ruggles of Red Gap.'" The Norman McLeod comedy about two impoverished English aristocrats (Alison Skipworth, Roland Young) who open a speakeasy in Manhattan bears no close resemblance to Wilson's story of Ruggles, the impeccable gentleman's gentleman who, lost in a game of "drawing poker," is forced to accompany his new employers[1] to Red Gap, Washington. There is one scene in *Profession* which displays the juxtaposition of very different languages to which Wilson was so attracted. When Tony (Roscoe Karns) explains to Lady Beulah (Skipworth) that the crowd is a fake one, paid "a buck a head" and not asked to "kick in for chow and alky," she is at first totally confused but picks up the lingo in time to use it on the prospective buyer for whom the deception has been staged.

The comedy of displacement, in which the idiom and the manners of one country confront those of another, is hardly a monopoly of Harry Leon Wilson (Leo McCarey once described *Peg o' My Heart* as *Ruggles* "in reverse"), but *Ruggles of Red Gap*, in its original form and its many adaptations, had been percolating through American popular culture for almost twenty years. Harry Leon Wilson was a very talented professional, one of those writers—like Booth Tarkington,

---

Planning the Anglo-American Grill. ZaSu Pitts, Charles Laughton, Charles Ruggles, Maude Eburne. (*Ruggles of Red Gap*, Paramount, 1935. The Museum of Modern Art/Film Stills Archive.)

like Irvin S. Cobb—who worried about his audience as well as his art, whose ordinary work was a cut above that of the more pedestrian hacks and whose best work gave still vital figures—Penrod, Judge Priest, Ruggles—to American culture. Such authors were the luminaries of American magazine writing in its great days—up through the 1930s, say—when the average American was still a reader and editors could depend on a general audience. These writers, these magazines were the original source of much of the Hollywood product of the 1930s—certainly of most of the films I am discussing in this book. When Regina Crewe, reviewing the movie, called Ruggles "the old Satevepost classic," there may have been a touch of wryness in the phrase, but it was essentially affectionate; more than that, it was a kind of shorthand, suggesting the nature of the story and its audience (which would have included many of Crewe's *New York American* readers), and a simple statement of fact. *Ruggles of Red Gap* began as a serial in the *Saturday Evening Post* on December 26, 1914. It was so successful when it was published as a novel in 1915 that Wilson turned out a number of stories using the same characters—published as *Somewhere in Red Gap* (1916)—and a later wartime batch, gathered as *Ma Pettengill* (1919).[2] Before the end of 1915, *Ruggles* had found its way to Broadway, in a version by Harrison Rhodes that Heywood Broun called "just about as amusing as a bad play can be," and it first emerged as a film from Essanay in 1918. The more celebrated silent version came from Paramount in 1923, directed by James Cruze—the same year he did *The Covered Wagon*—with Edward Everett Horton as Ruggles.[3]

So Mordaunt Hall harked back and someone at Paramount, perhaps nudged by Hall, harked back, and *Ruggles of Red Gap* was scheduled for a remake. There are so many elements in the novel that feed—and feed on—American attitudes toward the country, the individual, ways of behaving that it is a natural for the movies. In his theater column in *Commonweal*, Grenville Vernon backed into a highly laudatory review of the movie by first suggesting that the success of stories like Wilson's rested on "the serious belief of so many millions of Americans, that we are the salt of the earth and that bad manners and scorn of tradition are a sign of our virility." It is an accurate reading, I think, although I would play it in a less abrasive key. The novel gives us first the crude Americans in Paris and then the fastidious Englishman in Red Gap. Mark Twain had long since taught us that, although the innocent abroad is a comic figure, his presence is also a test of the culture he confronts; similarly the outsider can make no contribution to his new American environment until he correctly interprets the manner that at first confuses or offends him. In *Ruggles of Red Gap*, the deck is stacked in favor of the Americans in both Paris and Red Gap—necessarily so, given the provenance of both author and audience—but Wilson's target is no more the funny foreigner than it is the uncouth American. Even the jokes about art, classical music, the new drama, which have a familiar anti-intellectual air about them, are aimed at cultural pretenders rather than the arts themselves. The main satirical point of the book is that the real people, English and American, are immune to the demands of fashion and propriety, and the ones who worry about social position and reputation are quite willing to accept a servant's view of what is correct. The correlative of the book's antisnobbism is a more basic rejection of the kind of pretension that substitutes manner for substance, that denies the ideals on which this country was presumably founded. Ruggles, reading the Declaration of Independence for the first time, found it "snarky in the extreme and with no end of silly rot about equality," but it is the dramatic business of the book to convert him, to turn the gentleman's gentleman into a man in his own right.

The unstuffing of stuffed shirts and the turning of worms have always been central to popular comedy, but the combination of these two elements as they exist in *Ruggles of Red Gap* makes the 1915 novel particularly right for filming in the mid-1930s. It is the decade not only of Groucho Marx as Rufus T. Firefly, but of Lewis Stone as Judge Hardy; the same audience embraced both skepticism and platitude, embodied both American irreverence and American reverence. The two strains existed together in American films all through the decade, but if an accurate irreverence count could be taken, the comedies of the early 1930s would more clearly reflect a suspicion of men and institutions, those later in the decade temper that suspicion with a personal or a societal affirmation. *Nothing Sacred* is an atypical 1937 film, because, by then, even the wackiest screwball comedy carried an implicit assumption that some things are sacred. A year after Ruggles successfully opened the Anglo-American Grill in Red Gap, Mr. Deeds went to town.

It was time for *Ruggles of Red Gap* again. It was time too for Leo McCarey to move from *Duck Soup* to *Ruggles*, from the purposeful artificiality of the Marx Brothers comedy to the emphasis on character that marks McCarey films as different as his two 1937 movies, the sentimentally didactic *Make Way for Tomorrow* and *The Awful Truth*, which he once called "one of those My-God, my-husband jobs." In the chapter on *Duck Soup*, (pp. 69–74) I discuss McCarey's skill and inventiveness as gag director, the presumed contribution of the old Hal Roach hand to the Marx Brothers film. That skill remained a basic part of his directorial equipment all through his career; as Irene Dunne said, recalling work on *The Awful Truth*, "he was a great man for routines." Charles Laughton called him "the greatest comic mind now living" and pointed to a Laurel and Hardy comedy in which he kept the camera on the back of Hardy's neck "for fully 75 feet of film" while Hardy lay face down in a cake.[4] The most obvious Laurel and Hardy routine in *Ruggles of Red Gap*, one that McCarey invented on the set according to Laughton, is the sequence in which Ruggles (Laughton) and Egbert (Charles Ruggles), both a bit drunk, do an Alphonse-Gaston about who shall get into the carriage first. Egbert, who has an uncertain grasp of the master-servant relationship, insists that Ruggles get in first, which he does. Then, as Egbert steps up, Ruggles comes around the back of the carriage, having gone out the other door, and proper servant that he is, prepares to follow his master. Before he can climb in, however, Egbert appears from the back of the carriage, and the two of them bicker about precedence until Jeff Tuttle (James Burke), who has stepped through their argument and taken his seat, insists that Egbert give in so t at they can get underway. At this point, as Egbert starts to step up, Ruggles restrains him with his hand and steps in ahead of him. The thematic relevance of the gag and its dramatic content—drink beginning the job on Ruggles that Red Gap will finish—cannot disguise the fact that it is a set piece of comic business. Lifted out of context and played as a very short short, it would still be funny.

If the physical comedy of the Laurel and Hardy films carried over into McCarey's later work, his more familiar character comedy also had its roots in his Hal Roach days, in his work with Charley Chase and Laurel and Hardy. In *We Faw Down* (1928), for instance, he uses many close-ups and medium shots which focus on one or both of the comedians, using their facial expressions or their gestures to find the laughter in character rather than clowning. A single instance of many: when the two men come back from their escapade with the other women, not knowing that their wives have found them out, the camera concentrates on the slow change that passes across Ollie's face as he works up to mock anger at the accusations from his wife. Marvelously calculated, his altering expression conveys the combination of self-satisfaction and inept wiliness that are so much a part of the Hardy persona. McCarey's understanding of Laurel and Hardy prepared him for *Ruggles*. Wilson's characters are stereotypes—caricatures, even—as that kind of comic writing demands, and the marvel of the movie is that McCarey, holding to those stereotypes and retaining much of the broad comedy, turns them into characters that use and go beyond their stock-figure origins. Jean Renoir is supposed once to have said that McCarey was one of the few Hollywood directors who understood human beings.

One of the fascinations of *Ruggles of Red Gap* is that it is an almost perfect example of an adaptation of a novel into film which retains the central impulse of the original work while discarding or restructuring unusable characters, incidents, settings. One of the mysteries of the screenplay is that it is so neat a finished work despite the laying on of so many writing hands. Walter De Leon and Harlan Thompson are credited with a screenplay based on an adaptation by Humphrey Pearson, who seems an unlikely author to have been allowed near *Ruggles of Red Gap*. In *Red Salute* (1935), for which Pearson did the original story and helped write the screenplay, he turned the old chestnut about the quarreling, runaway couple who unwillingly fall in love into a didactic drama in which the student radical is necessarily the paid agent of a foreign power. Otis Ferguson was understandably acid in his review: "And the dialogue throughout suggests nothing so much as the triumph and angry clucking of five bridge-tables of D.A.R. delegates, reading antiphonally or in unison the week's crop of scare-heads from their respective local branches of the Hearst press." Given that ideational impulse, Pearson might have turned the amiable Americanism of *Ruggles* into flamboyant jingoism, but other attitudes prevailed.

De Leon and Thompson had both come to Hollywood from Broadway, where they had worked on undistinguished musicals, and were recognizable screenwriting hacks. First honors presumably to De Leon, not simply because he got first writing credit and the *New York Times* said he "had most to do with the screen play," but because he had worked on the films of such comedians as Joe Cook, Wheeler and Woolsey, and W. C. Fields (including *Six of a Kind* [1934], which McCarey directed and in which Charles Ruggles and Mary Boland got top billing) and had helped write the script to *Make Me a Star* (1932), then the most recent screen version of another perennial Harry Leon Wilson favorite, *Merton of the Movies* (1922). An undated biographical handout from the Lasky publicity department identifies Jack Cunningham, another Fields writer, as having done the/an adaptation of *Ruggles*, and the obituary of Cunningham in *Variety*, which may have been written from the publicity sheet, lists *Ruggles* as one of Cunningham's best-known works. According to Elsa Lanchester in *Charles Laughton and I*, their friend Arthur Macrae, the English playwright, "helped with the dialogue and wrote some of the funniest lines." There may have been a dozen other unidentified contributors, but I assume that the writer who brought it altogether was the director. After his Hal Roach days, McCarey had no screenwriting credits until the late 1930s, when he is listed as original author of his *Love Affair* (1939) and of *The Cowboy and the Lady* (1938), which H. C. Potter directed for Samuel Goldwyn after both William Wyler and McCarey refused to touch it

("What? Direct that crap!" McCarey is supposed to have said of his own story). The absence of 1930s credits is misleading, however, for McCarey is one of those directors who is famous for his improvisatory techniques, inventing on the set, writing while the film was in process. "Leo McCarey wrote an awful lot of it," Irene Dunne said of *The Awful Truth*. "While we sat on the set and waited." One does not have to be a confirmed auteurist to assume that *Ruggles* is primarily a McCarey film.

Years later, McCarey recalled having phoned Harry Leon Wilson at the height of the film's popularity, only to be asked, "What did you call me for—to apologize?" The recollection appears in an article on adaptation, a suitable anecdote to underscore the difficulty of that kind of writing, but I suspect that the Wilson line, if it is a fact and not an invention, was a joke. He had undergone adaptation too often and with no visible signs of suffering to be protective about his work. When George C. Tyler, who had produced the George S. Kaufman–Marc Connelly play version of *Merton of the Movies* (1922), sent Wilson a script, asking for an autograph, Wilson returned it with an inscription that said, in part, "True, I wrote the book, but you people did the play, I merely bought a cheap lot and sold out at an enormous profit after the town grew—me sitting around playing checkers while it was growing." It is difficult to imagine Wilson voicing the kind of regret expressed by Ben Lucien Burman over what happened to his *Steamboat Round the Bend* or Clarence Budington Kelland for the disappearance of his "Opera Hat" into *Mr. Deeds Goes to Town*. If Wilson experienced a twinge here for a lost line, a twinge there for a lost character, he—a playwright as well as a novelist—understood the demands of the process.

The first thing that had to go was the novel's narrative voice since the film spared us the voice-over that movie adaptations sometimes use to let us know that the protagonist is telling his own story. That meant the loss of one of the book's chief jokes, Ruggle's misunderstanding of American slang. When Egbert says, "There's more than one way to skin a cat," Ruggles, as narrator, can stop to wonder "why his mind should have flown to this brutal sport, if it be a sport." I confess to liking this example, although the device palls as the book goes on, and of course the film could not find a dramatic equivalent without reducing conversations to comic turns, the international-slang equivalent of the Abbott and Costello "Who's on First?" routine. In so far as the film depends on the confrontation of modes of speech, rather than ways of thinking, it transforms the narrator's remarks on unfamiliar phrases into nonverbal reactions, as when the presumably unflappable Ruggles has to absorb Egbert's description of Effie: "When she gets riled up—she'll fight a rattlesnake and give it the first two bites."

Or in lines that are definitional without overt explanation: Effie's compliment to Ruggles on his French when he pronounces *indubitably* so that every syllable can be heard, or the exasperation of Ma Pettingill (Maude Eburne) in the face of Ruggles's correctness—"Don't keep calling me madam." A second and more important result of robbing Ruggles of his narrator's function is that he becomes a great deal less obtuse than he is in the book. Although the novel assumes that he is clever enough to find his own success in Red Gap, it needs to keep him maddeningly unaware of the obvious events in the last half of the book if the work is to sustain the comic tone that is its presumed first virtue. Oddly enough, the conversion of Ruggles becomes much more touching in the film—and without losing the comedy—when the audience moves off, with the camera, simply to watch.

In the novel, Effie is married to Senator Floud, a character who is seldom around, and it is Cousin Egbert to whom she attempts to apply the high gloss of culture and fashion. Since her relationship to Egbert dramatically is that of a henpecking wife, the adapters sensibly jettisoned the Senator and married Egbert to Effie. In a similar attempt to tidy the family connections, they turned Ma Pettingill into Effie's mother which, since the other relationships of the book were sustained, makes the fastidious Belknap-Jackson Effie's brother-in-law. As with the Flouds, so with the English artistocrats; the Honourable George and the Earl of Brinstead are conflated into a single figure, the Earl of Burnstead (Roland Young), who not only loses Ruggles in the poker game as the Honourable George does, but wins Nell Kenner (Leila Hyams), as the Hon. George's older brother wins "Klondike Kate" Kenner. In thinning the cast of characters without losing any of the necessary types to make the book's comic point, the film is simply following a McCarey dictum which would not be stated until 1962: "An adapter is faced with time limits not only in the matter of compressing his material but also in holding the interest of the spectator." Such compression must also account for the film's discarding the scenes at the Adirondack camp and moving directly from Paris to Red Gap. There is, however, a more important structural change, a decided improvement on the novel. It has always seemed to me a little odd that the Americanization of Ruggles has to be done in two stages in the original; after he has opened his restaurant and become a successful American entrepreneur, Ruggles suddenly sides with Belknap-Jackson in his attempt to keep Kate Kenner from catching either the Hon. George or his brother. Ruggles is forced to learn a second time the lesson about equality and the importance of the individual. In the film, in which Ruggles never allies himself with Belknap-Jackson (Lucien Littlefield), the plots become parallel so that the opening of the restaurant, the engagement of his lordship to Nell and the defeat of snobbery all come together at the same time in a triumphant ending, in which the group—cleansed of Belknap-Jackson and his innocuous wife (Leota Lorraine)—sings "For He's a Jolly Good Fellow." If the adapters of *Ruggles* made something of a hash of Wilson's novel, they retained its main ingredients and served it up in a tasty dish quite proper to its new medium.

In 1937, McCarey told an interviewer that he had chosen Charles Laughton for the part of Ruggles because he had detected a "suggestion of humor" in *The Private Life of Henry VIII* (1932), "not exactly a comic piece." McCarey may have had a hand in the picking of Laughton for the last of his Paramount pictures, but his comment on *Henry VIII*, if we take it seriously, somewhat undercuts his image as "the greatest comic mind." I suspect, however, that it simply reflects the Hollywood compulsion, particularly noticeable among directors, producers, and studio heads, to have been in at the birth—of anything, of everything. Not only is *Henry VIII* obviously a comedy (consider the "chop and change" gag that follows the beheading of Merle Oberon's Anne Boleyn), but there is grotesque humor in many of the early roles with which Paramount ill-used the actor while making a star of him—Nero in *Sign of the Cross* (1932), Dr. Moreau in *The Island of Lost Souls* (1932), Horace H. Prin in *White Woman* (1933). Elsa Lanchester found him "very funny" in the latter in which "He gave one of those lewd performances with a sort of dirty red look in his eye." There is a ludicrous moment in *The Island of Lost Souls* in which he leans back on the lab table, up on one arm, legs crossed, a coy look on his face, like a parody odalisque. Dr. Moreau's bid for admiration within the context of the scene, it looks like nothing so much as a variation on the familiar Chaplin flirtation/placation gesture. It is either a consciously funny bit or else a remarkable piece of flamboyantly bad acting, and the admirable Laughton was always capable of both these effects, sometimes at the same instant, often in inappropriate places. Not exactly a comedian newly minted on the set of *Ruggles*, then, Laughton made the transplanted valet his most perfectly conceived comic character, and I would be tempted to drop the qualifying "comic" from that assertion.

When Laughton first appeared on Broadway in 1931, John Mason Brown, reviewing him in *Payment Deferred*, said, "He can be cross with a peppery violence, carnal with a grossness that is repellant, merry with the expansiveness of Falstaff, cruel with a hideousness that is sickening, and afraid with a whimpering terror that is almost unendurable." The sentence is intended as high compliment, the assumption being that these diverse elements add up to a single character, but this kind of catalogue, attached to any of his early movie roles, would be negative (and just) criticism. His Dr. Moreau, for instance, is a collection of histrionic fragments never formed into a complete character. It might be possible to take the blustering cheerfulness of his Sir William Porterhouse in *The Old Dark House* (1932) as the mask to the hurt, angry widower who exposes himself in a long confessional speech; but the physical bits—the tongue-lolling yawn, the hair ruffling, the dragging shuffle when he awakens, or the bit of swagger when he skitters out to close a window—are actor's exercises, cute but unattached to character. Even his Henry VIII seems less a whole than a collection of pieces—Henry as proud father, Henry as lubricious husband, Henry as comic butt (with Anne of Cleves), Henry as dainty feeder. I could— as an intellectual exercise—gather these scattered Henrys into a single figure, but, faced with the film, I cannot escape the sense that I am watching the performer, not the king.

Ruggles has no such effect on me. I am aware of Laughton as actor, of course, but my delight in the actor's choices in that film lies in the fact that they are so right that they seem to belong to the character. "He would have to know how . . . to *be* Captain Bligh," Mark Van Doren said, in his review of *Mutiny on the Bounty* (1935), "and how to be him in such fulness that no inconsistency appeared between the tyrant of the Bounty and the hero of the open boat on that impossible voyage to Timor." Van Doren thought he did "know how" in *Bounty*. In Ruggles, there are no such startlingly contradictory selves to be brought together. The need with that character is to allow the man to break out of the valet's shell—to let us see the break coming bit by bit—and to give a sense of the appealing vanity which belongs to both man and valet and which is presumably the root of his emergence. Implicit in the relationship between Ruggles and his lordship—his playing shepherd and keeper to a man who is presumably helpless about both social niceties and practical matters—is the suggestion that the servant is superior to the master, although Ruggles would never be able to express or even to recognize that superiority. We can see it, however. It is obvious from the beginning of the film, in the way Ruggles performs his part in his lordship's getting-up ritual. As he pours the cream and then the coffee, adds the sugar and stirs, he appears involved in an important routine that has only minimal reference to the man for whom it is being done. Vanity, then, but it should be given a more acceptable label—satisfaction in a job done properly. I may have a few doubts about Captain Bligh, despite Van Doren's eloquence, but Laughton certainly knew how to be Ruggles.

Learned how to be Ruggles, more exactly. Laughton sometimes affected an offhand attitude toward his work ("I have just 'muddled along,' clowning a lot and playing with the roles"), but he seems to have been an actor who concentrated on his characters with a sometimes frightening intensity. The Laughton who emerges from Charles Higham's biography is an unprofessional puffball of sensitivity, uncertain of his own ideas but impatient with those of his colleagues, difficult to work with, a trial to directors and fellow performers. That is almost certainly not the Laughton the biographer meant to convey, for I assume that Higham (and Elsa Lanchester, the puppet-master at his back) wanted us to see the actor as a perfectionist. Better to turn to Emlyn Williams or Bertolt Brecht for testimony on "his infinite capacity for taking pains," as Lanchester called it. Williams recalls Laughton backstage at the Apollo, spinning in his wheelchair ("back and round, round and back, frantic with frustration") to get the feel of Harry Heegan, the crippled soldier in Sean O'Casey's *The Silver Tassie* (1929), and later "alone and absorbed . . . pacing to and fro like a caged hobbledehoy, glaring and growling," trying to find his way into Perelli, the Italian gangster in Edgar Wallace's *On the Spot* (1930). Implicit in William's account of how Laughton tried to get to Perelli through his walk and his scowl is Brecht's later statement about Laughton at work with him on *Galileo* (1947): "He obstinately sought for the external: not for physics but for the physicist's behaviour." For Brecht, this is the correct approach, the way to exorcise the demon of empathy that might sidetrack the audience from thought.

For Laughton, it was simply the way he had to work. When C. A. Lejeune interviewed him on the set of *Rembrandt* in 1936, he talked as much about Gary Cooper, whom he had admired since they made *The Devil and the Deep* together in 1932 and whom he had just seen in *Mr. Deeds Goes to Town*, as he did about himself. "His is presentational acting, mine is representational. I get at a part from the outside. He gets at it from the inside. . . . His is the right way, if you can do it." Quentin Reynolds, interviewing Laughton while *Ruggles* was being made, concluded, "Laughton does not 'feel' or 'live' a part. Laughton *thinks* the part." The limitation of Laughton's approach is that he sometimes seems not to get beyond the costume, the makeup, the gestures. At his best, however, the external aspects become revelatory. A simple example from *If I Had a Million* (1932): as Laughton's downtrodden clerk opens the letter that will bring him his million dollars, the letter folds back on itself and he brushes it open again with the back of his hand. It is a neatening gesture that appears habitual, a comment on the routine of his job, his life, but it contains a hint of exasperation which helps prepare us for the long, methodical march to the president's office and the final release of the Bronx cheer. There is a similar simple but rich gesture in *Make Way for Tomorrow*. As the old couple

(Victor Moore, Beulah Bondi) sit at the table in the restaurant, he says "you kept your looks" and—we are looking at her from the rear, seeing just the right side of her face—her hand comes up and pulls at the edge of her high, lace collar. There are so many possibilities in that gesture: a gee-whiz response to the compliment or a modest oh-no. And I think, too, an automatic check to see that the neck is covered, not to reveal the flabbiness of age. A tiny, lovely moment, it may have been Bondi's own and it may have been Leo McCarey's. Certainly McCarey knew how to use it, as he knew how to use whatever Laughton, the representationalist, the thinking actor, brought to Ruggles. Laughton may not have felt Ruggles, but he lets us know that Ruggles feels.

Elsa Lanchester, who fit none of the conventional pigeonholes and thus found it difficult to find work in Hollywood while her husband was becoming a star, expressed her contempt for the way the industry considered performers. "Once you are typed it is almost impossible to get out of the rut—the rut that has been misnamed character acting," she wrote in *Charles Laughton and I*. For her, a character actor was a performer who was different in each role. Although she always seems to be Lanchester to me, whether she is the titular heroine of *The Bride of Frankenstein* (1935), Hendrickje Stoffels in *Rembrandt* (1936) or one of the batty sisters in *Ladies in Retirement* (1941)—as Laughton is always visible through his shifting roles—she is right that she and Laughton tried to be new characters in every play or film. What she failed to understand was that—at least, from the observer's point of view—that "rut" she deplored was one of the glories of Hollywood in the 1930s. The character actors, particularly the comedians, developed personae which they carried from film to film. Nor is this simply a Hollywood phenomenon, as Lanchester must have known from her work in the London theater; it is a refinement on the old stock-company practice of hiring performers for a spread of similar roles, not for a single part. The refinement comes as the specialist turns artist, when it is no longer the received sense of the role but the talent of the performer that defines the nature of his or her version of the stock figure. Although it must have been a delightful challenge for a performer like Roland Young to break completely with his conventional character to become Uriah Heep in *David Copperfield* (1935), the more obvious distinction of performers like Young lay in their skill within their familiar character, their command of voice and body, their manipulation of detail in a way that made these stock figures not only vivid but real, true, identifiable in the sense that Otis Ferguson celebrates in so many of his reviews. *Ruggles of Red Gap* is a gallery of such performers. Whether they came from Broadway—Mary Boland, Charles Ruggles, Roland Young, Maude Eburne—or grew up with the movie industry—ZaSu Pitts,

Lucien Littlefield—these comedians had spent years perfecting their comic specialities and the techniques that gave them both realistic and theatrical resonance (that let us say, at once, *how true* and *how clever*). They came to *Ruggles*, ready to mix Wilson's characters with theirs, and ready to meet a Ruggles, built from the costume in by an actor who had just been the tyrannical father in *The Barretts of Wimpole Street* (1934). Since the meeting was to be chaired by Leo McCarey, who must have known that an understanding of types is a first step to an understanding of human beings, the result is a film in which there is no visible line between approaches to character. The conflict of styles, rightly, belongs to the characters themselves.

The juxtaposition of styles comes at the beginning of the film—as soon as the place (Paris) and the time ("the Spring of 1908") are established. The film opens with matching two-character scenes—Ruggles and his lordship, Effie and Egbert—to establish at least the superficial difference between Red Gap and the "hoetay moonday," as Effie would and later does say. First we get a slow, quiet scene in which Ruggles opens the curtains and awakens his master, and they talk in fragmentary English (the servant's reserve encouraging the master's tendency toward incoherence) of his lordship's condition (a hangover, apparently) and his experiments with "drawing poker." His lordship is reluctant to tell Ruggles that he was the stakes in the poker game; the audience finds out—from Effie and Egbert—before Ruggles does. Young's restraint in these early scenes shows him as the "epitome of meiosis," to use Basil Wright's lovely phrase. As Lady Beulah said of her brother in *A Lady's Profession*, in a line which may have been written by Walter De Leon, "his expression is pleasant, but vacant." This is the muted version of Young's customary comic figure, one that will not emerge in full until he gets to Red Gap late in the film. The infectious bubble that fills his characters in their happier moments is necessarily absent in view of his impending loss of Ruggles. Otherwise the identifiers are all in place: the imperturbability suggested by the relaxed state of the body; the tendency to chew the ends off his sentences, swallowing as much as he spits out; his "lambent charm," as John Corbin called it when Young played General Burgoyne in *The Devil's Disciple* in 1923. There is already a contrast here between the professional dignity of Ruggles and the easy, if wary, manner of his lordship (the latter is, after all, the natural ally of Egbert), but for a moment he and Ruggles function as a pair to set off Effie and Egbert.

Egbert in long johns is busily packing while Effie hangs over him, demanding that he get dressed and go to pick up Ruggles. By the time this film was made, Charles Ruggles and Mary Boland were so firmly established as a husband-wife comedy team that Sara Hamilton could do a piece like "We Want a Divorce" for *Photoplay* in which they bicker in a producer's office, finally deciding to stay together because they understand one another; pure publicity and something of a bore, the article is an indication of the team's popularity and of the way in which the conventional roles had swallowed the performers. They first appeared as husband and wife in *The Night of June 13th* (1932), but it was not until their sequence in *If I Had a Million* later that year that their roles were defined, their promise as a team recognized. The sketch belongs primarily to Ruggles, the rabbit-loving, rabbit-like clerk in the elegant china store who, when he gets his million dollars, turns up in the shop, spiffily dressed, a rabbit on a leash, and proceeds to smash china, but with the preciseness, the delicacy proper to his character. A henpecked husband whose only escape is the bathroom, he is as much tormented by his wife—in a dream sequence and in reality—as he is by his autocratic boss. Even at this stage, the playing relationship between Ruggles and Boland is clear. He will be largely silent, she in full voice. Here she sees him off to work, her voice going on and on and on, until the door shuts behind him and abruptly cuts off the sound. Only then does he—can he—say, good-bye. This joke is an indication of a practice that would become part of their act; when he speaks in her presence, he seems to be talking to himself (like W. C. Fields with Kathleen Howard) and the simplest line may carry a load of resignation or a hint of defiance, although she will hear neither the line nor the implication. Although the wife is a relentless nag in *If I Had a Million*, a softening sets in after that, affection invades the henpeckery (see the end of *Six of a Kind*). They present not a Fieldsian view of marriage but a less harrowing kind of domestic comedy which accepts the nagging-wife joke but insists, as the title of their first post-*Million* movie indicates, that *Mama Loves Papa* (1933). After *Mama* and *Six of a Kind*, Paramount began to use them to rescue or to give comic substance to movies that existed not simply for the team's sake: *Melody in Spring* (1934), *The Pursuit of Happiness* (1934). Finally *Ruggles of Red Gap*.

Ruggles and Boland not only came to *Ruggles* with their teamwork established, but they came together as a pair with comic characterizations which had been developed before they ever got to Hollywood and which could be incorporated into their new husband-wife stereotypes. Charles Ruggles, who made his New York debut the year that the fictional Ruggles made his in *The Saturday Evening Post*, later said of his years as a successful Broadway farceur, "I became a standard type—the anemic, inoffensive Caspar Milquetoast with a wistful eyebrow and apologetic cough." The cough and the eyebrow served him at every stage of his career because all his characters—even the quietly forceful Philo Swift in *No Time for Comedy* (1940)—have hesitancy at their heart. His use of his body and his voice underlines this fact. Consider the little-boy droop with which his sulky, unsuccessful lover in *One Hour with You* (1932) responds when Colette (Jeanette MacDonald) orders him from the house, and the way his hands make tentative fists at his side without ever clenching. Consider that moment in *Million* when he stands, clutching a gigantic vase, while his customers decide that, no, it is not what they really want, and all that he can say is a polite *good day*. His voice rises within the delivery of the phrase, prying open his patience to let an unmistakable note of hopelessness enter.

On the surface, his Egbert is a marked variation on the usual Ruggles character. He wears a full mustache—a handlebar until he is tricked into having it clipped—instead of Ruggles's familiar neat, small one, and he speaks with a broad Western accent. He is crude, boisterous, outgoing—the cartoon American abroad. Yet, in the presence of Effie, he is completely deflated. His catchphrase "I can be pushed so fer and no ferther" is so insufficient a declaration that it is frequently cut off by Effie before he can finish it. Late in the film, after the celebrated recitation of the Gettysburg Address, Egbert tries to bring Lincoln to his aid but is no match for Effie's dismissive "equal to what." If he is dominant at the end of the film, it is less a transformation in him than in Effie, who, as one of the resident snobs, has to be cut to size. His way of coping is to escape, and early in the film, when he explains to Ruggles how he outsmarts Effie by copying his thoughts on art from a guidebook, he is more the naughty boy than the assertive husband. This side of him is emphasized later in the film in the scene in which he and "Earl," as he calls his lordship, shinny down a tree to escape Effie's formal dinner: the henpecked husband as Huck Finn.

Mary Boland, for all her commanding presence, is first of all a construction of words—words that roar, tumble, pour stumblingly out of her, losing meaning in the process, and words that cut because she sharpens them, syllable by syllable, with operatic pauses and dangerously pointed emphases. Take, for instance, the explosion of *B*s in the scene in which Effie, on the phone to the editor, learns that Egbert is at Nell Kenner's party. "Beer bust! What would my husband be doing at a . . ." she pauses to build a head of steam, ". . . Beer Bust!" She is not all bite, however; on her third repetition of the phrase ("He's at the beer bust"), which comes after she hangs up, the outrage is infected by disappointment. This hint of vulnerability whispers that an absent Egbert can be a victor too. This creature of Boland's came fully formed from the stage, as Brooks Atkinson's review of *The Vinegar Tree* (1930) indicates: "She is an orgy of affectations, a twister of lines, a bungler of words, a sore trial to her family and a great treat for an audience." It was her performance as Paula Ritter in *The Torch-Bearers* (1922) that tagged her "the new Mrs. Malaprop," she said in 1931, and her command of that kind of role was strengthened in *The Cradle Snatchers* (1925) and *The Vinegar Tree.* The character needed few adjustments to become the henpecking wife, particularly when—as in *Ruggles*—she has social and cultural pretensions.

Yet, Effie is not a social-climbing wife, like Irene Rich's Idy in *They Had to See Paris* (1929), whose natural grace is momentarily obscured by fashionable falsity, for one of the strongest elements in the Boland persona is a streak of vulgarity that will not be denied. Take a treasured moment from *Pride and Prejudice* (1940), in which Boland, who could seldom be accused of underplaying, is a reasonably restrained Mrs. Bennet. Pure Austenites may be uneasy in her presence, but Austenites who are also Bolandites will find that most of the time—as the put-upon mother, the too congenial hostess, the dominating wife, the woman offended by Darcy—her vulgarity is only that of Mrs. Bennet. There is, however, that scene in which, felled by social disaster, she lies on the chaise lounge, a tureen of chicken broth on a low table beside her. When the girls call from the window the news that Lydia is returning with husband, coach, and footmen, she rises with a single superb movement. She swerves in a long arc, kicking over soup and table as she goes, and comes up on her feet while poor Mr. Collins (Melville Cooper), who has come to comfort her, sits stupefied, barely missed in the grand sweep. Mrs. Bennet, meet Mary Boland. It is this quality in the comedian that is so right for Effie, indicating that she really belongs with Egbert and Ma Pettingill, not with Belknap-Jackson, and it is best displayed in the film when the character's insecure verbal control lets the real Effie break through. She gives herself away in her inspired French, as in the scene where she apologizes for the arrival of a drunken Egbert, with "Je suis mortifee. I'm traze amazed." And in her inability not to overexplain, as in her attempt to strengthen the bogus role of Colonel Marmaduke Ruggles, which the valet is forced to assume; he was "with the Black Watch in darkest Africa," she bubbles and, then, to Ruggles, "You were a Black Watchman, weren't you?"

Ruggles will bring them "tone—joi de vivre," she tells Egbert, and when he asks what the second is, she not only goes up a register and repeats "tone," but she makes a circle with her thumb and forefinger as though she were illustrating the word. In a very brief scene, the characters of Effie and Egbert are established, their conflict defined (for contemporary moviegoers, in part by the audience recognition on which the performers and the director depended) and the surface

differences between the Englishmen and the Flouds of Red Gap—
between Egbert's long underwear and his lordship's dressing gown—
is made clear. We can go back to his lordship's breakfast where the
news that Ruggles has been won by the Flouds causes only a slight
rattling as Ruggles returns the lid to a cut-glass container. He quickly
regains his professional mask. Their farewell is a model of English
understatement, touching for what it does not say. It is particularly
effective, I think, because it is preceded by a moment in which Young
is isolated at the center of the frame and stands, in three-quarter shot,
rubbing his finger along the edge of the table, comtemplatively, guilt-
ily, sadly: choose one or all.

Egbert has arrived by this time, has greeted his new valet with a
handshake and a "Mr. Ruggles" (he will call him "Bill" or "Colonel"
for the rest of the film), and his presence—like his bright, checked
suit—gives an extra fillip to the farewell, for Ruggles thinks he knows
now what he is going to as well as what he is leaving. There is a shot of
Egbert sniffling, which I wish had ended on the cutting-room floor, but
I understand what McCarey wants from it. Not simply an easy laugh,
but an indicator that Egbert can no more disguise his feelings than he
can wear comfortably the clothes and the pose that Ruggles and Effie
force on him. Beginning with the scene in the sidewalk café, Ruggles,
who imagines he is turning Egbert into at least the semblance of a
fashionable gentleman, is—bit by bit, step by step—transformed himself, trapped at first by his sense of duty, won over finally by Egbert's
openness and by his occasionally calculated innocence. This process is
first indicated by a physical incongruity. Laughton gives Ruggles a
bodily rigidity which reflects not only the valet's professional manner
but a quality of mind as well; he retains the physical characteristic all
through the film, even after he has begun to relax his inflexible ideas
about class and social correctness, so that the new Ruggles comes not
as a surface change but as a spirit within. At the beginning of the café
scene—Effie having left the two men—Egbert grabs Ruggles and drags
him across the street. Although he tries to retain his dignity and his
body clearly wants to remain its stiffly upright self, an ungainliness,
even a ludicrous kind of laxity, undermines the attempt; our eyes tell
us that the Ruggles redoubt is clearly not impregnable. At the table,
Egbert orders two beers and asks Ruggles to sit down. "It would never
do . . ." he tries to explain. Egbert, who knows all the American
platitudes (which, in this film, are more than platitudes), says, "You're
as good as I am and I'm as good as you are," and, when Ruggles still
hesitates, starts angrily to his feet with "Well, ain't I?" Ruggles, who
knows the servant's answer to that question, sits—straightbacked,
unbending, expressionless, sharing the space but not the table. "Don't

you ever smile?" Egbert asks, and the barest hint of a smile touches Ruggles's face. The artificial smile, assumed on demand, is a familiar device, used for pathos or for laughter, but here it has greater significance; Laughton will use degrees of smiling all through the film to show alterations in Ruggles's state of mind. Consider, for instance, the sudden infectious grin that breaks onto his face late in the film when, after having been fired by Belknap-Jackson, he realizes that Egbert and Ma want him to remain. It is on the face that the transformation of Ruggles is registered.

In the first stages, then, Ruggles's manner rejects the implications of the gestures toward equality forced upon him. With the arrival of Jeff Tuttle, we move toward a more genuine, if still involuntary, softening of Ruggles, drink not duty doing the job. Tuttle is an uncharacteristic role for James Burke. Usually, whether he played one of his perennial traffic cops (*It's a Gift* [1934]), a plainclothes or private detective (*It Happened One Night* [1934]), or a villain (*At the Circus* [1939]), he was taciturn, often with an edge of nastiness underneath. His Jeff is, if anything, louder that Charles Ruggles's Egbert, noisily convivial. He and Egbert greet one another with shouts, affectionate insults ("Well, you old sourdough . . . longhorn . . . mustang . . . coyote"), much pounding on one another, and the meeting ends with Egbert's riding Jeff piggyback while many a *yahoo* rends the air. The crowd, in delight or disapprobation, rise from their tables to watch this spectacle, and the camera catches Ruggles sitting alone, attempting not to be part of it. He has disappeared completely by the time Egbert and Jeff return to the table. We see him in the distance, standing far along a typical French street—a windowed store front, shrubs in tubs, a tree. A crowded scene, then, but he is the only person in it—a tiny figure, his dark suit making him stand out against a white doorway. His isolation conveys his uncertainty as, apparently torn between obligation and reason, he does not know whether to go or to stay. He comes at Egbert's call and is inescapably hooked. They move from beer to whiskee-soda ("That's French for highball," says Jeff), and before they leave the place, Ruggles quite suddenly opens his solemn face with a YA-HOO and a modestly triumphant smile. Then he is on his feet crying "yippy-yippy-yippy-yippy." More puppy dog, perhaps, than Western wild man, he is underway at least, moving toward that grand finish when Jeff and Egbert bring him home to an outraged Effie. As she begins her reprimand, he starts to laugh, and when she suggests that he had better go to bed, he leans against her, still laughing, and simply slides along her, first to his knees, then to the floor where we see him lying on his side, one leg up, one arm up, the other arm—hat still in hand—tucked under his head and now laughing uncontrollably. Egbert and Jeff Tuttle and whiskee-soda release the demon in Ruggles; it will take Red Gap to release the man.

The scene on the train is a fine example of McCarey at work, using business to sweeten exposition. We learn that Ma Pettingill is the source of the family money and that Belknap-Jackson is the town's social leader (Effie's version) and/or a scrounger who came from Boston to marry a fortune (Egbert's version), but we take in the information almost by accident; our attention is on Egbert's handkerchief which Ruggles folds and places in Egbert's breast pocket, refolds and replaces when Egbert pulls it out, only to see his efforts defeated when an excited Egbert blows his nose as the train comes into the station. Here we—and Ruggles—meet Ma and Belknap-Jackson. He is elegantly dressed, prissily well spoken, a meticulously detailed version of the self-centered prig that Lucien Littlefield did so well, snottier than the office manager who fires Ambrose (W. C. Fields) in *The Man on the Flying Trapeze* (1935), not quite so malevolent as Herr Schultz in *The Man I Killed* (1932: a.k.a. *Broken Lullaby*), in which the comic stereotype turns sinister. Ma Pettingill is a much more substantial role than the comic servants that Maude Eburne too often had to cope with (watch her scuttling through *The Guardsman* [1931], expressing wry disbelief in *To Be or Not to Be* [1942]), and she made the woman everything that Belknap-Jackson was not: robust, raucous, direct, sensible, appealingly vulgar. It is she who tells Ruggles on his arrival, "If you're a regular guy, you're okay with Red Gap."

Before Ruggles can become a regular guy, however, he has to become Colonel Marmaduke Ruggles, a fiction created by the diligent if incomplete reporting of the local editor (one of Clarence Wilson's nice crochety bits). The servant becomes the honored guest, the secret arbiter of taste becomes the visible darling of society. That Red Gap cannot tell a servant from a gentleman is not so much a comment on Red Gap as it is on the system that draws the class lines, that confuses books with covers. Ruggles reluctantly rises to the occasion and then—for a while, at least—finds that he enjoys the role. The neatest instance of the Colonel working on Ruggles, the dandiacal swagger he develops, comes in the scene in which he stops to visit Mrs. Judson (ZaSu Pitts). Faultlessly dressed in correct riding togs, he stops to chat with the lady in her garden and, when she asks him in to tea, the picture he has of himself tells him that he should vault her fence. He puts his hand on the top of the fence to boost himself, and both legs fly off the ground—but just barely. Superb execution, no results; he turns and goes through the gate. Both the abortive attempt and the recovery are done with great aplomb—Colonel Marmaduke Ruggles moving with assurance—and it is one of the most charming bits that Laughton has in the whole film.

Several things have begun to work on Ruggles even before the masquerade—the comfortable way he is received at Nell Kenner's beer bust, the impulse to return kick in the pants for kick in the pants[5] with Belknap-Jackson ("I coarsely gave way to the brute in me"). Most of all, his tentative courtship of Mrs. Judson. By 1935, with *Greed* and the possibility of using her mannerisms seriously ten years behind her, ZaSu Pitts had established a comic persona as marked as those of Ruggles, Boland, and Young. The audience knew her fluttering hands, her quavering near-whine, the forlorn look in her large, lovely eyes, and knew that her character would be soft, vulnerable, apparently helpless, but with an edge of toughness underneath. The best image of Pittsian vulnerability that I know is in the scene in *Mrs. Wiggs of the Cabbage Patch* (1934) in which her Miss Hazy stands beside Mr. Stubbins (W. C. Fields) as he eats the meal that will decide whether or not he will propose; her hand moves in his direction, tentatively, as though she might touch him and, then, it simply hovers a few inches from his shoulder. Although this Pitts is evident in many of Mrs. Judson's scenes—most noticeably the one in which she tells Egbert that she has driven Ruggles to suicide—there is iron in the character, whether she is defending her meat sauce or, exasperated with Ruggles, telling him to jump in the river "at the bend—it's deeper there." In the scene in the Silver Dollar in which Ruggles tells Egbert and Ma that he wants to "stand on his own feet," be neither a gentleman's gentleman nor a fake colonel, and in which he reveals himself to Mrs. Judson, they reach across the table and shake hands as though they have just met. And in a way they have.

It is at this point that the famous Gettysburg Address scene comes. McCarey told an interviewer that "The idea of it came to me in a night club when I heard a song about 'The Star Spangled Banner,' and how no one knows the words but 'the Argentines, the Portuguese, and the Greeks.'" Well, perhaps. Certainly, the recitation begins after it is determined that none of the Americans in the Silver Dollar remembers the words. Yet, the Gettysburg Address is used in the film as the Declaration of Independence is in the novel, an American document to mark the Americanization of Ruggles. At the end of the book, Ruggles is practicing to read the Declaration at the Fourth of July celebration. "It lends itself rather well to reciting," he says, but he is dead wrong. Beyond the preamble, the Declaration is an impossible piece to speak. The Gettysburg Address, designed by a man who knew how to combine simplicity with the best rhetorical devices, makes a sensible substitute, particularly when its content suits so well the thematic and dramatic purposes of the scene. However McCarey came to the scene, its use indicates directorial imagination and courage. To interrupt a lively and often very broad comedy to insert a set piece, very different in tone, is to risk losing the audience or disorienting them so that they cannot get back to the next loud laugh. A look at the reviews, almost all of which single out this scene for special praise, indicates the degree of his success, and Laughton's.

The effectiveness of the scene lies in the care with which it was designed and cut, and in its use of a familiar film device infuriatingly endemic to musicals. Customarily, when a performer begins to play or sing, the director, as though he is afraid the audience is too crass to understand that there is beauty at hand, moves his camera to the crowd to clue the proper reverential response. Thus, in *Show Boat* (1936), James Cruze almost wrecks Helen Morgan's great rendition of "Just My Bill" with banal reaction shots. In *Ruggles*, however, there is no plot need to prove that either the Gettysburg Address or Ruggles, as elocutionist, is star material. This is an occasion that is both personal and communal, and McCarey's manipulation of his crowd and his camera make that quite clear. The four principals are sitting in an alcove at the edge of the main part of the barroom. Sam, the bartender (Del Henderson), has just said, "What a fine bunch of Americans," having found no one who remembers Lincoln's words, when we see Ruggles in profile, his lips moving. Egbert, full-face toward us, is watching and, at his insistence, Ruggles begins to recite, as the camera holds the men in a two-shot. A three-shot, then—Egbert, Ma, and Mrs. Judson listening. A four-shot—Sam and his partner Harry and two men opposite them at the bar. We go back to a shot of Sam and Harry as they begin to move toward us—toward Ruggles's voice. When the camera pulls backs, we realize that they have reached the alcove end of the bar and that the other two men, whom we could not see, have come along their side of the bar as well. The speech, with the camera as its instrument, has moved out and begun to pull people in. The camera pans on the crowd as they gather at the edge of the alcove, turning it into a stage of sorts, and then it goes behind the crowd, to pick up the stragglers, Ruggles having become a voice only. The camera goes back to Ruggles, who was sitting when he began, and he rises on "the world will little note . . ." as though the text, the occasion were pulling him to his feet. The camera is on his face now, but not too close, a shot that catches him from the chest up. Then a selection of listening shots—the crowd, the three at the table, a close-up of Egbert, Sam and Harry once again—and finally back to Ruggles to finish on him from "of the people" to the end. The camera turns back to the crowd, embarrassed and moved, aware that something has happened which can be neither denied nor explained. "I'll buy a drink," Sam says, and, even then, there is no rush, no abrupt end to the scene. Men begin to peel off slowly and find their way to the bar. When next we see Ruggles and his friends, the four of them are standing at the bar, as though the alcove is not a suitable setting in which to discuss the restaurant Ruggles proposes, as though it has been hallowed far above McCarey's poor power to add or detract.

Ruggles, the new man, riding on the wave of Lincoln's words, sets to work and, with Mrs. Judson's help, begins to create his restaurant. When she says how awful the junk-cluttered building is when they begin to clean it, he says "It's wonderful." After his speech about his coming from a long line of gentleman's gentlemen and that "a man—a person of importance" has emerged from that line, she echoes, "It's wonderful." Yet, every conversion needs a testing—at least, dramatically—and Effie enters, washed in on a deluge of words, with the news that his lordship is coming and that—of course, of course—Ruggles will be needed. He begins to wilt back into the servant ("I'd be the first man in my family to let his family down"), and Mrs. Judson leaves him, a sponge of self-pity, with the suggestion about the bend in the river.

For the moment, the film concentrates on his lordship. The major scene is the one at Nell Kenner's, where he and Egbert go, after they climb down the tree. She ties his tie for him (Ruggles has, after all, not appeared) as he eyes her with amiable lubricity, Roland Young now rescued from the austerity of his early scenes. He has a rambling, flirtatious speech about how Nell reminds him of the most beautiful girl in England, whose name he somehow cannot remember and does Nell happen to know it, but the heart of the scene is their duet. She sings "Pretty Baby,"[6] while he, at the trap drum, is supposed to punctuate the pauses with *booms*. When her "I need a lovin' baby and it might as well be you" is followed by silence, she says "Do you mind?" and he says "Not at all," forgetting the double-*boom* he should have delivered. The scene is gentle, warm, wry, a love scene in the comic vein that Hollywood did so well, with a quality that gives it a continuing emotional validity missing, after fifty years, from so many of the heavy-breathing clinches of the period. Early in the film, we learn that his lordship is something of a ladies' man—or at least that Ruggles has had to rescue him from a number of designing women—but since Nell, for all the cluck-clucking of people like Belknap-Jackson, has the imprimatur of Egbert and the real folks of Red Gap, this is clearly the genuine item, all the preparation we need for the engagement at the end of the film.

Leila Hyams is particularly effective here, which is something of a surprise. She was very beautiful—the artist Henry Oliver dubbed her "The Golden Girl" in her modeling days—but she was a bland performer. Even so, she worked steadily until, still in her early thirties, she retired the year after *Ruggles* was released. Whether she was losing a husband to Lil (Jean Harlow) in *Red-Headed Woman* (1932) or being menaced by one of Dr. Moreau's beast-men in *The Island of Lost Souls*, there was a gentility about her that made her perfectly correct responses—anger, fear, disappointment—clear but oh so polite. A happy exception is the brief scene in *Part Time Wife* (1930: a.k.a. *The Shepper-Newfounder*) in which Betty and Jim, momentarily reconciled, become caught up in a laughing love chase around the living room. That Hyams is so alive in this scene is the more remarkable because Jim is played by Edmund Lowe, who was not only a very wooden leading man but, as Carole Lombard testified, one quite willing to sacrifice a youthful leading lady to keep the camera on himself. The key to Hyams's vivacity here is presumably the director of *Part Time Wife*— Leo McCarey. Certainly, in *Ruggles*, Hyams seems finally to have escaped the Listerine advertisement (she was the first pretty girl to warn us about "halitosis") and become a woman. More important, she establishes her presence as a performer. When the characters gather at the end, she is there not simply because Nell Kenner, the subplot love interest, has to have a seat at table, but because her scene with Young and the trap drum has earned her a place among Ruggles, Boland, and Eburne.

Whatever the Nell Kenner sequence contributes to the plot, however attractive it is in its own right, it is also a device for keeping Ruggles offscreen. He is out there, walking the streets, brooding, and although Laughton could clearly do a brood if the occasion demanded, McCarey is certainly correct in registering Ruggles's presence by his absence—the distress of Mrs. Judson, Egbert's call to action. After he returns and tells his former master what he has become (to the writers' credit, his lordship, with a touch of class indifference, has no idea what he is talking about), we are ready for the climactic opening of the Anglo-American Grill. It is a gala occasion; everyone is dressed to the nines. The Flouds have engaged a table—with Ma and the Belknap-Jacksons—to entertain his lordship, but when he arrives, belatedly, sporting a ten-gallon hat, he brings his newly won fiancée, and Nell Kenner is made a part of the group. Effie, impressed by Nell's ascent to the aristocracy and softened by the champagne Egbert has been pouring into her, is openly congenial. Only Belknap-Jackson is unregenerate. He has been waspish about everything, including the food (although certainly his request for catsup is a mistake: that would be

Egbert's way and lovable in him), but when he mutters "common dancer" of Nell, Ruggles orders him out of the restaurant. When he does not move quickly enough, Ruggles picks him up and hustles him out, turning then, professionally polite, to open the door for Mrs. Belknap-Jackson, who loyally follows. Having violated the sense of elegance he wanted for his restaurant and expecting public disapproval, he goes into the kitchen and says to Mrs. Judson, "So I'm a failure." The audience knows better, not only because this is Ruggles's movie, but because they have seen the only reaction registered by the camera; one of the socialite women at another table rises in outrage only to be pulled back to her seat by her husband. "For He's a Jolly Good Fellow" begins in the restaurant, and Egbert comes into the kitchen and drags out a reluctant Ruggles "to get in on this." Assuming the song is for his lordship, Ruggles joins in and, when the others stop, he goes on until Egbert says, "You old plate of soup, they're singing for you." There is just the tiniest roll of Laughton's eyes, a sidewise glance, and then the actor exudes the fullness of Ruggles's pride and pleasure.

The singing begins again and goes on through the corny ending which McCarey apparently could not avoid (see the clock ending of *The Awful Truth* with the male figurine following the female through her little door). Egbert pushes Ruggles back into the kitchen, peeks through the window and, presumably seeing Ruggles with Mrs. Judson, quickens the tempo with which he's been directing the singing. Ruggles wins Mrs. Judson, of course; we already know that when she corrects his "your meat sauce" to "our meat sauce." *Ruggles of Red Gap* is not a comic love story and needs no offscreen kiss to bring it to an end. It is a film about a man who wins his own sense of self, who becomes the "regular guy" of Ma Pettingill's greeting and proves himself "okay with Red Gap." Forget the final silliness and move back to the real ending of the film, when the singing recommences after Ruggles learns that he is the "jolly good fellow." The *of* in the title of the film and the book becomes a fact as the restaurant full of people—Red Gap—envelops him with song; it is proper that the two men in the four-shot with the bartenders in the Gettysburg Address scene, now having become waiters, join in the singing, for there are no longer servants and masters, only men and women, and the correct thing is no longer proper dress or prescribed manners or social position but goodness of heart.

There is no undertone here, as there is in *It's a Gift* and *Steamboat Round the Bend*, to question the happy ending, no suggestion that Lincoln's "proposition that all men are created equal" remains more proposition than practice. There is, however, what today might be called a subtext, for *Ruggles of Red Gap* is not only about the making of a man, it is about the making of a particular kind of 1930s comedy. When the singing begins again, McCarey intersperses shots of the room with close-ups of the principals, including Mrs. Judson, looking in from the kitchen. As we move from close-up to close-up, it becomes obvious that these are not only Ruggles's friends declaring their love, but performers being given their curtain call. *Ruggles of Red Gap* is a comic celebration not only of a persistent American myth but of the art of the character actor.

Notes

1. I almost said *owners*. In the film, when his lordship breaks the news to Ruggles that he is to go to America, the valet softly says "a country of slavery," a phrase which does neatly what the novel accomplishes in a long passage in which Ruggles contemplates the imaginary America he has conjured from a coon song heard in Brighton (Harry Leon Wilson, *Ruggles of Red Gap*, Garden City, N.Y., Doubleday, Page, 1915, p. 21).

2. The name is spelled "Pettingill" in the film credits and I use that form throughout the chapter. The movie also altered the name of the novel's Earl of Brinstead to Burnstead. When the novel was issued in paperback by Washington Square Press in 1951, "Pettingill" was the spelling of Ma's name. That usage may have derived from the film, but since Brinstead was still Brinstead, it is possible that a typographical error simply took over and swallowed the original.

3. Both silent versions have apparently disappeared. The four reels that remain of the original seven-reel *Beggar on Horseback* (1925), in which Cruze directed Horton, suggest that the 1923 *Ruggles* is an unfortunate loss.

4. Laughton did not name the film, but it is clearly *From Soup to Nuts* (1928). In that film Laurel and Hardy work as waiters for an elegant dinner party in a home that has a remarkable supply of gigantic iced cakes. Hardy falls face forward not once, but three times. It is presumably the first fall, the one in which Hardy lies longest with his face buried in the cake, to which Laughton referred. I have not counted the feet of film conveying the incident—and I doubt that Laughton did. Nor does Hardy remain immobile for a minute and a half, as Leo McCarey's recollection of the film suggests (in Serge Daney and Jean-Louis Noames, "Taking Chances," *Cahiers du Cinéma in English*, no. 7, [January 1967], 44), but he is beautifully buried for a long count of six. "I remained until the picture was run again to discover the name of the

director," Laughton recalled (Scoop Conlon, "He Directs for Laughs—and Gets 'Em," *Motion Picture*, 50 [September 1935], 54), ". . . His name was Leo McCarey!" As it happens, *From Soup to Nuts* is one of the Laurel and Hardy films on which McCarey's name does not appear, a fact that suggests that Laughton's memory may have been invented by the Paramount publicity department, but McCarey does claim the film as his, as his remarks in *Cahiers du Cinéma* indicate, and the example attributed to Laughton is valid even if the details are sketchy.

5. In the novel, Ruggles knocks Belknap-Jackson down after the irate little man kicks him, but the old Hal Roach hand in McCarey must have known the proper eye-for-an-eye for a film comedy.

6. Both "Pretty Baby" (1916) and "By the Light of the Silvery Moon" (1909), which Nell sings earlier in the film, were written after 1908, the year in which *Ruggles* is supposed to take place. Yet, verisimilitude has more to do with tonal truth than factual accuracy. The real musical mystery about *Ruggles of Red Gap* is that Ralph Rainger and Sam Coslow are listed for music and lyrics in the credits to the film, and there are no songs in the movie other than those that Nell Kenner sings and "For He's a Jolly Good Fellow," with none of which Rainger and Coslow have any connection. In filmmaking, there is many a slip. . . . and perhaps there once was a Rainger-Coslow song scheduled for *Ruggles*. The pressbook for *She Done Him Wrong* contains an article on Rainger, who wrote "A Guy What Takes His Time" for that film, in which a second Rainger song "Haven't Got No Peace of Mind" is mentioned. An inquiry to Mae West elicited a letter from her secretary (March 13, 1979) saying that "Piece of Mind" was cut from the script and never filmed.

7

Mr. Deeds
Goes to Town

· 1936 ·

"You know, I think this
wop's got something."
—Clark Gable

Back in 1941, when *Meet John Doe* was about to be released, *Good Housekeeping* published an article on Frank Capra which insisted that the director *"is* Deeds and Smith and Doe—a modest, simple, everyday person, unspoiled and unpretentious." Anyone who has read *The Name above the Title*, Capra's very lively but immodest and often pretentious autobiography, will suspect those adjectives. By 1941, Capra was one of the most successful and most visible directors in American films. He had just left Columbia, where for more than ten years he worked in apparent amiability with Harry Cohn, one of Hollywood's most celebrated tyrants. During that decade he had found his style, his themes, his audience, and the kind of commercial success that helped elevate Columbia to the status of a major studio. He had discovered, in Robert Riskin, a congenial collaborator who wrote the screenplays for most of the Capra films from *American Madness* (1932) to *Meet John Doe*. "Riskin says Capra is a great writer," *Good Housekeeping* reported. "Capra says Riskin is." Capra had gained complete artistic control of his films in an industry in which, as he said in a 1939 letter to the *New York Times*, "the director at present has no power." He would eventually lose the assurance that marks even his earliest films and repackage old goods for unpredictable audiences, but—even though the seeds of uncertainty may lie in his difficulty in ending *Doe*—he seemed, as the Second World War began, a perfect example of the

Longfellow Deeds in Mandrake Falls. Lionel Stander, Gary Cooper, Emma Dunn, Douglass Dumbrille. (*Mr. Deeds Goes to Town*, Columbia, 1936. The Museum of Modern Art/Film Stills Archive.)

persistent Andrew Carnegie, bobbin-boy-to-millionaire myth, the immigrant boy who reached the top of his profession and was rewarded with wealth and fame. "I just don't believe in failures," he said in 1973, explaining why he preferred comedy ("Victory over your environment") to tragedy, but there is a difference between comedic and Carnegian success. Despite the parallels that Stephen Handzo's biographical reading of *It's a Wonderful Life* (1946) found between George Bailey (James Stewart) and his creator, the description with which this paragraph opens seems more appropriate to Capra characters than to the director who rejoiced in seeing his name above the title.

There are critics—Leland A. Poague, for instance, intent on Capra's "visionary-poetic universe"—who would contend that those adjectives do not fully describe the Capra heroes either. It is true that Capra's films, like most good popular films, are more complex than reductive negative criticism implies. Yet, the *Good Housekeeping* phrase suggests the virtues that the Capra films espouse, admirable if unheroic qualities that earned the label "Capracorn" at least as early as 1941 when Margaret Case Harriman credited it to "one Hollywood wag." Again turning to unidentified Hollywood sources, Harriman said of "every Capra picture": "The moral, they add, is either that the common man is the true gentleman, or else that great wealth can bring great unhappiness, or else that true happiness comes from giving happiness to others." Capra is supposed to have responded to a question about these "aphorisms" with "Well, they're all true, aren't they?" A year earlier he had told Geoffrey T. Hellman that "the underlying idea of my movies is actually the Sermon on the Mount—a plus value of some kind along with entertainment." Hellman's profile, called with barely noticeable irony "Thinker in Hollywood," reflects the changes that marked Capra's work in the 1930s, his attempt to hold onto the entertainment value of his films even as he struggled to deal with his growing self-consciousness about ideas, particularly social ideas. Graham Greene, reviewing *You Can't Take It with You* (1938), said, "The director emerges as a rather muddled and sentimental idealist who feels—vaguely—that something is wrong with the social system." The muddle, the sentiment, and the vague discomfort become increasingly obvious as Capra moves from *Mr. Deeds Goes to Town* to *Lost Horizon* (1937) to *Mr. Smith Goes to Washington* (1939) to *Meet John Doe* to *It's a Wonderful Life*. Whether one holds with the overt optimism of these films or the covert pessimism that a critic like William S. Pechter finds, particularly in the last two, it is clear that, after *Deeds*, Capra never quite manages the playful tone—the "incidental human warmth and naturalness" that Otis Ferguson found in *Broadway Bill* (1934)—that holds its own against whatever thematic concerns emerge in the early films.

"I am interested most in characterizations," Frank Capra said in 1936. "The people must be real." In this article in *Stage*, in later interviews, in his autobiography, Capra continued to emphasize the primacy of character in his work and the need to match actor to role in the interest of both verisimilitude and comic effect. "This is the artistry of the film director:" he wrote in *The Name above the Title*. "Convince actors that they are real flesh and blood human beings living a story." His message to young directors was to "forget techniques, forget zoom lenses and subliminal cutting; remember only that you are telling your story not with gimmicks, but with *actors!*" In the 1970s, as though he had overstated the performance aspect of his films, he would remind interviewers that "I move the camera a lot more than you think" and "I use an awful lot of cinema tricks," but he would insist on the necessary invisibility of technique, on devices in the service of the story rather than for their own sake. It is startling in *The Strong Man* (1926) when the camera shoots from above, watching Paul (Harry Langdon) struggle to protect his virtue from the fake "little Mary" (Gertrude Astor), who is only trying to recover money from the lining of his coat. The unusual angle emphasizes both the luridness and the ludicrousness of the scene, but the surprise in it comes from the fact that one is aware of an abrupt change of perspective where, later, the camera can descend the stairs with Deeds while the viewer remains only vaguely aware of it. The growing body of Capra criticism is giving increasing attention to the director's methods, but the discussions tend to stick with Capra's first concerns. When Robert Sklar comments on the director's use of "medium shots and medium close-ups," for instance, it is to emphasize composition designed to "focus audience concentration on the characters in action." The neatest statement about Capra as filmmaker can be found in Otis Ferguson's review of *Deeds*: "He takes a plot with as few restrictions as possible (it has the necessary sentimental angle and forward motion but is fairly empty of anything else) and proceeds to fill it up with situations and characters from life—working the situations into some direct line with wonderful care both for their speed and clarity as parts and for their associative values, their cumulative effect in the whole story."

Plot is not quite as negligible as the Ferguson quotation suggests, although Capra himself said in the *Stage* piece, "To my mind plot is unimportant." He uses conventional stories, usually adapted from popular-magazine material: the ugly duckling, Damon Runyon variation (*Lady for a Day* [1933]), boy-meets-insults-wins-loses-gets-girl (*It Happened One Night* [1934]), the racetrack as pastoral retreat (*Broadway Bill*). Capra films work up audience anticipation and suspense, as good popular films should, but they do not do so through intricacies of plot or through any doubt about the eventual outcome. Although I knew that Peter (Clark Gable) would win Ellie (Claudette Colbert) the first time I saw *It Happened One Night* and although I have seen the film many times, I still feel a sense of excitement, of joy when she cuts and runs in the wedding scene, making her escape from the wrong husband to the right one. I am responding partly to the rhythm of conventional comedy plot in which the lovers finally overcome the obstacles, often self-imposed, that keep them apart, and partly to the visual image, the girl in the long wedding dress breaking ranks and moving obliquely across the lawn. More obviously, I am responding to Capra's success with actors, his way of presenting characters with which the audience can identify. Stephen Handzo is sensibly responsive to the best in Capra's work when he says of *Deeds*, "Surely, the face of Gary Cooper and *voice* of Jean Arthur are the film's real 'content.'" Sensible, that is, unless he is thinking of the performers as separate from the characters. Stars in the 1930s were often used to decorate movies, like figures on a wedding cake, when the impossible juxtaposition of their personalities with their parts kept them from being a contributive ingredient to the whole. With Capra this usually did not happen; he even turned the somewhat stuffy Warner Baxter into the playful Dan Brooks of *Broadway Bill*. The faces of Cooper and Deeds are inseparable, just as are the voices of Arthur and Babe Bennett. It is misleading, however, to overemphasize the leading characters, for the special quality of Capra is that his heroes and heroines, dragging the audience sympathy to the inevitable happy ending, move through a context of "situations and characters from life." The situations are sometimes simply gags—as one might expect from a former gag writer for Mack Sennett—and the characters are often caricatures, but the effect is finally that of comic realism, a verifiable sense of ordinary American life that somehow infects the fables. Take, for instance, the laconic stationmaster in *Deeds* (Spencer Charters) who greets John Cedar (Douglass Dumbrille) when he and his entourage first arrive in Mandrake Falls. He is based on a rural stereotype, which has its roots in both reality and the stage, and he disappears from the film as soon as he sees the Cedar party to Deeds's house, but in his brief appearance he helps give substance to the town and, through the way in which he hears and responds to questions, sets up an opposition of values that will be central to Deeds's confrontation with the city. Whatever point is made by or imposed on a Capra film, it gains resonance from the fact that it is carried by a vehicle that has the surface look of life.

In *The Name above the Title*, Capra described *Deeds* as "my first of a series of social-minded films." This is not strictly true. Early in *American Madness*, Matt (Pat O'Brien) tries to borrow ten dollars from one of the tellers with whom he works only to be greeted by, "Did you ever hear of the Depression?" A joking refusal, a touch of character comedy, the line does place in a larger social context a film in which a run on the bank is the chief crisis and in which a conflict of ideas about good banking leads to a resolution which is also a social-economic statement. This is not simply a retrospective appraisal of a film which is also a marital triangle and a mystery story; as early as 1935—before Capra turned into the post-*Deeds* "thinker"—John Stuart called *Madness* "about as close to timely social comment as the screen had yet dared to approach." Contrariwise, with *Deeds*. "I presumed to 'say' something to audiences for two hours," Capra said, but with a few exceptions— Robert Stebbins in *New Theatre*, the anonymous reviewer in *The New Statesman and Nation*—the reviewers presumed not to listen; at least, the very favorable first reviews tended to welcome the movie as another Capra comedy.

Clarence Budington Kelland's "Opera Hat" seems an odd work to turn to for a director about to embark on social-mindedness. An *American Magazine* serial, it is a tepid murder mystery, the solution of which seems not even to interest the author whose real concern lies in the fun he has with the conventions and the snobbery of opera. "Opera Hat" aside, Kelland is a likely enough source for Capra. Although the director was generally assumed to be liberal left politically (he was once temporarily denied security clearance for a job he was to do for the Defense Department) and the writer was a conservative Republican (national committeeman from Arizona, 1940–1956), the two men shared certain attitudes about small-town life and community responsibility. Kelland may have been more cynical about his material than Capra was; he once responded to an interviewer's paraphrase of his recurring story of the young man who triumphs when the girl teases him into action with "Why should I hunt up a new plot? I've made money out of that one all my life—and it's foolproof." Still, tiny homilies tend to invade even his innocuous fiction, and at his most didactic he uses his familiar plots to carry overt social messages.

The Stephen Howland stories Kelland did for *The Saturday Evening Post* in 1931 belong in the latter category. Howland is a small-town banker, a rock of integrity and wisdom holding fast against the Depression undertow; he regularly solves the personal and financial problems of his customers/clients/constituency, dosing them with uplift: "I don't want you to lose heart and faith in this town or in this country of ours, because everything is coming through sooner or later, and probably sooner." When he is not doing good, Howland is casting sheep's eyes at Mary Quayle, a cheeky young woman who works in the bank, who he thinks is too young for a forty-five-year-old bachelor.

Capra might have found just what he needed in Stephen Howland. In fact, a look at the last of the Howland stories, "Several Birds and One Stone," might make a suspicious person wonder if Capra or Robert Riskin had been leafing through the *Post* before *American Madness* took shape. Not only does Howland salvage a couple of the bank's debtors, but he invents a project—a kind of free-enterprise WPA operation—which brings a picnic park to the town and work to many of the unemployed; in his turn, he is rescued by the people he helped when they march into the bank and threaten to withdraw their money if the board replaces Howland as president with a young whippersnapper who has unwisely invested in German bonds instead of American grit. This is Capra's kind of banker, for both Tom Dickson in *Madness* and George Bailey in *It's a Wonderful Life* run "the small community bank, the personal bank," as Kelland called it in an article on his own disastrous adventures as the director of a suburban bank that had no Howland to save it.[1] Since trust breeds trust for Capra as well as Kelland, both Dickson and Bailey are saved from financial collapse by the men and women in whom they had faith. For an extra-Capraesque fillip, Howland gets his Mary Quayle, although she has to do the proposing. If we can watch Capra now, when we can no longer read Kelland, it is because Capra was an artist with great talent working in a medium that allowed him to convert Kelland's paper-doll characters into identifiable human beings.

"The opera stuff was just 'too-too' for me," Capra says in *Name*. "But—what would country-boy Deeds do with *twenty million dollars*? In the middle of the Great Depression? . . . That *did* interest me." So Columbia acquired "Opera Hat" and Capra and Riskin proceeded to junk most of it. They kept the name of the hero, his talent for greeting-card verse and his tuba, and the name of his small town, Mandrake Falls. There were other minor retentions and a few more extensive ones—the meeting with the opera board, the confrontation with the condescending writers, the subplot about the dead uncle's possible common-law wife. Although Riskin occasionally borrows a line ("We must give the wrong kind of shows"), these scenes in the film not only have a surface dissimilarity to Kelland's originals, they have a very different weight in the total work; what are continuing plot elements for Kelland become discrete incidents that help Capra and Riskin define their Deeds.

Mr. Deeds Goes to Town takes its time about introducing its hero. The film begins with an automobile speeding along a dangerously curving road and then going over an embankment. This is followed by a shot of a newspaper, its headline announcing the death of millionaire Martin

W. Semple. The juxtaposition of accident and death announcement drew a laugh from a class to whom I showed the film in the early 1970s. Their instinct was correct. Capra's exposition—the kind of shorthand which my generation of moviegoer simply absorbed without thinking—is so patently artificial that it might—*Deeds*'s being advertised as a classic comedy—be taken as a joke. What Capra intended, presumably, was a nicely impersonal opening, freeing the heir from a need to mourn and the audience from even a hint of uneasiness.

We then get a shot of the editor (George Bancroft), barking into the telephone, demanding to know who the Semple heir is, while Cornelius Cobb (Lionel Stander), the press agent whose job was to keep Semple's name out of the paper—as he later tells Deeds—tries to quiet him, and the senior Cedar says to hang up. The scene establishes something of the tone and the concerns of the city, to which Deeds will eventually go; introduces us to three of his antagonists, two of whom will become his allies; and points up the newspaper and the law firm as central to the developing story. A characteristic informational bridge, this one is particularly vivid—retrospectively as the characters become leading figures in the film, immediately through the force of the performers.

Bancroft had been in films since the early 1920s. His "Bull" Weed in *Underworld* (1927) was the best known of his silent roles, and he went on to play other brutes—gangsters usually—in three more films for Josef von Sternberg. In the largely forgotten movies in which he starred in the early 1930s, Bancroft's specialty was "the portrayal of guffawing killers," as Mordaunt Hall, surprised to find him playing comedy, said in his review of *Elmer and Elsie* (1934). Hall was somewhat obsessed by the Bancroft laugh, which can be heard echoing through the *Times* reviews of *Ladies Love Brutes* (1930), *The World and the Flesh* (1932), and *Blood Money* (1933). This hysteric note, quite at odds with Bancroft's performance in *Deeds*, sounds as late as 1940 when his villainous half-breed in *Northwest Mounted Police* chortles over his Gatling gun as he mows down the helpless Mounties. Bancroft's editor in *Deeds*—like his sheriff in *Stagecoach* (1939)—is a solid, reassuring presence whose rough exterior belies the understanding and the sympathy within. This character may have grown out of the less extravagant side of Bancroft's star turn, for either Hall or one of his assistants, reviewing pre-*Deeds* films that lacked the hypnotizing laugh, described Bancroft as "sentimentally tough" and a "tower of strength." Although he played the lead in some Columbia cheapies after his appearance in *Deeds*, the Capra film marked his transition into an honorable career as a featured performer—often, as here, a supporting player in more senses than one.

Stander, after a busy but undistinguished few years on stage, made his film debut as the poet in the Ben Hecht–Charles MacArthur *The Scoundrel* (1935), a role that provided the mix of working-class roughness and almost fastidious acidity that became standard Stander. In that film he used a verbal mannerism that would stay with him, a way of biting off his lines as though, despite the deep voice, the words were bunched up behind the teeth waiting to get out. His "I spy a native" when he and Cedar arrive in Mandrake Falls has the familiar Stander snarl-snap, but the nastiness, the near savagery of the poet in *The Scoundrel* is never allowed to emerge in Cobb, whose venom is on the surface just waiting to be milked off by Deeds's goodness; it would reappear in full, ugly flower in his press agent in *A Star Is Born* (1937). According to Stander, the role of Cobb was originally intended for Ned Sparks, a croak-voiced comedian who made a career of presumed sardonic sidekicks of somewhat innocent heroes (see his Happy McGuire in *Lady for a Day*), but since Sparks was a free-lance performer and Stander was under contract to Columbia, the latter got the role. "It was a good part," Stander said with uncharacteristic modesty, "and any competent actor would have given it gloss." Although Sparks gave me a great deal of pleasure as I grew up in 1930s movie houses, this is one role that I am not sorry he missed; the casting of Stander as Cobb resulted in a character more substantial than the familiar comedy turn Sparks would probably have made of it.

Douglass Dumbrille filled a wide variety of roles on stage in the 1920s, on screen in the 1930s (for Capra he had been a not quite raffish enough racetrack gambler in *Broadway Bill*), but he usually played villains, elegant, unctuous, venomous—sometimes all three at once. "Even his hands are oily," Deeds says in a scene in which Cedar tries to ingratiate himself with the young man by pretending admiration for his having tossed out the shyster representing Semple's alleged wife. Gary Cooper, as McGregor, had already tangled with Douglass Dumbrille, as Mohammed Khan, in *The Lives of a Bengal Lancer* (1935), and regular moviegoers in 1936 would immediately have recognized Deeds/Cooper's chief antagonist, despite Cedar's business suit. Not that familiarity with *Bengal Lancer* would have been necessary. Dumbrille is a beguilingly transparent villain; every comforting word, conciliatory gesture, effort at amiability is heavy with menace.

When Cedar and his party arrive in Mandrake Falls, they are greeted by a "Welcome to . . ." sign in doggerel, written, we later learn, by Longfellow Deeds. They are greeted, too, by the station attendant, a friendly enough man ("Morning, neighbor"), but one who comes and goes at his freight-tending chores as they try to talk to him. He responds directly to their questions, but the joke in the scene—heightened by the perennially surprised look that a wide-eyed

Spencer Charters brings to the character—is that his answers give the information requested but in ways that they do not expect. When they ask him if he knows Longfellow Deeds, he says that everyone around here knows Longfellow Deeds, and when they say they want to talk to Deeds, he assures them that that will be all right because he is "very democratic—talks to anybody." The gag is sustained even after he drives them to Deeds's house; when Mrs. Meredith wonders why he has brought them there, he says that, yes, he knows Deeds is in the park, but they asked for his house. "Can't read their minds if they don't say what they want."

A typical example of broad Capra character comedy, the scene is more important than any laughs that lie in it. The joke is based on the fact that the man's questioners do not take their own words literally, that they assume that their queries will initiate a flow of information beyond that specifically requested. The station attendant's abrupt answers deflect them, force them to begin again. It is this violation of assumptions, on a much more exalted level, that will set Deeds apart from most of the people he meets. When he finally puts in his appearance, he seems indifferent to their news about his inheritance, more interested in the new mouthpiece for his tuba and in their trying Mrs. Meredith's orange cake. To some people, such a reaction might tag Deeds not as naive and innocent but as mentally defective. "The boy must be a nitwit," says one of the lawyers early in the film, the first of a trail of "crazy" remarks leading to the sanity hearing. Yet, twenty million dollars lacks the reality of orange cake. The sum remains words coming from a too cordial stranger, and the new mouthpiece for his tuba is something that Deeds can hold in his hand. The thing that sets Deeds apart from Cedar and Cobb in this scene is not that he seems unable to take money seriously—not that he represents antimaterialistic values—but that he violates their expectations, fails to react in ways that seem appropriate to them. The fundamental difference between the city and the small town in *Deeds* may not lie in urban corruption compared to rural innocence, but in the fact that the clever city people, who think they have all the answers, do not even know how to frame the questions. The fiscal annunciation scene ends with Deeds and Mrs. Meredith alone. The news finally having begun to register, he asks the housekeeper if she realizes how much twenty million dollars is; she, putting first things first, says, "I don't care how much it is. You sit there and eat your lunch." A familiar movie cliché about the presumed housebound vision of maternal types, Mrs. Meredith's line is more than a tidy way to bring the scene to a close. It is a reprise of the station-attendant joke, another thematic statement.

Capra uses two standard film clichés to establish Deeds's likability before he ever appears: his housekeeper and his dog. Mrs. Meredith's primary function in the film is expositional; she explains to us as she explains to Cedar and company who and what Deeds is. She even gives a folksy, comic reading of one of his verses.[2] Yet, her protective bullying of Deeds and her automatic response to the visitors ("Sure I couldn't get you a glass of lemonade or something") establish a home-like atmosphere that tells an audience more about Deeds than her words do. Our acceptance of Deeds is made the easier by the casting of Emma Dunn in the housekeeper's role. She had been playing mothers since 1906 when, just past thirty, she was Ase to the much older Richard Mansfield's Peer Gynt—a performance, she was to claim in a 1915 interview, that saddled her with mother roles from then on. A tiny, cuddly woman, all warmth and spunk, she transferred her maternal instinct to the movies as early as 1920, and became one of a band of character actresses (Beryl Mercer, Mary Gordon) who made careers of mothers and surrogate mothers—housekeepers and landladies. As though Emma Dunn were not enough, Capra provides Deeds with a handsome English setter that goes to the door and rears up, paws high, waiting for the imminent entrance of its master. Dog lovers may wonder why Deeds does not take his devoted dog with him to New York—there is certainly room enough in his inherited Fifth Avenue mansion—but the dog, having done its work, disappears from the movie, as do the station attendant and Mrs. Meredith. They are of no further use to Capra, hence of no further use to Deeds. If the audience thinks of them at all, we are presumably to imagine them happy back in Mandrake Falls, which turns into an abstract absent paradise once Deeds gets to New York.

The ground well-prepared by the station attendant, the housekeeper, and the dog, Deeds arrives and plays his scene with the city visitors. His response to the news of his inheritance establishes him as an individual and as a man formed by his environment. He is a silly eccentric only if you are standing with Cedar and Cobb, for most of the comedy in the scene lies in their reactions. To them, his verbal games are as foolish as his preoccupation with his new mouthpiece, but there is a double edge in Capra's use of his poet's response to names and rhymes. When the lawyer introduces himself as the senior partner of Cedar, Cedar, Cedar, and Budington, Deeds says, "Budington must feel like an awful stranger,"[3] and then worries all through lunch because he cannot find a rhyme for Budington. The device is Kelland's although the rhyme his Longfellow Deeds seeks is for McGonigle; the substitution of Kelland's middle name in the movie is an inside joke presumably devised by Riskin or Capra. The unfound rhyme becomes a running joke in the movie, as it is in the Kelland serial, but it takes on special significance here when Deeds, discussing the simplicity of some rhymes, makes up a limerick on Cobb's name which ends, "And now poor Cobb is out of a job." Cobb, responding in good city fashion, assumes he is being fired until Deeds assures him that the verse is just an exercise in rhyming. Still, the exchange holds out the possibility of a Deeds who can act as well as react in unexpected ways. When Cedar tells him that he must come to the city right away, he does not question the lawyer's demand. His apparent docility suggests that Deeds is what Cedar thinks he is, a yokel who will be easy to manipulate, but the scene suggests a substantiality in him that will emerge fairly quickly after he gets to the city. The Cobb limerick is one evidence of this, but the presence of Gary Cooper is a more obvious indication that Deeds, as Otis Ferguson says, "is not the I-swan stooge of tradition but a solid character, shrewd and not to be trifled with."

By 1936, Cooper was an established star, popular with men and women alike, although not yet the institution he would become before his death in 1961. One of the persistent nontruths about him is that he was a laconic personality, on screen and off, a nonactor whose success lay in his likability rather than his skill. It is difficult to understand how that view of him survived, in the face of his reviews, the comments by professionals, the evidence on the screen itself. His physical grace is already plain in the tiny role in *Wings* (1927) which helped propel him to stardom. If an awkwardness emerges in later roles which ask that he do more than simply stand with casual authority—*The Virginian* (1929), *Morocco* (1930), *City Streets* (1931)—it is because in these early talkies he is still learning how to convey emotions effectively using the narrow range of gestures and voice changes he has at his command. "It was painful for me to make a gesture that was broader than the absolute minimum," he later recalled. In both *Morocco* and *City Streets*, he conveys his character's pleasure in the figure he cuts—particularly in his show-off scene with the gun in the latter—but he falls short of lust in both films and of the calm menace he is supposed to have in the scene in *City Streets* in which the Kid takes over the mob. By 1936, his authority as a performer and his sense of character are so perfected that he can give nuance to the simplest speech or movement. In *Desire*, the film that immediately preceded *Deeds*, he plays a love scene with Marlene Dietrich, who, as the far from innocent Madeleine, pretends to have run from him because she was afraid. His Tom Bradley does a little-boy bit, protesting that he did nothing, but when she says she saw it in his eyes, he says, "I didn't know it showed." It does show. In a film that does not take sex very seriously, he conveys the titular desire with a sureness that makes his presumably experienced legionnaire Tom Brown seem retrospectively to belong not in Sternberg's *Morocco* but in *Tom Brown's School Days*. The sense of self-satisfied repletion with which he murmurs, "But, I'm not a little boy anymore," when the Prince (John Halliday) awakens him after what has been—censorship or no—clearly a night of sex, is even more effective. Although Deeds may hanker after Babe Bennett, he is no Tom Bradley off on a footloose holiday to Spain. The emotions Cooper is called upon to display in *Deeds* may differ from those in *Desire*, but the Capra film does ask him to move easily and surely from suspicion to anger to delight to respect to sincerity to self-mockery to . . . which he does with a minimum of overt technical apparatus but with no lack of clarity. We always know what Deeds is thinking. One of the best examples can be found in the restaurant scene in which the "literati" invite Deeds and Babe to their table so that they can make fun of the millionaire poet from Mandrake Falls. At first he laughs with them, accepting the jokes as friendly ragging, but as he realizes their essential snottiness, his pleasure turns to anger. His amiable grin fades, his mouth tightens, his eyes grow hard. Cooper conveys the transition without histrionics. The scene is a perfect illustration of Cooper's technique as an actor.

"Shucks, I don't know anything about actin'," Cooper is supposed to have said in 1942. ". . . I don't act. I just learn my lines and do things the way I'd do 'em if I was the fellow I'm playin'." Despite the folksy, Cooper-image spelling Jerome Beatty gave to this quotation, it makes the essential point about acting that Charles Laughton made in 1936 when he compared his technique with Cooper's: "His is presentational acting. . . . He gets at [a part] from the inside." Years later, after he had put fake humility behind him and decided to talk as a professional, Cooper said, "Mr. [Lee] Strasberg himself once said that I was a Method actor without knowing it." Comments by performers who worked with Cooper—Walter Brennan, Akim Tamiroff, Lilli Palmer—and by directors—Howard Hawks, Sam Wood, even George Cukor, who never directed him—emphasize the deceptive simplicity of Cooper's acting. Typical statements about Cooper as performer are those of Walter Brennan ("All of his seeming carelessness and his apparent nonacting is carefully studied out") and Robert Preston ("But Cooper never made a move that wasn't thoroughly thought out and planned"). The "as told to" autobiography that appeared in *The Saturday Evening Post* in 1956, unlike a great many such star turns, gives much attention to Cooper's art. His best story about the difference between playing and being a character concerns the making of *The Real Glory* (1939). They had just shot a scene when the director (Henry Hathaway) was struck by a shadow at the window. He wanted to do the scene again, using the mysteriousness of the shadow, but Cooper insisted he could not play it because he did not know who the shadow belonged to and what its passing by had to do with his character. "I'd have had to substitute acting for characterization, and I found I could no longer play that way." It is this connection between actor and character that gives Longfellow Deeds his authenticity. Cooper's strengths become those of the character; Deed's innocence seems almost to belong to the performer. This symbiosis lets us recognize the substance in Deeds from his first appearance in the film.

Before Deeds, once established, gets to town, there is one more Mandrake Falls scene to play—the grand farewell at the railway station. The main joke in it is that, while the city folks fret that Deeds has not turned up, the camera finds him with the band, his tuba contributing its bit to "For He's a Jolly Good Fellow" and "Auld Lang Syne." The sentiment in the scene is underlined by Deeds's words ("Gosh, I got a lot of friends") and, less soupily, by a visual gag: the little boy who rides on Deeds's back as he plays his way to the train and has to be plucked off by Cobb as Deeds finally climbs aboard. For Capra watchers, fascinated by the director's ambivalent attitude toward "the little man," the scene has an interest far beyond its overt uses. John Raeburn has said that Capra shares with D. W. Griffith "the ability for individuating the members of a crowd while at the same time conveying a vivid sense of its collective nature." He was speaking specifically of *American Madness*, which better fits his remark. It certainly seems untrue for *Deeds*. Compared to the crowd that Preston Sturges got together to greet Woodrow Truesmith (Eddie Bracken) in *Hail the Conquering Hero* (1944), this is an amorphous melange of presumed good will. It has no more social reality than the collection of extras to whom Finley P. Haddock (Leon Errol) makes his farewell speech in *Finn and Hattie* (1931). Even Deeds, waving good-bye from the observation car, calls out only one name. Capra's largely faceless crowd might be explained away on the basis of function. One of the traditional uses of crowds in the movies is as backdrop for the principals and, since Mandrake Falls has already been defined by Mrs. Meredith, the station attendant, and Deeds himself, there is no ideational use for it. Yet the other important crowd in *Deeds*, the mass of unemployed who descend on the hero's mansion, has a similar lack of differentiation; except for Swenson (Christian Rub in his familiar Scandinavian comic turn) and the farmer chosen to thank Deeds (George "Gabby" Hayes), who emerge from the group, this is simply a mosaic of Depression faces. They have an accusatory function (a "social-minded" film, Capra said), but, unlike the carefully chosen "peasant" faces with which William Dieterle surrounded his conventional romance in *Blockade* (1938), their presence accuses neither the comic context nor the individualism that pervades both character and plot.

To understand the way Capra uses crowds in this film, it might be useful to consider his general approach to people en masse. With *Meet John Doe*, in which the crowd is easily swayed, moved by its need and by the machinations of the power-hungry publisher, and in which its changeability was one of the film's subjects, Capra's credentials as a populist and an optimist were called into doubt. "I have a definite feeling that the people are right," he told Geoffrey T. Hellman. "People's instincts are good, never bad. They're right as the soil, right as the clouds, right as rain." *Meet John Doe*—then called *The Life and Death of John Doe*—was at the preproduction stage when the Hellman piece appeared in 1940 (the year in which John Ford's *The Grapes of Wrath* reminded audiences that even the soil is not quite trustworthy), but when the film appeared it seemed—despite the uneasy happy ending—to question the inevitable rightness of the people. Recent critics, looking at Capra's use of the crowd under a less attractive name, have decided, as Leland A. Poague put it, that "The mob is *always* wrong in Capra. . . . The only instances in which the mob can be described as 'right' are when the mob-as-mob is broken down into individuals." Capra said much the same thing in 1971, commenting on conformism, "I'd rather see some individuals. That was the common man idea, I didn't think he was common. I thought he was a hell of a guy." The apparent conflict between Capra's presumed love for "the little man" and the ugliness he can manifest in the plural (as in *Meet John Doe*) lies in the fact that labels like "the people" and "the common man," which are collective terms or abstractions in general usage, obviously connote the individual for Capra. Although he could devise a comic character like Danker (Alan Hale) in *It Happened One Night*, who gives the hitchhiking lovers a ride and then steals their luggage and whose individuality is never in doubt, the individual hiding behind Capra's use of "the people" is obviously man at his best. Although a gathering can be benevolent (Deeds's farewell crowd), individuals tend to get lost in groups, and the group itself is potentially dangerous. As Tom Dickson says in *American Madness*, "You can't reason with a mob."

From very early in his career—in *The Strong Man*, for instance, with its contending mobs of good guys and bad guys—Capra has been fascinated by the unpredictability of people in large groups. In *Rain or Shine* (1930), the crowd laughs happily at Smiley Johnson's improvised circus, until, egged on by the villainous ringmaster who reminds them of the show they are not seeing, they turn into a vicious mob; the total destruction of the circus is frightening despite the ameliorating unreality signaled by the presence of Joe Cook and his stooges. *The Miracle Woman* (1931) provides even more instances of changes and counterchanges within a crowd. The story of a crooked evangelist (Barbara

Stanwyck), purified by the trusting love of a good blind man (David Manners), the film is full of touches a great deal more sophisticated than the saccharine plot. The crowd faces are strong here—suggesting *American Madness* rather than *Deeds*—and Capra lets the camera play over them during the meeting, communicating the need and the longing on which Sister Fallon and her partners are feeding. In the climactic fire scene, the crowd panics, becomes a mob, a dangerous gallery of hurrying feet, but the evangelist stands on stage, calling God's name in earnest now, and stops the scramble, gets singing started, sends the crowd moving in an orderly fashion toward the exits. She has to be rescued from the burning stage by the blind hero, and he collapses once he staggers to safety with her in his arms. They are picked up and put on stretchers, but their rescue is difficult because the crowd has now turned into a surging mass of curiosity, pushing so close that the police have to try to beat them back. At this point, someone begins to pray and the people fall to their knees; the mob becomes a congregation again, intoning the Lord's Prayer.

Capra's presentation of these changes suggests both an attitude toward crowd psychology and an instinct for the immediate dramatic needs of a scene. The former is reflected again in *American Madness* when the frightened depositors surge into the bank to withdraw their savings, only to be turned, stilled, pacified by the appearance of the men who believe in Tom Dickson and announce that they want to put money in the bank. The scene also—and most graphically—illustrates Capra's use of the mob as a dramatic device. This is one of the ugliest crowd scenes in the Capra canon. At one point, we see a woman collapse in the crush, sink until only her hand is visible beyond the cashier's wicket. She is presumably trampled, but Capra and the film completely forget her. No one picks up her mangled body or even tells us that she survived, for the dramatic truth in the scene is the reversal that alters the nature of the mob, and the crowd simply melts away, an indication that all is well. Capra is no more interested in them once they have performed their task in the film than he is in Deeds's dog. It is this aspect of Capra's work that makes it difficult to argue the ideational fine points of the director's beliefs at any isolated moment in his films. The crowds in *Deeds* need neither the vividness of those in *The Miracle Woman* and *American Madness* nor the heavy burden of meaning that the people carry in *Meet John Doe*, for they appear in scenes that are about the hero rather than the crowds themselves.

One of the endearing clichés of 1930s comedy (sophisticated urban subgenre) was the stock opening in which nervously bright music, shots of busy streets, and a few unmistakable landmarks identified

New York City as place and idea. That is not the town to which Deeds goes, so—after a brief scene on the train—Capra gives us a shot of the train descending into the mouth of hell (the tunnel just beyond the 125th Street Station). Although Deeds and Babe will eventually ride on the open top of a Fifth Avenue bus and visit Grant's Tomb, Capra is not interested in New York as New York, but as a testing place for his hero. Its quality is defined not by location shots of the real city, but by three interior scenes which precede our first look at Deeds in his new home. In the lawyers' office, we learn not only that the firm expects to manage Deeds, but, as the worried Budington indicates, that they need control to cover their misuse of Semple funds. In the second scene we meet Deeds's languid Semple cousin (Jameson Thomas) and his querulous wife (Mayo Methot), whom Cedar will eventually use against Deeds, and know at first glance that they are unworthy candidates for the inheritance. The third and most important of the scenes takes us into the newspaper office and introduces us to the heroine/villain.

The editor has gathered a large group of reporters and photographers in his office and is berating them for not having come up with anything on the Semple heir. There is something absurd about the suggestion that a major metropolitan daily would be marshaling so large a force to so little purpose in 1936 (is there anyone left to cover the Rhineland, Ethiopia, Spain, the Berlin Olympics or the grander gossip of Edward VIII's impending abdication?), but, as the front-page stories that follow indicate, newspapers—at least in 1930s comedies—were concerned primarily with the shenanigans of the very rich.[4] Capra, who would worry about the political implications of a too powerful press in *Mr. Smith Goes to Washington* and *Meet John Doe*, is on more familiar comedy ground in *Deeds*. He and Riskin had already been that route in *Platinum Blonde* (1931) and *It Happened One Night*. In fact, the "Cinderella Man" label that Babe Bennett hangs on the new millionaire comes from *Platinum Blonde*,[5] where it is used more appropriately since Stew Smith (Robert Williams) leaves the kitchen hearth (the newsroom) to marry the Long Island princess (Jean Harlow), even if he does not live happily ever after. Capra may intend some criticism of the irresponsibility and the casual cruelty of the press, but there is no satiric harshness in *Deeds*—not even the amiable acidity of *The Whole Town's Talking* (1935), for which Riskin helped write the screenplay, and *Nothing Sacred* (1937).

The main business of the newspaper scene is to establish the special nature, the separateness of Babe Bennett. The other reporters, all male, form an undifferentiated clump, an effect that is heightened by the fact that most of them are, for some unexplained reason, wearing their outer garments. We first see Babe when the camera, which has been on the editor at his desk, pulls back to show her leaning against the glass partition that divides the office from the newsroom. Although other people cut between Babe and MacWade—a copyboy leaving papers on his desk, for instance—the two of them share the frame in a way that places her with the editor rather than with the journalistic hoi polloi bunched together in front of his desk. She plays with a bit of rope all during the scene, jerking it in an attempt to tie a knot with just one hand and finally succeeding. Although the activity is a show of indifference that indicates her professional status on the paper, it is also a child's game. There is an edge of little-girl rebellion in Jean Arthur's personality, and the device tells the audience that, although Babe is willing to go after Deeds for a month's vacation with pay, she is potentially on the side of the angels. A similar effect comes from her playing with a coin in a later scene with the editor; she tries to do a trick with it, drops it, almost disappears from the frame as she looks for it, rummages under the seat of the chair where it could not possibly have got. All this softens the fact that at this stage she still says that Deeds is "the original" sap.

After *Deeds*, Jean Arthur became the leading working-girl heroine in film comedy. Her persona, the soft-spoken but sharp-tongued young woman, was malleable enough to be either befuddled (*Easy Living*, 1937) or efficient, when she had to outsmart or to look after one of Capra's innocents—Deeds, Smith. She was beautiful in an unconventional, tomboyish way, but her most distinctive feature was her voice, which had an odd throaty quality that was a cross between sandpaper and a caress. She had a number of devices that she used with remarkable skill—a near stammer for emotional occasions, for instance, and an incredibly effective catch in the throat. She managed both of these at once in a lovely moment in *The More the Merrier* (1943) in which her Connie Milligan, having caught Dingle (Charles Coburn) reading her diary aloud to Joe (Joel McCrea), calls him *contemptible* and orders him from the house. Outrage about to turn into tears. Very funny-sad. She was a long time arriving at the kind of skill that made her a star in the late 1930s. If her 1908 birthdate is accurate (some references say 1905), she made her film debut at fifteen as the heroine's cousin in John Ford's *Cameo Kirby*, a role so tiny that you have to look quickly to see her at all. Then followed the long, slow climb through comedies, Westerns, featured roles, leads in secondary films that marked the career of other comedians like Carole Lombard and Myrna Loy. Dropped by Paramount in 1932, she went to Broadway where she played in a handful of unsuccessful plays, but where she attracted enough attention to be brought home to Hollywood by Columbia. It was there that she found her persona in *The Whole Town's Talking*. Her

"Bill" Clark refuses to conform to the office rules, and the director (John Ford, again) uses both business (feet on the desk, the newspaper) and physical placement (the way she tips her chair into other people's space), as Capra would in *Deeds*, to separate her from her nondescript colleagues. It is tempting to give Riskin credit for Arthur's discovery of her essential comedic self, but his cowriter on *Town*, Jo Swerling, had written a similar part in *Platinum Blonde* (to which Riskin contributed dialogue) for Loretta Young, who filled it less comfortably than Arthur would. It is more likely that *Town* was one of those happy Hollywood accidents, the joining of performer and character in a union that gave birth to a string of similar roles that would become both more complex and increasingly funny. In *Deeds*, Arthur has to move from Babe Bennett's brittleness to the soupy softness of Mary Dawson, the alias she assumes to get close to Deeds, and then as she responds to the simplicity she at first derides, she has to find a middle ground in which Babe can be tough enough to fight for him at the sanity hearing, soft enough to want to lean on him.

When we see Deeds for the first time in the city, he is in his bedroom, undergoing a fitting for a suit. The setting is a fine invention for the scene in which the Deeds who will not let himself be victimized by "strangers, politicians, moochers," as he later says, must finally emerge from his amiability. There is something ludicrous about a man pinned-up in an unfinished suit, and the air of foolishness is heightened when the tailor hovering around him is played by Franklin Pangborn at his fluttery best.[6] There is a suggestion of physical entrapment to go with the pressure of demands that bedevil Deeds. The scene is devised as a series of related interruptive actions, parentheses within parentheses. Cedar is here to get Deeds's power of attorney, and Deeds, who mutters, "It isn't natural," cannot understand why the lawyer is willing to act as his investment analyst as well as his legal adviser for no extra fee. At this point, they are interrupted by Hallor (Charles Lane in one of his aggressive, ferrety characterizations), who represents the late uncle's alleged wife. Deeds gives a sympathetic ear to the story, but before he can act on the lawyer's surprising news, he must move on to the opera board, which is meeting in his library. The spokesman for the group is played by Edwin Maxwell at his most supercilious, but he has no more luck condescending to Deeds than he did to Rufus T. Firefly (Groucho Marx) in *Duck Soup*. The heart of the scene lies in an echo of Deeds's earlier remark to Cedar. When it becomes clear that the board expects him to pick up the opera's deficit "naturally," he says, "Excuse me, gentlemen, there's nothing natural about that." Later, when Deeds goes on a binge with Morrow (Walter

Catlett), the drunken poet, we are told that they were discovered, wandering the streets in their shorts, shouting, "Back to nature." Since we never see them, those shorts are a bit unnecessary, nakedness being closer to nature. This fastidious touch aside, the story stands in the way of a too neat reading that might want to do something about the natural (Deeds and Mandrake Falls) versus the artificial (the city). The slippery meaning of "natural" in Deeds's scenes with Cedar and the opera board again emphasizes the difference between the ways Deeds and the others use language. Besides, had Riskin wished to press the point, any offspring of Martin W. Semple's presumed affair with Hallor's client would properly be called a natural child.

Leaving the opera board in disarray, Deeds returns to the bedroom to find that Hallor, insensitive to Deeds's initial response, is talking compromise; so he throws him out. Has him thrown out actually, but not before he grabs him by the lapel and threatens him. This is the first evidence of a strain of violence in Deeds which erupts when he cleans up on the poets in the "literati" scene and again at the end of the film when with a single punch and the judge's blessing he bowls over the three Cedars and Budington. Some critics have suggested that this is a blemish on the pure hero Deeds was never meant to be, as though Deeds's behavior were other than a convention of popular drama (see Harold Lloyd's decking the bully at the end of *Grandma's Boy*, 1922). After the battle of the poets, Cobb tells Deeds, "Socking people is no solution for anything." Although Deeds says "Sometimes it is the only solution," his punches are not solutions for Capra, the movie, or the audience; they are evidence that he refuses to be a patsy. It is on the ejection of Hallor that Cedar offers his "oily" handshake which elicits only a request from Deeds that he get the books straightened out. The scene not only ranges Deeds against his enemies, but introduces his allies. Cobb's "lamb bites wolf" and his handshake are taken straight, by Deeds and the audience, and from then on he is on Deeds's side. In this scene, too, we meet Walter (Raymond Walburn in an unfamiliar role, minus the delightful bluster that Capra had already used in *Broadway Bill*), the valet whose services so distress Deeds. This material comes directly from Kelland—although it might have been borrowed from *They Had to See Paris* (1929) or *Ruggles of Red Gap* (1935)—and Walter becomes the servant as friend. In the scene in which the farmer makes his "we think you're swell" speech for Deeds, Walter is standing next to the speaker, smiling in pride and agreement.

The innocent, not-so-innocent Deeds, unwilling to be taken in by Cedar, Hallor, and the opera board, is ripe for the film's betrayal plot. He is vulnerable to Babe Bennett's deception for two reasons. When she stages her fake collapse outside his mansion, she, as Mary Dawson, appears to be the lady in distress that Mrs. Meredith says at the beginning of the film he "has a lot of foolish notions about saving." This borrowing from Kelland disappears fairly early (the last reference comes in the park scene in which they improvise their duet), and Mary develops into another refugee from a small town, a girl he can trust in a give-me world. As Babe's stories—based on the brawl with the poets, the binge with Morrow, his chasing fire engines—reduce him to a front-page joke, the millionaire as country bumpkin, he turns to her alter ego because "You think about a man's feelings." Their scenes together, which resemble conventional love scenes in romantic comedies, allow him to voice his ideas without embarrassment. It is easy to mock lines like his lament for city people ("They work so hard at living they forget how to live") or his response to the attacks on him ("What puzzles me is why people seem to get so much pleasure out of hurting each other. Why don't they try liking each other"), but his platitudes are full of admirable sentiments, as Babe comes to understand, and they certainly are correct for the character of Deeds. One may squirm a little to hear spoken what should be dramatized, but there is none of the sense of the ridiculous that pervades so much of *Lost Horizon* in which Capra and Riskin put lines like "Be kind" in the mouth of the High Lama (Sam Jaffe) and back up his commonplaces with Dmitri Tiomkin's message-from-heaven music. Even in his bromides, Deeds is his own man. As Deeds falls in love with Mary Dawson, Babe Bennett falls in love with him. The film gives her the required sentimentally cynical friend (Ruth Donnelly) to whom she can express her distress at what she is doing. The courtship culminates in the engagement scene on the apartment steps in which Deeds gives her the poem he has written for her and which Arthur, since Babe is both moved and embarrassed, reads in a barely audible voice. It is a conventionally sentimental poem—*angel* figures prominently in it—that is as impeccable in its sentiments as it is bad aesthetically. It is suitable to both characters—the kind of poem Deeds would write and one that Babe accepts for its obvious sincerity. Before Babe can remove the obstacle that stands between them—can, with the blessing of her understanding editor, confess her duplicity—Cobb discovers the identity of Mary Dawson. Deeds, crushed, is ready to cut and run to Mandrake Falls.

It is at this point, finally, that Capra's "social-minded" film begins, and a very brief one it is. As Deeds comes down the stairs to make his escape from the wicked city, he is confronted by the farmer (John Wray) who threatens and fails to kill him. While the farmer eats the elegant lunch Deeds has had prepared for Babe, Deeds sits watching, saying nothing, only nodding when the man wonders if he can take some of the food home to his family. This scene, effectively played by

Cooper, almost masks the fact that Deeds's discovery of the Depression comes rather late in the decade as well as the movie. However late, it gives him an opportunity to return to the decision, made early in the film, to do good with the money that he does not need. I am not quite sure how all those farmless farmers made their way to New York City (Swenson says he is from "South Dakota North"), but here they are, and Deeds is prepared to meet their problem by giving each of them ten acres, seed, a horse and a cow, and, if they work the land successfully for three years, the farm becomes theirs. A combination of rich man's charity and self-help, Deeds's plan is a throwback to the homestead movement earlier in the decade. In *Flight From the City*, Ralph Borsodi explained how he and his family moved to the country

Longfellow Deeds in New York. Gary Cooper, Jean Arthur. (*Mr. Deeds Goes to Town*, Columbia, 1936. The Museum of Modern Art/Film Stills Archive.)

in 1920 and became self-sufficient and went on to indicate that their personal solution might be a desirable public one in the face of the Depression; in an article in the *Nation* in 1933, the year his book was published, Borsodi described a project he had organized, backed by a "responsible group of Dayton citizens," to help solve local unemployment in terms that would be rewarding for the participants. Whether Riskin and Capra had ever heard of the homestead movement, it is obvious that it would be attractive to Deeds since it contained both a way to help the hungry farmers and a reinforcement of his anticity impulses. In the sanity hearing, Cedar emphasizes the economic-political situation ("an undercurrent of social unrest") and, trying to turn Deeds into a radical, suggests that his project "will rock the foundations of our entire government system." Deeds is about as radical as John Crowe Ransom was when he called for "the self-subsistent or agrarian economy" in 1932, and the government, its foundations unrocked, had been experimenting with subsistence homesteads since 1933. When Deeds finally comes to defend himself, he does so by comparing himself to a man in a boat who has to decide whether to save the drowning (the farmers) or aid those who are simply tired of rowing (his Semple cousins). The greater-need dilemma aside, the heart of his metaphor is the assumption that the good neighbor is the good samaritan. As Capra said years later, he wanted to see with *Deeds* "what statements you could make about a man being his brother's keeper." If the simplicity of Capra's ideas stood in the way of his film's making a sophisticated political point, so too did his need to use this "social-minded" segment as simply another element in the movie's comic pattern. When Deeds is arrested—just as the farmers formally thank him, of course—he sees the insanity charges as a reinforcement of the betrayal he suffered at Babe Bennett's hands, a societal endorsement of personal venality and duplicity. The stage is set for the last two episodes in Deeds's confrontation with the city—his withdrawal from society and his return.

In her review of *Deeds*, Regina Crewe, who liked the film for the most part, began to get nervous toward the end because "they're making some sort of symbolic character of Mr. Cooper, and this part isn't amusing." Riskin and Capra certainly provide lines and significant shots enough to suggest that Crewe is right. "I'm crucifying him," Babe Bennett says to her friend Mabel, who answers that "people have been crucified before." Later, when Babe tries to get in to see Deeds, Cobb snarls, "You crucified him for a couple of stinking headlines." Like the only other crucifiee likely to be called to mind by Mabel's answer to Babe, Deeds refuses to defend himself, and Capra elevates his silence to iconography by shooting Deeds in silhouette against the window, unmoved, unmoving. There is an earlier hint both of Deeds's behavior and Capra's visualization of it in the scene in which, having confirmed Cobb's unmasking of Mary Dawson, Deeds goes silent and moves to the window where the camera catches him in accusatory profile. Ironic capital could be made of the fact that the judge in the sanity hearing is played by H. B. Warner, a former Christ—in Cecil B. DeMille's *The King of Kings* (1927)—but the apparently intentional Deeds/Christ analogy is no real use to the film. Deeds's withdrawal is like that of Panama (Jack Holt) in Capra's *Flight* (1929), in which his disillusionment sends him to sulk in his tent until, convinced that Lefty (Ralph Graves) is a true friend, he flies to the latter's rescue. "Why shouldn't he keep quiet?" Babe asks rhetorically and then explains to the hearing that Deeds's words were always turned against him by reporters, among whom she was the worst offender.

At the hearing, Deeds refuses to speak at all while Cedar uses Babe's articles, a parade of witnesses, a psychiatric expert to prove that Deeds is crazy. As the psychiatrist performs, using roller-coaster charts to illustrate the nature of manic depression, Deeds's heretofore immobile face is invaded with disbelief, not so much a smile as a grimace brought on by a slight downturn of one side of his mouth. Although the audience knows that he is back among the living, he persists in silence and the judge, who has been sympathetic to him throughout, is about to assign him to an asylum when another outburst from Babe gives him a chance to invite her to the stand. In an attempt to undermine her testimony, Cedar gets her to admit—she is under oath—that she loves Deeds. It is this admission that frees Deeds, of course, but before he can speak, first the editor, then Cobb, then a representative group of the farmers stand up to give their support. With so much evidence that the world is not as unreliable as the Cedars, Deeds decides, echoing the editor and Cobb, "to get in my two-cents worth." He defends his eccentricities by comparing them to the tics that he sees among the people in the hearing room. He gets the Faulkner sisters (Margaret Seddon, Margaret McWade), whom Cedar has imported from Mandrake Falls to use against him, to admit that everyone in the court, including the judge, is "pixilated." He explains his program with the farmers rationally and caps the explanation with the audience-condoned irrationality of the punch to Cedar's jaw. The judge, unmoved by the violence, declares him "The sanest man who ever walked into this court." There is no contest really—Cedar and company are sitting ducks—but the audience has been teased so long that Deeds's folksy bravura is accepted (and intended) as the victory of the good guys over the bad guys. The crowd goes wild and carries Deeds in triumph on their shoulders. Babe, lost in the confusion, sits sniffling in the deserted courtroom until Deeds runs in and sweeps her into his arms. Fade out on the Faulkner sisters and their insistence that the lovers are "pixilated."

In 1938, Ben Ray Redman, just back from an apparently frustrating period as executive assistant to an unidentified studio head, wrote an article which emphasized Hollywood's tendency to sidestep issues. *Mr. Deeds Goes to Town* was daring enough to admit "that there are those who have and those who have not" he said; "but the 'comedy angle' was entrusted with the burden of blanketing the picture's more serious implications." His remark reinforces one of the reigning clichés about movies in the 1930s: that they provided escape for audiences who were seriously troubled in their own lives. Of course, they did. One of the primary functions of popular art at all times is to find metaphorical solutions to real problems. By substituting the personal for the larger social dislocation, such art can and is expected to dish up the happy ending that is so hard to come by in real life. In *The Cinema of Frank Capra*, Leland A. Poague adds a touch of class to that aesthetic fact by invoking F. M. Cornford and Northrop Frye, by relating the Capra plots to Frye's "comic mythos." The continuing appeal of Capra's films may well lie in their place on the classic comic line which preoccupies Poague, but in the 1930s his escape endings had political significance too.

The happy ending of *Deeds*, the hero's apparent victory over greed and selfishness, functions as the kind of political statement most clearly revealed by Walt Disney's *Three Little Pigs* (1933) and the hit song, "Who's Afraid of the Big Bad Wolf?" which swept the country when the cartoon was released. After the despair and the sense of helplessness that weighed on the country at the beginning of the 1930s, a new mood began to take over. The official voice of the New Deal, middle-class plays and fiction, radical literature—all shared an assumption that solutions were possible. *Mr. Deeds Goes to Town* did not and could not have been expected to solve the problems of the farmer made landless by the Depression, but when the film allowed Deeds to escape "the looney bin," as Redman so genteely put it, and win Babe Bennett, it became part of the atmosphere of social optimism that prevailed despite the deprivation and the suffering of the period. Although it was probably not what Capra meant when he called his film "social-minded," choosing to be "pixilated" is a political act.

Notes

1. According to both Riskin (Jerry D. Lewis, "Top Story Man," *Collier's* 107 [March 29, 1941], 84) and Capra (Richard Schickel, *The Men Who Made the Movies*, New York, Atheneum, 1975, pp. 68–69), the model for Dickson was not a fictional banker but the very real A. P. Giannini, whom Riskin describes as "an interesting man who believed in lending money on a man's character if he didn't have the ordinary bank's idea of security." It is difficult to think of the Bank of America (then, the Bank of Italy) as an institution built on personal banking, but, as Bob Thomas makes clear in *King Cohn* (New York, Putnam's, 1967, pp. 30, 78), it was the friendly neighborhood support of Harry Cohn and Columbia.

2. A son's greeting to a mother, waiting for word from her absent boy, the Riskin/Capra/Deeds lines are so unlike greeting card verse, in style and in content, that they are not really parody of the genre. They would be more suitable as a joke about an aspiring greeting-card versifier who could not find the proper voice, and Deeds, we are told, is a success at the trade. Kelland has the same problem in "Opera Hat," for his offerings are also too outrageous.

3. Capra seems to accept Deeds's view of the matter in his casting. When we finally meet the members of the firm we find that the other two Cedars are played by Pierre Watkin and Stanley Andrews, actors as tall as Dumbrille and with the same edge of elegant nastiness, and Budington is played by tiny Arthur Hoyt, whom Capra had used earlier in *American Madness* and *It Happened One Night*.

4. For a more detailed discussion of this phenomenon, see the chapter on *Libeled Lady*, particularly pp. 219–21.

5. Capra and Riskin also borrow from *Blonde* the scene in which Deeds assembles the staff to test the echo in the grand hall. Stew Smith and the butler (Halliwell Hobbes) play such a scene in the earlier movie, and the version in *Deeds* ends with the butler (Barnett Parker) raising a final echo for himself, just as the butler does in *Blonde*. It is a familiar enough joke even before *Blonde*. Pike (Will Rogers) calls trains to test the echo in the entrance hall of "our chateau" in *They Had to See Paris* (1929), and Johnny Case uses an echo joke to make fun of the Seton mansion in Philip Barry's 1928 play, *Holiday*.

6. Pangborn is given a tiny bit of business which has nothing to do with the scene but is a good example of the kind of character touch that Capra liked to use. Marooned in a sea of contention, momentarily without occupation as Deeds faces the problem of his uncle's alleged wife, Pangborn, as though to judge the material, reaches out and

lightly touches the lapel of the angry lawyer's overcoat. The gesture comes quickly, is so underemphasized that it is easy to miss, but, once seen, it takes on a significance beyond anything that Capra intended. It is a better advertisement for Capra the director than the woolly ideas that encumber his later films.

My Man Godfrey

· 1936 ·

"La Cava isn't much interested in plot—as plot," Quentin Reynolds wrote in 1938. "He is interested in the way people behave under ordinary and extraordinary conditions." Those lines may seem more appropriate to *Stage Door* (1937), the immediate trigger for the Reynolds comment, than to *My Man Godfrey*, stuffed as it is with a great many stories stumbling toward denouement and with the kind of character that gave "screwball comedy" its good name. Yet, in Gregory La Cava's hands, the characters become more than the comic stereotypes on which they are based, become, as *Time* said in its review, "the most completely realistic set of rich crazy people seen on the screen for some time." William Powell, who played the title role, later said, "Probably no one ever lived who was like Godfrey. But La Cava . . . made the man seem quite plausible." La Cava put the emphasis elsewhere: "Give me real people to work with, people like Bill Powell and Carole Lombard, and we'll give you a picture. . . . real people, not dressed-up puppets."

La Cava's indifference to plot as plot can be seen in *Godfrey* in his handling of the story of the missing pearls. Cornelia, the bratty daughter of the rich family for whom Godfrey works, hides her pearls beneath his mattress where the police will presumably find them and punish him for not being properly responsive to her advances. In conventional jewel-robbery films, of which William Powell saw his share, the director tends to treat the jewels as central figures, but no

---

Godfrey as "the forgotten man." William Powell, Carole Lombard. (*My Man Godfrey*, Universal, 1936. The Museum of Modern Art/Film Stills Archive.)

such thing in *Godfrey*. How and when Godfrey discovered and removed the pearls is never shown. Observant moviegoers will have
noticed that when Cornelia plants the jewels, she first pulls open a
bureau drawer which she leaves open and then, having turned to the
mattress, she only half straightens the cover on the bed. The fastid-
iousness of Godfrey, established in his manner, his dress, and his
speech, as well as in the austerity of his room, explains why he would
have discovered the pearls, but there is no "oh-ho" from the camera,
concentrating on the open drawer, the wrinkled spread. We never
even see Godfrey return to his room. Perhaps La Cava wants to tease
the audience in the search scene, in which a presumably tipsy Godfrey
helps the police hunt for the jewels (there is a lovely shot across the
detectives at the bed which picks up a befuddled Godfrey looking into
a vase of flowers), but the emotional texture of the scene makes it
necessary that Cornelia, who insists that they look under the mattress,
be the recipient of the unwelcome surprise. The comic focus of the
scene is on Godfrey, the character emphasis on Cornelia and her
father, who, on Cornelia's "But they must be there," realizes that
something fishy is afoot and gets rid of the detectives. The pearls and
an explanation eventually emerge, but it is obvious that La Cava is
interested in Cornelia's jewels only as a contributive but not very
important element in the tangle of plots which make up *My Man
Godfrey*. The story of a derelict picked up in a shack settlement at the
city dump and turned into a butler for the rich and zany Bullock family,
Godfrey is five movies at once, all of them rooted in popular drama and
film.

THE BATTY FAMILY STORY. The reviewers in at least four of the New
York City papers—*Times, American, Sun, Daily News*—were reminded
of *Three-Cornered Moon* (1933), although why so tepid a comedy stuck
in their minds for three years I do not know. *Moon* is the story of the
cunningly irresponsible Rimplegars of Brooklyn and how, wiped out
in the crash, they cope with the Depression. To suggest a real setting
for the silliness, the director, Elliot Nugent, uses a Depression mon-
tage and a nasty scene in which the man in the shoe factory (Sam
Hardy) indicates that Elizabeth (Claudette Colbert) can keep her job
only if she has sex with him, but when the Rimplegars—Elizabeth, her
three brothers, her mother (Mary Boland in a Billie Burke role)—start
to do their crazy family bits, it as though the director, the performers,
the film itself ran up a flag proclaiming, "Now, we will be funny." The
artificial effect is heightened by the fact that the movie is so obviously a
filmed play, based on the Gertrude Tonkonogy comedy that had a
moderate success on Broadway early in 1933. The Bullocks, in contrast,
are simply a family that behaves outrageously, each member certain

that he or she alone is rational. La Cava, unlike Nugent, knows how to use the strong personalities of the performers—Eugene Pallette, Alice Brady, Carole Lombard, Gail Patrick—to present the Bullocks, never to allow the kind of complicity between actor and audience that often takes place in the theater but which works in the movies only with comedians like the Marx Brothers who are never really intended to become their characters. One went to the movies to see Lombard, of course, but not to see Lombard saying, *look, I'm Lombard*.

Convincingly presented or artificially manipulated, "real people" or "dressed-up puppets," rich crazies became standard in 1930s comedies, particularly after the success of *Godfrey*. Mary Gray (Ginger Rogers) in La Cava's *Fifth Avenue Girl* (1939) could say, "Rich people are just poor people with money," but that slight difference has aesthetic consequences. It becomes possible to dress the buffoons elegantly, house them exquisitely, and an audience, faced with the wealth-foolishness combination, could take vicarious pleasure in the luxury, condescend to the well-fed clowns and sympathize with them when their eccentricities were recognized as harmless and/or rectifiable. If the craziness is seen as a function of wealth in the 1930s, it is because irresponsibility in that decade was most easily identified in terms of the cushion that money put under it. The genre is older than the Depression, however, and the specialness of the crazy families in earlier comedies is likely to be seen in artistic rather than financial terms, in such plays as Noel Coward's *Hay Fever* (1925) and the George S. Kaufman–Edna Ferber *The Royal Family* (1927), which was filmed as *The Royal Family of Broadway* (1930).

THE MYSTERIOUS STRANGER STORY. One of the advantages of a houseful of foible-ridden individuals is that the appearance of an outsider can be used as a device for their regeneration. Godfrey serves that function in the La Cava film. It belongs to that group of films and plays in which characters, motivated by their own needs, take up residence in a household where their presence alters the behavior of the family. *Tovarich*, in which two aristocratic Russian émigrés become a live-in couple, is a popular example from the mid-1930s, almost contemporaneous with *Godfrey*. Robert E. Sherwood's adaptation of Jacques Deval's 1933 Parisian success opened in London shortly before the Eric Hatch novel on which *Godfrey* was based began running as a serial in *Liberty*; by the time the Sherwood-Deval play reached New York, the film had been released. I am not suggesting a direct connection; Hatch's aristocratic bum and Duval's hungry aristocrats are simply examples of a long line of servants, children, distant relatives, animals even who work their reformational magic in popular literature and drama. La Cava was so taken with the story that he used it again in

Fifth Avenue Girl, in which Mary Gray brings stability to the wealthy Bordens.

THE MAKING OF GODFREY SMITH. Godfrey Parke, of the Boston Parkes, was so cushioned against any genuine crisis that, after discovering his wife's infidelity, he gave her everything he had and began the slow, suicidal slide toward the river. Saved by the example of his fellow residents at the city dump ("there are two kinds of people. Those who fight the idea of being pushed into the river—and the other kind"), he began to rebuild himself as Godfrey Smith, a reconstruction that he finished by doing an honest job of work as the Bullock butler. This plot, the conventional uncovering of the strong man in the weak shell, is not dramatized in *Godfrey*. It is verbalized. The reason, of course, is that Godfrey's function in the other plots demands that he be a figure exuding authority and assurance.

THE WINNING OF GODFREY SMITH. Irene Bullock gets her Godfrey in still another version of the story of the relentless woman trapping her reluctantly willing man. The editors of *Liberty* presumably saw this as the primary plot, for they named their serialization of the Eric Hatch novel, which was called *My Man Godfrey* in book form, "Irene, the Stubborn Girl,"[1] *Bringing Up Baby* (1938) is a purer example of this genre, its central dramatic action uncluttered by competing plots.

THE DEPRESSION FILM. In the six months that passed between the opening in New York of *Mr. Deeds Goes to Town* and the appearance of *My Man Godfrey*, the reviewers apparently became more responsive to the social nuances of film comedy. Most of the *Godfrey* reviews—unlike those for *Deeds*—commented on the unemployment theme in the La Cava movie. In some cases, *Godfrey* was linked directly to *Deeds*, as in the *Brooklyn Eagle* review, which complained that "like 'Mr. Deeds' the solution offered by the producers for the reclamation of 'the forgotten man' is hilarious [sic] inept." Most of the reviewers simply registered the fact of the serious social theme and shuddered as *News-Week* did when it complained, "Unfortunately, the scenarists . . . retard the action occasionally by expressing their sympathy for the unemployed." Since the film begins on the city dump and ends on the city dump, it is understandable that the reviewers gave some attention to the social frame of the other plots. As for the action-retarding speeches of Godfrey, they are no more direct than the ones that Deeds delivers at the sanity hearing, but Deeds's messages are meshed with something that is happening to him on the screen as we watch; Godfrey's are the result of changes in him that have already occurred. Both films share the personal rather than the institutional approach to social problems.

Four of the five stories described above are present in the Eric Hatch original. "It's surprising how closely the picture follows the novel," Hatch told an interviewer shortly after the movie opened in New York, but that is something of an overstatement. The initial situation—the derelict turned butler—is retained, as are the setting and the characters. Many of the latter are greatly changed—Mr. Bullock, Mrs. Bullock's "protégé" Carlo, the maid Molly—and all of them are strengthened; Godfrey is so bland in Hatch's original that he is almost nonexistent. A number of events, references, lines, suggestions make their way from book to film (only the scavenger-hunt opening is an important borrowing), but that is hardly surprising considering that Hatch had a hand in the screenplay. Much of the detail was altered or junked and one important element added. "They discovered the story had social significance," Hatch said. "I didn't know it had social significance when I wrote it. We didn't know it was in the script either. But I heard it was in the picture, and it is. It surprised me all right." The tone of these remarks may reflect the interviewer—Eileen Creelman, whose later review would regret that the film discovered "social significance, economics" in the last reel—but it suggests the kind of flippancy that occasionally surfaces in Hatch's story. He says of the men who shared the shack village with Godfrey: "All of them belong to that new class of people so absurdly named by some moron who probably wanted to write a song: 'Forgotten Men.'" The sentence is a mildly joking reference to *Gold Diggers of 1933*, in which Joan Blondell and a host of associates sang "Remember My Forgotten Man" and Busby Berkeley staged a war-hero-to-breadline number, but the "moron" seems to needle not Harry Warren and Al Dubin, who wrote the song, but Roosevelt, who had promised to help "the forgotten man at the bottom of the economic pyramid" during the 1932 campaign. I may be placing far too much weight on the line, for I suspect that neither Hatch nor his readers saw in it all the implications I find there. It does, however, suggest that the "light fictioneer," as *Collier's* would call Hatch years later, was consciously separating his work from any kind of social point. Today, Hatch is one of the literary forgotten men; not even *My Man Godfrey*, his most successful book, is available. He is remembered—insofar as he is remembered—because of his connection with the film version of *Godfrey* and as one of the script writers for *Topper* (1937). His minor virtues as a popular writer seem very fragile when one turns again to *My Man Godfrey*. Its cardboard characters, its labored cuteness, its lack of verbal wit suggest that not only the social significance but the comedic success of the film lies primarily with his collaborators—with Morrie Ryskind and Gregory La Cava.

Before Ryskind came to Hatch's Bullocks, he had established himself as a writer for the professionally mad Marx Brothers. He had worked with George S. Kaufman, uncredited, on *The Cocoanuts* (1925) and, credited, on *Animal Crackers* (1928); had adapted both those musicals for the movies (1929, 1930); and, again with Kaufman, had done the screenplay for *A Night at the Opera* (1935). In a 1970 interview, Groucho Marx, dissociating himself from S. J. Perelman, as he often did in his last years, dismissed Perelman as "a dramatist" and cited Kaufman and Ryskind as writers of drama rather than unanchored funny dialogue. In the same interview, speaking of the scene in *Animal Crackers* in which Captain Spaulding (Groucho) and Ravelli (Chico) decide to search the house next door and, finding that there is none, start making plans to build, he said, "We had a fellow named Morrie Ryskind who had a Lewis Carroll quality about him. He could take lunacy and build it up." The lunacy of *Godfrey* is not that of Carroll (unless the disconnected logic of Mrs. Bullock's speeches be seen as distant echoes of Carroll's verbal games) nor that of the Marxes; however outrageous, it has its roots in character, plot, and social setting. Although Ryskind would go on to write successful sentimental screenplays like *Penny Serenade* (1941) and *Claudia* (1943), he had no experience with comedy drama when he came to *Godfrey*, unless Eddie Cantor's *Palmy Days* (1931) can be said to fit that category or unless his contribution to *Ceiling Zero* (1936) be seen as a first attempt at the form.

Ryskind had begun as a writer of light verse and as a literary odd-jobsman. In the latter capacity, for instance, he did a "Fictionalized Version" of *Thou Art the Man* (1920), a Paramount Artcraft film, in which he both told the story and mocked it at the same time—a double effect that let him retain his credentials as a clever young man even while he did hackwork. The poems collected in *Unaccustomed As I Am* (1921), some of them written as early as 1914 when he was still in his teens, are conventional light verse-satirical, gently ironic, tentatively sentimental, occasionally serious. It is the kind of popular poetry that flourished in the 1910s and 1920s, that Christopher Morley and Franklin P. Adams printed in their potpourri columns (Ryskind contributed to "The Conning Tower"), that infested the early issues of the *New Yorker*, the pages of *Judge*, *Life*, *Vanity Fair*. Ryskind was hardly turning out poetry for the ages, but he was finding his place in a milieu which would lead him to Broadway and finally to Hollywood. He contributed his first revue sketch to *The Forty-Niners* (1922), a concoction from the Algonquin Round Table which put him in the company of Kaufman, Heywood Broun, Ring Lardner, Robert Benchley, Dorothy Parker, Robert E. Sherwood, Marc Connelly. By the late 1920s, he was regularly providing lyrics, sketches, and book material for Broadway musicals. In the early 1930s, he was best known not for the Marx Brothers shows but for the satirical musicals he wrote with Kaufman and George and Ira Gershwin—*Strike Up the Band* (1930), *Of Thee I Sing* (1931), *Let 'Em Eat Cake* (1933). As early as 1925, Ryskind had contributed a sketch on the home life of the Coolidges to *Garrick Gaieties*, but it is on the basis of the Kaufman-Gershwin shows that he gained a reputation as a satirist who dealt with contemporary social and political problems. This Ryskind may have had a hand in discovering the "social significance" that Hatch never knew was in his story.

The underlying assumption of both *Of Thee I Sing* and *Let 'Em Eat Cake* is that governments are always corrupt, the public endlessly gullible. This is a sound enough basis on which to stack a pile of jokes drawn from the contemporary scene, but not one on which to build a satiric structure with a consistent political point of view. Insofar as *Godfrey* has one—the triumph of private enterprise that the bum-cum-butler brings to the city dump—it may reflect the distrust of government that was about as close as the musical-comedy philosopher ever came to a political position. In 1932, Ryskind wrote satiric pieces for the *Nation* based on the assumption, generally held by leftists of all persuasions, that Roosevelt and Hoover were indistinguishable. By 1938, when he wrote that he was shunned by Hollywood liberals because he questioned "the Divine Birth of Mr. Roosevelt," he was already en route to the extreme conservatism that marked his activities and his writing in the 1940s and 1950s. This transition may help explain lines in *Godfrey* like Mike's remark at the beginning of the film: "If them cops would stick to their own racket and leave honest guys alone, we'd get somewhere in this country without a lot of this relief and all that stuff." Yet, Mike's sentiments are hardly in conflict with the ideas of Godfrey, and it needs no embryonic right-winger to promulgate the doctrine of Deedsian self-help. It was popular enough in the mid-1930s, particularly in movie houses (see Shirley Temple at work in *Just around the Corner* [1938]).

Gregory La Cava, who was less political than Ryskind, told an interviewer in 1940 that he had no immediate plans for a film: "Lord knows I don't want to do anything weighty, but I'd like a film to have some social significance." The La Cava film that followed—*Unfinished Business* (1941)—is the story of a woman who marries the wrong brother, a romance that only an imaginative critical reading could find socially significant. La Cava's one relentlessly political film is the very odd *Gabriel over the White House* (1933), which the director made for William Randolph Hearst's Cosmopolitan Productions. Cosmopolitan was primarily a means to the glorification of Marion Davies, Hearst's mistress, but in this case the company—presumably Hearst himself—

wanted to peddle ideas rather than celebrate the lady. *Gabriel* is the story of a corrupt president (Walter Huston) who, brushed by the hand of death, reforms and brings peace and prosperity to the troubled country, but does so through a strong presidency that looks very like a dictatorship. Walter Lippmann called it "a dramatization of Mr. Hearst's editorials." If the film is to be taken as a La Cava movie, it will not be for its political content, but because the emergence of the savior president from the amiably tacky politician follows a pattern that can be found in so many of his films: hypnotism makes a man of the milquetoast Elmer Finch (W. C. Fields) in *Running Wild* (1927); a symphony of city sounds—building noises, a typewriter, a squeaking desk chair, the office boy's shoes—sends James Bates (Lee Tracy) back to the carnival where he belongs in *The Half-Naked Truth* (1932); the suicide of Kaye (Andrea Leeds) calls up the real actress in the stagey poseur of Terry Randall (Katharine Hepburn) in *Stage Door*. The social point in *Godfrey* seems less central to La Cava's work than the hero's discovery of himself.

The difficulty of assigning the political part—or any part—of the film to Ryskind lies in La Cava's improvisational method. A veteran of the silent film (he first attracted attention for the Richard Dix comedies he directed in 1925 and 1926), he carried the standard practice of those days into the talkies. William Powell said of La Cava's direction of *Godfrey*, "Every morning he'd give us some dialogue that he'd written during the night, and it was good dialogue." La Cava, whose name also appears as writer on many of the films he directed, was quite capable of turning out dialogue, but Powell's account may be a rather specific statement about the more general fact that La Cava did not feel comfortable tied to a script, that he wanted to feel free to go where the story and the characters took him. There were so many sprightly accounts in 1941 of his day-to-day script-making—*Life, Time, Christian Science Monitor*—that they read like plants from the Universal publicity office, pushing *Unfinished Business*. There is fact in the flack, however, as can be seen in the message David O. Selznick sent to John Wharton in 1937, when he was considering trying to sign La Cava to a producer-director contract with Selznick International: "La Cava would drive me crazy as a director with the rewriting he does on set, for as you know I don't like any projection-room surprises or shocks, but if he were his own producer we could take the chance that he would shock himself." He was his own producer on *Godfrey*, but—or so he told an interviewer—he wore whiskers and was stern as producer and "clowned as director." Hatch said that he spent three months in Hollywood working with La Cava and Ryskind on the script of *Godfrey*. "We put down as little as possible in writing," he told Eileen Creelman. "Greg works that way. He made few changes while he was shooting. But we did most of our work by discussion rather than writing." When Hatch returned to New York—before shooting began—he bought a dress shirt, "tore off one cuff, and mailed it to Greg as the final shooting script." Variations on this off-the-cuff joke would turn up in later La Cava articles, but this is evidently where it began. Presumably, once Hatch had departed, La Cava and Ryskind continued to work together on the film. In answer to a 1970 questionnaire from *Film Comment*, Ryskind listed La Cava and George Stevens as the two most congenial directors he ever worked with. "I cannot complain that my work was tampered with," he said. "If La Cava and I disagreed on the thrust of a scene, we'd shoot it both ways." He also said "I usually worked on set with director," and La Cava had told Bosley Crowther back in 1937— speaking of *Stage Door*, in a remark that may also apply to *Godfrey*— "Morrie Ryskind came in as my scenarist shortly before we began shooting. And together we put the picture into shape on the set." The published script of *Godfrey* is so close to the finished picture—unlike, say, the version of *It Happened One Night* which John Gassner and Dudley Nichols also printed in *Twenty Best Film Plays*—that it was presumably put together after the movie was finished.

La Cava is a deceptively simple director, for shots like the one with Godfrey and the vase of flowers do not call attention to themselves. He is capable of flamboyance, as in the slow-motion sequence in *Feel My Pulse* (1928), in which the gangsters, felled by a container of chloroform, collapse in a wonderfully lazy dance, one of the last to settle— plainly a professional acrobat—floating in a marvelous back flip. Or in the opening of *The Half-Naked Truth*, in which the camera is with the high-dive man at the top of the tower and follows his leap into the water below. Even this is trickiness with a purpose, an indication of the razzle-dazzle that will carry Bates and Teresita (Lupe Velez) from the carnival to success in New York. The neatness with which La Cava makes his effects can be illustrated by one of the few good scenes in *Gabriel over the White House*. The president and his nephew (Dickie Moore) play around his office, hunting for a hidden marshmallow, their half-heard dialogue an accompaniment to the action, while in the aural foreground a radio carries an impassioned speech on behalf of the unemployed. It is a likable scene, but unattractive in the context of the president's implicit indifference to the victims of the Depression.

There are three even simpler examples of La Cava effects in *So's Your Old Man* (1926). This film, like most of La Cava's, has occasional longueurs, most noticeably the extended exposition scene between Sam Bisbee (Fields) and the Princess (Alice Joyce) on the train. I can forgive the tediousness of that scene, however, for the sake of the mouth-to-ear sequence in which large close-ups that show only part of the faces illustrate how gossip about Bisbee and the strange lady spreads through the town. La Cava then uses a number of shots to indicate the way in which his fellow townsmen react to Bisbee, who has no idea of what he is supposed to have done. The best of these shows him walking toward three substantial ladies. As they approach in rank, spread across the sidewalk, they suddenly wheel to the left and file past him, forming an arc that emphasizes Bisbee in isolation. The third example presents the juveniles (Buddy Rogers, Kittens Reichert), who are temporarily separated by the refusal of the hero's mother to let her son court the Bisbee daughter. We get a shot of the young man, mooning at the Bisbee fence, and one of the girl, languishing in the swing, until she realizes he is there and pretends to read a book. Visual story-telling at its most precise.

The scene with the juveniles is hardly complex (what young-love subplot would be in a silent comedy?), but La Cava manages not only to signal a conventional situation but to suggest the involvement of real people. His preoccupation with character obviously reaches back to the beginning of his career. The scene in *So's Your Old Man* in which Mrs. Murchison stands at the door of her limousine, delivering a nonstop harangue at Bisbee, not only establishes the character—the stridency in the genteel social leader—but suggests that Julia Ralph, had she had the advantage of sound, might have proved a Fields nagger in the Kathleen Howard–Cora Witherspoon league. By the 1930s, La Cava had so developed his sense of character and of the relationship between character and performer that his approach might safely be dignified as aesthetic theory. Not that he used such terms, but in interview after interview in the mid-1930s, he identified—a sentence here, an answer there—his methodology. "I don't believe the screen is a great medium for acting," he said in 1935. "But it does reflect personality." Jean Dixon, who played Molly in *Godfrey*, reminiscing about La Cava after his death, said that she was warned, when she first went to the director for a role, not to mention her Broadway experience. It was not until she reported to the set—the unidentified film was presumably *She Married Her Boss* (1935)—that she discovered that the eight leading performers were all unprofessed stage veterans. It is a nice story and a reflection of La Cava's distrust of actors—that is, of technique—but I doubt that La Cava was quite as innocent of his performers' pasts as Dixon suggested. A director would have had to live in total isolation not to know that Helen Hayes, whom he directed in *What Every Woman Knows* in 1934, was a stage star, or that Alice Brady had crowned a long theatrical career with her performance as Lavinia in Eugene O'Neill's *Mourning Becomes Electra* (1931). Stage performers who made the transition to the screen needed neither to hide nor to discard their technique, but to discover that the camera called for something else as well. Brady knew this long before she came to La Cava and *Godfrey*. "A real actress has to have a method, not be just herself," she said in 1914, when she was a new star on Broadway, but in 1925, after her first film career had come to an end, she wrote, "I think a much stronger personality is necessary to succeed on the screen than on the stage."

For La Cava it was not the strength of the personality but the usable elements in it that counted. "The temperamental player's subconscious mind is always working," he said in an article in *Photoplay*. "Vivid imaginations, elemental emotions. Such players can be aroused to the necessary emotional pitch and feeling." His example comes from his work with Claudette Colbert on *Private Worlds* (1935). He considered her a "nice girl," a type who "never becomes a splendid actress until she overcomes conventional thinking and acting." They fought over how a scene should be played ("Why couldn't I see the feminist viewpoint?") and then he let her loose to play it her way, which she did but with the anger of their argument coloring her performance. His use of terms like "subconscious" and "psycho-analyzing" are somewhat misleading, for what he seems to have done as a director is not so much to excavate the hidden self as to recognize and take advantage of that aspect of a performer's personality that best suited the character. Pandro S. Berman, the producer of *Stage Door*, said of La Cava's work with Katharine Hepburn, "He saw her eagerness, awkwardness, enthusiasm, grace, and purity of spirit. Every word of dialogue he wrote for her was based on her own odd, exaggerated speech patterns." Commenting on Hepburn as an actress in 1938, La Cava said, "She's a mechanized actress. . . . She's got to think a thing through. She's got to arrive at a situation by intellect." He was not so much criticizing in these remarks ("She is good"), as describing a method other than his own. The interesting thing is that, looking at Hepburn's Terry Randall, one realizes that La Cava used not only the qualities Berman listed but the intense intellection itself. What may be a neutral quality or even a virtue in the performer is transformed in the character, particularly in the early part of the film, into abrasiveness, an almost accidental callousness.

Although there is not the kind of specific testimony that one gets about the La Cava–Hepburn interaction, William Powell's performance as Godfrey seems a direct reflection of the La Cava method. Although the Powell remark on La Cava quoted early in this chapter gives no indication of it, his comments in the same article on his customary approach to a scene suggest that he would have had trouble adjusting to the way the director worked: "It doesn't come natural to me to memorize a couple of pages of dialogue in a few minutes. I take that scene to bed with me and read it and read it. I figure out every bit of business that might go well with that scene. That's all subject to the director's approval, of course. But I can't hop right on a set and ad lib bits of business." In fact, according to La Cava, Powell at first "took violent exception" to the director's day-to-day approach, but, after having blown some preprepared lines, he became a convert. Powell had been making movies since 1922, when he made his film debut in the John Barrymore *Sherlock Holmes*, so he can hardly have been a stranger to improvisation; he had even acted for La Cava before in *Feel My Pulse*. Yet, Powell regularly emphasized the way he worked out his character before he faced the camera—a legacy, perhaps, of his ten years in stock and on Broadway (1912–1922). A reporter in *Screenland*, presumably having been primed by Powell, wrote in 1930, "He studies his characterization long before he attempts to play it. Therefore, he knows what his character would do under any circumstance." Elinor Hughes made a similar point in a less flattering way when she said that Powell lacked good looks and so "chose to use his brains, since his profile was out of the question." The weight of all these quotations may suggest a Powell who did not need and could not have worked with La Cava, but there is a difference between those at the beginning and those at the end of the paragraph. The early ones suggest a concern with lines, business, the detail of the moment; the later ones a preoccupation with character. This preoccupation is the meeting ground for Powell and La Cava.

To find Godfrey La Cava's way is to find that quality in Powell that can be used to modify the prevailing screen image of the actor. He had gone through several stages in his career. A celebrated villain in his last years on stage and in the silents, he had become, when film let him use his voice, a villain who won audience sympathy despite (or because of) his elegant nastiness. This transition can be seen taking place as early as *Feel My Pulse*. When his Phil Todd menaces Barbara Manning (Bebe Daniels) in her bedroom, he is the leering villain of old, but in his earlier attempt to win the girl with words, his wonderfully persuasive way of talking, at once sincere and mocking, suggests the manner that will become familiar when his voice can actually be heard; at this point, it is the cock of his head, the set of his mouth, the use of his body that conveys the later Powell. Paramount would turn him into a hero by casting him as Philo Vance in a series of films beginning with *The Canary Murder Case* (1929), but it was not until he got to MGM and *The Thin Man* (1934) that he found the persona that made Quentin

Reynolds call his *Collier's* piece on Powell "Smoothie." "I'm supposed to drip with polish and slide with suavity," he said in 1931, denying the image. After *The Thin Man*, adjectives like "charming, gay, casual" (from Reynolds) began to join the "suave" that had haunted Powell's reviews for years. Insouciant is what the character is—clearly intelligent, but giving the impression, usually false, that he is almost too relaxed to put his mind to work. It shows physically in a kind of looseness that his body suggests despite the fact that he carries himself with the elegance necessary to do justice to his well-tailored clothes. This is Nick Charles and Bill Chandler in *Libeled Lady*, but it is not Godfrey, although they all have a certain urbanity in common. This character can be seen only once in the La Cava film when Godfrey comes in a little drunk and jauntily crosses the kitchen singing, "Blithely," as the screenplay says, "For tomorrow may bring sorrow/ So tonight let us be gay!"[2]

According to an article in *Motion Picture*, Powell leaped at the chance to play Nick Charles because "the detective was a person he appreciated and understood. They talked the same language." There are obviously points at which William Powell and Nick Charles touch, but when one reads through a great many fan magazine articles on Powell, a different person emerges. One does not go to such magazines in search of biographical and psychological truth, of course, but cumulatively a little of it must appear. Whether Powell is talking about women or his art, repeating familiar anecdotes about his early career or making up new ones, being funny or being serious, two qualities come across. One of them would be called ponderousness if we were not talking about the professionally casual William Powell, and the other a kind of self-mockery that seems to hedge every platitude. These are what La Cava must have seen in Powell and helped him give to Godfrey. Gravity is what Powell's Godfrey has, and a kind of wryness that allows him to indicate that he knows how ludicrous the whole charade is. Surrounded as he is by the flamboyant Bullocks, Godfrey sometimes seems to be little more than a reaction character. Yet, he is the moral center of the movie and the stability that keeps the craziness of the Bullock scenes from collapsing into disintegration, ideational or aesthetic. Such a character could quickly turn prig if he did not see the humor of the whole thing, and Godfrey conveys the necessary awareness of self and situation. There may have been hints of such a character in some scenes in *The Great Ziegfeld*, which had been released earlier in 1936, but they tend to be weighed down with the solemnity that infects show-business biographies on screen. In *My Man Godfrey*, an important variation on the Powell image really takes shape—one that he could build on later for *Life with Father* and *The Senator Was Indiscreet* (both 1947)—and La Cava seems to have been the catalyst if not the creator. As Powell once said, "Actually that was La Cava's picture."

La Cava's picture begins with an art deco cityscape with flashing lights (the credits), and then the camera moves from the studied artificiality of that opening to the city dump, still stylized, all light and shadow, and finally to a realistic shot of the back of a truck dumping a load of trash. Charles Previn's sprightly music under the credits slows, then stops to mark the transition. The screenplay says that "shabby men are seen searching the ground for something of value," but the phrase is too genteel. Garbage pickers are what we see, and it takes no strong penchant for symbols to make the connection between one kind of refuse and another. The harshness implicit in the juxtaposition is taken away almost as soon as it is presented. The film has a social point to make, but it will not do so through photographic realism. This human dumping ground is where Godfrey discovered that there are salvable virtues even in a flaccid Parke of Boston, and the special quality of the place is established at the expense of the social symbol. It is made obvious in the cheerful opening exchange between Godfrey and Mike (Pat Flaherty)—by the corny joke about prosperity around the corner and Mike's mock-elegant farewell ("Bon soir"). By the time Mike exits, the audience has taken in the fact that Godfrey is unshaven, dressed in tattered clothes—a clear violation of the William Powell image—but the casualness of the exchange and the contemplative way he sits by the fire suggest that this is an exterior state, easily alterable.

He is ready to face the Bullock girls, who are about to descend on his home in search of "the forgotten man," the final item in the charity scavenger hunt in which, characteristically, the sisters are on opposing sides. Cornelia arrives first, with Faithful George in tow—an innocuous character innocuously played by Robert Light—but Irene gets there in time to watch her sister's humiliation at Godfrey's hands, to laugh happily as she backs away from him and falls over an ash-pile: "I've wanted to do that ever since I was six years old." In this first scene the characters of the two women are quickly established, their basic differences and their rivalry. In the Hatch original, Irene is the older sister, but here, where nothing specific is said about their ages, she appears to be the younger. I called Cornelia "bratty" at the beginning of this chapter, influenced presumably by Godfrey's attack on her in the cocktail-bar scene—"the Park Avenue brat—a spoiled child who has grown up in ease and luxury, who always had her own way"—but it is Irene who behaves like an unhappy child through much of the film. Cornelia is proud, disdainful, unpleasant, but apparently self-possessed. Irene, on the other hand, is not only given to childish tantrums but to a child's openness, a willingness to accept people (Godfrey, the bum, in this scene) without any thought of class, money, milieu. It is true that she is not very bright, but her ignorance of the simplest economic and social facts becomes a kind of innocence. It is this quality—and her capacity for excitement—that is shown at the beginning: the good child, not the bad one.

These two women are familiar figures, traditional rivals for the man who, refusing to abide by empty conventions, is rejected by the rigid, condescending, often greedy sister and so falls into the arms of the more attractive one. In *Holiday* (1930), Linda Seton (Ann Harding) goes off with Johnny Case (Robert Ames) when her sister Julia (Mary Astor) makes it clear that she wants him not on her own terms but on those of her banker father (Katharine Hepburn picks up Cary Grant after Doris Nolan dumps him in the more celebrated 1938 version of Philip Barry's play). In *Broadway Bill* (1934), Alice Higgins (Myrna Loy) wins the husband of her sister Margaret (Helen Vinson), when Dan (Warner Baxter) deserts the family business for the racetrack. In *Mississippi* (1935), Lucy Rumford (Joan Bennett) sticks by and finally wins Tom Grayson (Bing Crosby), when he refuses to fight a duel for her haughty sister Elvira (Gail Patrick). Both women have to be very beautiful, and, for the sake of contrast, one should be blonde, one brunette. The losing sister usually has the edge in elegance, a plastic brilliance that momentarily clouds the hero's eye, keeps him from recognizing that Miss Right is prettier, inside and out. This is not the precise plot of *Godfrey*, although Cornelia does make a play for Irene's butler at one point, but the types fit the specifications exactly.

Gail Patrick had already been nastily brunette to Joan Bennett's endearing blondeness in *Mississippi*, but it was in *Godfrey*, paired with Lombard, that she established herself as a type. She came to Hollywood in 1932, one of the finalists in a contest to choose the Panther Woman for *The Island of Lost Souls*. Kathleen Burke got the role (and seemed more foolish than feline in it), but Patrick was given a contract by Paramount and put in *The Mysterious Rider* (1933), one of that company's frequent remakes of the Zane Grey novel. The recurring Patrick story of the 1930s is a transformation tale about how the pretty but gauche Alabama college girl was turned into the resplendent Patrick of the second half of the decade. Johnny Engstead, who did still photography at Paramount, "had more to do with developing me than anyone else," she told *Motion Picture*. He used her in a great deal of studio filler-publicity and steered her to beauty experts who remade her image and a voice coach who helped her get rid of "an accent like Pick and Pat," as Kyle Crichton called it. "By 1936, the true Gail Patrick began to emerge," a *Photoplay* beauty column said. A press release back in 1932 explained that the new contract player had not won the contest because "she hasn't the panther qualities," but the emergent Patrick was panther enough—sleek, glistening, dangerous. These distinguishing marks are evident in her Cornelia, but La Cava is interested in the vulnerability beneath the nastiness. He never allows her the icy bitchiness she has in *Stage Door* (where Ginger Rogers is her blonde antagonist). Even when she is being most outrageous—when she demands that Godfrey clean her shoe with his handkerchief, for instance—there is a defiant note in her that prepares us for the moment near the end when she crumbles under his kindness and understanding. Cornelia cries and Patrick, who has seemed all surface, makes us believe it. In the opening scene with Godfrey, however, she treats him as though he were a commodity; prouder than he is hungry, he frightens her away.

Little sister Lombard, five years older than Patrick, had already made twenty-two movies—not counting the two-reelers she did for Mack Sennett—by the year Patrick tried to turn panther. She had even done one with La Cava in her Pathé days—*Big News* (1929), a newspaper melodrama in which she played the wife of a heavy-drinking reporter (Robert Armstrong). In Sennett's *Run, Girl, Run* (1928), there is a hint of the Lombard to come in the way she walks onto the field, her arms swinging lightly, or sits up abruptly and shouts (in a silent) at Daphne Pollard. Although I can see the accomplished comedian of the last half of the 1930s burried under the baby fat of Sennett's flirtatious athlete, I do not know the early Lombard talkies well enough to testify to any prophecy they may contain. Leonard Maltin, whose general admiration for the actress gives special weight to his negative words, says, "Knowing what we do about her talent, beauty, and vivacity, it's frustrating to see a drab, lifeless Lombard in a succession of films that range from dull to mediocre."

It was customary in the mid-1930's to see John Barrymore, Lombard's costar in *Twentieth Century* (1934) as the key to her release as a performer. Barrymore "taught her to forget herself and to put her every thought into the thing she was doing," said a typical fanmagazine piece. More recently, with directors in the ascendant, Howard Hawks recalled how he convinced her to quit acting, to do, as Lily Garland, what she would do as Carole Lombard. Whether it was Barrymore or Hawks, the combination of the two of them, or the trigger of a flamboyant role in a good Ben Hecht–Charles MacArthur script, what the playing of Lily Garland taught Lombard was to put into her character some of the electricity, the irreverence, the vulgarity, the sense of hilarity that marked her as a not very private person, a pet subject of the gossip columns. She would grow as a comedian after *Twentieth Century*; her demure and troubled girl at the beginning of the film lacks the subtlety of the Hazel Flagg we see at the beginning of *Nothing Sacred* (1937). Yet, much of her comic equipment is already on display in the earlier film—the calculated hysterics, the shouts of outrage or triumph, the sponge-faced crying, the overacting of fake sentiment, the physicality. Lombard, the comedian, might almost be said to have been born in the scene in which Lily rears back across the bed and uses her feet to spar with Oscar (Barrymore), her legs going in little peddling movements which turn into real jabs toward him— aimed too high, for the Production Code's sake, although Barrymore cradles his crotch at one point to signal the true target. The almost grotesque devices that I have just listed may seem appropriate only to a grandly temperamental star like Lily Garland, but Lombard continued to use them, to modulate them to fit a wide range of characters who share a desire to reorganize the world around them, to make it understand their particular graces even if they have to shout, cry, and punch their way to the center of attention. Thus, Irene Bullock, trying to catch Godfrey's eye, is a sister to Lily Garland, trying to maim Oscar Jaffe. In later roles, the Lombard characters would be forced to undergo abrupt emotional shifts, but the ground is already laid in *Twentieth Century*. In one brief scene Lily moves from patently fake sincerity to a very real tantrum to an undercut throwaway; she begins by playing up to George (Ralph Forbes at his dullest), but moves to a scream which she cuts off abruptly to order the maid out of her way.

In a volume called *Breaking into the Movies*, which came out in 1927, the year Lombard went to work for Sennett, Louise Fazenda, a Sennett Bathing Beauty of an earlier generation, wrote a piece called "The Comedienne," in which she discussed the conscious choice that a performer must make if she decides to be funny: "she must reconcile herself to the loss of any praises her beauty might elicit; she must erase the last vestige of physical vanity, and replace it with pride in her particular type of work." Fazenda overstates the case even for her generation—think of Mabel Normand—and her stricture is particularly out of place in a decade in which a woman did not have to look like Marie Dressler to be praised as a comedian. Yet, the remarks are somehow appropriate to Lombard. One of the loveliest women in Hollywood in the 1930s, she consciously made herself awkward, ungainly, strident in ways that her glamorous fellow comedians usually avoided. As Regina Crewe said in her review of *Godfrey*, "Not every star of Carole's magnitude would go so goofy for her art." One of my favorite images of Lombard is in *True Confession* (1937). In the scene in which Helen learns that her priggishly honest husband (Fred MacMurray) has refused to take the case of a man because he is guilty, Lombard lets out her marvelous whine-scream, and its grating quality is somehow intensified by the fact that she is shot head-on across a typewriter as she holds the telephone in one hand, a half-eaten sandwich in the other. There is one superb example in *Godfrey* of the kind of gorgeous grossness of which Lombard was capable. It comes at the end of the ludicrous party during which Irene has elaborately communicated her heartbreak to Godfrey, who remains intent on his professional duties as butler. Through her mother's wafty comments and the ponderous confusions of Tommy Gray (Alan Mowbray in one of his expert embodiments of fatuousness), she learns—or thinks she learns—that Godfrey has an Indian wife and five children, and in retaliation announces her marriage to Charlie Van Rumpel (Grady Sutton). When Godfrey politely congratulates her, she bursts into tears and runs and sits on the stair, watching Godfrey through the railing. We and the camera look back at her—a prisoner in her self-made jail—as she cries and chews on her black handkerchief, pulling it down across her chin as she holds it in her teeth. Then she takes it out of her mouth and wipes her nose on it.

Although Lombard was willing to make herself ugly, she also saw to it that her beauty was not kept secret. According to Leonard Maltin, Travis Banton designed twenty-four gowns for her to wear in *Godfrey*, and Ted Tetzlaff, her favorite cameraman, was on hand to see that she was properly photographed. She first worked with Tetzlaff when she was loaned to Columbia for *Brief Moment* in 1933 and again when she did *Lady by Choice* there in 1934. Presumably at her insistence, he did all her films (except for the technicolor *Nothing Sacred*) from *Rumba* (1935) to *Fools for Scandal* (1938); he went on to become the director of a string of unprepossessing movies. In the first scene in *Godfrey*, the fires around the dump become an occasion for chiaroscuro that allows just a little light on Powell, more on Lombard, highlighting her face and her gown, the fine lines of both. In this first scene, then, we get not only the foolishness and the sweetness of the character, but her beauty. All through the film, her physical loveliness is balanced against the way it is allowed to be violated—by blubbery tears, by being stuck under a shower. Sometimes the gorgeousness goes hand-in-hand with the joke. Just before the party scene, hurt the Godfrey has told her never to enter his room, Irene milks every word, every gesture in her attempt to convey the meaninglessness of it all. She stands in the open French doors, one hand resting high on the white frame, her gaze dreamily upward, and then moves to assume the same tragic pose against a tall white pedestal topped by a vine in a large white vase. One hardly needs Cornelia's "I learned it in dramatic school. It's number eight, isn't it?" to emphasize the falsity of the attitude. Yet, Banton's black dress against all that whiteness, Tetzlaff's caressing camera, Lombard's undeniable beauty make something exquisite of a comic moment which La Cava does not hold long, moving quickly on to other poses, other gestures, other insistences that, however beautiful, Irene is much more fascinating in other ways.

"By letting my lips hang open just a trifle, widening my eyes and elevating the eyebrows," Lombard told a *New York Post* interviewer, "I managed to get the expression of foolish expectancy to fit Irene's habit of greeting the most obvious facts of life with breathless surprise and delight." This is the Irene of the initial scene. After a brief conversation that reveals both her obtuseness (she wonders why Godfrey lives on the dump "when there are so many other nice places") and her surprising sensitivity ("I don't want to play any more games with human beings as objects"), Godfrey decides to be her "forgotten man."

The film brings them and us to the Waldorf-Ritz, the fictional substitute for the real Waldorf of the book, and the most impressive scene in the movie. The ballroom is awash with richly dressed men and women who push their way through the pandemonium carrying, dragging, leading (Mrs. Bullock has a goat on a rope) all kinds of animate and inanimate objects that fit Irene's earlier description of a scavenger hunt as a search for "something that nobody wants." At the center of this chaos, a record keeper stands on a high platform, a figure of authority who—wonderfully played by Franklin Pangborn in a mixture of bossiness and hysterical helplessness—comes across as a kind of Lord of Misrule. The scavenger hunt in the film makes a strong satirical comment out of what, in the Hatch original, was little more than an implementing device. LaCava and Ryskind give Godfrey a denunciatory speech, unnecessarily spelling out the significance of a scene that is already obvious in the emptiness at the heart of its cacophony. Besides, they have earlier provided choral comment in the exchange between Bullock and another man at the bar. When his fellow observer-drinker says, "This place slightly resembles an insane asylum," Bullock answers, "Well—all you need to start an asylum is an empty room and the right kind of people." Later, when we and Godfrey move into the Bullock mansion, the craziness of the Bullocks will become domesticated as both the protagonist and the audience attach themselves to the family. Here, the Bullocks seem part of a larger societal madness that a film with a different ending in mind would insist on as more than a momentary social comment. It is difficult to hear poetry in a dramatic context and even more difficult to recognize it, but it is appropriate that when Carlo tries to read to Mrs. Bullock in a later scene, he chooses Tennyson's "The Lotos-Eaters."

The scene in the ballroom, whatever its general satirical point, is also an occasion to meet the other Bullocks. Angelica, the mother, is neither the "elderly woman" of the screenplay nor the "dizzy old gal" Bullock's bar companion calls her. Dizzy, she is, but, in the person of Alice Brady,[3] she is attractive enough to deserve the tipsy Godfrey's compliment later in the movie, "I hope you'll forgive me, madam, but you seem to be looking younger every day." The correctness of Angelica as a character is that she is clearly the mother of both Irene and Cornelia. The discontinuity in her thought processes, the speech that seems to be built on word associations, the sense of almost cosmic irrelevance that hovers over her clearly indicate the source of Irene's mental powers and practices, but she also has Irene's charm much of the time. When it fades, it is because another, thoroughly self-absorbed Angelica—Cornelia's mother—breaks through. She has one of those wretched little dogs with which society ladies were identified in 1930s movies and comic strips, and in one scene, having just read about a murder in the newspaper, she says, "If anyone ever drowned my 'booful' in the bathtub, his mama would be very, very cross, yes she would." Since the audience knows neither murderer nor victim, the dehumanization is abstract, but she displays the same callousness of mind when she says of Irene's infatuation with Godfrey, and in his presence, "He's the only thing she's shown any affection for since her Pomeranian died last summer."

This creature is simply a variation on the kind of character Alice Brady had been playing since her return to the movies in *When Ladies Meet* (1933). After her success in the high art of *Mourning Becomes Electra*, Brady found herself, as Arthur Pollock put it, "happily cast as the light-headed mother" in *Mademoiselle* (1932), a role which presumably led to her call to Hollywood. "When I did my first stage comedy in *Mademoiselle*," she said later in a burst of fiction (John Mason Brown: "Alice Brady returned last evening to the realm of farcical comedy in which she has few peers"), "I hadn't the foggiest notion of how to be funny. . . . I just thought I'd flap my hands about even more than normally and 'talk silly'. I did—and I've lived off of it for six years." There were reviewers—Richard Watts, Jr., John S. Cohen, Jr.—who would have agreed about the amateurishness implicit in her comment; both found her performance in *Should Ladies Behave?* (1933) artificial compared to the inspired silliness of Mary Boland in the Broadway original, Paul Osborn's *The Vinegar Tree* (1930). Anyone who has watched Brady trying to cope with the one-joke character she played in

The Gay Divorcee (1934) knows that she could be pedestrian if either the role or the director let her succumb to mannerism. Laura in *Should Ladies Behave?* is a character with greater potential, at once funny and touching, with an edge of aggression in the foolishness and a hint of mockery in the pathos—as one might expect from a creation of Paul Osborn. Brady never achieves a Laura with substance enough to anchor the comedy or to suggest the possibility of pain. The most successful scene is the one in which Laura imposes a game of Twenty Questions on her unwilling family and guests and disrupts the game while scolding the others for not obeying the rules, a funny sequence which illustrates how impossible the character can be. For the most part she is brisk and brittle whether she is going for laughs or for a possible lump in the throat. In *Godfrey*, however, there is an odd edge of reserve in Angelica's foolishness which suggests, although the role is smaller, a much more substantial character than her Laura. I suspect that much of the credit should go to La Cava.

Angelica is accompanied not only by a goat but by Carlo, her protégé. According to a 1939 article in the *Brooklyn Eagle*, the character was to be an "insidious" gigolo, but Will Hays disapproved; instead, Carlo is the suffering artist appalled at the taint of money, the hungry freeloader always first at table. In the scene in which Bullock first tries to discuss the possibility of financial difficulties, Carlo cries out in artistic pain ("Oh, money, money, money! the Frankenstein monster that destroys souls") and retreats to the window where he remains, back to the room, moaning occasionally, until Angelica calls for him to "come and get some nice hors d'oeuvres"; he turns abruptly and moves briskly to the goodies. In the Hatch original, Godfrey surprises Mrs. Bullock and her Carlo "having a perfect whale of a kissing bee," and not even the adolescent prose disguises the nature of their relationship. In the film, he seems more like what Zoe in Arthur Wing Pinero's *Mid-Channel* (1909) calls a "tame robin." He sings *Otchi tchornia* for Angelica, reads Tennyson to her, escorts her to concerts and on scavenger hunts, is generally on hand, but La Cava never suggests that there are services beyond that. Carlo, despite the Italianate name, speaks with a beguiling Russian accent for he is played by Mischa Auer, who here found the voice and the character that would serve him for the rest of his career.

Auer had been in films since 1928. A photograph of him in the Standard Casting Directory for January 1931, shows him in stock comedy makeup as the "Greckian Ambassador" in *The Royal Bed* (1930). In the June–July 1932 edition, he is mustacheless, all in black, in a soulful pose that seems to call out for serious roles. He had begun to get them—after his fashion. In *Tarzan, the Fearless* (1933), he simply looks disconcerted, as though his mind were somewhere offscreen, while he reads the few portentous lines he has before he releases Tarzan (Buster Crabbe) and his chums from the underground emerald city he rules as high priest. In *Gabriel over the White House*, on the other hand, he plays straight as a radical newspaperman who makes a stunning if unlikely indictment of the government at the president's press conference. There is always the possibility of satire invading such a role. In *Winterset* (1936), which came out after *Godfrey*, he again plays a radical, mounting a soapbox to denounce oppression when the policeman breaks up the spontaneous party that has sprung up around the organ grinder. The words are mostly Maxwell Anderson's and the film shares the radical's point of view, but Auer is using a heavy accent which gives a comic reading to the part. Such, at least, was my reaction when I resaw the film in 1982, but I may have been carrying my own *Godfrey*-created Auer to *Winterset*. It was the La Cava film that firmly established him as a comedian. "Forget about the Academy Awards," William Powell is supposed to have told him. "Make them laugh and you'll be around a long time." Much has been made of Auer's monkey imitation in *Godfrey*—Carlo's attempt to cheer up an unhappy Irene— and that scene is almost certainly the one that fixed the actor as a funnyman. To me, however, it is the least interesting thing about Auer's Carlo. I am more impressed that La Cava seemed to recognize that the intensity Auer shows in *Gabriel*, could—given a half turn— come out as high-Russian, mock tragedy. A joke about art, a joke about money, perhaps a joke about sex. Carlo is very much at home among the Bullocks.

The same cannot be said for Alexander Bullock. It is characteristic of him that, when we meet him, he is on the edge of the action, an observer rather than a participant. In later scenes, shared with Molly and Godfrey, we see him trying to cope while the Bullock ladies lie abed. Even when he is with the family, he is anchorless, buffeted by their language and their indifference, unless a particular incident (Cornelia and the pearls) forces him to act decisively. He does command attention in the scene in which he announces the complete collapse of the Bullock Enterprises and in which he finally throws Carlo out of the house, but his dominant role is quickly taken over by Godfrey, who has been buying stock on the sly and has saved the company and who has to have center stage to tie up his own loose ends. Bullock is not developed as a character to the extent that Walter Connolly's Alfred Borden is in *Fifth Avenue Girl*, but he is a solid enough outline to be filled by Eugene Pallette, an expert at the bark and rumble of stifled outrage. This is not the Pallette of *Steamboat Round the Bend*, the assured innocent that La Cava had made use of in *The Half-Naked Truth*, but one of the put-upon businessmen that he had been playing at least since *It Pays to Advertise* (1931), in which Lombard is the daughter-in-law who helps outsmart him. In repose, his exasperation stilled, Pallette could convey a kind of prickly sadness which is appropriate to his role in *Godfrey*. In the scavenger-hunt scene, while Angelica babbles on about what they still need to find, ignoring his going-home noises, he snarls, "if you want a forgotten man—you'll find me home in bed." It is not simply a comic line.

Hired as a butler, Godfrey spends the rest of the film proving his worth to himself and making himself necessary to the Bullocks. Even the sardonic maid Molly falls in love with him. Jean Dixon, whom John

Godfrey as the perfect butler. William Powell, Eugene Pallette, Jean Dixon. (*My Man Godfrey*, Universal, 1936. The Museum of Modern Art/Film Stills Archive.)

Mason Brown called "one of the most hilariously acid comediennes in our theatre," made her reputation in two of the best tough-sentimental roles in American comedy—Lucille Sears in the George S. Kaufman–Ring Lardner *June Moon* (1929) and Mary Daniels in the Kaufman–Moss Hart *Once in a Lifetime* (1930). Like Helen Broderick and Ruth Donnelly, two other celebrated Broadway wisecrackers, Dixon brought her specialty to Hollywood. She could be nasty; in the packing scene in *She Married Her Boss,* as she tries to hurry her friend Julia (Claudette Colbert) to her version of happiness, her remarks to the distraught little girl (Edith Fellows) are not funny, simply mean. More often, there was a kind of softness in Dixon's playing—her comic lines in the 1938 *Holiday* are almost gentle—that made it easy for her to move from a sharp remark to a comforting one. In *Godfrey,* her Molly not only gives the newcomer a tart-tongued rundown on the Bullock family, but she plays a crying scene with Irene, in which both women lament their unrequited love for Godfrey, which is at once touching and very funny. Dixon, in *Godfrey,* has—as Andre Sennwald said of her in *I'll Love You Always* (1935)—"an acid kindliness, if that is possible."

When the camera is not calling out attention to Godfrey, as he moves with authority through the Bullock chaos, it focuses most of its attention on Irene and her puppy-dog persistence in forcing herself on the butler of her choice. The paragraphs above are sprinkled with instances of Lombard's Irene in love, but there are two scenes toward the end of the film which display attractive if contradictory sides of the character and the remarkable skill of the performer. In the first, a love scene of sorts, she is helping Godfrey do the dishes. The situation allows Powell to make Godfrey a touch less formal than usual, and Lombard works at a speed appropriate not to the job but to the momentary thoughts that come into Irene's head. The arhythmical stops and starts are in part an indication that she is a rich girl who knows little about doing dishes, but these hesitations also reflect her attempt to accept that Godfrey will be leaving, a soft avowal of love that is more communicative than the lines she speaks. When she turns away, crying, and says, "I won't cry, I promise"—and Lombard was very good at that kind of ruefulness—the reality of her love is obvious as it never is with the tragic poseur of the party or the screaming child who will not respond to Carlo's monkey act. Shortly after the dish-washing scene, when Irene thinks she has heard Godfrey make an assignation with Cornelia, she stages a faint which ends with his sticking her under the shower. She takes his act as a confession of love and, while he is tendering and Angelica accepting his resignation, they are scarcely audible since Irene, soaking wet and radiant, is bouncing all over the room, chanting "Godfrey loves me!" Not since *Running*

Wild, when La Cava let Fields's Elmer Finch jump around the room, on and off the furniture, shouting (in a silent film), "I'm a lion," had there been so infectious a presentation of jubilance.

In the final family scene, three of the five films in *Godfrey* reach a conclusion as the batty family is shown tamed by the no longer strange stranger and Godfrey explains, once again, what his job with the Bullocks had done for him. We then go to the city dump to bring the Depression film to an end; there, the former derelicts—thanks to Godfrey, Tommy Gray, and Cornelia's pearls—are profitably employed in a business of their own and making plans for steam-heated quarters which will make this the most luxurious dump in the country. Finally, Irene arrives, bearing a basket of food, and the film ends with the inevitable marriage. *Komos. Gamos*. What could be more classical? The ancient comedy ending which signals the replenishment of the man, the family, the society.

Or does it? A careful look at the last two scenes is necessary before an official happy ending can be declared. There are grating elements in both of them.

Godfrey's plans for his friends at the dump are kept from the audience all during the film, their existence only indicated by unrevealing conversations between him and Tommy Gray. When we finally get to the site of his social experiment, the dump has become as art deco as the artificial opening of the film. A lavish nightclub called The Dump is in operation and, as the limousines unload the idle rich, a uniformed Mike ("without a lot of this relief") opens the door for them. There may be a certain utility in solving social problems by tapping into the decadence of its most useless members, and the film may be making that sardonic point (the mayor is one of the guests). That the movie may be sending up social comedies like *Mr. Deeds Goes to Town* is suggested by a last exchange between Godfrey and Tommy in which Godfrey asks for funds to build a dock to bring in the "yachting trade." Just before his final exit, Tommy says, "you're nuts," an echo of his earlier suggestion that Godfrey see a brain specialist; one might well recall Bullock's remark from earlier in the film: "I sometimes wonder whether my whole family has gone mad or whether it's me." It is at least a possibility in a film like this that solutions turn out to be as crazy as problems.

The romantic ending is somewhat colored by the fact that the Irene we see is a very aggressive one, simply riding over Godfrey's objections. Although she is very much in control of herself and the situation, she is likely to remind us of the hysterically demanding woman of the noisier early scenes. The reviewers tended to describe her in highly unflattering terms which suggest that sensible Godfrey may be in for more than he can handle. Regina Crewe, who called her "a man-mad psychopathic moron," wondered if Godfrey should not have been allowed to marry Cornelia. Certainly the very end of the film lacks the tenderness of the traditional fade-out. Irene, busy placing everyone for the ceremony, drags Godfrey to his feet and says, "Stand still, Godfrey, it'll all be over in a minute."

Although I am drawn to a satiric reading of these two scenes, I do not think it really holds. La Cava is less blunt in his use of disquieting elements. He is willing to use sentiment and sardonicism in the same film, letting each feed on the other without destroying it. At the end of *Primrose Path* (1940), the corrupt old grandmother (Queenie Vassar) remains mean-spirited and ugly in the face of the traditional happy ending, but La Cava does not let this touch of comic nastiness drain the traditional meaning from the announced honeymoon of Ellie May (Ginger Rogers) and Ed (Joel McCrea). The nightclub in *Godfrey* may be a joke, but the solution itself—reclamation through work—is fully embedded in the film as a whole. All Godfrey's little homilies on the innate worth of his fellow derelicts, on what being a butler has meant to him, on the value of occupation ("I can only hope that you'll use those high spirits in a more constructive way," he says to the transformed Cornelia) are seriously intended. He is not Polonius, nor was meant to be. As for his final union with Irene, we know that he is destined/doomed to marry her from the first scene, in which he responds to the best qualities in her. Given a second look, the last line turns out to be an old friend. It is simply a variation on Ann's possession line at the end of *Man and Superman*: "Never mind her, dear. Go on talking." Bernard Shaw presents the protesting Jack Tanner as an accomplice in his own entrapment, and the marriage as fulfillment for the couple, the audience, and—if we believe the dream act—the human race. La Cava recognizes that Godfrey is the same kind of reluctant lover. When Irene speaks her last line, it can be heard as a declaration of love as well as of triumph and—"it'll all be over in a minute"—an indication that it is time for the movie to end. As Shaw's last stage direction says, *Universal laughter*.

Notes

1. When the Morrie Ryskind–Eric Hatch screenplay was published by John Gassner and Dudley Nichols in their *Twenty Best Film Plays* (New York, Crown, 1943), a note (p. 131) incorrectly identified the *Liberty* title as "1011 Fifth Avenue." That is the address of the Bullock

mansion, although the published text of the screenplay has both Irene and Godfrey say "1011 Fiftieth" (p. 139), an impossible New York address. A number of film scholars simply repeat the misinformation or miscopy it; Richard Corliss, for instance, calls the story "1101 Fifth Avenue" in *Talking Pictures* (New York, Penguin, 1975, p. 293). The Gassner-Nichols note also gives an incorrect date for the book publication of the novel—1936 instead of 1935.

2. Why the University of Pennsylvania drinking song—even with one line slightly changed—should emerge in a movie put together by people with no Penn connections, I do not know. Actually, the song "The Glorious Highball" (words and music by G. B. Brigham) dates from 1903 when, as the cover of the sheet music says, it was sung with success by Alva E. Laing, Baritone. It was taken over by Wesleyan, but when the team from that college came to Philadelphia to play in 1906, T. H. "Monty" Montgomery appropriated it and it has been identified with the University of Pennsylvania ever since. It must have had some special appeal to Powell—the sentiments? the tune?—for he had used it on a similar tipsy occasion earlier in *The Thin Man*.

3. Generational note. In 1975, I commented in class on Brady's beauty in the bedroom scene in which Godfrey first serves her breakfast and in which Tetzlaff photographs her with loving care. The class laughed, presumably because mothers are not beautiful and because I was far too old to make such a judgment. She was only in her early forties then, I pointed out, scarcely old enough to be mother of two big girls like Lombard and Patrick. When that had no effect, I topped it with the information that Eugene Pallette in *Godfrey* was younger than Paul Newman was at the time of the lecture. Surprise, disbelief, but no real shuffling of prefixed categories. I understand these nuances because, although built on modified Pallette lines, I was born in Newman's year.

Libeled Lady

· 1936 ·

"I didn't distort the truth. I heightened the composition."
—Chris in *Too Hot to Handle*

"It is not even melodrama," Theodore Dreiser complained; "it's just tomfoolery. Chasing men around the table and in and out doors and windows to get a newspaper story." He is speaking of *The Front Page*, one of the popular 1931 films he chose to illustrate that "Hollywood has no interest in encouraging the people to think or to know." Dreiser's description is reasonably accurate and his larger assumption is sound enough, but he clearly misses the point about *The Front Page*. Of course, it is "tomfoolery," for the film is a vigorous and very faithful adaptation of the Ben Hecht–Charles MacArthur play (1928), one of the most successful and certainly the most influential of the newspaper farces. It is melodrama as well—whatever Dreiser says—and romance. "This story is laid in a Mythical Kingdom," the film's opening title announces. This may be the moviemakers' sly comment on their own commercial discretion, on the fact that the city in the film is never specifically identified as Chicago. Yet, the designation is truthful in a deeper sense. *The Front Page* provided the setting which was to become confused with reality and established the newspaper stereotype which would haunt the stage and screen into the 1940s. "Back in Hildy Johnson's time," Nicholas von Hoffman wrote in 1976, invoking the reporter hero of *The Front Page*, " . . . we were crooked and inaccurate but rather more loved than now." The line between fact and fiction is further muddied by the fact that Hildy Johnson and Walter Burns, the play's demon editor, as well as a number of the minor characters,

Newspaperman and abandoned bride. Spencer Tracy, Jean Harlow. (*Libeled Lady*, MGM, 1936. The Museum of Modern Art/Film Stills Archive.)

borrowed the names and the behavior of real reporters whom Hecht
and MacArthur had known in their Chicago days.

The hard-drinking, fast-talking, wisecracking reporter, loyal only to
the editor he love-hates, whose only moral imperative is to get the
story before anyone else does, became a very usable cliché, suitable for
anything from a star turn to a comic walk-on. Hecht's newsroom—like
Frank Capra's small town—may have had its roots in an actual milieu,
but it was one that distance had softened, sweetened. In *A Child of the
Century*, Ben Hecht told how a relative brought him, at sixteen, to the
Chicago Journal office in search of a job. "We entered a large barnlike
room full of desks and long tables, piled with typewriters and crumpled newspapers. There were many men in shirt sleeves. Some of
them were bellowing, others sprawled in chairs asleep, with their hats
down over their eyes." (Archer Winsten on *Libeled Lady*: "A special
medal should be minted for Director Jack Conway who has permitted a
newspaper office to be shown in which only two reporters wear their
hats indoors.") Hecht was hired and, as he described his wait for an
assignment, he added more color to the picture.

> The smell of ink, the drunks coming in with seven A.M.
> hangovers and sucking therapeutically on oranges, the
> clanging of a mysterious bell above Mr. Dunne's head, the
> air of swashbuckle—hats tilted, feet up on top of typewrit-
> ers, faces breathing out liquor fumes like dragons—these
> matters held me shyly spellbound.

An adolescent's first impression became a young man's home and
school. Hecht wrote a great deal about his newspaper days, but he
always seemed able to find new anecdotes to embody his unvarying
enthusiasm for a time and a place and a calling that were like no others.
Newspaper memoirs share with the war stories of graying veterans
and the recollections of overweight ex-athletes the conviction that
there were giants in those days. "Our friendship was based, largely,
on the nostalgia we shared," Hecht said in *Charlie*. "We were all fools
to have left Chicago." But since Chicago was their youth, they had
very little choice. It is just accident or luck or good timing that the
Hecht-MacArthur valentine to their twenty-year-old selves passed
quickly into the mythology of popular culture.

There are thorns on these Chicago roses, of course, and it is possible
to see *The Front Page* as satire. The reporters are not only witty,
amusing, lovable, but they are dishonest, callous, casually vicious (as
when they goad Mollie Malloy into jumping out the window). They
deal in stories, not facts. At the end of the play, when the escaped

criminal is finally discovered hidden in the rolltop desk, each of them phones in a lurid account of the spiritless capture, tuned to the presumed trashy tastes of his readers—a deservedly celebrated scene which was heightened in the film version by Lewis Milestone's clever play with close-ups, as one after another of the reporters tips onto the screen, his momentary presence underlined by a fragment of his call. Burns is the most outrageous of the lot and Hildy Johnson, who imagines that he wants to escape to a home and a nine-to-five job, is Burns's victim, his apprentice, his other self. The unsavory side of the Hecht-MacArthur stereotype became standard in films; ineptitude, corruption, insensibility were as likely as charm to turn up as characteristics of the movie newspaperman. Robert Benchley's comic bit as the gossip reporter in *Dancing Lady* (1933) is to search his vest pockets, continually in search of the pencil he never finds. Walter Catlett's Bingy in *Platinum Blonde* (1931) accepts fifty dollars to kill a story. "Jo Swerling and I stole a column from *Front Page*," said Frank Capra. In *Laughter* (1930), the reporters—nondescript middle-aged men—are so eager to call in the news that the rich Mrs. Gibson (Nancy Carroll) has turned up at the suicide's door, that they invade a stranger's darkened apartment and, when a shocked woman sits up in bed, one of them tells her to shut up, he's on the phone. Occasionally, a newspaperman commits a crime that cannot be forgiven, as in *The Murder Man* (1935), in which the star reporter (Spencer Tracy) turns out to be the murderer. Sometimes, the edge of nastiness in a film—*The Whole Town's Talking* (1935)—or the touch of earnestness—*Mr. Deeds Goes to Town* (1936)— suggests real culpability among journalists, but for the most part the legacy of *The Front Page* is that antisocial behavior is just part of the fun. "For innocent is what we were," Hecht said, recalling the Chicago days; "not in our doings but in our point of view." *The Front Page* is never seriously satirical because its tone reflects the attitude of its authors: "We were both writing of people we had loved, and of an employment that had been like none other was ever to be." The play's descendants—the newspaper farces that crowded the screen during the 1930s—became more likably larcenous, farther removed from reality.

If *The Front Page* deals, however gingerly, with murder, political chicanery, and the incompetence of the police and the courts, Hollywood's favorite variation on the newspaper farce is more likely to concern itself with the newsworthiness of the very rich. The runaway-heiress-meets-reporter story—*It Happened One Night* (1934), *Love Is News* (1937)—is only the most romantic form of the film that assumes— *Platinum Blonde*, *Deeds*—that newspaper readers care deeply about what the fancy folk are up to. This presumed reader concern is more than an artificial device to move the plot. Whether dictated by the demands of the readers or the inclinations of the men on the city desk, scandal journalism flourished in the 1930s (as it does in the 1980s). Both Barbara Hutton and Doris Duke came into their fortunes in 1933, the year that found about twenty million people on relief, but readers were supposed to and apparently did want to know the details of their investiture. In 1936, the year of *Libeled Lady*, the battle over custody of the Vanderbilt heir, the trials of Baby Gloria, filled the papers, stole space from less demanding stories like the latest divorce of Adolph B. Spreckels, Jr., "the California sugar heir," who was going to win his suit against "vivacious Gloria Debevoise Spreckels, 18" by unveiling a diary said to be "hotter than Boccaccio's 'Decameron'." How the newspapers loved the labels *heir* and *heiress*. The *Mirror* even used "Gardener's Son, Heiress Eloped" as a headline on its account of the secret marriage of nineteen-year-old Carol Thorne-Smith, although she almost certainly belonged somewhat lower in the financial hierarchy, was more correctly the missing debutante of the *New York American* story.

Perhaps the marriage of Anne Gould, "heiress to a railroad fortune," to Herman H. Elsbury, a "dude wrangler," can best illustrate the newspapers' fondness for the frivolous rich. Although this was the twenty-two-year-old Gould's second marriage and she was the great granddaughter of Jay Gould, she was not the stuff of popular legend as Barbara Hutton and Doris Duke and Baby Gloria were. Yet her marriage to her cowboy was considered important news although it was played a little tongue-in-cheek, at least by the *Mirror*, which reported that the groom wore "a ten-gallon hat, chaps, spurs and a cowy aroma." The *Times* discreetly put the item on page 19, but the *American* had it on page 3, and the *Mirror* had it on 4, much of the space on page 3, their prime sensational page, having been commandeered by "Bruno's Death House Story," an exclusive interview that a *Mirror* editor had obtained from the man convicted of kidnapping and murdering the Lindbergh baby. Both the *World-Telegram* and the *Sun* put the story on the front page with a picture of the bride. Since her photograph was the only one on the front of the *World-Telegram*, Anne Gould was the first point of focus for every reader; in the *Sun* she had to share the space with the murderers of Samuel Druckman, but the editors made up for this dereliction by setting a sly "On Second Honeymoon" above her likeness. Looking at these news stories almost fifty years after the nonevent, one wonders who could really have cared that Anne Gould had married a cowboy. The playful tone in the stories, like the punching luridness in the Vanderbilt and Spreckels news, suggests that, for both the writers and the readers, these were a kind of elaborate fiction, accidentally attached to real people. The cowboy-heiress marriage was, after all, a favorite Hollywood plot both before and after the Gould-Elsbury alliance. Gary Cooper played the upwardly mobile cowboy twice, when he married Carole Lombard in *I Take This Woman* (1931) and Merle Oberon in *The Cowboy and the Lady* (1938).

The newspaper comedies, with the editors and reporters relentlessly in search of scandal among the rich, were reflections of journalistic reality—although the Gould marriage was reported largely through wire-service stories filed from Cheyenne. They were also unvoiced admissions that the fictions of the newsroom and the fictions of the screening room met on the common ground of the Hecht-MacArthur "Mythical Kingdom." The roster of Hollywood writers was filled with former newspapermen.

When Metro-Goldwyn-Mayer decided to do its newspaper farce, it turned to one such writer—Maurine Watkins, a Chicago reporter who had got to Hollywood by way of Broadway. Watkins's reputation rests on a single work, the sardonic play *Chicago* (1926). She had been a police reporter in Chicago a journalistic generation after Hecht and MacArthur and had made something of a sensation by getting an interview from Leopold and Loeb shortly before they confessed to the thrill murder that gave them a permanent place in what devotees like to call the annals of crime. She gave up the newsroom to go to Yale and study with George Pierce Baker, and it was there that *Chicago* took shape. It is an account of the marketing of Roxie Hart, a murderess who gets off through the manipulations of a clever lawyer and is made famous by a reporter who would have been called a *Front Page* stereotype if the Watkins play had not preceded the Hecht-MacArthur comedy by a year-and-a-half. Watkins's only other Broadway play was *Revelry* (1927), an adaptation of a Samuel Hopkinson Adams novel which was probably given to Watkins because it was supposed to do for/to Washington what she did for/to Chicago in her play; Brooks Atkinson dismissed it as "a scissors and paste-pot structure of scenes." Her Hollywood credits—*Libeled Lady* aside—are uninteresting except for her first movie, *Up the River* (1930), the film that brought Spencer Tracy to Hollywood. John Ford told Peter Bogdanovich that "Sheehan [head of production at Fox] wanted to do a great picture about a prison break, so he had some woman write the story and it was just a bunch of junk." The director's casual male chauvinism[1] has its ludicrous side since Watkins almost certainly knew more about prisons than Ford and the actor William Collier, Sr., who, according to Ford, helped him rewrite the script as a comedy. Judging by *Chicago*, Watkins could have handled Ford's comedy, and she was given screenplay credit, but *Chicago* may be one of those flukes that emerge occasionally in American theater, its author a one-play playwright.

There is *Libeled Lady*, of course. The author of *Chicago* seems a likely choice to write a newspaper farce, but there are so many writing names in the credits that it is impossible to assign the movie to a single pen. Wallace Sullivan, who had a hand in a number of undistinguished films, is credited with the story on which the screenplay was based, and not only Maurine Watkins but Howard Emmett Rogers and George Oppenheimer worked the material over. Rogers had been a screenwriter since 1924. He contributed to several of the Gregory La Cava silents—W. C. Fields's *So's Your Old Man* (1926), Richard Dix's *Paradise for Two* (1927), Bebe Daniels's *Feel My Pulse* (1928). Having worked with Anita Loos on *Hold Your Man* (1933) and *The Girl from Missouri* (1934), both Jean Harlow films, and written the screenplay for *Whipsaw* (1935), which starred Myrna Loy and Spencer Tracy, he might be presumed to have some experience writing lines for the *Libeled Lady* performers. Yet the comedy of the two Harlow films turns to soap opera and *Whipsaw* is sentimental melodrama; none of the three is preparation for the consistency of tone of *Libeled Lady*. Perhaps that is where George Oppenheimer came in. A man of many careers (he was one of the founders of Viking Press), in his Hollywood days he "was often put on as a polish man." So said George Seaton, one of Oppenheimer's cowriters on *A Day at the Races* (1937). "He was sort of the local Noel Coward when it came to comedies," Seaton added, a remark that seems irrelevant to the very American sound of *Libeled Lady* and a touch ironic when one remembers that Brooks Atkinson, in his generally favorable comment on *Here Today* (1927), found the Oppenheimer farce "inferior to 'Private Lives' and even 'Hay Fever.'" Polish-man Oppenheimer brings up the rear of so many multiple screen credits that Bronislau Kaper is supposed to have said on meeting him, "I always thought your name was 'and George Oppenheimer.'"

When all these cooks managed to perfect rather than spoil the broth of *Libeled Lady*, it was ready for a director to serve up. The assignment went to Jack Conway. Conway is a director whose thirty years of film work is too easily dismissed by too many film commentators. "He was a factory-man, turning scripts into films with a minimum of fuss (ie. in his case, originality, personality or liveliness)." Thus Markku Salmi in his remarks accompanying the Conway filmography in *Film Dope*. What he means is that the director was an Irving Thalberg regular; "the MGM team spirit was strong in Conway," Samuel Marx said in *Mayer and Thalberg*. What Thalberg expected of his directors was that they put the scripts he gave them onto the screen, making the best use of the MGM performers, and that they not make the mistake of assuming that film was a medium of individual artistic expression. "Thalberg mistrusted men who preferred their own concepts to his," Marx wrote.

No one wants to declare Conway a major director, but it is easy to agree with Ben Hecht that he is "one of the best of the town's unsung talents." He was efficient and often imaginative, and he surely does not deserve the retrospective belittlement that has come to him in recent years. The accounts of *Red-Headed Woman* (1932) and *Viva Villa!* (1934) are cases in point. In her mean-spirited autobiography, *Kiss Hollywood Good-by*, Anita Loos tells how clever she and clever Thalberg joined forces to make a smart comedy out of Katharine Brush's "highly forgettable best seller" *Red-Headed Woman*. "I'll direct this if you insist," she has Conway say, "but take my word, Irving, people are going to laugh at it," and an avuncular Thalberg warns the director, "I'll have Nita stay on the set to keep reminding you that the picture's a comedy." Her portrait of Conway as a stupid man is not only smugly condescending but highly suspect when one recalls that earlier the same year Conway directed the Barrymore boys in *Arsene Lupin*, a film that moved from comedy to melodrama with no obvious strain on the director.

Viva Villa! is a more difficult case. Howard Hawks began directing the film on location in Mexico, but production came to a halt when Lee Tracy, who was playing the American reporter, got drunk and urinated from a hotel balcony. Tracy was rescued from the local authorities but fired from the picture. Hawks either "abruptly quit the production" or was fired because he would not "bear witness against Tracy" (this last is the Hawksian version). Stuart Erwin took the Lee Tracy role, and Jack Conway, loyal company man, was called in to take over from Hawks. According to Peter Bogdanovich, whose source is Hawks, "the story and all the exteriors were done by Hawks; the interiors, except for those shot in Mexico, were not." The film's chief strength is thespic not directorial (Wallace Beery as Villa), and its most identifiable style is the high rhetoric and the reportorial snappiness of Ben Hecht. Credit for directing should probably be split between Hawks and Conway with a piece of the action assigned to Richard Rosson, who headed the second unit. The prim snottiness of Louis B. Mayer (the Screen Directors Guild did not exist in 1934) cut out Hawks completely and gave Conway full credit. Time and a casual contempt for Conway's work seem to be reversing the decision. Andrew Sarris concluded that "this film is far superior to any of Conway's other work" and so gave it to Hawks; John Wayne, presenting an honorary Oscar to the director in 1975, simply spoke of Hawks's *Viva Villa!* as though Conway's name were not on it at all. Which of the two men, I ask myself, shot the nice bit at the end of the film in which, having heard the gunfire that fatally wounds Villa, Emilio (George E. Stone) seems to be trying to come to the aid of his hero, but using his umbrella as a protective shield at the same time. A distant shot, it could be Hawks's; in the setting in which the surrounding scenes between Villa and Johnny (Erwin) are played, it is more likely Conway's. It certainly has more to recommend it than the conventional action sequences, such as those in which the horsemen ride over the camera or, approaching in pairs, fan apart to pass on either side; or all those portentous shots of massing peons. It is understandable that Hawks continued to be annoyed by what happened to him on *Viva Villa!* long after the film had come and gone, but now that both Hawks and Conway have passed into history, the old wrongs done Hawks on *Viva Villa!* can surely be rectified without the propitiating sacrifice of Jack Conway.

In a piece on young directors in 1916, *Photoplay* described Conway as "a 'comer' whose arrival is close at hand." He had begun as an actor in stock ("When I was young I was an actor, and a very bad actor") and then in the movies. He was an assistant to D. W. Griffith on *The Birth of a Nation* (1915) and began his career as director that year. His first full-length film was *The Penitentes* (1915), which, as *Photoplay* so elegantly put it, "won him his first meed of fame." He joined MGM in 1925 with *The Only Thing*, the first of two films he did that year based on Elinor Glyn stories. Although he occasionally directed an MGM cultural giant—*A Tale of Two Cities* (1935)—and worked in all genres, his best films are his comedies, *Arsene Lupin, Red-Headed Woman, The Girl From Missouri, Too Hot to Handle* (1938), *Love Crazy* (1941). These films are not likely to turn up on anyone's list of the best Hollywood comedies, but there are some very good sequences in all of them, scenes that depend as much on the director's skill as they do on the talent of the writers and the performers. Whatever their virtues, they cannot compare to *Libeled Lady*. Spencer Tracy once dismissed films like *Libeled Lady* with "They're the 'fun-on-the-farm' studio items. They amuse, but the serious fans think they're silly, and then they dig into Hollywood." Both Tracy and his "serious fans" were wrong, of course. *Libeled Lady* has survived in a way that more sincere Tracy films like *Boys Town* (1938) have not. *Libeled Lady* is one of the most perfectly realized films of its kind to come out of Hollywood in the 1930s. Trivial in content, artificial in form, it underlines the triviality, announces the artificiality. The stereotypical characters are given some degree of humanity through the personality and the skill of the performers, but the film itself, the director and his editor (Frederick Y. Smith) constantly remind the viewers, is all artifice and is meant to be. Jack Conway surpassed himself in *Libeled Lady* and made the movie that Katharine Hepburn is supposed to have called the "Funniest damned thing I've ever seen in my life."

The film is defined by the opening credits. The first shot shows the four stars, the women elegantly dressed (Harlow trimmed in fur, of course), the men top-hatted, walking toward the audience, arm-in-arm, laughing and sharing the laugh. They are ranged across the screen left to right—Jean Harlow, William Powell, Myrna Loy, Spencer Tracy—in the order of their billing rather than in the romantic pairing—Harlow and Tracy, Loy and Powell—that the plot will provide. The stars, not the characters, are being presented to the audience. Snatches of the wedding march can be heard in the music to which they move and, then, under the credits, the wedding music segues into "Who?" The newspaper farce is almost too fragile a form to exist on its own (see the melodrama mixed into *The Front Page*), and the writers of *Libeled Lady* have stirred in a second Hollywood standard, the marital mix-up comedy. The music signals that fact and, by its gaiety, indicates the tone of all that is to follow.

The music is by William Axt, who was often listed in credits as Dr. William Axt, although the provenance of the title is somewhat clouded; the only indication I have seen of his musical education is a biographical note that says, "Studied in Germany under great masters." He and David Mendoza—they were coconductors at the Capitol Theater in New York—wrote music for several of the more ambitious silent films—*The Big Parade* (1925), *Ben-Hur* (1926), and *Don Juan* (1926). The first composer to be given a studio contract, Axt was hired by MGM where, in 1930, he organized the music department. His own credits indicate that he provided the background music for a wide variety of films—comedies, mysteries, melodramas—but not for the cosseted classics that gave MGM its air of overstuffed elegance. He was, like Jack Conway, a competent, nonshowy professional. When I think of *Dinner at Eight* (1933), *The Thin Man* (1934), or *The Girl From Missouri*, the music does not come to mind, but Axt's musical games on *Libeled Lady* not only contribute to the cheerful artificiality of the film, but do so by calling attention to themselves in a positive way. Too often, one remembers scores because they are intrusive or showily obvious, as with Axt's contribution to *Gabriel over the White House* (1933). The music in that film is either conventionally patriotic or conventionally spiritual, depending on whether we are getting an American government scene or a shot of the moving curtain that heralds Gabriel's presence. There is none of the wit that Axt brought to

Libeled Lady. Take his second use of the wedding march. Gladys Benton (Harlow), having been left at the altar once again by Warren Haggerty (Tracy), storms into the newspaper office in full regalia—train, orange blossoms, and all. She cuts across the city room with a purposeful stride while the sound track pours out the wedding march; as she enters Haggerty's editorial cubicle and slams the door behind her, the music stops abruptly, as though it were a character left outside. Or take a less grandiloquent bit of playfulness. As Connie Allenbury (Loy), Bill Chandler (Powell), and her father (Walter Connolly) set out to fish, they walk in file along the stream, the music a spirited hippity-hop vaguely reminiscent of the Laurel and Hardy theme; at least, it has that kind of promise in it—adventure, assurance, impending disaster—and the trio *are* en route to Powell's celebrated slapstick fishing scene.

The film proper begins with a standard shot of presses rolling. *Libeled Lady* is so unembarrassed in its use of the devices of the genre that there is even a "Stop the presses!" scene, although the famous words are never spoken. The telephone rings in the pressroom, a laconic "O.K.," a pushed button, and the presses come to a halt, letting us see, then read in close-up the front page of the *New York Evening Star.* There is a photograph of Connie Allenbury and a headline proclaiming that a "Peer's Wife" has found her husband with a "Rich Playgirl." The story, we quickly discover, is untrue, an invention of the paper's London correspondent in his cups, but one truck is already on the street and it is too late to kill the edition completely. The editorial room, in an uproar, is trying to find Haggerty. Exposition, pure and simple, one might say, conditioned by so many headline-introduced movie plots (see *Mr. Deeds Goes to Town*), but the purity and the simplicity is a little too calculated here. *Libeled Lady* is set up so that the audience meets each of the four principals, after an anticipatory lead-in that builds up expectation that is never quite fulfilled. It is as though each of them entered by sliding down a fireman's pole, like Groucho Marx in *Duck Soup* (1933), when we expected them to enter regally at the head of the stairs.

The movie finds Haggerty before his colleagues do. The reluctant bridegroom is putting the final touches to his formal clothes. Resplendent above the waist, he is wearing shorts below, an incongruity gag that is also an indication of his hesitation about getting on with the joyful occasion. He is engaged in badinage with his Japanese houseboy, who appears in the film only once after this—to pick up the wedding suit at the office where he is instructed to throw it in the ash can. Haggerty looks at himself in the mirror and says, "There'll be no reprieve from the governor this time," and then he toasts himself, "Here's to the last mile." On that line, character gives way to performer again. Any moviegoer who had read the often told story of the Milwaukee boy who made his way to Broadway and then to Hollywood would remember that John Ford had signed Tracy for *Up the River* after having seen his performance as Killer Mears in John Wexley's *The Last Mile* (1930). Warren Haggerty is a far cry from Killer Mears, a fast-talking newspaper stereotype rather than an embittered and suicidal prisoner, but the line is a signal that there is an actor here, that the man who had just firmly established his place as a star in the MGM hierarchy with his performance as the priest in *San Francisco* (1936) was both ready and able to gambol with the other giants. Over the years, Spencer Tracy has become almost everyone's example of movie acting at its best; his apparently natural behavior uses a minimum of gesture and voice differentiation to suggest complex emotion or to make comic points. "Look, kid," George Cukor is supposed to have said to Paulette Goddard, "just forget those female tricks of yours and try to give me the best imitation you can of *Spencer Tracy!*"

The natural Tracy is the one most recognized by critics, moviegoers, fellow performers, but there has never been—as there sometimes was with Gary Cooper—any suggestion that the apparent easiness of the performer was anything other than art. In his biography of Tracy, Larry Swindell tells some anecdotes in which the Tracy of the films can be seen taking shape in his early roles on the stage. Lynne Overman, whom Tracy replaced in a stock production of *The Nervous Wreck* (1924), is supposed to have told him, "Don't decide to make a move until you do it, and don't move at all unless it's instinctive." George M. Cohan is supposed to have challenged Tracy to discover the mannerisms of Grant Mitchell, the star of *The Baby Cyclone* (1927), and then insisted, "Of course he has mannerisms, and you're a dead duck without them. That's Grant's style. He doesn't do anything, he only suggests." It is always difficult, years after the fact, to confirm this kind of acting influence. On the screen, both Overman, a marvelous comedian with a voice that promises disaster, and the often finicky Mitchell seem more mannered than Tracy, and as for Lionel Barrymore, who Bill Davidson says gave Tracy "tips on underplaying," he signals his professional intentions like a baseball star who announces the fence over which he will knock the ball.

Under whatever tutelage, through whatever experience, Tracy had developed, by the time he got to Hollywood, a skill that let him display, often in mediocre material, a tough-tender charm that was not simply the marketable quality of a potential star performer but the personality of the characters he played. In *Me and My Gal* (1932), for instance, the teasing exchanges between Dan (Tracy) and Helen (Joan Bennett), the policeman and the waitress, make a routine gangster

228 • Chapter Nine

drama a great deal sprightlier than the material might suggest; of course, it helped to have Arthur Kober writing the lines and Raoul Walsh directing. "His acting of these hard-drinking, saddened, humorous parts is as certain as a mathematical formula," Graham Greene said in his review of *The Murder Man*, the first film Tracy did after he moved from Fox to MGM. By this time, his ability was widely accepted, although his admirers sometimes praised him by suggesting that his talent was a secret kept from the ordinary moviegoer. *The New Statesman and Nation*, reviewing *Libeled Lady*, called him "perhaps the expert's favourite film actor, after Groucho Marx" as against William Powell, "everybody's film favourite." In 1938, *Time*, reviewing *Test Pilot*, called him "cinema's No. 1 actors' actor," and Ed Sullivan used the same phrase as title of an article on Tracy he did for *Pictorial Review*. Tracy was soon to become Father Flanagan, Henry M. Stanley, Major Robert Rogers, Thomas Edison, even Dr. Jekyll and Mr. Hyde, and although his humanizing skill kept most of those personages from turning into wax-museum figures, the gruff, warm, irreverent, incipiently brutal persona that he carried from his lightweight Fox films into Warren Haggerty would disappear until it reemerged in the comedies he did with Katharine Hepburn in the 1940s and 1950s. There it was played in a new key, however, for those are character comedies, and *Libeled Lady* is farce.

The copyboy arrives in time to rescue Haggerty from his impending wedding (his muttered "good old governor" completes the "last mile" routine) and after a flaccid joke about his being pantsless, the film takes us to the office where a very different Haggerty is shown. The only remnant of the wryly softspoken groom is his dress suit which he will shortly remove as he has his earlier manner. He berates his assistant, snaps out commands, gives every impression of intense (and largely meaningless) activity. Much of the shouting is exposition that the audience needs, but the texture of the scene shows us Haggerty alive. He goes into his private cubicle ostensibly for a drink. Drinking plays no part in the film; the gesture is *Libeled Lady*'s way of winking and saying, hard-drinking newspaperman—get it?

Haggerty really goes into his private space so that Gladys will have a door to slam when she arrives. The lead-in to her appearance is quite different from the one with Haggerty. The whole staff of the *Evening Star* is looking for him. No one is looking for her. A wedding is presumably about to take place and there must be a bride around somewhere, but the movie insists on her presence by her absence, teases by not telling us anything. When she arrives in full cry, she is not only the very angry Gladys, but Jean Harlow doing one of the things she did best, using outrage to lift vulgarity to an art. According to Curtis F. Brown in his *Jean Harlow*, the actress developed her walk, with the help of Victor Fleming, in *Red Dust* (1932). Whatever its origins, that walk is a marvel. It contains little of the teasing seductiveness that Hollywood sex goddesses are supposed to display. Her sexuality is direct and matter-of-fact; she moves like an athlete. Fueled by the character's anger, as it is in *Libeled Lady*, the walk has the determination of a line drive. The photographs of Harlow—particularly those in which the makeup is discreetly minimal—remind me how lovely she was, but when I think of her I see her as Lola Burns in *Bombshell* (1933), moving at a near-run across the lawn of the mansion, a remembered scene which, if it was ever in the film, was not there the last time I saw it.

At the time of Jean Harlow's death in 1937, she was generally accepted as a fine comedian, which is why so many reviewers heaved sighs of relief when *Libeled Lady* opened and rescued the actress from films like her earlier 1936 movies—*Riffraff*, *Wife vs. Secretary*, *Suzy*—in which she was expected to play serious (i.e., soapy) roles. When one considers the long apprentice career of performers like Myrna Loy and Jean Arthur, the rapidity of Harlow's rise is remarkable; yet, as her reviews show, the critics edged slowly toward her banner. Richard Watts, Jr., not one of her early admirers, praising her in *Red Dust*, recalled that, yes, she had been "almost terrifyingly effective" in *Red-Headed Woman*, but that "was merely a triumph of casting and fearlessness." The next year, in a Sunday piece tracing his growing admiration for the actress, he was now—with *Dinner at Eight*—ready to call her "the most entertaining comedienne in motion pictures." There is early evidence of what, in the right films, with the right direction, she would become. In the Laurel and Hardy *Double Whoopee* (1929), she plays a bit in which she steps from a limousine, helped by the purringly polite Hardy while Laurel closes the door on her skirt. Skirtless, she then enters the hotel and crosses the lobby, secure in her own elegance. She has no elaborate funny business; that is left to the stars. Yet, she is more than a pretty prop. Hers is a straight-man role and she is *in* the scene so fully that the future comic Harlow is already there in embryo. Seeing Harlow in *Double Whoopee*, looking back from *Bombshell* and *Libeled Lady*, is like seeing Carole Lombard in Mack Sennett's *Run, Girl, Run* (1928), looking back from *My Man Godfrey* (1936) and *Nothing Sacred* (1937). It is odd, in retrospect, that between their beginnings with Hal Roach and Sennett, the two comedians had to work their way through roles that disguised their talent. In Harlow's case, she became a celebrity in the process, playing variations on the heroine of *Hell's*

Angels (1930), whose presence presumably fed the sexual fantasies of the male audience and certainly sent a great many women to beauty shops to duplicate her "platinum blonde" hair.

Despite the promise of *Double Whoopee*, there is little evidence of the performer to come in such 1931 films as *The Secret Six* and *Public Enemy*. As Anne Courtland in the fomer, she has a genteel name and a genteel voice, both at odds with the gangster's moll she plays. The comic overtones in her mouthing of phrases like "but you must realize" are not intentional; they lie in the incongruity and in our retrospective knowledge of what she will do with that voice later. She does have comic lines—"Sure I understand you—you're no crossword puzzle"—but she lacks the tough assurance that will allow her a year later to make a joke and a defensive weapon of such weak throwaways in *Red-Headed Woman* and *Red Dust*. Her society girl in *Platinum Blonde* loses her temper in one scene, when her newly acquired reporter husband (Robert Williams) fails to assimilate properly, and one can hear, just under the unbelievable Long Island veneer, the strident voice of the woman in *Bombshell* and *Dinner at Eight*. In *Platinum Blonde*, she has not yet learned to use her two voices—the appealingly coarse one and the hoity-toity one—but by *Bombshell*, she makes the transition from one to another with ease, using the jumps as both character and comic devices. Consider, for instance, the scene at the beginning of the film when, beset by incompetent servants and blood-sucking relatives, she bursts into flamboyant anger, only to stop in mid-diatribe to drip saccharine on the intruding interviewer from *Photoplay*; or the single line in which she combines both voices at once in soliciting the sympathy of the reporter with, "As one lady to another, isn't that a load of clams." In *Libeled Lady*, she uses her genteel voice whenever she wants to impress Bill Chandler or when she sides with Bill against Haggerty. "Don't shout, Warren, we're not used to it," she delicately says in a scene with the three of them in the newspaper office, the setting of our first full-throated meeting of her.

When, after her success in *Red-Headed Woman*, Harlow was recognized as a comedian, it became customary for ruminative critics to talk about her and Mae West as allies in the comic assault on sex. "She was rowdy and ribald," said John Chapin Mosher. "She was doing for the flapper what Mae West was doing for the mature siren." It was apparently a comparison that rankled because, almost thirty years after Harlow's death, West would tell an interviewer that Harlow was "merely acting sex." The comparison is more apparent than real. Harlow was never—not even in *Red-Headed Woman* and *Dinner at Eight*—the predator that West played. For all her brassiness, it is vulnerability that makes the Harlow characters so attractive. She was presumably the most desirable woman in America, yet in her screen roles she is a woman whose personal and social longings are casually ignored; she is a sexual convenience but she can hardly command the full attention of the male who has a rubber plantation (*Red Dust*) or a newspaper (*Libeled Lady*) to run. She is passed over, temporarily at least, for women with more class (Mary Astor's Barbara Willis in *Red Dust*, Rosalind Russell's Sybil Barclay in *China Seas* [1935]). She can trade self-protective wisecracks with a man, but her attachment is likely to be quicker, deeper, more lasting. Until the epiphany hits Eddie Hall (Clark Gable) in *Hold Your Man* and leads him to true love, murder, and two reels of treacle, he treats the smitten Ruby (Harlow) casually, as sex object and bait for his badger game. Reduced to plot and to character relationships, the Harlow films imply a dark underside to the audience admiration for the star. The desirable woman becomes the victim. As in the Marilyn Monroe films later, the woman's humiliation is part of the male sexual success. One of the saddest and funniest scenes that Monroe ever played is the one in *Some Like It Hot* (1959), in which Sugar Kane (Monroe) tells Joe/Josephine (Tony Curtis in drag) about her unhappy love affair with the saxophone player who abused her when she brought home cole slaw instead of potato salad: "So he threw it right in my face." Unlike the Mae West films, in which the men tend to be jokes, in the Harlow films the star is the comic butt. The triumph of Harlow as a comic performer is that she used the vulnerability of her characters as a soft, sweet center for a tough-shelled performance in which the vitality, the beauty, the wit, the vulgarity formed the prevailing image.

Gladys in *Libeled Lady* may be seen as a distillation of the Harlow role: Powell prefers Loy; Tracy prefers his job; Harlow cracks wise, screams on occasion, is very funny, usually gorgeous, and finally a bit touching. The sadness in the character surfaces at the end of the film in her what-about-Gladys? speech in which she attacks Bill, then Warren, finally Connie, for her money and the assurance that goes with it. *Libeled Lady*, being a farce, cannot linger over such character revelation, so the film stumbles hurriedly to its incredible happy ending. Yet it does, for a moment, state directly what has been obvious throughout—that Gladys is only a thing, if a pretty thing. This fact provides the chief device of the plot, Bill's plan to marry a willing woman (in name only, of course) so that they can trap Connie into an alienation-of-affections situation that will make the libelous news story true after all; without consulting Gladys, Haggerty volunteers her for the role. The best visual image of Gladys's position comes in the scene in which the fishing instructor (E. E. Clive) prepares Bill for his visit to Allenbury's fishing camp. To teach Bill to cast against hazards, the instructor stands on the sofa, his arms outstreched—a branched tree behind the fisherman—and places Gladys downstream to Bill's left—a boulder in the stream. As she leans against a table, she says wryly, "Remember, there's a man on second," and of course gets a hook in the seat of her marvelous, floppy-legged white lounging pajamas.[2] The nastiest instance of Gladys's place in the scheme of things comes immediately before her unhappy denunciation of the other characters. When it looks as though Connie's libel suit is going to be called off, Haggerty pushes Gladys aside to thank Connie. Like the male dominance games that Howard Hawks lets Cary Grant and Rosalind Russell play in the early scenes in *His Girl Friday* (1940), the action here is not calculated; both the ugliness and the comedy lie in the casualness of the gesture. When Connie says that Haggerty has forgotten something, he reaches around Gladys to get his hat from the chair behind her. Jokes seldom work singly in *Libeled Lady*, and this one carries an echo of the earlier scene in the Allenbury mansion in which first Haggerty, then Bill exit at a run, hesitate at the door, turn back to pick up a hat, a routine that is funny only because of the nicely timed repetition. Yet, the chief emphasis in the thank-you scene is on Gladys as glamorous patsy, a role that is indicated in her first scene.

Despite the fire-eating entrance and the initial shouting match, the dominant note of the quarrel lies in the line, which will be repeated as the film goes on, "If you don't want to marry me, just say so." Gladys's position is emphasized with the entrance of the publisher, Hollis Bane. He comes in on one of those am-I-running-a-newspaper-or-a-lunatic-asylum lines so popular with 1930s movie tycoons and, when she reacts with "You just took the words out of my mouth," he turns on her: "Get rid of this woman." Bane might have been played with flamboyance (see Walter Connolly in *Nothing Sacred*), but Charley Grapewin does him almost quietly, snapping his lines so that there is more bite than rhetorical flourish to them. When they connect, as this one does, they have a lethal quality. Gladys shouts that she will not be talked to like a house detective, which brings not a defense but a query from Haggerty: "How do you know how a house detective talks?" Her answer, that she can read, is less close to this exchange than preparation for a later Gladys scene which begins with a shot of *Real Love Stories*.[3] The reading joke is picked up once again in the scene in which Haggerty explains to her that he will not be able to take her out while Bill is in England—no hint of scandal can be allowed to touch the newly married and soon to be wronged Mrs. Chandler—and that she must entertain herself; Bill, with whom she has been quarreling ever since the ceremony, murmurs, "Maybe you can learn to read."

At the end of her initial scene, Gladys is given one last image of rejection. As Haggerty and Bane turn back to their work, as the whole newspaper goes about its business, she is left deserted in the center of the editorial room. "And this is supposed to be the happiest day in a girl's life," she says—a lament, not a question—but the copyboy, who is characterized in his few appearances by his slowness and his literalness, thinks she needs an answer. On his *yes*, she gives him a marvelous look compounded of despair and a desire to clobber him. Harlow's ability to look messages was one of her comic talents. Take the scene in which she is racing toward the Allenbury estate, urging the taxi driver to go faster. In his review of the film, Otis Ferguson asks "and what was this she said to the taxi driver when he told her I can go faster lady but the cab can't." So far as I can hear she says nothing; whatever word Ferguson imagined is implicit in her look.

The build to Loy is still another kind of tease. Haggerty on the telephone does a long, sweet, explanatory speech—spirit of fair play and all that—but when we go abruptly to London it is not Connie but her father on the phone. According to Larry Swindell, Walter Connolly got the part of Mr. Allenbury at the insistence of Spencer Tracy, who had played with him in *A Man's Castle* (1933). With or without Tracy's benediction, Connolly was in great demand at this time and was consistently singled out for praise, often for work in movies the reviewers dismissed. Max Reinhardt is supposed to have called him "the greatest character actor on stage or screen." The German director cast Connolly as Bottom in his production of *A Midsummer Night's Dream* in the Hollywood Bowl in 1934, a role that went to James Cagney when Reinhardt made his film version of the play the next year. Connolly's Shakespearian credits go back at least as far as 1912 when he traveled with the E. H. Sothern–Julia Marlowe company. The reputation he built in New York in the 1920s was for versatility and meticulousness in the creation of character. Brooks Atkinson called his performance in *The Late Christopher Bean* (1932) "the quintessence of the comic spirit." By the time he came to Sidney Howard's play, Connolly had made his first trip to Hollywood.

A fleshy man with prominent jowls, Connolly was not a fat man—as he sometimes seems in my memory. The falsely remembered rotundity is not bulk, but presence. When Connolly was on the screen, it was easy to let one's eyes wander away from the star. The *Literary Digest* reported in 1935, "In a nation-wide popularity-poll of motion-picture players, he overwhelmingly defeated no less than a dozen beautiful young men." Connolly commanded his space even when he was doing nothing but reacting to the other characters. Perhaps that *even* should read *especially*, for Connolly was a great reactor. With the barest modifications of his downturned mouth, he could convey exasperation, bewilderment, resignation, comic despair. His eyes were marvelously expressive, and he used his eyebrows like signal flags. Sometimes, as in *Lady by Choice* (1934), in which his judge's role was mere decoration, his lifted eyebrows were all that he had to play with, but it was on that film, Carole Lombard once said, that she learned from Connolly how to pace her comic delivery. The most distinctive thing about Connolly was his voice, which sounded as though it were being strained through a mouthful of flannel. This quality was particularly useful when he played rage, when his anger seemed to bunch in the back of his throat, choking him in its explosive attempt to escape, or when he played delight, when joy seemed to bubble through a barrier that let it out in steam-engine spurts. In *Libeled Lady*, he plays one of his indulgent millionaire fathers—as in *It Happened One Night*—but here, with more footage than he has in the Capra film, he and Loy can establish a closeness, a comradeship between father and daughter that *Night* lacks. In part that sense of relatedness grows out of the two performers, for some of the same quality can be found in *Broadway Bill* (1934), even though J. L. Higgins in that film is, on the surface at least, a much more tyrannical figure than Allenbury. In only one scene of *Libeled Lady* do we get a glimpse of the business man Allenbury presumably is—the political opponent of Hollis Bane. For the rest, when he is not being the good father, he is being the passionate angler.

Having insisted on the preemptive force of Connolly's playing, I must now deny it. In the telephone scene, we watch Connolly, but our attention is really on Loy. Connie sits on her father's desk, back to the camera, bouncing a tennis ball, while he talks, or listens, to New York. The ball bounces on the desk until Allenbury catches it. At one point, she puts her finger in his ear. This teasing, which might suggest frivolity in the character to match the original news story, is a joke shared with her father about their response to the sincerity Haggerty is pouring on them. A confirmed realist might point out that she could not possibly know what is being said on the phone, but the audience knows, and the tone in the scene plays on that knowledge; we wait for Haggerty to fall over his sweet reason as though he were a personage about to step on a banana peel. When Connie begins to speak, her head is buried in the tennis sweater which she is pulling off, and our first look at her, her hair becomingly mussed, comes as she tells the lawyer to inform them that the libel suit is for five million dollars.

Myrna Loy had been in the movies since 1925, had moved from minuscule roles to wicked ladies to evil exotics—Chinese, Gypsy, Eurasian. After seeing her in *Skyline* (1931), Irving Thalberg brought her to MGM, but once she got there she continued to be a utility other woman. A popular Loy-Thalberg anecdote concerns his famous career changing interview with her, held a year or so after she came to MGM. In the kind of platitudes that often passed for Thalbergian wisdom he told her that "there is something holding you back . . . there seems to be a veil between you and the audience," and presumably she sprinted out of his office, tore off the veil, and—presto!—became a star. I suspect that the true story is less dramatic. As with so many performers of the period (Carole Lombard for example), she had to prove her talent on loan to other studios—*Love Me Tonight* (Paramount, 1932), *The Animal Kingdom* (RKO, 1932), *Topaze* (RKO, 1933). "It was Rouben Mamoulian who first gave me a comedy bit in 'Love Me Tonight,'" she told an interviewer in 1936, "and that, I think, was the turning point of my career." Pare Lorentz, reviewing the Mamoulian film, said, "Myrna Loy is for once melted down to an easy natural manner, which makes her twice as comely," a remark that seems even stronger when one remembers that a few months earlier, reviewing *Arrowsmith* (1932), he chided John Ford and Sidney Howard for adding to Sinclair Lewis's story "a menace in the form of a well-dressed woman." The unidentified "menace" was played by Loy, presumably still unmelted, unnatural, although looking at *Arrowsmith* now one can see the outlines of the Loy persona to come. Her performance is somewhat metallic, but a neat, clean statement of a type that would gain polish in a few years, soften, take on humor and self-irony. The process is under way in *Love Me Tonight*, where it can best be seen not in her occasional comic lines but in the countess's amused and almost wordless participation in the confrontation between her cousin (Charles Ruggles) and his father (C. Aubrey Smith).

"No one person really discovered me," Loy said in 1973, not denying Mamoulian's recognition of her but extending the process. "I was discovered over and over, every time a director saw some quality he could bring out in me that I didn't even know I had." At MGM, it was W. S. Van Dyke who mined her best qualities ("Nobody ever pays any attention to W. S. Van Dyke," Loy said in 1980, "But he was a fabulous director") in *Penthouse* (1933), *The Prizefighter and the Lady* (1933), *Manhattan Melodrama* (1934), *The Thin Man* (1934). "I'm not even a lady," Loy's Gertie Waxted says in *Penthouse*, but she is—far too ladylike, in speech and manner, for the company she keeps. A whore with a heart of gold, she wins the love of Jackson Durant (Warner Baxter), but it is not in the plot but the dialogue that the film is prophetic. Similar banter (both films were written by Frances Goodrich and Albert Hackett) works much better in *The Thin Man*, in which Nora Charles, a millionaire's daughter, seems a better vehicle for the developing Loy style than Gertie Waxted and in which William Powell is a more relaxed partner than Baxter. After the surprising success of *The Thin Man* (it was a studio quickie, shot in twelve days), MGM cranked up its star-making machinery and took advantage of the personality that audiences had already embraced.

Attempts to define Loy's quality as a performer almost always turn into descriptions of Nora Charles and the other "perfect wife" characters she played and emphasize her warmth, her wryness, her amused understanding of male idiosyncrasies. Alva Johnston tried to do more than that in a piece he did for *Woman's Home Companion* in 1935. The article is awash with biographical inaccuracies, but it is sound criticism when he turns to comic technique. "Miss Loy is almost perfect in her delivery of a good line," he said. "When she has a funny thing to say, she does not give any intimation that it is going to be funny. It takes the audience a fraction of a second to discover that she has been clever." Then, to explain the "almost" in the first sentence, he added, "She is not quite perfect because after a smart line she will sometimes look up brightly, as if pleased with herself and expecting a little applause." Since Johnston said that W. C. Fields was the only comedian at the time who was perfect at the technique of speaking a funny line without either signaling it before hand or underlining it afterwards and since Johnston was one of Fields's most insistent admirers, he put Myrna Loy in very heady company. *Libeled Lady* is full of examples of Loy's unheralded comic lines, particularly in her early exchanges with William Powell. For me, however, the most impressive one comes late in the film in a scene with Spencer Tracy. Haggerty, no longer convinced that the Allenburys can be beaten by chicanery, comes to make a direct appeal to Connie. When he finishes his soupily hightoned plea on behalf of the men and women who will lose their jobs if the suit is successful, Connie says, as though genuinely interested, "You write the editorials, don't you?" If her comic lines are delivered with minimal emphasis, she has voice tricks for other occasions that help explain why she comes across as a happy mix of wit and sentiment. In *Stamboul Quest* (1934), a foolishness about international spies, George Brent's American, beginning to suspect that his bumptious charm is not working on Loy's wordly spy, asks if she has been laughing at him all along. "A little bit, perhaps," she answers, "but very tenderly." Loy almost caresses *tenderly*. The best example in *Libeled Lady* is in the garden scene toward the end of the movie in which the Connie-Bill romance is about to reach its culmination. "We've had such fun together—such happy times," Connie says. The line, pure cliché, escapes its bromidic origins through the incredible thing Loy does with the word *happy*; she trips it somehow into a playful skip and a throatcatch in one.[4] Even Fields could not do that.

The announced libel suit sets off a search for Bill Chandler, the best libel man who ever worked for the *Evening Star*. That search—shots of editors in Washington, Denver, San Francisco, a broadcaster in Singapore—is the introduction to the last of the principals, the last of the stars. The copyboy, whom no one has asked, finally volunteers the information that Bill is in town, at the Grand Plaza. Haggerty, who had fired Bill because he thought he knew more about the newspaper business than anyone else (Bane: "And he was right") and who wants to rehire him on the cheap, is disturbed at the news, assuming that Bill must be in the money if he is staying at such a good hotel. We go to a close-up of a hotel statement indicating that Bill owes $745.60 in back rent. Cut, finally, to Bill Chandler, to William Powell. He is standing in the lobby, reading the bad news with obvious equanimity, when Warren comes up and pokes him. "Warren Haggerty," Bill says, " . . . a stab in the back spells Haggerty." This line, like Haggerty's earlier description of Bill as "a conceited, double-crossing heel," indicates that theirs is one of the favorite Hollywood relationships, the standard acrimoniously friendly rivalry (Captain Flagg and Sergeant Quirt in whatever profession), and it is developed that way in the film, on a basis of mutual distrust. Their competitive relationship is kept on the periphery of the action for most of the movie since it is Bill's courtship of the two women that is most central to the plot. Yet, it is proper that we first meet Bill with Warren, watch him outsmart the Haggerty who so wants to be clever, for Bill is essentially a con man. He spends most of the movie in one pose or another, exuding sincerity as he manipulates Connie, Gladys, Warren, Mr. Allenbury. He sets out to deceive Connie, to compromise her so that she will have to drop the libel suit, and, having fallen in love with her, continues to deceive her until almost the end of the film so that she will not know that he is connected with the *Star*. After the initial antagonism with Gladys, he becomes so sweet and understanding with her that Gladys, unused to a kind word, becomes first his ally in postponing the action against Connie, finally a jealous wife in earnest. He convinces—or at least tries to convince—Haggerty that he is concerned only with the problems of the *Star*, and he makes Allenbury believe that he is a seasoned fisherman, legitimizing the deception by winning his slapstick battle with the giant trout Allenbury has been after for years.

In discussing William Powell in the chapter on *My Man Godfrey* (see pp. 199–202), I tried to differentiate between brands of Powell suavity, between the weightier Godfrey, the lighter Nick Charles. Bill Chandler belongs with Nick Charles. The reviewer in the *New Statesman* described Frank Morgan's comic technique—"that trick of voluble forced jollity cut short, contradicted, and resumed"—and suggested that Powell, who had just appeared with Morgan in *The Great Ziegfeld* (1936), was doing "a close and clever imitation" of the comedian. I can understand the English critic's point without quite accepting it. In the dinner on shipboard, for instance, Bill regularly initiates a verbal approach to the Allenburys, is cut short by Connie, retreats, regroups, and tries again. Although Powell plays somewhat broadly in this scene, he never approximates the befuddled con men so beautifully created by Morgan—think of *Dimples* (1936) or *The Wizard of Oz* (1939) rather than *Ziegfeld*. Chandler is still feeling his way in this scene, but for most of the movie what Powell conveys is the character's self-awareness, his amusement at his own games. This can be seen even in the romantic scenes with Connie—the moments when the film comes closest to turning sentimental—and it is so obvious in the scenes with Gladys that it would be sad if it were not so funny. The playfulness belongs to the character, but it is also a function of Powell's partnership with Myrna Loy. She serves for the pair of them as Powell does for the eccentric family in *My Man Godfrey*. *Solidity* is too heavy a word for Loy, but—call it *stillness*, call it *reserve*—she has a quality that makes her a fixed point around which Powell can practice his "light cat-dancing style." They made fourteen films together (*Libeled Lady* was the fifth) and, almost forty years after they first appeared together in *Manhattan Melodrama*, Loy was to remember: "From the very first scene we did together . . . we felt that particular magic there was between us. There was this feeling of rhythm, of complete understanding, and an instinct of how each of us could bring out the best in the other." This quality is only occasionally visible in the preposterousness of *Manhattan Melodrama*; their "best" was to show at its strongest in the comedies, beginning with *The Thin Man*. Their team playing pervades *Libeled Lady*, and the wry affection of Bill and Connie provides a softer beat against which Bill's scenes with Gladys and/or Warren take on greater comic force.

Once the four main characters are introduced, the film settles down to its primary task, carrying them at a brisk run through plot and counterplot, pausing only for extended comic sequences (Bill's marriage to Gladys, their fake fond farewell, the trout-stream slapstick). The marital mixup is transcended (rather than resolved), and the film ends as the four of them, now properly paired, talk noisily all at once. Connolly's face looms large on the screen, shouting a final "QUIET," for all the world as though he were Porky Pig, bringing a Looney Tunes to an end with "Th-th-that's all, folks!"

Libeled Lady was not only one of MGM's most successful movies commercially—outdrawing presumably classier offerings such as *Camille, Anna Karenina,* and *A Tale of Two Cities* (all 1935)—but it was generally pleasing to reviewers as well. An occasional doubtful note did creep into the notices, questioning not the effectiveness of the film but the implicit ugliness of this band of lovable characters. Otis Ferguson, of all critics, complained that the movie "is a bit mean to some of its characters." The anonymous reviewer in the *New Statesman* called

Moving in on the libeled lady. Myrna Loy, William Powell. (*Libeled Lady*, MGM, 1936. The Museum of Modern Art/Film Stills Archive.)

the film "a story of a biter getting bit," and proceeded to define his terms: "For 'newspaper' read scandal-sheet; for 'biter' read out-smarted crook; for love interest substitute Hollywood's whole pack of wisecracks, complications, shady business and noisy divorce: that'll give you a fair idea of the picture." That is not an inaccurate description. Looked at objectively, Bill Chandler is a professional trickster; Warren Haggerty is a manipulator intent on survival, not journalistic truth; Connie Allenbury is an overprotected rich girl with the icy self-possession that implies ("I simply can't be bothered with people I meet on a boat"); Gladys Benton is a willing victim and finally a would-be dog in the manger.

It is, of course, neither desirable nor possible to look at the characters objectively. Three aesthetic forces interfere. Vincent Canby touched on two of them in his recent reconsideration of *Libeled Lady*. Speaking of MGM's overt allegiance to the studio setting, he wrote,

> This sort of stylization, which certainly didn't appear to be stylization in the 30's, has the effect of intensifying the dramatic experience by removing it from a distracting reality. The characters become larger-than-life by being both what they are (actors/stars) and what they represent.

In another kind of film the simultaneity of performer and character can be disconcerting (why is Clark Gable pretending to be Parnell?), but here it is a contribution to the total effect of the movie. Not only do the stars share audience attention with the characters they play, but their presence, their charm cleanses the characters of negative attributes. This process is heightened by the artificiality of the film, in part a product of the "stylization" to which Canby referred. He is wrong to suggest that it was not apparent to 1930s audiences, for—as most of my discussion of the film suggests—*Libeled Lady* is conscious artifice, advertising itself by word and visual image. When a director allows a character to say metaphorically that there are going to be fireworks and then cuts to actual fireworks—as Haggerty does just before Gladys leaves in anger for the charity fair at the Allenbury estate—the bridge between the scenes is obviously a gag; whether the audience groans or laughs, the corniness of the device is its point.

The third element in the sweetening of *Libeled Lady* is the hovering presence of the *Evening Star*. When, at the beginning of the film, Haggerty tries to save the situation, he calls for a new front page to replace the Allenbury story. "War Threatens Europe," he suggests as a headline. When the assistant asks, "What country?" he answers, "Flip a nickel." On that exchange we are back in Hecht-MacArthur country.

Later, as Bill and Warren sit plotting the attack on Connie Allenbury, they use phrases like "America's playgirl" and "fat-headed old father," which suggest that, even though they know how stories get into the paper, they come to believe their own inventions. Warren Haggerty is not Walter Burns, nor was meant to be, and his friend and rival is no Hildy Johnson, but *Libeled Lady*, for all that it wanders rather far away from the newsroom, is still a newspaper farce, which means that whatever Bill and Warren do they are protected by the built-in innocence of the genre. *Libeled Lady* is a completely amoral film, but the amorality is transformed into delight.

Notes

1. When Robert Garland used the phrase "Maurine Watkins and a couple of other fellows" in his review of *Libeled Lady* (*New York American*, October 31, 1936, p. 11), he probably meant it as a compliment if he meant it at all; Garland, not the most careful writer on a New York daily, may have made the neat remark by accident. It was years later that Watkins was to fall prey to an unconscious antifemale reaction when, with the alteration of a single letter, Maurine Watkins became Maurice Watkins in Donald Deschner's *The Films of Spencer Tracy* (New York, Citadel, 1968, p. 69), in the Hecht filmography in Richard Corliss's *The Hollywood Screenwriters* (New York, Discus-Avon, 1972, p. 89), in Julian Fox's *Films and Filming* piece on John Ford ("A Man's World," 19 [April 1973], 36), and in Dan Ford's *Pappy: The Life of John Ford* (Englewood Cliffs, N.J., Prentice-Hall, 1979, p. 53). The latter appeared after the success of the musical version of *Chicago* (1975), an event which made Maurine Watkins rather more visible than she had been for several decades.

2. From the precredits opening shot, it is obvious that Dolly Tree's costumes are going to be an important element in the film. Tree dresses both Loy and Harlow with great care, making the always attractive Harlow costumes just a touch flashy, not at all right for Loy's richly restrained Connie Allenbury. Connie could never wear the fur-trimmed suit that Gladys carries with such angry grace when she heads for a showdown at the Allenbury estate, and Gladys would not be caught dead in the simple and rather unbecoming print dress that Connie wears in the flapjack scene at the fishing camp. This preoccupation with clothes is not simply the studio's attempt to make its film as attractive as possible. It is almost a subject, certainly a characterizing device, of the movie. In *Red-Headed Woman*—the Brush novel even more than the film—Lillian Andrews's constant search for some-

thing impressive to wear is not simply an old campaigner's desire for
the most effective weapons but an indication of the arriviste's uncertainty about her position. There is some of that in Gladys, but it is
broadly comic here. During a discussion of how she and Haggety will
surprise Bill and Connie at the fishing camp, she gets sidetracked into a
consideration of what she should wear (not even *Vogue* prescribed the
correct costume for catching one's husband with another woman) and
decides on the pink ("I look awfully cute in pink"). Later, when Bill is
trying to protect Connie by insisting that there is not enough evidence
to support a charge, that they would be thrown out of court, Gladys
says not if she wears blue ("I'm awfully appealing in blue"). One of the
attractions of a film like *Libeled Lady* now, almost fifty years after it was
made, is archaeological. It is an animated fashion museum, evoking a
period as automobiles, furnishings, even ways of speaking do. The
gown that Loy wears in the charity-ball scene is a case in point. Both
the cloth, which to my untrained eye looks like shimmering brocade,
and the discreet daring of the single strap across the shoulder (and Loy
has the shoulders to wear it) mark it as the height of fashion, now
become a period piece. Yet, it is not so purely 1930s as the pajamas that
triggered this footnote, with the ornate G C (Gladys is Mrs. Bill Chandler at this point) that serves as a catch. These voluminous pajamas,
the legs in repose almost a skirt, are an unmistakable sign of the
decade. When Irene (Carole Lombard) enters the sitting room in *My
Man Godfrey*, complaining that no one has noticed her new pajamas,
her costume says 1930s to me more clearly than the film's references to
the Depression although—in the circles in which I grew up—I saw
plenty of evidences of the Depression and no "turquoise-blue-and-
silver tea pajamas," like those that Lillian wears in Katharine Brush's
novel (New York, Farrar & Rinehart, 1931, p. 121). The costume seems
particularly to belong to Harlow. Gwen in *Public Enemy* is most Harlow
in the aborted love scene with Tom (James Cagney), less for what she
does than for the slithery formal trousers she wears. As *Motion Picture*
told us, Harlow was the "first movie star to wear pajamas on Hollywood Boulevard." (Muriel Babcock, "The Headline Career of Jean
Harlow," *Motion Picture*, 44 [December 1932], 73).

3. This is Harlow's "last mile" scene. Although her resplendent
white negligee lacks the acres of frill that decorate the one that Kitty
Packard wears to greet her doctor/lover (Edmund Lowe) in *Dinner at
Eight*, the setting is likely to suggest the earlier movie to Harlow fans. It
will certainly recall the celebrated *Time* magazine cover of August 19,
1935—a fantasy in white. A white Harlow sits on a white chair, dressed
all in white—a low-cut robe with cuffs as big as a majorette's pom-
poms. The white rug and the white bedspread pick up the texture as

well as the color of the cuffs. The dazzling quality is emphasized by a patch of gray shadow under the left side of the chair, and a startling circle of black; the mirror of her looking glass, held down, facing the camera, reflects the intense light on her and thus photographs black. It could be called "Jean Harlow" just as another famous sitting lady is routinely called "Whistler's Mother," but the *Time* cover might more properly borrow the abstract title of the painting, substitute *white* for *gray*, and call itself "Arrangement in White and Black."

4. Connie's line is retained in *Easy to Wed* (1946), the unfortunate musical remake of *Libeled Lady*. To get a sense of the special quality of Loy as performer, compare her reading of the line with that of Esther Williams, for whom it is little more than eight words in a row.

NOTHING SACRED

· 1937 ·

I'll write them a farce, half gall, half candy,
And call it, "*Sic transit gloria mundi.*"
—Peer Gynt

William A. Wellman was one of the names Frank Capra mentioned in a 1975 interview when he listed the directors he admired. "He's a man who talks like he wants you to think he knows nothing," Capra said, "but he knows a great deal about a lot of things." One of the things he—or Ben Hecht, who wrote the screenplay to *Nothing Sacred*, or David O. Selznick, who produced it, or all three men—knew a lot about was Capra's *Mr. Deeds Goes to Town* (1936). Neither the reviewers in 1937 nor commentators since have noticed the way *Sacred* plays off *Deeds*, but the connection between the films is not only implicit in the concepts on which the two movies are based, but explicit in some of the scenes.

Nothing Sacred, like *Deeds*, moves from New England to New York City to tell its story of the rural innocent who goes to town. Mount Ida, Arkansas, of James H. Street's original story, becomes Warsaw, Vermont, of the film, perhaps so that it will have a superficial resemblance to the Mandrake Falls in which Deeds lives. In *Nothing Sacred* the sexes of the principals are reversed; the knowing big-city newspaperperson is Wally Cook (Frederic March) and it is Hazel Flagg (Carole Lombard), whom he brings to New York. She is supposed to be dying of radium poisoning and Cook, who is in disgrace with his publisher because his last bit of chicanery was found out, plans to reingratiate himself with Oliver Stone (Walter Connolly) by bringing Hazel to New York as the guest of the *Morning Star* so that the newspaper can batten on the last

City slickers. Walter Connolly, Fredric March. (*Nothing Sacred*, Selznick International, 1937. The Museum of Modern Art/Film Stills Archive.)

brave days of a doomed and beautiful young woman. This is not simply the story of a tough newspaperman softened by guilt and love, as Babe Bennett (Jean Arthur) is in the Capra film; *Nothing Sacred* is *Deeds* turned inside out in a more basic way. Hazel Flagg is the manipulator; Wally Cook, the innocent. New York City, as saccharine as it is fraudulent, is cotton candy to the hardtack of Warsaw, Vermont.

Wellman, like Capra, introduces us to his film's New England village, but it is not the idealized small town of Capra's movie. When Wally Cook arrives in Warsaw, he plays a scene with the baggageman which is a parody of the one that Cedar and company have in *Deeds*. The character in *Sacred* is as laconic as the one in *Deeds*, but where the latter is briskly and busily at work, the former is stretched out on the luggage wagon taking his ease. Olin Howland's performance embodies two elements that seem to reflect different stages of his show-business career. He made his broadway reputation as a dancer-comedian in musicals like *Leave It to Jane* (1917) and *Linger Longer Letty* (1919). It may be this background that allows him to use his lazily sprawling body in *Sacred* to convey such indifference to the questioning presence of Wally Cook. His face has more malevolent work to do, and its alliance is with the other film bits that Howland regularly played. "If you try to be funny you're usually not as funny as you may think," he told an interviewer. "Just let the comedy sneak out." In his one scene in *Little Women* (1933), his Mr. Davis, the prim schoolmaster, communicates a rigidity that is at once personal and regional. Even as he agrees not to tell Marmee about the misbehavior of Amy (Joan Bennett), his ungiving face seems to deny his act of Christmas charity. The lack of expression that masks Mr. Davis's grudging kindness in *Little Women* becomes the vehicle for suspicion and greed in *Sacred*. Unlike the amiable if precise character Spencer Charters plays in *Deeds*, Howland's baggageman not only refuses to take Cook to Hazel Flagg but tells him to go back to New York. No one in town will talk to him, the man explains, and he would not have done so except that he expected to be paid. Then, he tests the coin Cook gives him by sounding it on his makeshift bed.

The second *Deeds* echo comes with Cook's arrival at the house/office of the local doctor. His housekeeper is not the motherly figure that Emma Dunn plays in *Deeds*, urging the guests to have lunch. She is an icily self-contained figure who can spare him only two *yeps*—carrying on the monosyllabic joke begun at the railway station and continued in the scene with the lady in the drugstore (Margaret Hamilton)—and, when he asks to be announced to Dr. Enoch Downer (Charles Winninger), she says, "Tell him yourself," and continues to make ineffectual dabs at the furniture with her feather duster.

Between the direct *Deeds* references of the baggageman and the housekeeper, *Sacred* provides a number of additional images to emphasize how different the Hecht-Wellman small town is from the Capra one. Two ladies, one very tall, one very short, nod toward Cook, dismissing him with the gesture; to a critic beset by Capra allusions, the spinsterish women might recall the "pixilated" Faulkner sisters of *Deeds*, but such a comic duo is familiar enough (see the town gossips in *You're Telling Me* [1934]) to suggest that likenesses can be pressed too far. A group of children riding on the back of an ice wagon pelt Cook with bits of ice. His interview with the drustore proprietor becomes a slightly more animated repetition of the exchange with the baggageman. Margaret Hamilton, still two years from the witch in *The Wizard of Oz* (1939) that would haunt the rest of her career, was already established as a character actress whose simplest phrase, whose every look carried an edge of acid. "At the first dirty look shot by Miss Margaret Hamilton at her mother-in-law," Robert Benchley said in his review of Rose Franken's *Another Language* (1932), the play in which Hamilton made her highly successful Broadway debut, "the audience straightened up and began to pay attention." Within the somewhat narrow range suggested by her physical type ("I'm glad I'm homely," she told an interviewer in 1951. " . . . My face has given me lots of work."), she proved herself a versatile performer, but moviemakers quickly learned the value of an actress who wore self-satisfied rectitude like a badge of office and who spoke with a bite that might have cut through tenpenny nails. One has only to see her in *Nothing Sacred*, a tiny figure unassailable in the redoubt of her rocker, to know that Wally Cook has run into another wall of silence. She answers *nope* to his every question, except when he asks, "Mind if I sit down?" He slides uncertainly onto one of the stools at the soda fountain despite her negative *yep*, but gets no closer to finding Hazel Flagg. She finally agrees that he has "tooken" up her time and that it is probably worth something; she accepts his money.

The payments to the baggageman and the drugstore woman are more than simple jokes about Vermont canniness, just as the treatment of Wally Cook in this scene goes beyond the rejection of the stranger by an enclosed community. In *Deeds*, the main character's relaxed attitude toward money is shown as a product of the Mandrake Falls setting and is contrasted to the greed and the dishonesty of the big city. Warsaw, unlike Mandrake Falls, is a place where the only old-fashioned virtues are pecuniary ones. It is a company town for the Paragon Watch Company, for whom Hazel Flagg works and in whose factory she would have contracted the radium poisoning she is presumed to have at this point, and the townspeople, shutting out the New York newspaperman, are protecting the company, the poisoned rock on which the town is built. *Nothing Sacred* does little with this point. It is not a social comedy , even to the extent that *Deeds* and *My Man Godfrey* (1936) are, and it certainly does not upend *Deeds* to the extent of setting up an idealized city to balance the evil small town. Ben Hecht suggests a continuum of corruption that embraces town and city, country bumpkin and city slicker, heroine and hero, in a world in which, as the title says, nothing is sacred.

Wellman often said that he could no longer look at his pictures, but he made one exception in an interview with *Focus on Film*: "I can watch *Nothing Sacred* forever." He picked the best bit from the Warsaw scenes for special comment. "I'm very proud of that kid jumping out and biting March on the leg." As Cook walks along a benevolent-looking street (Technicolor contributes to the mythic surface that the actions undermine), a child darts out of a white-picket-fenced front yard, sinks his teeth in the reporter's leg and scurries back to sanctuary. "It was really a midget," Wellman said, "and I knew which one to get because I'd done the tail end of a Tarzan picture a little while before." Although I cannot find Billy Barty's name in the credits to *Tarzan Escapes* (1936), which Wellman finished shooting after Richard Thorpe fell ill, that is the actor he means, then the best known midget performer in Hollywood. If, as Barty said in a 1981 interview, he is six years younger than Mickey Rooney, with whom he played in the Mickey McGuire comedies in the late 1920s, he would have been about eleven years old when he made *Nothing Sacred*. He appears to be about five. The film uses none of the special qualities that Busby Berkeley found in him a few years earlier, that child–old man lubriciousness that the boy shows in the "Honeymoon Hotel" number in *Footlight Parade* (1933) or the scene in *Gold Diggers of 1933* in which he leeringly raises the scrim curtain behind which the chorus girls are undressing. Wellman does not even want the smart-alecky behavior implicit in the still in *Harpo Speaks!* in which Harpo, in drag in a nurse's uniform, tangles with both Billy Barty and Tom Kennedy in a sequence presumably and unhappily discarded from *Monkey Business* (1931). What Wellman needs in *Nothing Sacred* is a performer who can be a five-year-old but move with relentless efficiency, attacking and retreating in an instant while the audience gasps in pleased surprise. Mark Van Doren was so taken with the "brief, noiseless, and surprising" scene that he called his review of the movie "Boy Bites Man" and labeled the event "the symbol through which the context is remembered."

After responding to the startling rightness of the biting scene, Van Doren lost it in a far too narrow reading of the film; he decided that the bite stood for Vermont's and Ben Hecht's "contempt for the metropolitan press" and that it was "the one gesture capable of discharging all the venom accumulated in his heart through years of impotently hating newspapers." As I suggested in the discussion of *The Front Page* in the chapter on *Libeled Lady* (see pp. 217–19), there was more love than hate in Ben Hecht's attitude toward the cruel sentimentality of journalism. In any case, despite the fact that a great many reviewers joined Van Doren in the misconception that *Nothing Sacred* was primarily a satire about newspapers, the targets of the barbed wit are so many and so indiscriminate that Billy Barty's scene can be lifted to a symbol only if one emphasizes the gratuitousness of the action. Then it stands not so much for the ideational content of the film as the behavior of the moviemakers, who bite everyone who happens to pass. If I were to isolate a single image from the film to represent the attitude of the movie toward man and society, I would turn away from Barty's bite, for all that I admire it; put Warsaw, Vermont, behind me; and go to the nightclub scene which comes later in the film, when Wally Cook shows New York to Hazel Flagg and Hazel Flagg to New York.

The nightclub—designed by Lyle Wheeler with a ceiling by special-effects man Jack Cosgrove—is elegant to look at, but it is pure sleaziness at the heart. The lights outside proclaim both HAZEL FLAGG NIGHT and TOOTSIES OF ALL NATIONS. The show consists of a presentation of the great heroines of history—Lady Godiva, Catherine of Russia, Pocahontas, a Dutch girl who saved Holland—leading up to applause for Hazel Flagg. The heroines are nearly nude show girls who ride in on horseback, but the vulgar triumph of the sequence is Frank Fay as the master of ceremonies. "Fay was brilliant, sardonic, and contemptuous of most of mankind," Marian Spitzer said in her book on the Palace Theatre, a description that suggests that he would have been right at home in *Nothing Sacred* even if he had not been asked to do a variation on the act that made him famous. The son of stock-company performers who was carried into show business when he was a small child, Fay had developed by the 1920s the routine that made him a vaudeville headliner. He served as master of ceremonies, but he interrupted acts as well as introduced them, wandered in and out of the proceedings, mixing outlandish anecdotes with pointed comments on the other performers delivered in a deceptively innocent manner. He came to Hollywood in 1929 to do his familiar bit in one of those all-star movie revues of the period, Warner's *Show of Shows*. He had a brief film career after that but quickly sank into obscurity, pushed along by the fondness for drink that had dogged him even in his most successful days. In 1935, he turned up in *Stars over Broadway* as the m.c. of an amateur hour in one of those radio-based musicals of the period in which Hollywood tried to co-opt the competition. If *Stars* was a step to *Sacred*, it served a useful purpose, for Frank Fay might have been invented for his role in the Wellman film. Jerry Stagg, commenting on Fay's contribution to the success of *Artists and Models* (1923), called him a comedian "whose face was a promising leer to begin with, and whose exquisite sense of timing could convert the Lord's Prayer into a suggestive piece." Take a line of his from *Nothing Sacred*, one that looks totally innocuous on the page: "Catherine the Great, who saved Russia—and she could do it too." There is nothing funny about this comment on the Catherine momentarily in the spotlight, but it is somehow fetid in context which makes it, by nightclub standards, a comic line. Burton Rascoe once described Fay's speciality as "the humor of anticlimax," which is clearly the case here. The hesitation after "Russia" signals that a joke is to follow, but when the second half of the sentence comes it proves to be surprisingly harmless except that Fay's voice caresses the phrase in a suggestive way. The line becomes nasty partly because it is not at all dirty in the expected sense.

This is the perfect setting for an image by which *Nothing Sacred* can represent itself. The Dutch boy who put his finger in the leaking dike and saved his country has here become the Dutch girl so that she can find a place among the scantily clad horsewomen. When Fay introduces Katinka (Jinx Falkenburg, the celebrated cover girl) to the crowd, he tells the story of her heroic action and then says, "Show them the finger, babe." She lifts her hand above her head so that we can see that one finger, presumably a casualty, is tied with a white rag by way of bandage, but that tepid joke is only the screen for the real one. The finger she lifts is the middle one and, since this film gives the finger to everyone and everything, it is a gestural obscenity that is also a substantive comment. Such a sign would be completely commonplace in a 1980s film, but in 1937 it was outrageous. In Section V ("Profanity") of The Production Code in operation then, "finger (the)" was expressly forbidden. Someone over in the Hays office went momentarily deaf and blind, seduced presumably by Fay's gift for disguising double entendre and by the white rag that obscured the classic lift of the middle finger. As though intent on seeing how far they could go with the game, Hecht and Wellman reprised the theme in the scene in which Oliver Stone learns that Hazel Flagg does not have radium poisoning. When he is told that she has pneumonia and a temperature of 106, his outrage turns to gratification and he calls this presumed punishment on the fraudulent Hazel "the finger of God." His choice of this phrase where "the hand of God" might more conventionally be used evokes not the Sistine Chapel ceiling but the uplifted finger of Katinka.

How did Selznick International, which was newly launched in 1936 with *Little Lord Fauntleroy*, find its way to *Nothing Sacred*. At first glance, it might seem that, following the success of *A Star Is Born* (1937), the producer (Selznick), the director (Wellman), the star (March), the cameraman (W. Howard Greene), and the technical staff of that film set out to do for New York in *Nothing Sacred* what they had done for Hollywood in the less romantic, less sentimental scenes in *Star*. Yet, if Wellman's chronology is correct in his interview with Richard Schickel,[1] "the Ben Hecht thing" was scheduled before Selznick decided to do *A Star Is Born*. According to Ronald Haver in *David O. Selznick's Hollywood*, John Hay Whitney, Selznick's New York moneyman,[2] thought they should do a screwball comedy; Selznick agreed on the understanding that he could hire Ben Hecht to do the script. Whitney, who is said to have disliked Hecht, a feeling that was apparently mutual, wired, "If you're absolutely convinced that there no one else who can do the job, then go ahead and hire him." Hecht, screenwriting was a high-paying chore that was best finished quickly as possible, its rewards monetary rather than artistic. "Writi a good movie brings a writer about as much fame as steering a bicy he said, a typical Hecht dismissal denied by the reviews of *N Sacred*, most of which discussed it as a Hecht film; there was even a piece in *Stage* which used his screenplay to illustrate the joys of reading movies. Critics today are likely to take *Nothing Sacred* or *Scarface* (1932) more seriously than Hechtian high art, like his novel *Eric Dorn* (1921). "Much as I do not admire Mr. Ben Hecht," Otis Ferguson wrote in his review of *It's a Wonderful World* (1939), "I must insist that he is one of the most brilliant writers in pictures . . . and has been proving it for years." Selznick seems to have agreed. In 1936, instructing the New York office to write into Sidney Howard's contract for *Gone with the Wind* availability clauses to allow "almost daily collaboration with myself," he said, "the only exception in my entire producing career in which I have had any success in leaving a writer more or less alone has been in the case of Hecht." According to the filmography prepared by Steven Fuller and Rose Caylor, Hecht's widow, the writer had been an uncredited contributor to *Topaze* (1933), which Selznick produced at RKO, and had done the screenplay for *Viva Villa!* (1934), one of Selznick's MGM films. In a letter to Louis B. Mayer about *Villa*, Selznick suggested a $5000 bonus for Hecht if he finished the script in fifteen days, "for doing in two weeks what it would take a lesser man to do, with certainly infinitely poorer results, in six or eight weeks."

In *A Child of the Century*, Hecht said that he did the *Sacred* screenplay "in two weeks . . . on trains between New York and Hollywood." The process was not quite that simple. He first submitted an outline about a group of unattractive rich people, which Selznick rejected, suggesting instead that he look at a short story on which Selznick had just taken an option. Already bought by *Cosmopolitan*, "Letter to the Editor," as the story was then called, was the first fiction by James H. Street, who would go on to write historical novels such as the best-selling *Tap Roots* (1942) and dog stories such as "The Biscuit Eater" (1939). "Letter," which was published as "Nothing Sacred" a month before the film was released, reflects Street's background as a New York newspaperman rather than the rural settings of his better-known works. It also suggests that he was not exaggerating years later when he told the *Raleigh News and Observer*, "I not only hadn't ever written a short-story, I hadn't read 20 in my life." About all that Hecht salvaged from the Street story was the device—the false diagnosis of radium poisoning—and the idea that "a little gal from Mount Ida, Arkansas" could outsmart "the hottest newspaper in the hottest circuit of the world," as Street's rather gentle city editor put it. On this fragile base, Hecht built a script which even he later admitted was one of the ten or so of his seventy movies that "were not entirely waste product." Not that the script was his alone. Never a man to labor long in "the Hollywood jute mills," Hecht left the screenplay unfinished—if we are to believe Bob Thomas's *Selznick*—or at least with an ending that did not satisfy the producer. As was his way (consider the confused writing credits for *Gone with the Wind*), Selznick called on George S. Kaufman, Moss Hart, Sidney Howard, Robert Sherwood—or so various sources insist—before turning to Ring Lardner, Jr., and and Budd Schulberg, the embyro writers who are supposed to have saved the ending of *A Star Is Born*. Schulberg became ill and Lardner was assigned to work with George Oppenheimer (see chap. 9, p. 222), "on loan from MGM for the purpose"; the two men devised an ending which, if it falls short of the best of *Nothing Sacred*, at least brings the film to an acceptable close.

In 1966, William A. Wellman told an interviewer that on "the few great pictures . . . the two who were really responsible . . . were the writer and the director," and he later talked about sitting around with "these fine writers—Ben Hecht, Ernie Gann and so on" doctoring their scripts to fit the immediate needs of a shot. Although the image conjured by the last remark hardly squares with Hecht's portrait of himself as a hack who turned in his copy and ran, Wellman, who after all had writing credits of his own—*The Robin Hood of El Dorado* (1936), *A Star Is Born*, *The Last Gangster* (1937), *Gallant Journey* (1946)—obviously contributed to those scripts on which his name did not appear. He may even have invented the biting scene that he remembered so fondly from *Nothing Sacred*. Since it is not in the copy of the screenplay in the Museum of Modern Art film archives, it was added later, but whose idea it was remains lost in the cloudy land of collaboration. Wellman did claim—but, then, so did Darryl F. Zanuck—to have invented the grapefruit in the face that made the James Cagney–Mae Clarke breakfast scene in *Public Enemy* (1931) so notorious. Although Wellman, whose directorial credits go back to his work with Dustin Farnum and Buck Jones in the mid-1920s, worked in all genres, he is best known for his war and adventure films. He would do some interesting comedies in the 1940s, including *Roxie Hart* (1942), to which Hecht is supposed to have been an uncredited contributor, but there is nothing in his pre-1937 work to prepare us for *Nothing Sacred*. Conventional comedy does crop up in some of his dramas, as in El Brendel's supposedly funny recruit in *Wings*, and there is a distant nod to Charlie Chaplin in the department store scene in *Public Enemy*, in which Tom and Matt, as boys, escape their pursuers by making clever use of the escalator and the bulk of two large women. Still, in the Wellman canon, *Nothing Sacred* is one of a kind.

Wellman later enlarged on his writer-director remarks by saying, "You see, pictures that still live, that are still successful, are made with the combination of a writer and a director and a producer." He was speaking of Zanuck at that moment, but he might have been talking about Selznick, of whom he liked to say, "I didn't make pictures for him, I made them with him." Wellman, who was riding high at Paramount after the success of *Wings*, was presumably largely responsible for Selznick's being hired there as a producer in 1928, the first important step toward his later eminence. The next year, Wellman worked with Selznick on *Chinatown Nights* and *The Man I Love*, and later, at RKO, on *The Conquerors* (1932), but it was not until *Star* and *Sacred*, the two he did for Selznick International, that their work together was more than routine. The closeness of their collaboration is best shown perhaps by the story of Wellman and his writer's Oscar. When he and Robert Carson received the Academy Award for original story, for *A Star Is Born*, he put the statue down on Selznick's table and said "either sarcastically or honestly" that it belonged to the producer. There was presumably the same kind of close cooperation on *Nothing Sacred* although a look at the Selznick credits suggests that he was only a little better prepared for that kind of comedy than Wellman was. He had worked with Gregory La Cava (*The Half-Naked Truth* [1932]) and Harry d'Arrast (*Topaze* [1933]) at RKO, and had even produced a film featuring Jack Pearl, Jimmy Durante, ZaSu Pitts, and Ted Healy and the Three Stooges at MGM (*Meet the Baron* [1933]) but by the time he left MGM, he had become best known as the producer of loving transformations of classic novels, notably the big three of 1935: *David Copperfield, Anna Karenina, A Tale of Two Cities.* "You wanted comedy," he wired Jock Whitney, when production on *Nothing Sacred* began, "— Boy you're going to get it. . . . After this one I am either the new Mack Sennett or I return to Dr. Eliot." Although *Little Lord Fauntleroy* and *The Prisoner of Zenda* (1937) hardly belong on the good doctor's five-foot shelf, Selznick remained more Eliot than Sennett. His one post-*Sacred* comedy was the very gentle *The Young in Heart* (1938). He would go on to burn Atlanta, but he was essentially too romantic to play with "the finger of God."

"Let's see the finger." The first shots of *Nothing Sacred* include the fountain at Rockefeller Center, a section of a skyscraper, Times Square at night—conventional shots made unconventional by the use of Technicolor. The audience is not allowed simply to take pleasure in familiar sights in glamorous new garb because superimposed on the scenes are titles that proclaim (the ellipses mark the movement from view to view) "THIS IS NEW YORK, Skyscraper Champion of the World . . . where the Slickers and Know-It-Alls peddle gold bricks to each other . . . and where Truth crushed to earth rises again more phony than a glass eye." This opening indicates not only the tone of the film, but that it will quite willingly eschew subtlety when the spirit moves the filmmakers—although these lines are almost austere compared to the extended version that *Stage* quoted from the Hecht screenplay.

The film then takes us to a banquet where Wally Cook sits, apparently drunk, and Oliver Stone pontificates about the "twenty-seven halls of learning and culture" that the *Morning Star*'s very own "potentate of the Orient" will build. We are thus introduced to two of the principals and the performers who embody them. Despite Cook's present condition, he is not quite the stereotype that the Hecht of *The Front Page* helped establish, which may be why it was possible for Fredric March to fill the role. March was an unusual performer, popular and busy all during the 1930s, but there were always critics and moviegoers who found him a less interesting actor than his admirers insisted he was. Otis Ferguson was consistently harsh about March until *Mary of Scotland* (1936), even when he liked the actor's work; he praised Richard Boleslawski's *Les Miserables* (1935) because the director made "something more than a silly paper bag out of Fredric March." Even Selznick seems to have had some doubt about using him as Vronsky in *Anna Karenina*: "I begged for Gable, but I got March." The division between March watchers goes back as far as the 1920s when the actor was beginning to make his way on Broadway. Alexander

Woollcott found him "extraordinarily good in the absurd central role" in Jack McClellan's *The Half-Caste* (1926), but Alan Dale, more laconic in his review, wrote, "Frederic³ March played the boy, and wore a nice white suit." He signed with Paramount in 1928 and spent five years vacillating between terrible and promising films. From the beginning, fan magazines pushed his career. In a typical piece in *Motion Picture Classic* in 1931, Elisabeth Goldbeck said that "there is nobody else in pictures who can approach him as the humorous, volatile, insubordinate and completely charming person he was in 'Laughter' and 'The Royal Family.'" By 1937, he was so established as a romantic actor that one had almost to turn back to those two 1930 films to find a precedent for March in comedy.

There was *Design for Living* (1933), but Ben Hecht's reworking of Noel Coward for Ernst Lubitsch was more amiable than outrageous. Nor do the two earlier films provide a suitable foretaste of *Nothing Sacred*. March's performance as Tony Cavendish is a touch too genteel in *The Royal Family of Broadway*, as the Edna Ferber–George S. Kaufman *The Royal Family* was renamed, presumably so that the folks in the boondocks would not think it a film about nontheatrical kings and queens. March had been playing the role on stage in Los Angeles when Paramount hired him, and when the film appeared he was generally praised, particularly for his impression of John Barrymore. There is one fine moment in the film when Tony's niece (Mary Brian) asks him angrily if *he* has had a baby; he answers, "You've uncovered my secret dream," fluting wildly and displaying gestures straight out of silent melodrama. Otherwise he storms around, busy vocally and physically, but this Tony lacks the insane note that the script calls for, the one that Barrymore displays so enthusiastically in *Twentieth Century* (1934). March is much more at home with Paul Lockridge in *Laughter*— a film that he often listed as one of his favorites—because the flamboyance of the artist, as written by Donald Ogden Stewart and directed by Harry d'Arrast, is little more than a restrained playfulness. It is ideological rather than demonic. *Laughter* has earned a retroactive reputation as "a screwball comedy, entirely out of its period," as John Paxton said in 1939, but it is no such thing. Stewart has called it "a comedy of marriage, another version of the 'youth vs. age' theme," a description that is generically correct without being accurate; the conflict is really between money/propriety and art/openness/freedom/ laughter. The touch of solemnity in Paul Lockridge's boyishness, the note of rectitude that sounds in his "laughter" speech suggest that the March of *Laughter* anticipates his Norman Maine in *A Star Is Born* more than he does his Wally Cook. Those qualities are more likely to be played as a joke in *Nothing Sacred*, except for the end of the film when

Cook makes his "flash-in-the-pan" speech on the transience of celebrity. The film presumably takes those sentiments seriously, but even their presentation is undercut, as Wally and Hazel get into an argument over just how admired she was, one that almost ends with her taking another sock at him.

The somewhat convoluted look at March's career in the paragraphs above grows out of my own misgivings about the actor. Looking back at his most famous 1930s roles, I find it hard to warm to the performer in his anthonyadversity—"sunk in the costume things," as he put it—and even in a film like *Laughter*, in which his performance is correct for that kind of comedy, the reserve in the character tends to become reservations about the actor. Yet, he seems right for Wally Cook because Wellman and the script are able to use his weaknesses as well as his undeniable skill. In his essay on Ben Hecht in *Talking Pictures*, Richard Corliss does his usual clever butchery on *Nothing Sacred*, branching out from the author to take in some of the performers, particularly March with his "vegetable magnetism." Cook is supposed to be "the vibrant, immoral center" of the film, according to Corliss, and March plays the reporter as "a wounded faun, a klutz, a Ralph Bellamy!" Corliss is wrong on the first point,[4] since Hazel Flagg is clearly the "immoral center," but he is right in his overstatement about March's performance. Yet, March is not failing the stereotype, as Corliss suggests. I doubt that March could have played a reporter like Pat O'Brien's Hildy Johnson in *The Front Page* (1931) or Spencer Tracy's Warren Haggerty in *Libeled Lady* (1936), but Wally Cook was surely never intended as a Hildy Johnson. Before he sets out for Warsaw he is given a boastful speech in which he tells Oliver that, if he fails to get a story, "You can put me back in short pants and make me marbles editor." The line—and the emphatic gesture that accompanies its delivery—hints at a vigor that is not in the role, just as Cook's initial drunkenness refers to the stereotypical newspaperman without the character's ever embracing that convention. If any residual grains of the stereotype remain after Wally Cook confronts the citizens of Warsaw, they are swept away in the scene at the wrestling match in which, as Hazel stands to take the homage of the wrestlers, the now guilty Wally, still seated, clasps and kisses her hand. Cook is not the protagonist of a newspaper farce, but the naive city boy being taken by the country slicker in a foolish variation on the seduction of the innocent. Even in the celebrated slugging match between Wally and Hazel (it was featured in many of the advertisements and the pressbook offered a photographic spread heralding it "Battle of the Century"), the heroine gets to knock out the hero.

If the reporter in *Nothing Sacred* has other stereotypical rows to hoe, the publisher is conventional enough, a lovely combination of unscrupulousness and sanctimoniousness. According to Ronald Haver, Selznick asked Hecht to "tone down" the Oliver Stone character, afraid that it "might insult his friends in publishing." If Oliver Stone has been smoothed toward blandness, the character must have been written in pure venom in the Hecht original. In the film, he is at his nasty best in the scene, following Hazel's collapse in the nightclub, in which he, Cook, and Dr. Downer hover over her bed; he says, in Walter Connolly's most concerned voice, "I don't want you to spare our feelings. We go to press in fifteen minutes." Except when he is angry, he speaks in the worst kind of journalistic platitudes. "The life blood of a newspaper is its integrity," he lectures Wally and Hazel, once all the schemes have collapsed. Undeterred by Wally's reminder that he wrote that speech for Stone to give at a convention in Cleveland, the publisher moves smoothly from "integrity" to an insistence that—for the sake of all those people who look up to her (that is, for the *Morning Star* and its circulation)—Hazel, who is finally tired of dissembling, must not confess the deception.

In his biography of Carole Lombard, Larry Swindell said that Connolly was cast as Oliver Stone at the actress's suggestion. Since the two performers had played together in *No More Orchids* (1932) and *Lady by Choice* (1934) and since Lombard professed to have learned a lot from Connolly on the second film, Swindell's contention may well be true. Connolly was an excellent choice in any case, not simply because of his ability (see pp. 233–34), but—given the *Deeds* echoes—because he was an old Frank Capra hand, having played irascible but soft-hearted fathers for the director twice in 1934—in *It Happened One Night* and *Broadway Bill*. Elsewhere, for other directors, Connolly could be amiably tricky—for Howard Hawks in *Twentieth Century*—or grandiloquently wrathful—for Lewis Milestone in *The Captain Hates the Sea* (1934)—but for any moviegoer who recognized the implications of the scene between Cook and the baggageman, Connolly would come trailing clouds of Capra and his unctuous Oliver Stone would be all the funnier. Connolly is so effective as Oliver Stone that his conscienceless newsreel executive in *Too Hot to Handle* (1938) seems a splenetic reprise of the earlier role. Although Connolly had a fine talent for the tonal nuances of public plausibility, he had perfected a verbal device which served him whenever excitement or anger stifled his character's measured if larcenous solemnity. Stone and Cook have been planning an elaborate state funeral for the presumably dying Hazel and when they learn that she has gone to commit suicide, Cook tries to call for help while Stone, more relentless in his concerns, shouts into the intercom, "Get the governor. Tell him we want that holiday tomorrow." On "want," Connolly's voice rises to an almost falsetto scream and breaks there, letting him slide, articulation still intact, to the end of the sentence.

Within the film as a whole, Oliver Stone, because of his pose of public responsibility, comes across as more corrupt than Wally Cook. Cook is essentially a prankster, a perpetrator of elaborate confidence games with the emphasis on *game*. The opening joke, that a Harlem bootblack is being passed off as a foreign prince, suggests the kind of trick, described by Ben Hecht in *Charlie*, in which Charles MacArthur convinced his gullible boss on the Hearst Sunday supplement that two young women were nonagenarians. It is, then, an unwitting Oliver Stone who waxes in self-satisfied eloquence as he introduces the cultural benefactor at the beginning of the film. Troy Brown, who plays the fake sultan, has little to do in this scene. An immense man with little movie experience, Brown was a comedian whose stock in trade was the contrast between his size and his lightness of foot. His one real scene in *Sacred* comes much later when, restored to his character as Ernest Walker, he leans his great bulk against the double doors and gently forces his way into Hazel's hotel suite. He calls someone—presumably a sweetie other than the wife of the opening sequence—to see what kind of flowers she likes ("Don't worry, honey—they all the same price") and then proceeds to fill a florist's box from the bouquets that have been sent by Hazel's admirers; his eye falls on Hazel's fake suicide note and, crying, he calls Stone to initiate the voice-breaking scene described above. Ernest Walker proves as sentimentally dishonest as the New York that has taken Hazel to its heart.

In the opening scene, Troy Brown has only one line—"Peace be unto you, my friends—peace and the blessings of culture." The fraudulent prince has scarcely got the words out when a disturbance can be heard, and a large black woman with several children of various sizes, comes hurrying down the stairs, calling out, "That's him. That's my husband." Hecht, if he wrote the sultan's line, may have intended the reiterated *peace* to suggest the greeting ritually used by the followers of Father Divine and thus to prepare for the unmasking. Not that the spectators would have had time to absorb the implications of the word before the disruptive entrance of Mrs. Walker. The force of the scene lies in the surprise it provides—and in the commanding presence of Hattie McDaniel, who makes this brief appearance as the wife. Only two years away from the role in *Gone with the Wind* which would bring her an Academy Award, McDaniel had established herself not only in the Mammy stereotype—*Judge Priest* (1934), *Show Boat* (1936)—

but in much more interesting variations on the black servant—*Blonde Venus* (1932), *Alice Adams* (1935). It may seem odd for a performer who had played a part as important as the one McDaniel had in *Show Boat* to be given a one-line walk-on, but in Hollywood in the 1930s, character actors in general, black actors in particular, often found themselves playing large roles one day, barely noticeable bits the next; in *Libeled Lady*, for instance, McDaniel, as a hotel maid, has no lines at all, is only a silent witness to the counterfeit touching farewells of Bill (William Powell) and Gladys (Jean Harlow). Her scene in *Sacred* was originally a more extended one, as the screenplay at the Museum of Modern Art indicates, but if it was filmed (a collection of stills showing the black children playing with the film's principals suggest that it was), it was later cut. That may have been unfortunate for the performer, but it was good for the movie. The exposure of the film's first fraud depends for its effectiveness not only on the arrival of Mrs. Walker, but on an abrupt cut from her revelation to the front page of the rival *Dispatch*. That page, incidentally, carries not only a shot of Walker "in rental robes" but one of him outside his bootblack stand above which hangs a sign that allows the filmmakers a very period joke: "Ernest Walker. Best Shine in Harlem."

Oliver Stone responds to the fiasco of the "learning and culture" banquet—which means to the *Dispatch's* making a fool of the *Morning Star*—by removing Wally Cook "from the land of the living." On Stone's spoken threat, the film cuts to the reporter stuck behind a tiny desk which bears a nameplate proclaiming him "obituary editor." That this is an unlikely desk ornament for a newspaper office bothers the filmmakers no more than the equally unbelievable statement that Cook has a five-year contract that will not allow him to quit the *Morning Star* (Hollywood had a way of thinking in terms of the highly paid bondage in which studios held actors); the label on the desk allowed the movie to use a joke as exposition. The idea of Cook as obituary editor probably came from the Street story, although Hecht uses it in a very different way. In the original, the girl from Mount Ida and one of the reporters assigned to show her the town fall in love (as Hazel and Wally do in the movie); at the end of the story, the kindly city editor, promising to bring them together, refuses to show the girl "what Joe wrote" because, he says, winking, "You see, Joe is our obituary editor!" Hecht takes Street's only joke and separates it from the context of the girl who is supposed to be dying, attaches it as punishment to Wally Cook before Hazel Flagg ever enters the film. The brief sequence in which Cook is in that limbo is little more than a series of visual gags. Wedged between two banks of files (the obituary editor in the newspaper morgue?), Cook becomes little more than a piece of furniture.

Someone at the water fountain throws a paper cup which lands on his hat; a girl leaning over to look into a file drawer plants her behind on his typewriter keys; a copyboy hits him with the flapping ends of the sheets he is carrying; a rain of photographs falls on him; two men move him and his chair aside to get by with a filing cabinet. The scene is a comic interlude within a comedy, a bit of horseplay which is almost affectionate. It quickly gives way to the film's more pervasive sardonic tone as Cook goes off to Vermont to get Hazel Flagg and his next big story.

Having undergone the introduction to Warsaw described at the beginning of this chapter, Cook comes finally to Dr. Downer. His presence elicits an explosion as Downer attacks the newspaper business in general, the *Morning Star* in particular in a burst of high moral vituperation that begins as a stock denunciation of journalistic evils, but turns out to be his grievance at not having won a *Morning Star* contest to pick the six greatest Americans. He cannot forgive them the one-dollar consolation prize. His flamboyant anger in the scene with Cook modulates into low-level irritability which surfaces on other occasions as in his defensive abruptness in the scene in which he tells Hazel about his misdiagnosis: "I don't chew my cabbage twice." It is in this scene that we get our first clear sense that Dr. Downer is as deceitful as he is incompetent, or would be if he had the courage of his lack of convictions. When a disappointed Hazel learns that she is not dying—she was going to use the two hundred dollars insurance money for a last fling in New York—she suggests that Downer not tell the company: "I know it sounds a little dishonest." He refuses because he is certain that they would get caught, and then he adds, almost as an afterthought, "and besides, there's the ethics." There is no question of "ethics" when Wally Cook makes his offer to Hazel Flagg. Downer's practice is not tied to the *Morning Star*, as it is to the Paragon Watch Company, and besides the paper cheated him out of the prize money he is sure was rightfully his. He accompanies Hazel to New York, thus giving medical credibility to her fake illness, and shows no sign of misgivings until late in the film when the deception begins to come to pieces. Add that he is a drunk—we see him take a swig from a jug marked poison— and he is as neat a collection of rural virtues, Hecht-Wellman variety, as one could imagine.

Drunken doctors were familiar characters in 1930s movies, where they were usually played by Thomas Mitchell and almost always regained their sobriety long enough to perform a bit of heroic medical sleight-of-hand (as in *Stagecoach* [1939] or *The Hurricane* [1937], another of Ben Hecht's uncredited scripts). But even redeemable drunkenness stayed away from country doctors. This was a decade in which that kindly, twinkly creature on Norman Rockwell magazine covers prevailed as a public image and in which readers made a best seller of Arthur E. Hertzler's *The Horse and Buggy Doctor* (1938). Country doctors in the movies may occasionally have been at odds with their society (Will Rogers in *Dr. Bull* [1933]), but they were suffering from misunderstanding, not malpractice. Dr. Enoch Downer is the decade's most determined assault on the country-doctor stereotype. Dr. Stall (Harlan Briggs), the old charlatan who helps Egbert Sousè (W. C. Fields) sequester J. Pinkerton Snoopington (Franklin Pangborn) in *The Bank Dick* (1940), is benign by comparison.

Nothing Sacred's use of Dr. Downer is the more interesting in the face of that film's introduction of a standard comic type, the foreign specialist. As that figure is usually presented he is both inept and pompous (see the offstage alienist in *The Front Page*, whose restaging of the crime leads to the escape of Earl Williams), but Dr. Eggelhoffer and his three colleagues are clearly competent enough to know that Hazel Flagg is not suffering from radium poisoning. Yet, they are presented as standard caricatures. The three consulting doctors are automatons as yes men, figures whose joke lies in their rigidity. One of them was played by Monty Woolley, who was obviously hired for his beard, not for his acid delivery, which was being introduced to moviegoers in *Live, Love and Learn* (1937) at about the time *Nothing Sacred* was released and which, in *The Man Who Came to Dinner*, would shortly make him a star on Broadway (1939) and in Hollywood (1941). Dr. Eggelhoffer was played by Sig Rumann, who, having just appeared as Dr. Leopold X. Steinberg in *A Day at the Races* (1937), had become the very model of the dialect comic doctor. When Siegfried Rumann[5] came to Hollywood in 1934, after having established himself as a dramatic actor in Germany and in New York (notably as Preysing in *Grand Hotel* [1930]), he was heralded by Fox's Winfield Sheehan as "one of the best and most versatile actors I have ever known," a worthy successor of Lon Chaney and Emil Jannings. Although his stern father in *The Wedding Night* (1935) is too conventional to put him in the Chaney-Jannings class, it reflects Sheehan's initial intention to use Rumann as a serious actor. In later years he occasionally got roles like Dutchman in *Only Angels Have Wings* (1939), in which he was both an affectionate joke and a sympathetic character, but once he ran afoul of the Marx Brothers in *A Night at the Opera* (1935) he pretty much became Herman Bing's rival as Hollywood's leading German dialect comedian. Dr. Eggelhoffer meets Dr. Downer in one scene in *Nothing Sacred*, and although it is hardly the kind of confrontation that Rumann had been playing with Groucho Marx, it is distantly like those in *Opera* and *Races*; the Rumann character remains the comic butt although his antagonist loses none of his own disreputable character. Dr. Downer, after his outing in the rowboat (he was supposed surreptitiously to save Hazel from her fake suicide), is soaking his feet and himself to ward off a cold. Dr. Eggelhoffer may expect a medical discussion; what he gets is a drunken rendition of "All the darkies am a weepin'/Massa's in the cold, cold ground."

The strength of Dr. Downer as a satirical character lies not simply in its conception, but in Charles Winninger's performance in the role. Winninger was as right for Downer as Walter Connolly was for Oliver Stone. Will Rogers, in a nostalgic column in 1935, said of his old *Ziegfeld Follies* associate, "Where in America is there . . . a Charley Winninger who could do anything ever done on stage, every musical instrument, a dandy acrobat." Rogers, of course, meant where among the new performers, for Winninger was still flourishing; he had just done *Revenge with Music* (1934) on Broadway and was about to reestablish his now-and-again film career which would carry him into the 1950s, when one of his last movies was *The Sun Shines Bright* (1953), a remake of *Judge Priest*, which found him in the role that Rogers had created originally. "I've done everything from the physic show, as it used to be called, up through the circus, vaudeville, musical comedy, straight drama (including Shakespeare and the Greeks) to grand opera," Winninger wrote in 1934. He made his Broadway debut as a German dialect comedian in *The Yankee Girl* (1910), but he was best known for his work in *No, No, Nanette* (1925) and as Captain Andy in *Show Boat* (1927), a role he repeated in the 1936 film version and in a radio series based on the character. The best anthology of Winninger's comic range, of his physical and vocal skills, can be found in *Show Boat* in the scene in which the mountain man, unfamiliar with theater, shoots at the villain, and Captain Andy has to act out the rest of the play, doing all the characters (including the heroine's sister) and staging a fight in which he plays both the opponents in a grand bit of acrobatic knockabout. His vocal devices can also be seen elsewhere in that film. At one point, unwilling to listen to gossip from Parthy (Helen Westley), he says, "I say fergit it, and when I say fergit it, fergit it," and on the third *fergit it*, his voice rises and then descends into an outraged whisper. His inspired use of calculated pauses can be seen in the New Year's Eve scene in which, a little drunk, he calls out "Hap . . . [long rest, then very explosively] . . . py New Year." That was so celebrated a Winninger bit that he used it outside *Show Boat*, in *Every Day's a Holiday* (1938) for instance. Winninger's control of both body and voice are in evidence all through *Nothing Sacred*—his anger at the *Morning Star* is as much physical as verbal—but his appearance is one of his strong points as Dr. Downer. In 1937, as for many years before and after, Winninger was a round-faced little man, his pink-white face crowned with a boyish mass of untidy white hair. In *Nothing Sacred* he looks like a demonic baby. In Hazel's hangover scene, she is beset by remorse for her behavior and moans an accusation, "Why did you let me come to New York?" She adds, "You were always as honest as you look." On that line, Winninger flashes a marvelously innocent corrupt smile that sums up the whole character.

The Hazel Flagg that we meet in her initial scene with Dr. Downer has an air of innocence that makes her expression of regret that she is well ("Now, I've got to stay in Warsaw") and her suggestion that they swindle the company sound like the proper sentiments for a simple

Country slickers. Carole Lombard, Charles Winninger. (*Nothing Sacred*, Selznick International, 1937. The Museum of Modern Art/Film Stills Archive.)

country girl. *Simple* is the word, for Hecht and Wellman are playing with the idea that the conventional rural heroine is a vehicle for stupidity as well as a mask for chicanery. In the scene with Cook outside Downer's house, the reporter sees just the surface, bemused by her beauty and the idea of her impending death, and responds to her forlorn "It's sort of too late" in a nice confusion of meanings. She is lamenting her lost trip to New York; he hears "too late" through his misinformation about her fatal disase. When she finally understands that he and the *Morning Star* are offering her New York after all, she frisks like a puppy, runs awkwardly and excitedly to tell Enoch. Her immediate and amoral response to Downer's bad-good news and Cook's good-bad news is characteristic of Hazel for the rest of the film. She bridles—a barely perceptible reaction—whenever Wally uses the words *fake* and *phony*, which he often does, meaning New York, not her, and she luxuriates in the public acclaim, becoming what she pretends to be. She gets annoyed when Cook's growing disgust at his role begins to get in the way of the treats New York is offering her, as in the nightclub scene when his snarling reference to the pleasures of a wake elicits her "Let's not talk shop." Even at the end, she reacts to his speech about the inevitable passing of her celebrity with "They loved me." During the last part of the film, her growing distress at her situation, as the initial deception breeds still more subterfuges, has nothing to do with morality. It is simply that a new desire—her love for Wally—is in conflict with her pleasure in her New York reception. She is sorry for her actions only to the extent that she fears Wally's disapproval.

"She was the only really beautiful woman who was also a comedienne," Wellman said of Carole Lombard and—on another occasion—"She could do anything—you could do everything *with* her." To illustrate this last remark, Julian Fox, who was interviewing the director, pointed to a scene in which she willingly adopts what Wellman described as "A very unladylike position." Fox identified this as Hazel's hangover scene, but he was clearly thinking of the one in which she meets the dignitaries who want her to go on with her lie—as the photograph on the page preceding the one with the quotation indicates. "It was [Wellman's] idea that she sit in that curiously straddled position. . . . Knees wide apart, toes turned out, slumped forward and pouting into the middle distance, this glimpse of Lombard seems to increase her attraction and vulnerability, where many stars would have appeared frankly ridiculous." The women that Lombard played in her most characteristic comedies—*Twentieth Century*, *My Man Godfrey* (1936), *Nothing Sacred*, *True Confession* (1937), *To Be or Not to Be* (1942)—seem to me about as vulnerable as the lovable leopard in

Bringing up Baby (1938), but otherwise Fox's description is sound enough. Elsewhere in this book (see chap. 8, pp. 204–7). I have talked at some length about Lombard as a performer. Here it seems necessary to do little more than to reiterate that her willingness to make herself ludicrous—the fist fight that is supposed to raise her temperature and confirm her nonexistent pneumonia, the love scene that she and March play soaking wet—is finally less important to *Nothing Sacred* than her uncanny ability to convey naiveté and calculation in a single speech. Hazel Flagg may be a touch brighter than Lombard's Irene Bullock in *My Man Godfrey*, but they share a sense of expectation and delight, of bewilderment when plans go awry, of implacable determination that is perfectly suited to the talent and the personality of Carole Lombard. Her strength plays to March's weakness, her toughness to his softness, and the Hecht-Wellman upending of the little-girl-from-the-country story retains its tonal quality even when Wally tries to assume the male prerogative, Hazel to dwindle to conventional dependence.

Once the film has established the four principals and nailed down the central assumption that, city and country, society is motivated by greed and activated by fraud, *Nothing Sacred* takes Hazel to New York and divides its time between her reception and the tangled when-once-we-practice-to-deceive plot in which she tries to extricate herself from her untenable position. In the first scene between Hazel and Wally, he tells her that New York will like her and, when she asks, "Just because I'm dying?," he says *no*—"You'll be a symbol of courage and heroism"—while his discomfort answers *yes*. "There is also a new sort of fame in our day that has never quite been known before," Hecht wrote in *A Child of the Century*. "It is fame seemingly invented out of whole cloth, based on nothing and needing only a press agent to keep it alive." Wally Cook says, "I used to love New York when it went gaga over some phony celebrity." The combination of curiosity and sentimentality (the master of ceremonies in the nightclub scene oozes that Hazel Flagg "has wrung tears and cheers from the great stone heart of the city") in New York's warm welcome of Hazel has all the depth and integrity of a bored crowd hurrying to a fire or a wreck. If the tearful ordinary citizen has nothing to gain but momentary diversion from Hazel, the more knowing people are able to use her to build their circulation (*Morning Star*), entice customers (the nightclub), strengthen their public image (the mayor who gives her the key to the city, the woman whose study group has changed its subject from "the menace of Communism to the inspiration of Hazel Flagg"). It is the self-protectiveness of this group that provides a way out for Hazel when her own schemes fail.

She tries to stage a suicide so that she can disappear without Wally's finding out that she has been lying; with his help, she attempts to fool Oliver Stone with pneumonia to replace the by now exploded radium poisoning. Finally, seeing no way out, she tries to tell the truth, but the civic leaders to whom she confesses join Stone in persuading her to silence. She mutters sadly that she would just like to go away and die, alone, like an elephant. We go to the front page of the *Morning Star*, which shouts that Hazel is missing and prints her farewell note, which includes the elephant line. Hazel and Wally are discovered on shipboard, newly married, hiding behind dark glasses, when a cable from Stone tells them how lovely her memorial day was. That would seem to be an appropriate ending for the film, but Selznick and Wellman, presumably with an authorial assist from Lardner and Oppenheimer, go beyond the fitting finish. A woman recognizes Hazel and when she denies any connection with "that fake," the woman lectures her primly for disparaging "one of the most gallant girls that ever lived." The joke in the exchange is that the woman is played by Hedda Hopper, who by this time was known less as an actress than as a professional Hollywood gossip, second only to Louella Parsons in her misuse of her journalistic power. Her attack on Hazel elicits Wally's assurance that Hazel Flagg, the celebrity, will soon be forgotten, a message that his bride does not want and the movie does not need. The film has already said the same thing more effectively in a neat variation on one of the standard clichés about yesterday's news. We watch a poet (Leonid Kinsky) in the throes of creation, then cut to the *Morning Star*, the finished poem front-page center; a fish is placed across the page and the paper folded around it. I have never been able to decide whether the very last scene in which a slightly drunk Dr. Downer wanders to a porthole and screams that the hotel is flooded, is simply a closing bit of foolishness or a conscious withdrawal from a lapse into message that might imply a narrower theme for the film than the title suggests.

"What fills me with tumultuous applause, what makes me tingle with respect," Katharine Best wrote in *Stage*, in an article which has the most complete list of the satirical targets in *Nothing Sacred*, "is the pristine purity of its villainies." Her celebration of "the healthiest, most sustained hate" to be found in recent movies is echoed by Basil Wright in the *Spectator*, who found "at the least a demi-cauldron of good honest hate" in the film. The English critics were fortunate enough to have a revival of Ben Jonson's *Volpone* in town to give their reviews a classical point of reference. Peter Galway, in the *New Statesman and Nation*, said, "there is more than a slight resemblance between the scarifying play at the Westminster and the scarifying movie at the Pavilion," and added, to indicate his assumption about the source of the venom, "O rare Ben Hecht!" Words like *contempt, sardonic,* and *ghoulish* appear in other reviews, but the contemporary notices, despite comments on the film's presumed satiric intentions, tended to emphasize its funniness, which means finally its harmlessness. Basil Wright, who after all found only a "demi-cauldron," concluded:

> There is indeed a fundamental distaste for humanity here, which might have given the film something approaching the lusty hatred of a play like *Volpone*; but this the producers, quite rightly doubtful of the public stomach, have carefully avoided.

I distrust the "fundamental distaste" here, as I do the "hate" in the quotations above, for Hecht and Wellman are not moralists excoriating evil; there is an edge of fondness that colors their larcenous portrait. The film's consistent and unflattering view of man is one of its sources of strength, but its continuing popularity rests in part on the delight that the chicanery provides. Stefan Zweig was on to something basic about *Volpone* when he let Mosca come out a winner in his adaptation of the play (1925)—think of the triumphant ending of Maurice Tourneur's film version (1940)—for the punishments that Jonson visits on his mountebanks have always seemed more ideational than dramatically necessary. In *Nothing Sacred*, Hecht and Wellman never even pretend to Ben Jonson's high moral purpose. They come across as—to use Hecht's description of Charles Dickens and Mark Twain—"Two such jolly and bitter men!" Emphasis on the compound. The last time I saw *Nothing Sacred* with an audience was at a film club, the members of which seem more interested in nostalgia than film art. As we filed out, one benign-looking elderly lady said to another, "Now that's what a comedy should be." Meaning sweet, I think, not venomous.

There are two elements at work in *Nothing Sacred* to make it acceptable to the "public stomach," although I suspect that the gentling has more to do with the temperament of the filmmakers than the commercial considerations Wright implied.[6] The first of the softeners is the love story, but it is not quite trustworthy as a tool to take the edge off the film's sharpness. Boy does get girl, as comedy says he should, and the audience clearly roots for them, but both Wellman and Hecht toy with the conventions. Lombard and March play part of their first scene together with their heads hidden behind the limb of a tree, and their first kiss, which comes after Hazel saves her would-be rescuer from drowning, is seen as a shot of a packing box from which her wriggling feet protrude. This scene, in which they declare their mutual love, is played with both the principals dripping wet. The big scene between Hazel and Wally is their temperature-building sparring match; when Oliver Stone, who would like to have a crack at her himself, says, "You hit her," Wally answers, "That's entirely different. I love her." Hecht, who has always had an ambiguous relationship with metaphor (we are presumably to take seriously the incredible lines of the playwright in *Angels over Broadway* [1940] and of the poet in *Specter of the Rose* [1946]), treats his own images as fair game here. The "fire alarm" that Hecht's very *Front Page* reporter in *Viva Villa!* says he follows becomes "love" in the sailboat scene in which Wally tells Hazel he is no longer vulnerable, that not since his teens has he waited for that alarm to sound. After their packing-box kiss, he says, "The greatest fire since Rome," and then to cap the joke they are driven home on a fire engine. The closest we got to "love, honor, and obey" in the film is Wally's "I'm going to show you cards and spades in lying for the next fifty years," and we last see them together, but in disguise, still dissembling. No wonder *The Literary Digest* said, "the romance seems just as phony as the rest of the goings on."

With William A. Wellman it is sometimes difficult to define the precise tone of a scene. For me, the most outrageous one he ever filmed is the great showman's farewell to his public in *Buffalo Bill* (1944). Bill, on horseback in the center of the arena, makes a moving speech which ends with his blessing on the audience. The camera turns to a sea of small boys, one of whom, on crutches, struggles to his feet and—a misplaced Tiny Tim—shouts, "And God bless you, Buffalo Bill!" In his interview with Richard Schickel, Wellman said that the scene was the "fakiest thing I ever heard," but that his deal with Darryl F. Zanuck locked him into a script he could not change and so he shot the scene although he "damn near vomited." Shot it straight presumably, although I see it as more sardonic than anything in *Nothing Sacred*. With *Buffalo Bill* in mind, it is possible to assume that Wellman's attitude toward the love story in *Nothing Sacred* approaches that of the woman at the film club. Even if one absorbs it into the general thematic pattern of the movie—as I did in the paragraph above—its very existence and its embodiment in the attractive presences of Lombard and March help lighten the film.

More important in tempering the acidity of *Nothing Sacred* are the comic devices that abound—old jokes and old routines, some of them corny, some of them superbly performed, that depend for their humor not at all on the satiric side of the film. The obituary-editor scene described above is a good example. So, too, are things like the squirrel that escapes from one of the schoolchildren who have come to serenade Hazel and turns up on her pillow, as though it had been conjured by her hangover, and the tall lady in the nightclub dancing with the tiny man who looks around her as she flips her hips from side to side. Spit in the eye might seem appropriate to the Hecht-Wellman vision, but the scene in the drugstore becomes less nasty, more obviously a comic turn when, after the woman gets Cook in the eye, he returns the favor, spraying on "tooken," a word he has borrowed from her. Maxie Rosenbloom, former light heavyweight champion turned buffoon, appears to be in the film primarily for the moment in which he re-arranges his cauliflower ear to fit the telephone receiver. Best of all is Charles Winninger's bag of vaudeville tricks. In Dr. Downer's angry first scene with Cook, Winninger twice leans toward March, his body almost a forty-five degree angle with the floor, and hovers precariously until March catches him. He repeats the routine—once leaning back-wards—in later scenes with Lombard. It is one of the finest vaudeville leans I have seen in films, rivaled only by the one that Walter Catlett, another *Follies* veteran, uses when his drunken poet confronts the hero of *Mr. Deeds Goes to Town*. Also in the Cook scene, Winninger does an extended routine with a door that will not stay shut. He slams it behind the offending reporter, slams it again, kicks it shut, and, when it insists on staying open, snaps his fingers by way of dismissal—of both Cook and the door. Routines with recalcitrant inanimate objects can be characterizing devices (see W. C. Fields), but, although this one may emphasize Downer's irascibility, it has less to do with the con man in the character than it does with the Winninger skills that Will Rogers remembered so fondly.

The primary effect of *Nothing Sacred* is a double one. It declares that the world is unvaryingly corrupt and invites us to delight in that corruption. The members of the audience who take pleasure in the Hecht-Wellman collection of self-seeking tricksters—the fakes and phonies, as the movie calls them—are not responding out of the inherent evil in their own hearts (not necessarily, at least), but are reacting to devices, designed primarily to amuse. It may seem odd to introduce a movie like *Steamboat Round the Bend* (1935) into a discussion of *Nothing Sacred*, but there is a kind of reverse comparison that may explain why Charles Winninger's Dr. Downer, say, affects me as Eugene Pallette's Sheriff Rufe does in *Steamboat*. The Will Rogers film is sentimental comedy which is subversive at the center; *Nothing Sacred* is a subversive comedy softened by uncomplicated laughter.

Notes

1. Wellman is a particularly good argument for caution in the face of oral history and autobiography. For one thing, he loved to tell the story of how a shy Gary Cooper, after the shooting of his one scene in *Wings* (1927), asked to do it over because he had been picking his nose; Wellman assured him that he might well pick his nose to stardom. I have never been able to detect even the simplest feint toward nose-picking in the Cooper scene in *Wings*. More interesting is the transformation over the years of Wellman's experience in the Lafayette Flying Corps in World War I. For Wellman, his few months as a combat pilot are what Hecht's prewar Chicago newspaper days were for him, the period of truest, happiest experience (that is, youth) and an anecdotal source for the rest of his life. (Those two closet romantics should really have got together on a film less relentlessly comic than *Nothing Sacred*.) In interviews in the 1960s and 1970s and in his autobiography, *A Short Time for Insanity* (New York, Hawthorne, 1974), Wellman told again and again his favorite war stories. Unlike the run-of-reminiscence war veteran, Wellman provided a comparison for his anecdotes. In 1918, discharged from the Foreign Legion because of injuries suffered when his plane was shot down, he returned to the United States and wrote *Go, Get 'Em!* (Boston, Page, 1918), a book that is at once a description of his training, an account of his adventures, and since the war was still in progress, a call to arms ("Wake up, America, and stretch your wings, the wings of Victory!" [p. 284]). It is possible that the stories in *Go, Get 'Em!* have been somewhat sanitized for an audience that persisted in seeing American soldiers as, to use Wellman's words about his friend Tommy Hitchcock, "'clean'—mentally, morally, physically" (p. 43), and that the raunchier, boozier later versions have a different kind of truth to them. Yet, the message from Woodrow Wilson that he and Hitchcock dropped over the enemy trenches could not have been an announcement of America's entry into the war, as he later recalled (*Short Time*, p. 222), because the United States had declared war on Germany before he sailed for Europe on May 22, 1917. What the young man's book shares with the old man's anecdotes is a sense of the exhilaration of flying and a deep attachment to comrades in arms. That continuity helps explain why—artistic truth being what it is—I cheerfully make use of assertions, stories, quotations that might weigh a little light if assayed for factual truth.

2. Whitney was both chairman of the board of Selznick International and president of Pioneer Pictures, the company that controlled

the Technicolor process, owned the Technicolor cameras, did the filming, and retained the ownership of both *Star* and *Sacred*.

3. Born Ernest Frederick McIntyre Bickel, he was Frederick Bickel until John Cromwell, who directed him in the Chicago company of *Tarnish* (1924), convinced him that Bickel was no name for an actor. Once he had hit on March, a shortening of his mother's maiden name, Marcher, he (or reviewers, or typesetters) hesitated between Frederic and Fredric. Thus Dale gave him an "e" although he is without one in the cast list accompanying the review.

4. He is also wrong when he says, apropos the ice-throwing kids, that "local children stone the reporter from the back of a covered wagon" (Richard Corliss, *Talking Pictures*, New York, Penguin, 1975, p. 16).

5. Siegfried became Sig with *The Princess Comes Across* (1936), the first film in which he appeared with Carole Lombard. The second *n* in Rumann disappeared during the early 1940s when—as the credits for Rumann listed in the *New York Times* during 1942 and 1943 indicate— he vacillated between one and two *n*s. On that score, *Nothing Sacred* was ahead of its time since he was Sig Ruman in some of the credit lists, but that was a typographical error; he is plainly a two-*n* Rumann in the onscreen credits.

6. If it was commerce at work, it failed. The audience that had embraced the straightforward amorality of *Libeled Lady* and made it one of the most successful pictures of 1936, did not take to *Nothing Sacred* despite the favorable reviews. Ronald Haver (*David O. Selznick's Hollywood*, New York, Knopf, 1980, p. 218) says that it lost four thousand dollars in its first year. The film's growing reputation as one of the best of the 1930s comedies suggests that, in this instance at least, the critics knew better than the public.

Bringing Up Baby

· 1938 ·

"They are setting up Howard Hawks for the waxworks."
—Archer Winsten, 1962

There is a story told about William Faulkner that once a reporter came to Oxford to ask his opinion about an arcane exegetical article that had appeared in one of the academic quarterlies. Once the critical point had been explained to him, Faulkner is supposed to have said, "Back in the twenties, we wore raincoats with deep pockets so that we could carry a bottle on each side." And then he closed the door. None of the Faulkner specialists I consulted—Malcolm Cowley, Joseph Blotner, James B. Meriwether—knew the story, but all of them were familiar with the raincoat and the variation of the anecdote in which Shakespeare or the Bible goes in one pocket, a bottle in the other. My version is presumably apocryphal—I have long since forgotten who told it to me—but a parable does not have to be factual to be true; Cowley—bless him—assured me, "I believe every word of it." Certainly, it reflects the kind of authorial uneasiness—a form of self-assurance—apparent in the juxtaposition Faulkner used in a 1948 *New York Times* interview. As a young writer he had "an old trenchcoat with a pocket big enough for a whiskey bottle," he said. "Now I get stacks of letters asking what I eat for breakfast and what about curves and linear discreteness." Twice in that short interview, Ralph Thompson quoted the novelist as having said, "I'm just a writer." Ernest Hemingway took a similar line in his interview with George Plimpton. "It would be impossible for me to make generalizations about a shelf of novels or a wisp of snipe or a gaggle of geese," the novelist said and then, after

A confusion of purses. Tala Birell, Katharine Hepburn, Fritz Feld, Cary Grant. (*Bringing Up Baby*, RKO, 1938. The Museum of Modern Art/Film Stills Archive.)

having made a few generalizations despite the impossibility, he added, "The most essential gift for a good writer is a built-in, shock-proof, shit detector." To test the validity of his own work, he meant, but within the immediate context the implications for the critical process are enormous.

If two such self-conscious artists as Faulkner and Hemingway shied away from their explicators, how much more appropriate that reaction is to their friend Howard Hawks, the director who never ceased to wear "the mask of the commerical film-maker," as Andrew Sarris put it. Of couse, that may not have been a mask. Hawks was understandably pleased when the French intellectuals took up his work ("I'm very glad that they like it"), but there is a touch of suspicion in his pleasure: "I get open-mouthed and wonder where they find some of the stuff that they say about me. All I'm doing is telling a story." That last line, in variations, runs all through the Hawks interviews of the 1960s and 1970s as he insists not only that he just told stories, but that he put what he liked on screen—people and situations—and found that audiences liked the same thing. As early as 1956, he was already sidestepping potentially difficult questions from his admirers on the *Cahiers du Cinéma* with his insistence on the primacy of story and "on subjects that interest me." There is something a bit ingenuous about this attitude—as there is with Faulkner and Hemingway—because Hawks was always ready to talk about his movies, about "how I make them, but not why," a practice that often degenerated into well-turned anecdotes about working with Carole Lombard, Lauren Bacall, John Wayne. "It is hard enough to write books and stories," Hemingway told Plimpton, "without being asked to explain them as well."

There is little point in reviving the quarrel over auteurism at this point. The aggressive eclecticism of this volume, the emphasis on the multiplicity of contributors that provides the texture of a Hollywood film, indicates that I find the auteur theory as limiting as any closed critical method. Still, I agree with Hawks, who told Richard Schickel, "any director that I think is any good puts a stamp on his work," particularly when I recall that one of the directors he consistently praised was his old friend Victor Fleming, who has never found a prominent place among serious auteurists. I stir these ancient critical waters not because I doubt that "the *Cahiers* camp-follower and the ex-*Cahiers* film-maker," to use Peter John Dyer's phrase, can tell a Hawks from a handsaw, but because their evocations of the Hawksian vision, the legacy of Jacques Rivette's 1953 *Cahiers* article, obscure a film like *Bringing Up Baby*. Rivette's essay ("one of the rare *classics* of the critical literature," said Olivier Eyquem in 1977) was undeniably seminal, giving birth both to the recognition of Hawks as a serious director

and to pervasive ideas that have clung to Hawks criticism ever since
the article appeared. Rivette's essay, reread today, is not very startling;
it is not so much a coherent piece as a grand appreciation scattered
with undeveloped insights. Rivette's reactions to Hawks's works were
embroidered by American and English critics (Andrew Sarris's 1962
Sight and Sound article), echoed and re-echoed by French critics (Henri
Agel, Jean-Claude Missiaen), solidified finally into critical clichés
which have the shorthand valdity of bumperstickers (Michel Ciment's
1977 *Positif* essay). The primary assumption of this critical line is that
Hawks has a dark view of man and his possibilities ("bitter," says
Sarris; "tragic," says Peter Bogdanovich) that can be seen most clearly
in his comedies, which are exercises in degradation, the reversion of
man to infantilism, savagery, bestiality. "The word 'fun' crops up
constantly in Hawks's interviews and scripts," says Peter Wollen in
Signs and Meaning in the Cinema. "It masks his despair." There comes
that mask again. Not that Hawksian criticism is quite as monolithic as
this paragraph suggests. This reading of Hawks has been challenged
not only by critics like Pauline Kael and Manny Farber, whose fondness for the director falls a great deal short of idolatry, but by those like
Dyer and John Belton, who take Hawks as seriously as Sarris does but
look at him with different eyes. Belton goes so far as to speak of
"overall optimism" and "positive human values." Bertrand Tavernier,
like Rivette a critic turned filmmaker, says, "it is equally stupid to make
of Hawks an unshakable pessimist." In the Hawksian subtext there are
many mansions.

The implications of *Cahiers* consciousness for the Hawks comedies
are particularly unhelpful. When Sarris says that *Bringing Up Baby*
"passes beyond the customary lunacy of the period into a bestial
Walpurgisnacht," I try to believe that he feels more horror than delight
as Susan (Katharine Hepburn) and David (Cary Grant) stumble
through the Connecticut woods in search of the elusive leopard, but I
cannot help feeling that he is building a critical castle in the air out of
material from the Rivette brickworks. What one might do for the dark
underside of Mitchell Leisen by attaching the proper labels to the
automat scene in *Easy Living* (1937). "I have to confess that I am quite
unable to join in the laughter of a packed theater," Rivette said, "when
I am riveted by the calculated twists of a fable (*Monkey Business*) which
sets out—gaily, logically, and with an unholy abandon—to chronicle
the fatal stages in the degradation of a superior mind."[1] I have to
confess that I am also unable to join in the laughter at *Monkey Business*,
but that is not because I have sighted the beasties at the bottom of my
psyche, as Robin Wood suggests when he says that the excesses of
Hawks's 1952 comedy are only for "those stable enough to accept

them." At the risk of exposing my apparently fragile stability, I will go along with Hawks, who said, "*Monkey Business* went too far, became too fanciful and not funny enough." Hawks's reputation as a director of comedies rests—or should rest—on *Twentieth Century* (1934), *Bringing Up Baby*, and *His Girl Friday* (1940). *Ball of Fire* (1941), despite its covey of charming character comedians, is at once static and strained, its enclosed setting, unlike those of *Twentieth Century* and *His Girl Friday*, lacking the verbal vigor that Ben Hecht and Charles MacArthur gave to Hawks's other comic boxes. Some of the mobility of *Bringing Up Baby* gets into *Monkey Business* and the even more flaccid *I Was a Male War Bride* (1949), but both those films punch like a stand-up comic trapped on stage at a humor convention with only a collection of mother-in-law jokes.

De gustibus non est disputandum, as the spider said to the fly, but I cannot help feeling that the appeal of the late comedies for some Hawks commentators lies in their suitability for Hawksian generalizations about civilization/maturity/stability *in extremis*. If they do not quite fit such a thesis, they can be made to fit with a touch of retrospective editing, as in Rivette's awarding "a superior mind" to Professor Barnaby Fulton in *Monkey Business*. There is no evidence on screen that we are to take Barnaby, the most outrageous of the Cary Grant–Howard Hawks absent-minded professors, as an intelligence more commanding than that of, say, Holofernes in *Love's Labour's Lost*. This kind of doctoring of the evidence is an attempt to impose a reasoned statement on the recognition that Hawks's comedies—farces, really—splash around in the underground stream of irrationality and impulse that flows beneath our carefully landscaped surfaces. "I see no need . . . for the asumption that this director's view of the world is pessimistic," wrote V. F. Perkins. "All comedy is more or less 'black.'" The Hawksian descent seems to reflect less the bitterness of the director's vision than it does the demand of the genre. As Eric Bentley said in "The Psychology of Farce," "The dynamic of farce proper derives from the interplay between the mask (of actuality) and the real face (of primitive instinct)." Who was that degraded *savant* I saw you with last night? That was no degraded *savant*, that was my comic butt.

Hawks, like any accomplished farceur, may give us a glimpse into the psychological abyss, but I agree with Perkins: "His comedies do not lament human degradation so much as celebrate human resilience." The Susan-dog-leopard combination in *Bringing Up Baby* that drags David, kicking and screaming, from his refuge/prison may be an example of "the lure of irresponsiblity," to use Robin Wood's chapter title, but within the context of the film the disorder is not only aesthetically satisfying—that is, funny—but ideationally healthy, therapeutic rather than frightening. It seems to me more rewarding to see *Bringing Up Baby* in the particular context of American movie comedy than from the presumed Hawksian worldview. It is a liberation comedy in which a too rigid character is released from the shackles of society, his profession, his monomania through the manipulations of an unbuttoned character, a savior who sometimes looks like a predator. In this case, girl gets boy. *Ball of Fire*, in which Sugarpuss O'Shea (Barbara Stanwyck) wins Professor Potts (Gary Cooper) in the flesh and his avuncular colleagues in spirit, is a Hawks variation on the theme. The year of *Fire*, Stanwyck, as the shipboard gambler, performed the same rescue operation on the shy millionaire (Henry Fonda) in Preston Sturges's *The Lady Eve*. Ernst Lubitsch's *Ninotchka* (1939), which had a better Billy Wilder–Charles Brackett script than the one they provided for *Ball of Fire*, is the same story with the sexes switched; this time the Russian theoretician (Greta Garbo) is corrupted (that is, humanized) by the Parisian playboy (Melvyn Douglas)—but, then, the sexual awakening of the cautious maiden has long been a staple of popular drama. The comedy of liberation does not have to be a love story, as *Topper* (1937) indicates when the playful ghosts of Marion and George Kerby (Constance Bennett, Cary Grant) work to eradicate the rigidities of their banker friend (Roland Young). If we start dragging in films about the sweetening of the sour old man (*The Little Colonel* [1935], *Wee Willie Winkle* [1937]) or the democratizing of the rich little boy (*Captains Courageous* [1937], for which Hawks claimed script credit), we begin to edge into sentimental melodrama. It is enough to recognize that the psychological subbasment of *Bringing Up Baby* is crowded with familiar Hollywood comedies.

Bringing Up Baby began as a short story in *Collier's* (April 10, 1937). The author, Hagar Wilde, had been contributing to popular magazines, particularly *Collier's*, since 1930 and had written two indifferently received novels, *Break-up* (1931) and *Stand Clear of Thunder* (1933). *The Saturday Review of Literature* labeled the latter a "'Smart' novel" and dismissed it as "Easy to read and forget." One might say the same thing for "Bringing Up Baby" if it were not that Wilde's somewhat innocuous story contains the seeds for much of the later film. In her original version, Suzan, as Wilde spelled it, and David are a pair of rich young lovers who settle their differences and nail down Suzan's inheritance at the same time. David is largely faceless, but Hepburn's Susan exists in embryo in Suzan, and the story also gave the film Aunt Elizabeth; George, a fox terrier who became a wire-haired for the movie; and the panther Baby, who became a leopard in the film. "Leopards are intelligent, affectionate and quick to respond to attention," said Mme Olga Celeste, the trainer of Nissa, the film's Baby, in a publicity piece ostensibly about the relative merits of the large cats as performing animals.[2] A number of details (Baby's fondness for "I Can't Give You Anything but Love, Baby"; the attempt to sing the leopard down from a neighbor's roof) found their way from the story to the movie, as did Wilde's one good verbal joke—Susan's confusion about the note from her brother, whether his saying that Baby liked dogs meant as friends or as food.

The Wilde story was just what RKO needed for Hepburn to follow the successful *Stage Door* (1937), and those two free-lancers, Howard Hawks and Cary Grant, signed on—Hawks as producer as well as director. Wilde, who got her first screen credit on *Baby*, worked on the script of the film, but Dudley Nichols, an old Hollywood hand, was assigned to the movie as well. He had been doing a lot of work for RKO, de-versing Maxwell Anderson's *Mary of Scotland* (1936), in which Hepburn played the queen; jettisoning the point of Sean O'Casey's *The Plough and the Stars* (1936), which brought Barry Fitzgerald to Hollywood; becoming entrapped in the historic sources of *Toast of New York* (1937), in which Cary Grant had precious little to do. Nichols is best known for the ambitious scripts he did for John Ford, like *The Informer* (1935) and *Stagecoach* (1939), but there is some comedy in *Toast*—lame, despite the presence of accomplished comedians like Jack Oakie and Donald Meek—which reminds one that Nichols was once presumed to have, in the company the Lamar Trotti, a talent for fashioning scripts to the personality of character comedians like Will Rogers (*Judge Priest* [1934], *Life begins at Forty* [1935], *Steamboat Round the Bend* [1935]), May Robson (*You Can't Buy Everything* [1934]) and even Herbert Mundin (*Call It Luck* [1934]). There is nothing in this catalogue to suggest that Dudley Nichols is a likely choice to write a screwball comedy. Wilde would have an authorial hand in *I Was a Male War Bride*, and Nichols went on to do two scripts for Hawks—*Air Force* (1943) and *The Big Sky* (1952)—which suggests a closer writer-director relationship than probably existed. In a 1971 interview about his work with writers all that Hawks had to say about Nichols was that he "was an excellent writer," a too formal compliment when one recalls Hawks's anecdotal expansiveness whenever he was asked about William Faulkner, Ben Hecht, or Leigh Brackett. Even so, Hawks may have been the not-so-secret ingredient in the preparation of the screenplay which—or so Hawks said—Harold Lloyd called "the best constructed comedy he had ever seen."

The David of Hagar Wilde's original story is provided with a last name (Huxley), a profession (paleontology), a goal (to finish the reconstruction of a brontosaurus skeleton) and a stereotypical surface (absent-minded professor). The name is a mild joke, no more significant than calling the colleges in *Horse Feathers* (1932) Huxley and Darwin.[3] A more useful joke is the one attached to our first view of David. "Dr. Huxley is thinking," says his associate, and we are shown the scientist high on a scaffold, contemplating a bone; what we see is Cary Grant in the pose of Rodin's *The Thinker*. It was a standard image for cartoonists who wanted a gag about either the exclusiveness or the vulnerability of thought—and for filmmakers, as well. In *Million Dollar Legs* (1932), for instance, when Mata Machree (Lyda Roberti), the irresistible siren, rests for a moment on the base of *The Thinker*, the statue turns and says, "How can I think?" Our first glimpse of Professor Huxley is a joke so familiar that it does the work of initial characterization.

The Cary Grant of *Bringing Up Baby* had come a long way from the slightly animated mannequin I discussed in the chapter on *She Done Him Wrong* (see pp. 39–40). He had put behind him both Paramount and the "straight-up-and-down" roles he usually played there and was now recognized as an accomplished comedian. It is generally accepted that *Sylvia Scarlett* (1936), which he made on loan to RKO, was the film that marked the change in him as a performer. "For once," Grant wrote years later, "the audiences and the critics did not see me as a nice young man, with regular features and a heart of gold." *Scarlett*, a project dear to the hearts of George Cukor and Katharine Hepburn, was such a disaster at the box office that those involved in it continued to speak slightingly about it for years. Producer Pandro S. Berman: "by far the worst picture I ever made, and the greatest catastrophe of Kate's thirties' career." Seen today, the film is a fascinating if not quite successful work, wonderfully attractive in its early scenes and sprinkled throughout with effective moments, like the drunken run through the rain of the jealous Henry Scarlett (Edmund Gwenn). Jimmy Monkley's laugh at the end of the film is pure Grant, and the characterization throughout suggests the actor who would emerge within a year. The special quality of the performance lies not in mannerisms—although Grant developed his share of those over the years—but in manner, an air of easiness which allows Grant to use his voice and his body to define the character and to assert himself as actor. That he could still be as wooden as he was in *Toast of New York* suggests that he needed directors more accomplished than Rowland V. Lee to release his personality and to channel it properly, which may have been what Grant had in mind when he said of his work with Cukor on *Scarlett*, "I learned comedy timing from George."

Grant had a way of tossing bouquets to his colleagues as though he constantly saw himself as a learner, but his professional education must have begun when, as fourteen-year-old Archie Leach, he joined the Pender Troupe, whose "stilt pantomime" brought him to the United States in 1920. He presumably acquired a vocabulary of physical and vocal devices as he worked his way through English music hall, American vaudeville, the musical comedy stage, and his long string of Paramount movies. "I strove to make everything I did at least *appear* relaxed," he said of his days with Bob Pender. Relaxation plus conscious striving, then; nature and artifice joined. "A delicious personality who has learned to do certain things marvelously well," Katharine Hepburn said, distinguishing between Grant and those costars—Spencer Tracy, Humphrey Bogart—she considered actors. Pauline Kael described some of those things when she wrote, "Once he realized that each movement could be stylized for humor, the eyepopping, the cocked head, the forward lunge, and the slightly ungainly stride became as certain as the pen strokes of a master cartoonist." The strokes could get out of hand, as Grant's performance in *Arsenic and Old Lace* (1944) indicates. With *Bringing Up Baby*, Grant was at his best; even when he was falling down he never gave the sense that he was pushing for effect.

Grant had played comedy at Paramount—the movies with Mae West and such tepid offerings as *Kiss and Make Up* and *Ladies Should Listen* (both 1934), in which Edward Everett Horton out-farced him—but it was not until 1937, with *Topper* and *The Awful Truth*, that his charm and his skill joined forces to establish his individual quality as a comedian. When *Bringing Up Baby* first appeared, reviewers, open-mouthed at a slapstick Hepburn, simply nodded in pleasure at Grant, "an adept by now at knockabout," as Basil Wright put it. So far as I have been able to discover, only the reviewer in *St. Nicholas* noticed that he had changed roles with *Baby*: "It is funny to have the suave, man-about-townish Cary Grant as that bespectacled and bewildered professor." The suave Grant would return for *Holiday* (1938) and *The Philadelphia Story* (1940) and in the movies he did for Alfred Hitchcock, but with *Baby* he found a comic persona that would serve him well for the rest of his career. He established his command of a type beset by circumstances and other characters, a comic butt who floundered, stumbled, sputtered his way to the necessary happy ending. Myrna Loy, who played with Grant in *The Bachelor and the Bobby Soxer* (1947) and *Mr. Blandings Builds His Dream House* (1948), said, "With Cary I played it so that he was the long-suffering one, you know; he's very good at that, terribly funny." Hawks told his *Cahiers* interviewers in 1967, "I love to put my characters into embarrassing situations."

When Hawks approached Grant for the role of David Huxley, he is supposed to have said, "I wouldn't know how to tackle it. I'm not an intellectual type." Hawks removed his doubts by saying, "You've seen Harold Lloyd, haven't you?" Although David Huxley begins as the conventional absent-minded professor, that characterization is not sustained as the film progresses. Less naive than the characters that Harold Lloyd usually played, Grant's David is still "the innocent abroad," as Hawks put it, and like the Lloyd character he confronts obstacles head-on only to meet increasing confusion. The horn-rimmed glasses are only the most overt of the borrowings from Lloyd. There is no abrupt division between the David of the opening and the later protagonist as butt, for David now and then displays the kind of professional propriety that his colleague-fiancée would expect of him. The best example comes after Susan has introduced David to Baby and David, refusing to go with her to take the leopard to Connecticut, stalks out, not knowing in his righteous indignation that Baby has followed him. As he marches down the street, Baby at his heels, Grant gives David an impressively stiff walk, all prude and professor, that makes the inevitable deflation the funnier.

The first extended scene in the film comes when David, now off his scaffold, joins his colleagues for the good news that the intercostal clavicle—a bone named for sound, not sense—has been found and the skeleton can finally be finished. There is standard exposition in the sequence—David and Alice are to be married the next day, David has an appointment to play golf with Mr. Peabody, who represents a woman with a million dollars to give away—but it is more important as a way of defining David as an incipient rebel, a man waiting for the rescue operation that he does not know he needs. The most obvious device here is David's bride-to-be, a relentlessly earthbound young woman wonderfully named Alice Swallow (Virginia Walker). How appropriate that, at the end of the movie, she breaks her engagement because David is too flighty: "You're a butterfly." In answer to a question from Peter Bogdanovich about his presumed "annoyance with scientists and academicians," Hawks dismissed the suggestion and answered, on aesthetic rather than ideational grounds, "the fun of it is to do a characterization, something very close to caricature. . . . If you don't do a caricature, you don't have a character." This remark about David fits most of the figures in the film. It is particularly suitable to Alice Swallow. She is an attractive woman, dressed in a dark tailored suit, not so much mannish as metallic in her obvious efficiency; here is the obsessive concentration on professional goals that commentators sometimes assign to David. In his delight at the news about the intercostal clavicle, he embraces Alice, who reprimands him: "There is a time and place for everything." Despite the phrase, there is apparently no time and no place for some things because, as they segue into a discussion of their forthcoming marriage, she says she sees it as an extension of his work, with "no domestic entanglements of any kind." Grant gives David a barely perceptible double take at this point, and the professor, who like the audience hears "sex" in "of any kind," moves into a discussion of children. She gestures toward the dinosaur skeleton as the child they will produce. The somewhat muted desire reflected in David's doubt is set against the unsexed Miss Swallow (fear of flying?), and the audience knows that he will have to find a more congenial mate, one not averse to "entanglements."

David's escape is not simply—not even primarily—from sexual repression. Alice Swallow may never become a mother, but she treats David as though he were a child; she resembles Hollywood's idea of the old-maid schoolteacher trying to impose order on her unwilling students. When David says of his meeting with Mr. Peabody, "I'll wow him. I'll knock him for a loop," she prissily cautions him, "No slang. Remember who and what you are." Finding "who and what" he is will become the burden of the film, and Susan helps him realize that he exists more in his unquenchable slang than he does in his dinosaur (although litle boys build models and collect skeletons, too). Irene Dunne, who played with Grant in *The Awful Truth* and *My Favorite Wife* (1940), recalled, "Cary was quite a mumbler. He'd go mmm-mmm-mm. He'd throw in little yeses and nos and mumbles all the way through." This is certainly true of Grant's performance in *Bringing Up Baby*, but in the initial scene his embryonic interjections are signals of what is bubbling just beneath the surface. In some ways, the most revealing line he has in the opening sequence is his response to Alice's dismissal of "entanglements": "Well, gee whiz, Alice. . . ." David Huxley may be a slightly repressed man in need of sexual awakening—and he does get his bone back at the end of the film—but he is more obviously Huck Finn trying to escape the civilizing influence of Aunt Sally/Alice Swallow and waiting for Susan Vance to show him the way so that he can light out for the territory.

We next see David on the golf course where, still unable to differentiate between work and play, he tries to talk money to Mr. Peabody (George Irving), who wants to get on with the game. It is here that he and we first see Susan Vance, who hits the ball with so authoritative a swing—Hepburn played tournament golf in her Connecticut youth—that we are left with the suspicion that, however dithery Susan gets, there is a center of control that knows exactly what she is doing. In the course of the film, she emerges as an energetic young woman as prone to accident as David but without his sense of being put upon. "After all the fun we've had," she says forlornly, when David tries to dismiss her after the string of slapstick disasters that befall them in the hunt for

Baby. There is a kind of desperate logic to her thought processes, obvious in her actions (driving off in someone else's car, which she does three times) and in her lines. Their argument over David's golf ball, which she appropriates as her own, provides ample illustration. When he explains that his balls are marked with a circle and hers with two dots, she says, "I'm not superstitious about such things." Pressing his case, he tries to get her to look closely at the contested ball, insisting that it is a circle, and she says, "Of course. Do you think it would roll if it were square?" On paper, those lines look as bland as the printed versions of the exchanges between Groucho and Chico Marx, but the joke lies not in the line itself but in the assurance with which she casts herself as the voice of reason, him as a kind of lunatic. "Your golf ball, your car—is there anything in the world that doesn't belong to you?" she asks, dismissing his protests as she settles herself in his car and, then, with his befuddled help, extricates it from the parking lot at the expense of a crumpled fender and drives away with him on the running board: "I'll be with you in a minute, Mr. Peabody."

The Susan of this scene is a fair sample of the Susan to come. The actions become more outrageous, the physical behavior more frenetic, the verbal quality more intricate, but the character—and her relationship to David—is already clear. This creature was, as the reviewers said, a surprise from Katharine Hepburn. *Life* said that "she leaps bravely into a new and daffy domain already conquered by Carole Lombard and equals Miss Lombard's best," which, considering *Life*'s devotion to Lombard, is a high compliment. Today, largely because *Bringing Up Baby, Holiday, The Philadelphia Story*, and the comedies she did with Spencer Tracy are among her best-remembered films, Hepburn is considered as much a comedian as she is a serious actress. Early in her career—despite the touches of comedy in some of her films and the obvious attempts at packaged charm—she was seen primarily as an emotional actress. Frances Robinson-Duff, her first voice coach, would say years later that, when she first looked at the wet and bedraggled girl who had come through the rain to study with her, "something inside whispered, 'Duse. She looks like Duse.'" George Cukor, looking at her screen test, is supposed to have said, "She'll be greater than Garbo," or so Adela Rogers St. Johns reported in 1934; the story which Cukor would often tell later had apparently not yet taken shape—his assertion that it was the way she handled a glass that, in an otherwise ghastly test, showed her potential. The Hepburn story is so familiar that surely everyone knows how, after a rocky beginning on stage (1928–31), she found Broadway success as the Amazon queen in Julian Thompson's *The Warrior's Husband* (1932) and was carried off to Hollywood where, in a very different kind of role, guided by Cukor and

helped by John Barrymore ("I learned a tremendous lot from Barrymore"), she found instant stardom through her role as the daughter in
A Bill of Divorcement (1932).

Reviewing *Christopher Strong* (1933), Hepburn's second film, Regina
Crewe wrote, "That troubled, masque-like face, the high, strident,
raucous rasping voice, the straight, broad-shouldered boyish figure—
perhaps they all may grate upon you, but they compel attention, and
they fascinate an audience." Crewe here recognized what would become increasingly obvious during the 1930s—that Hepburn, whose
mannerisms could be off-putting, was an undeniable presence on both
screen and stage. George Jean Nathan, who regularly attacked her as
an actress, admitted that she had "the gift of fascinating the attention
and making it her own." Frank S. Nugent, stung by the reactions to his
negative review of *Quality Street* (1937), could cry out in his *Times*
Sunday piece that "Miss Hepburn, personally, gives me, personally,
the jitters," but in his list of her acting sins he describes with some
accuracy the characteristic Hepburn way of speaking, moving, gestur-
ing. In someone else's typewriter, on some other occasion, Nugent's
catalogue might be seen simply as the devices available to an actress
making the most of her physical and vocal possibilities. "Tricks she
has," wrote Alan Jackson in that short-lived, elegant fan magazine
Cinema Arts.

> There is the breathless voice, the unshed tear, the flat high
> monotone for excitement. But it is unfair to accuse her of
> relying for effect on a set of mannerisms only. In every one
> of her movies, even the poorest, there are moments when
> she is completely the part she plays.

Those moments are rare in *Quality Street* (Nugent was right about that
one) or in a soaper like *Break of Hearts* (1935), but when Hepburn's
mannerisms fed into her material and when she had directors who
could both control her and draw out her best qualities—Cukor (*Divorcement, Sylvia Scarlett, Holiday*), Lowell Sherman (*Morning Glory*
[1933]), George Stevens (*Alice Adams* [1935], not *Quality Street*), Gregory La Cava (*Stage Door* [1937])—she gave performances that remain as
impressive as the surer, more mature ones that began to take shape in
the 1940s.

Bringing Up Baby is such an occasion. Susan Vance has all the worst
qualities of Hepburn's 1930s heroines—the aggressiveness, the unbot-
tled effervescence, the calculated helplessness, the relentless certainty—but Hepburn and Howard Hawks, taking advantage of the
actress's most jarring mannerisms, make Susan completely attractive.

Even her "somewhat carnivorous smile," as J. C. Furnas called it in 1933, is a virtue here since Susan is going to devour David and make him like it. Ruth Suckow, momentarily turned movie commentator in 1936, said of Hepburn:

> In her wilfulness, her tomboyishness, her piquant face, her tinny little voice, in her very eccentricities, there might be found a concrete definition of the intense individualism of the spoiled little rich girl of this era. It is a role which Miss Hepburn suggests, but does not play.

Hepburn did play her the next year, as Terry Randall in *Stage Door*, but events— chiefly the suicide of Kaye (Andrea Leeds)—transformed the character, separated the individual from the spoiled rich girl, turned the amateur into a professional. Hepburn plays her again in *Bringing Up Baby*, but this time all the rich girl's most unsavory characteristics— including her apparent indifference to the needs of the other characters and the rules of society—are channeled into the demands of farce, the impulse toward a liberating disorder.

The slapstick setting entails a great deal of physical action—almost constant movement—on the part of both the character and the actress. "She has an amazing body—like a boxer," Hawks said of Hepburn. ". . . She's always in perfect balance. . . . This gives her an amazing sense of timing. I've never seen a girl that had that odd rhythm and control." Although this is undeniable, I find myself thinking of Susan Vance in vocal terms and, on that ground, she recalls the earlier Hepburn heroines. She can stop to caress a line as in her response/repetition to news of David's impending wedding. "Engaged . . . to be . . . married," she says, her moue and her falsely congratulatory smile telling us that the hesitations mean both *alas* and *that's what you think*. More often, the words simply pour from her, a flood that will finally drown David. In that torrent there are echoes of Eva Lovelace in *Morning Glory* and even Jo in *Little Women* (1933). Susan is never as naive as Eva, but the rush of her plans and suggestions sometimes sounds like the marvelous scene in the office of Louis Easton (Adolphe Menjou) when Eva, fresh from Franklin ("Franklin, Vermont, to go into the loathsome details"), talks everyone's head off. Perhaps because *Little Women* seems as artificial to me as the Christmas card it sometimes resembles, Jo is a more difficult case. Sliding down bannisters, slipping on the ice, Hepburn's Jo is self-consciously boyish ("Christopher Columbus!") and perhaps should be, but she never seems genuinely physical, as Susan is. On the other hand, when the grown-up Jo and Professor Bhaer (Paul Lukas) return from the opera, her chattering excitement has a nonstop quality suitable to Susan, although it is used here not for the character's sake but as a set-up for the news of Beth's illness. Of all the earlier Hepburn characters, however, it is Alice Adams that come closest vocally to Susan. As conscientiously Hoosier as Booth Tarkington, I always find it difficult to understand how Hepburn's Connecticut cuckoo got into the very midwestern nest of the Adams family (Fred Stone, Ann Shoemaker, Frank Albertson), but once my initial shock passes, I realize that the film and Hepburn catch exactly the desperate and desperately cheerful note of Tarkington's Alice. The best of the speeches is the one at the Palmer party when, thinking that someone is listening, she bubbles in fake admiration at what a marvelous dancer her brother is, shaking her pathetic bouquet of violets coquettishly in his face. There is a similar intense effort at lightness in the scene in the flower shop, in the one before the mirror when she brushes off imaginary suitors, even in her attempt to keep up the conversation at their disastrous dinner party, although the latter is too fragmented for Alice in full flight. In *Baby*, in which Susan has the assurance of complete self-absorption, there is the same kind of sparkling vehemence with the note of hysteria removed.

The drive of Susan's voice is important not simply as a defining element of her character but because it is in some sense the energizing force which pushes along the plot and at the same time, through the confusion she engenders, undercuts the action, emphasizing the stops and starts within the relentless forward thrust of the film. The only thing remotely like Susan's voice is the screech of May Robson, as Aunt Elizabeth, who, when she is in full cry, suggests her splenetic Queen of Hearts in *Alice in Wonderland* (1933). The movie is marked by a pattern of failed speech. Walter Catlett's Constable Slocum talks in involuntary parentheses; in both the scene on the village street and the one in jail, he starts a speech which a remark of Susan's interrupts, sending him off on a sidetrack until he fumes his way back to his original point. Charles Ruggles's Major Applegate keeps falling over the meaning of his sentences, as in the confusion over his name and David's assumed one (Mr. Bone); when he and Aunt Elizabeth arrive at the jail to rescue Susan, he explains, "I'm the niece. I'm the aunt. I'm Major . . . ," and he stammers his way to a correct identification. Barry Fitzgerald's Gogarty constantly talks to himself in a barely understandable mutter, half Irish, half drink, a conscious use of a device that Joseph Holloway saw as a defect in 1926 when he complained that Fitzgerald, as Captain Boyle in *The Plough and the Stars*, "fails to articulate clearly in his longer speeches." The verbal tricks employed by these three comedians contribute to neatly detailed comic turns, and, since popular theater has always been willing to interrupt the story for a funny bit, they do not need to find justification in the larger scheme of the film. Yet, they have that, too. The film is a cacophony of sound in which rational speech is almost impossible. Once David is dragged into Susan's world, he is enveloped by chaos that is aural as well as physical, and his only method of asserting himself is to join the screamers. This is best demonstrated in the scene, right after Aunt Elizabeth's arrival in Connecticut, when David sits on the stairway, trying to force a word of his own into the solid wall of noise around him. Both Susan and her aunt are shouting unintelligibly, and the irascible George is barking at the shrill top of his terrier voice. On his third try—his third cry of "Quiet"—David shuts them up, but not until he stomps heavily on Susan's foot and throws a scare into Aunt Elizabeth and Mrs. Gogarty (Leona Roberts). His is not the voice of sweet reason. Gee whiz, as he would say, this is the stubterranean David emerging to knock them, momentarily, for a loop.

That David is also revealed physically in the supper club scene, the one which follows the golf course debacle. When David arrives to meet Mr. Peabody, he goes through a routine that denies the image of Cary Grant, impeccable in his tails. Faced with a decision—to check or not to check—he dissolves in uncertainty, first withholding the hat, then offering it to the hatcheck girl, dropping it in the process, bumping heads with the girl as both try to pick it up, finally choosing to keep it. He is uncomfortable here because, unlike Susan, he does not recognize that all settings are playgrounds. She is at the bar learning a new game; the bartender is teaching her how to hold an olive on the flat of the hand, tap it so that the olive flies up and then catch it in the mouth. The bartender is played by Billy Bevan, a busy character actor who could be impressive given a substantial part, as in *The Long Voyage Home* (1940), in which his nasty saloonkeeper reveals the villainy in his cordiality by the hardness around his eyes. More often, he was cast for his voice (Cockney) or his look (his round face, his mustache). One of my best childhood memories of Bevan is his being shot out of a palm tree by besieging Arabs in *The Lost Patrol* (1934). His role in *Baby* is minuscule, but it is useful to the film because he brings a commonsense practicality to his pedagogic role which makes him, next to Mr. Peabody, the sanest character in the film. Yet, his relative sobriety is in the interests of foolishness—the olive game—and his presence ideally should remind the audience not of *The Lost Patrol* but of the string of two-reelers he starred in for Mack Sennett (1920–29). Practicing her new skill, Susan leans well back on the barstool and misses, just as the unsuspecting David comes along and slips on the fugitive olive. "You're sitting on your hat," she says. The choice of Billy Bevan as the bartender may have been no more significant than that of George Humbert as the headwaiter—a case of typecasting—but I like to think that his being there is *Bringing Up Baby*'s nod to its ancient antecedents. It is proper that Bevan and the spirit of Sennett should hover over the film's first pratfall.

At this point Susan begins to stalk David in earnest, but as she follows him she pauses at a table to pick up some olives and continue working on her new trick. Here she and we meet the first of the second-string eccentrics that people the film—Dr. Lehmann, a psychiatrist. "I think the picture had a great fault and I learned an awful lot from it," Hawks would say years later. "There were no normal people in it. Everyone you met was a screwball." He had forgotten Mr. Peabody, which is easy to do, but that character is all the normality that the film needs. Hawks was wrong in any case. Had the gardener or the constable been less than "way off center," as Hawks put it, the film would have moved away from farce, and as it approached conventional comedy the lunatic behavior of Susan would have been tested against reality—or what passes for reality in ordinary life. As Dr. Lehmann says. "All people who behave strangely are not insane," an eye-of-the-beholder platitude which takes on greater resonance as we see character after character indicating (the finger making circles alongside the head) that some other character—usually David—is crazy. An enterprising critic might make much of the fact that among Hawks's screwballs are representatives of psychiatry and the law, but that way lies the possibility that *Bringing Up Baby* is a satire, which I do not for a moment believe. Constable Slocum and Dr. Lehmann do pool their ineptitudes in the jail scene, positing official irrationality against that of the prisoners, but they are in fact not opponents but allies of Susan, Aunt Elizabeth, Major Applegate, Gogarty, co-contributors to the general disorder which David does not want to recognize as his home.

Fritz Feld, who played Dr. Lehmann, said in 1978, "I don't burlesque the characters I portray," and his statement may be accurate if we can walk the fine line between burlesque and caricature, can find exaggeration rather than mockery in that string of exasperated waiters and hotel clerks he played over the years. One has only to watch unsure performers play farce, to see them sending up signals to the audience—look, look, we are being very funny—to understand that Feld and the other first-rate comics in *Baby* allow us to recognize the human origins in the overstatement of their characters. Yet, here, necessarily, the outlandish becomes the norm. "He has a pronounced leaning toward the unusual and the grotesque," said a *Boston Herald* interviewer in 1925, when Feld was in that city playing the Piper in Max Reinhardt's production of *The Miracle*; years later, in a volume celebrating the centenary of the famous German director, Feld recalled that when he worked with Reinhardt "I played grotesque parts— devils and hunchbacks; and comedy characters." After the American tour of *The Miracle*, Feld stayed in this country and went to Hollywood, at first to play heavies, then the comic roles with which he became identified. Feld was very adept at making comedy and character out of explosive sounds. When Helen (Carole Lombard) in *True Confession* (1937) asks the butler of her lecherous new employer, "Where does his secretary usually do most of her work," Feld delivers a marvelous "HAH!" that says more than a paragraph of explanation.

In *Baby*, however, where most of the other comics are juggling vocal devices, Feld establishes his credentials as one of the crazies with a soundless tic. At the end of the word "insane," in the sentence quoted above, he lifts his eyebrows, making his eyes seem very large, and blinks a few times. His one verbal characteristic is the precision of his speech which emphasizes his professional (in)competence. When Susan asks him why a man would follow a woman simply to fight with her (her interpretation of her encounters with David), Dr. Lehmann has a snap diagnosis to offer and the jargon to couch it in—an explanation of the way "the love impulse" is often expressed "in terms of conflict." It needs no psychiatrist (particularly one named *layman*) to explain what has been clear to popular comedy at least since Beatrice and Benedick fought their way to the altar. Dr. Lehmann is used not to explain the love story of *Bringing Up Baby*, which in a way he does, but as the comic doctor of farce. The voice of scientific reason as he talks to Susan, he is vainly attempting her olive trick when she next passes his table; "missed," she mutters. Much later, when, thanks to the wonders of farce coincidence, Baby takes to Dr. Lehmann's roof, the doctor interprets Susan's factual statement—"There's a leopard on your roof"—as a symptom; he oozes professional self-satisfaction when he appears, trying to lure Susan inside by condescending to her presumed hallucination. "There's a million dollars at stake," she says (Aunt Elizabeth is Mr. Peabody's prospective donor); he assures her that it is in the house, "all in one-dollar bills," obvious gibberish that is all the more lunatic for his pointing to an imaginary leopard when she and we know there is nothing at all on that roof, Baby having jumped down. It is an old comic device to confront the limited knowledge of a character with the fuller knowledge of the audience and make a fool out of him in the process, particularly suitable for the braggart who cannot see danger approaching, the henpecked husband who does not know his wife is in the room, the comic detective certain of his solution (Edgar Kennedy's Inspector Darsey in *True Confession*), and, of course, the doctor who becomes the patient. In the extreme form of the latter, the wrong man is carted off, but here it is enough to establish Dr. Lehmann as another comic butt, a fitting victim of Susan's implacability. No wonder she twice steals his car.

After her first meeting with Dr. Lehmann, Susan walks off with his wife's purse, but this mistake has less to do with the psychiatrist as patsy than it does with Susan's knack for getting David into situations in which he earnestly performs a task that makes him appear dishonest, dangerous, unstable. Realizing that the purse is not hers, she gives it to David to hold ("I wanted him to stay here") even though she was to walk past the Lehmann table to reclaim her own purse at the bar. Not wanting to be tied to her with anything as substantial as a piece of property, he follows her to return the purse just as Mrs. Lehmann, presumably back from the ladies' room (in real life, she would have taken her purse with her), returns to her table and discovers her loss. David is forced to defend the purse against the accusatory Lehmanns until Susan returns and says airily that it is not hers. Later, when he races to her apartment to save her from an invented attack by Baby, when he tries to persuade the zoo that there is a leopard loose in Connecticut, when he has to assume an alias without knowing what name or history Susan has given him, he is only doing extended variations on the purse routine, acting correctly under circumstances which are defined by Susan's words or actions.

Susan does attempt to apologize in the nightclub, a gesture which leads to the comic high-point of the scene. Trying to stop his retreat so that she can force the apology on him, she grabs the tail of his coat which rips ("You've torn your coat") and then, finally angry at his continual rejection, she storms off and, since he is standing on the edge of her dress, has a neat wedge torn out of the back of it. The ripped or lost skirt is a staple of farce, on stage and screen. In Cary Grant's first film, *This Is the Night* (1932), there is a running gag in which the clumsy servant (Irving Bacon) of the would-be seducer (Roland Young) regularly removes the skirt of the willing seducee (Thelma Todd), by catching it in a car door, a suitcase, wherever; on the first occasion, since this is the Paramount of the Ernst Lubitsch-Maurice Chevalier comedies, the screen erupts into the celebratory singing of the Ralph Rainger-George Marion, Jr., "Madame Has Lost Her Dress." The joke of the missed skirt finds its best form on those occasions when the woman is unaware of her state and must be protected surreptitiously by gentlemen who want to shield her from prying eyes, as in *Double Whoopee* (1929) in which Stan Laurel and Oliver Hardy try to cover up Jean Harlow. That is the joke in *Baby*. When David tries to tell Susan what has happened, she talks right through his words. He backs her against a pillar, protectively if menacingly. When she escapes, he follows and makes an incredible and slightly erotic attempt to cover her with his hat. He tries to stand behind her, but she marches off in fury, fanning the back of her dress as she goes, and only then discovers what has happened. Her cry for help at this point is indicative of another pattern in the film, Susan's need to be rescued by her klutz-cum-hero from her self-created confusions. At the end of the film, for instance, she drags the angry, spitting wild leopard into the jail, thinking she has captured Baby, and has to be saved by an involuntarily intrepid David. In the club, he steps behind her, snaps a command ("begin on the left foot") and the two of them exit in precise and rapid lockstep while the startled lawyer looks on. "I'll be with you in a minute, Mr. Peabody."

However ludicrous, that exit is an indication that the two antagonists know how to play together. It is not simply that Hepburn and Grant perform well as a team; in *Holiday*, for instance, it is only in the scenes in the playroom that they approximate the almost kinetic sense of a couple that Susan and David convey even when they are at one another's throats. Hawks is particularly adept at revealing character through the physical relationship of his performers on screen, a standard film practice which depends on an immediate action held tightly within a frame. What is going on in the search for Baby, for instance, has nothing to do with the offscreen leopard and everything to do with Susan and David, who are so convincingly filmed as a unit although they may not yet know that the bond has been forged. Not that contiguity necessarily means community. David and Alice Swallow can share space on the screen without ever being together in the sense that David and Susan are. In the opening sequence of the film, David, Alice, and the older male assistant are lined up in a way that reminds me of many scenes in *Ceiling Zero* (1936). That film, which a number of critics award an honorable place in the Hawks canon, seems to me one of his most awkward movies, the static filming of a stage play in which the two-shots and three-shots ideally should but in fact do not establish the relationship among characters. When Dizzy (James Cagney), Jake (Pat O'Brien), and Texas (Stuart Erwin) play a comic palship scene together, I have less a sense of the celebrated Hawksian male bonding than of three actors doing a scene. A similar three-shot works at the beginning of *Baby* because the characters do not belong together. The older assistant has no function in the film and disappears after that first scene, and Alice is defined as the wrong mate for David. The frame can use the shared space to suggest separation rather than closeness.

David's inextricable attachment to Susan is shown throughout the film by almost involuntary approaches, shared gestures and movements, instances of the body cooperating while the voice protests.

Most of the Susan-David scenes are done as two-shots and, even when there are more figures visible, the others are likely to become spectators of a shared action, as in the exit from the nightclub or the dinner party in which Aunt Elizabeth and Major Applegate are a kind of addled audience until, sucked in by the constant movement of Susan and David, they become a comic pair themselves, most happily in the moment when he says, "Shall we run?" and, arm in arm, they make a trotting exit from the dining room. Although the end of the film, the final embrace, is implicit in almost every sequence, however disruptive it may appear to be, the movie is sprinkled with overt indications of the way Susan and David work as a pair. One of the most interesting comes in the scene in which David learns that George has carried off the intercostal clavicle. As he wanders the house, calling "George," she follows him, repeating the name until he says, "Oh, stop it, Susan, you sound like an echo." She then begins to say "nice dog" when he says "George," but it is the same chirpy echo voice, and it is physical echo as well since she is on his heels as though attached by invisible rods that let his movements control hers. There is similar physical business a little earlier when he exits in anger because she repeats that he is good-looking without his glasses when he is trying to impress on her the seriousness of their situation; she follows, as though they are marching to the same beat, repeating "What did I say?" Both sequences recall the exit from the nightclub.

The nightclub scene is followed by a relatively quiet one which marks a transition in Susan's attitude toward David; she is now going to help him, a decision that will eventuate in even more disasters. It turns out that she knows Mr. Peabody well—calls him Boopie—and proposes that they go to his house in Riverdale to give David a chance finally to make his case for the donation (in fact, to keep him from meeting Alice Swallow at Carnegie Hall). They finally get to the Peabody house—after having passed it six times because, as she says, it was such a nice night for a drive—and when there is no answer to the bell, she acts with characteristic Susan directness. She throws gravel at Boopie's window and, when that does not seem to arouse him, hunts for a larger stone which, since he comes out on the balcony just as she lets fly, hits him on the head. They run away. "In moments of quiet, I am strangely drawn to you," David says as they part, but he adds that there have been no quiet moments. "Privately, I'm convinced that I have some dignity," he insists, as he turns away from the car and falls flat on his face.

"I did see Mr. Peabody, but I didn't see him," David says to Alice Swallow on the phone. "I did talk to him, but I didn't talk to him."

From this point on the reliability of language and the solidity of truth are going to become as tenuous as David's dignity, as uncertain as the principals are on their feet. Susan, who has called to ask "Do you want a leopard?" falls down as she tries to shoo Baby back into the bathroom. David, who has not believed the leopard story, asks if she is hurt and, just on the point of saying *no*, she realizes what he is thinking, cries out in apparent fright, knocks down a tray full of dishes, runs the receiver along the firescreen. He screams that he is coming and, the phone still in his hand, falls headlong in his precipitate race to the rescue. Not even stopping to put down the newly arrived intercostal clavicle (George could hardly steal the bone if they did not have it with them in Connecticut), he reaches her apartment only to find her dressed to travel. Convinced at last that there is a leopard but annoyed at Susan's deception, he refuses to help her, but he spends the film insisting that he will not do things which he does do. In short order, they are on the road, he complaining, she asserting "I've had a wonderful time." This exchange comes after they have run into a truck load of fowl and failed to restrain Baby, even by holding his tail and singing the presumably soothing "I Can't Give You Anything but Love, Baby." This sequence—like the earlier gravel-throwing scene—is both strained and restrained compared to the demented doings which will follow their arrival in Connecticut, but it gets its comic substance not from the rather weak joke but from the aspect of the characters (the placid Baby, the contented Susan, the fuming feather-covered David) and from its verbal and visual connections with future scenes. David is unhappy at having had to pay for Baby's snack, particularly annoyed that the leopard should have eaten two swans at $150 a pair. There seems to be little comic point to the item until the jail scene and Susan's sudden transformation into a tough-talking gangster's moll ready to rat on Jerry the Nipper (David) because he cheated on her, "a regular Don Swan."

The feathers are more important. They are sticking to David because he had to struggle to get Baby out of a pond, a scene which, oddly enough considering the film's devotion to slapstick, we do not get to see. This is another instance—like the torn coat—of Hawks's use of a modification in costume to emphasize the ludicrousness of David's situation. The device will be pushed much farther once they arrive in Connecticut and, Susan having sent his suit to the cleaners, he is forced to wear first her dressing gown, then an ill-fitting pair of her brother's riding pants which make him look even more foolish. It is that dressing gown that is particularly dear to the hearts of Hawks critics interested in the reversal of sex roles in the director's work. It is true that his heroines are frequently the aggressors, but if we were to go into an emasculation song and dance every time a man put on women's clothes in a play or movie the psycho-critical follies would run for months. Asked why he so often put Cary Grant into women's clothes, Hawks said, "he's funny in women's clothes because he doesn't try to be at all feminine. He just proceeds the way he is: disgusted with himself. I think Cary is funny when he's disgusted— that was the only reason for doing it." That statement is probably a touch too innocent since Hawks elsewhere claimed to have advised Josef von Sternberg to dress Marlene Dietrich as a man in *Morocco* (1930) and let her kiss another woman. He is obviously aware of the dramatic and comedic use of sexual ambiguity which is not at all the same thing as recording "the emasculation of sexes in the modern world to the point of transvestism," which is what Andrew Sarris thought Hawks was up to in *I Was a Male War Bride*. Since Grant also wears women's clothes in *My Favorite Wife*, does that mean that Garson Kanin shares the Hawksian vision or are some directors allowed to use the familiar device as a gag? One is tempted to start a catalogue of actors in drag from Wallace Beery, an unlikely woman in silent comedies, through William Powell, amusing as his own sister in *Love Crazy* (1941), to whoever is wearing women's clothes at your neighborhood movie house as you read this.

Perhaps it is better to stick to the scene in *Baby*, however, for it provides a reference to its theatrical antecedents. David, in Susan's dressing gown, answers the door when Aunt Elizabeth arrives and, when she asks why he is dressed that way, he shouts "I just went gay all of a sudden" and does a ridiculous leap high into the air. That line gets a particular laugh these days, now that *gay* no longer means simply *joyous*, and significant nods from the more literal Hawks admirers. In 1938, however, *gay* was not a common term for *homosexual* and, if such a joke were intended, it had a limited audience and nothing at all to do with either serious ideas about role reversal or the familiar joke about a man's dressing up in women's clothes. More revealing, I think, is David's remark when Susan explains to her aunt that he is a friend of her brother's from Brazil and that he has had a breakdown; he mutters to himself, "I'm a nut from Brazil." In Brandon Thomas's *Charley's Aunt* (1892), surely one of the best-loved drag farces, the bogus aunt is described as being from Brazil, "where the nuts come from." Although that line is often quoted, I doubt that it was much more familiar to the general movie audience than the special meaning of *gay*. Even so, it seems to me that David's mumbled variation is a way of identifying him, in terms both of women's clothes and the complications of farce, with a character that had been familiar to stage audiences since 1892 and had already been twice translated to the screen, played in one instance (1930) by Charles Ruggles, *Baby*'s inane big-game hunter.

David's uncertain dignity is going to be tested more severly than it can be by anything as ordinary as his wearing Susan's dressing gown. Once they get to Connecticut, the plot not so much thickens as explodes. George (the lovable Asta of the Thin Man movies as a malevolent little beast) runs off with the intercostal clavicle and presumably buries it somewhere on the grounds. The drunken Gogarty—perhaps because the writers have borrowed an idea from Benson in Bella and Samuel Spewack's *Boy Meets Girl* (1935)—leaves the door open when he goes for a spare bottle and allows Baby to escape. In search of dog, bone, and leopard, David is forced to scramble around the countryside, slipping, sliding, fussing, fuming, once disappearing in a waterhole when Susan assures him that the creek is shallow and they can wade across; she gets as wet as he does but her spirits are not dampened until he offers to send her away. Meanwhile a second, vicious leopard has escaped from a circus conveniently in the neighborhood, a development that not only allows Barry Fitzgerald and Charles Ruggles to share a braggart-coward turn, but prepares for the end of the adventure—which is not quite the end of the film. Eventually, as so aften happens in 1930s comedies, everyone ends up at the jail—Constable Slocum, his dimwitted associate (John Kelly), and Dr. Lehmann on one side of the bars, Aunt Elizabeth, Major Applegate, Gogarty, David, and sometimes Susan on the other. It is customary at this point to drag everyone before a magistrate of some kind, usually a rustic, avuncular, sharp-tongued old darling (Slim Summerville in *Love Is News* [1937]) who will sort out the complications and bring the lovers together. No such thing in *Bringing Up Baby*. The ubiquitous Mr. Peabody arrives in time to free the prisoners, but the sequence cannot end until David, in the best Harold Lloyd tradition, is allowed to become a hero by saving Susan from the nasty leopard that she mistook for Baby. That done, he faints dead away.

An ending, but not the end. Back in his museum, rejected by the shocked Miss Swallow, David hears Susan coming and hurries to the doubtful safety of the scaffolding on which we first saw him. Susan climbs a tall ladder on the other side of the brontosaurus and, from that vantage point, tells him she has retrieved the missing bone and apologizes for all that happened, confessing "I was only trying to keep you near me." Suddenly he says that that was "the best day I ever had in my whole life." He uses the world *like*, he uses the word *love* and Susan, entranced, begins to rock back and forth on the ladder, he swaying as she does, until the ladder leans too precariously and she clambers onto the skeleton which collapses just as she gets a hold on the edge of the scaffolding. He pulls her to safety. She rides verbally across his protests (four years of work in collapse), mows him down by putting words in his mouth. He accepts the inevitable. They embrace.

Happy ending? The genre says *yes*, but some Hawksians say *no*. I am not thinking of those critics who see the film in Spenglerian terms as the decline of civilization, but of Robin Wood, who so often writes good sense about Hawks and other directors. He says *Baby* is "perhaps the funniest of Hawks's comedies" and calls it the triumph of the Id over the Superego, a feasible description of a plot that I prefer to discuss in other terms. Then, suddenly, he becomes quite prim and says "one is forced also to contemplate Hepburn as a suitable life-partner for him. One can only feel uneasy, and question whether the triumph of total irresponsibility the film appears to be offering as fitting resolution is in fact acceptable." One is forced to do no such thing. If one had to worry about how lovers were going to get on after the final curtain, the last fade-out, it would surely be necessary to question the appropriateness of Sugarpuss O'Shea as "life-partner" to Professor Potts in *Ball of Fire*, a union that Wood blesses presumably because the film is more discreet in its balancing of the forces of order and disorder. Yet, characters have no existence once a film comes to an end. Wood sounds like all those fusty critics who wondered how Nora was going to earn a living after she walked out on Torvald in *A Doll House*. It is the final image that counts—the door-slam heard round the world, the kiss over the crumbled brontosaurus—and it can be perceived only within the terms that the work itself provides. The film clearly makes Susan the savior, Alice Swallow the jailer; the movement throughout is toward David's recognition that—"Gee whiz"—he belongs among the crazies. Wood's phrasing of his uneasiness suggests that the film advocates irresponsibility, but all that it does is follow its initial assumptions to their inevitable conclusion. In conventional farce the characters usually pass through disorder to return to normality, but *Bringing Up Baby* is a variation on the form. It is one of a number of 1930s comedies in which the ending is an act of destruction which, given the context, is an affirmation of release, self-discovery, found love. In Gregory La Cava's *She Married Her Boss* (1935), for instance, Richard (Melvyn Douglas) and Julia (Claudette Colbert) throw bricks through the windows of the department store which has kept in thrall him, as owner, and her, as secretary, and drive off to catch a boat to freedom. It would be as pointless to worry about their act of vandalism as it is to fret about the now routed scientist who never really was at home in the person of David Huxley.

Happy ending? Of course. He lost his skeleton, but Susan helped him get his bone back.

Notes

1. The apparently accidental pun in this sentence—Rivetted/riveted—which would work in French as well seems very appropriate. It suggests that the French critic is not seeing the film that I see on screen, that he is up to intellectual monkey business of his own.

2. Hawks would say years later, "We had two or three leopards, but even the tamest one wasn't any fun" (Michael Goodman and Naomi Wise, "An Interview with Howard Hawks," *Take One*, 3 [November–December, 1971], 21). The RKO publicity department would have had to invent a Nissa—a personality leopard—even if she had not existed. One of the canned news features in the *Bringing Up Baby* pressbook accompanying the film's release in England was a mock movie-star piece in which Nissa was described as married to another trained leopard named Midnight. She refused, the article asserted, to let marriage interfere with her career. At the risk of being called a sentimentalist, I elect to stay with Nissa, if only to have an individual on which to hang Otis Ferguson's high praise. After warm words for the performances of Cary Grant, Barry Fitzgerald, Walter Catlett, and May Robson, he wrote, "the leopard was better than any of them, but is it art?" (*The Film Criticism of Otis Ferguson*, Philadelphia, Temple University Press, 1971, p. 216). Besides, Hawks, like most Hollywood rememberers, has an uneasy grasp of fact. At the same question-and-answer session at which he mentioned the several leopards, he said that the fight scene between John Barrymore and Carole Lombard in *Twentieth Century* "was the first scene she had ever done in a picture" (p. 20). *Century* was Lombard's thirty-fifth film, not counting the shorts she had done for Mack Sennett.

3. The name of Mr. Peabody, a good New England name for the lawyer, one of the few apparently normal characters in the film, almost certainly comes from the Peabody Museum of Natural History at Yale. According to *Showplace* (2 [March 3, 1938], 7), the program of the Radio City Music Hall, Harold Hendee, research director at RKO, copied David's brontosaurus from the one in New Haven. That is not even a joke, just an instance of the allusiveness of 1930s comedies.

12

DESTRY RIDES AGAIN

· 1939 ·

"I love happy endings. I do."
—Marlene Dietrich

There was a *gemütlich* gathering one day on the set of *Destry Rides Again*. Marlene Dietrich, who just happened to have a copy of one of Karl May's novels in her bag, pulled out the book, and she and Hungarian-born Joe Pasternak, the producer of the film, waxed nostalgic about what Dr. May and his vision of the American West meant to European children. James Stewart, Brian Donlevy, and Charles Winninger stood around and fueled the discussion with straight lines masked as mild witticisms or expressions of surprise. It may well be that the *causerie* took place only in the head of a publicist for Universal (the title and the translation, put in Dietrich's mouth, seem to me neither German nor Karl May), but the *New York Times* presented it in charming detail, and it is an almost perfect image of the collection of talent that put together *Destry Rides Again*. Almost perfect, because— had their names been known to a wider public—both Felix Jackson (Felix Joachimson), the chief scriptwriter, and Frederick Hollander (Friedrich Holländer),[1] who wrote the songs for the film, should have been invited to take part in the May seminar. This European contingent, whatever its memories of Karl May, was professionally innocent of the Western, but the American contributors—except for director George Marshall and cameraman Hal Mohr, old Western hands—were not much more knowledgeable about the genre. Some of the performers had appeared in Westerns, but stars and supporting players alike

---

The bad guys toast a soaking-wet Frenchy. Warren Hymer, Brian Donlevy, Samuel S. Hinds, Marlene Dietrich, Allen Jenkins, Billy Gilbert, et al. (*Destry Rides Again*, Universal, 1939. The Museum of Modern Art/Film Stills Archive.)

were so identified with other genres that one can understand Anthony Bower's complaint that "a distinguished set of players has been miscast." Bower, like Graham Greene in his review, had come to *Destry* stunned by the beauty of a documentary called *Dark Rapture*, so he may be, as Greene admitted he was, an imperfect observer. Still, Bower is right to the extent that the new context forced familiar screen personalities to play unexpected variations on their accepted stereotypes. Bower and Greene notwithstanding, the *Destry* company, most of them not at home on the range, managed to turn out one of the best comedy Westerns ever to come out of Hollywood.

The phrase "comedy Western" may be somewhat imprecise, particularly at a time when, on the trail of Mel Brooks, moviemakers have accepted and youthful audiences embraced grotesque farcical overstatement as the standard of comedy. That Brooks's *Blazing Saddles* (1974) was, among other things, a parody of *Destry Rides Again* suggests the distance between even an austere example of the current genre and the 1939 film. There are critics—Sheridan Morley, for instance—who see *Destry* as a satire, but it certainly does not belong with the burlesques which have shadowed Westerns since the genre broke screen. These have never had much use for subtlety, as *The Daredevil* (1923) indicates. In that film—a joke about making Westerns rather than about the genre itself—a bucking horse sends Ben Turpin flying in one of those mechanical gags that Mack Sennett so doted on. A great many good comedians managed to go West—Buster Keaton, Laurel and Hardy, and—after *Destry*—the Marx Brothers, W. C. Fields and Mae West. Will Rogers kidded the Western for Hal Roach—*Two Wagons, Both Covered* (1923) and *Uncensored Movies* (1923)—but he had already made films for Samuel Goldwyn—*Jubilo* (1919), for instance— which were much closer in tone to *Destry Rides Again*. Graham Greene complained that *Destry* "doesn't take itself quite seriously enough," but that is precisely what it does do. Just seriously enough. It belongs to the multigenre film represented in this volume by *She Done Him Wrong* (1933) and *Steamboat Round the Bend* (1935). The characters in *Destry* are essentially comic and most of them are played by established comedians, but neither the roles nor the performers suggest parody. The comedy becomes an essential part of the drama, and, in turn, "the staple elements of Western melodrama," which William Boehnel, like so many reviewers, found in the film, become transformed by both the conception and the playing of the characters. When Jerry Wald and Richard Macaulay chose to include *Destry* in their *The Best Pictures, 1939–1940*, an unfortunately unsuccessful attempt to imitate Burns Mantle's *Best Plays* series, they had to find a suitable pigeonhole for it, having already filled the categories of comedy (*Ninotchka*) and comedy-drama (*Mr. Smith Goes to Washington*). They classified it under "Action," but they qualified the label in their remarks, indicating that although the film "has all the trappings of the action formula," it "was done with such high good humor by all concerned that it stood apart from the year's crop of super-Westerns, many of which were more expensively mounted."

Most of the reviewers, faced with *Destry*, relaxed and enjoyed themselves, passing out praise all around. Howard Barnes, however, chose to lay the success of the film to Joe Pasternak's supervision, calling the producer "as shrewd a showman with a six-shooter spectacle as he is with comedy of adolescence." It is a good guess, although Pasternak's contribution seems to have consisted primarily of bringing the right group of people together and providing them with a congenial working situation. "The single element which I sought to instill in every venture," he said in his autobiography, "was a sense of joyful, equal collaboration." In his account of the making of *Destry*, he explains that he was warned about Dietrich's lost popularity and "shy, likable, and apparently soft" James Stewart's inappropriateness as a "Western hero," but that he insisted they be used. Such was his position at Universal at the time that opposition was not likely to be more than token. Pasternak had been in the movie business since 1923, when he went to work for Paramount, and he had been with Universal since 1926. He was sent to run the company's Berlin office and it was there, in 1930, that he produced his first film. From 1930 to 1935, he made films for Universal, first in Germany, then in Hungary. When he returned to Hollywood to work he was at first uneasy about how he would fit into the home studio, but he discovered, invented, introduced—whatever the verb—Deanna Durbin in *Three Smart Girls* (1936), directed by Henry Koster, a veteran of the Pasternak European years, and then packaged her in a series of hits that made her a star and Universal a pot of money. At the end of the decade, he could pretty much have his own way at Universal.

"My idea of a good story, or a good picture, is one that leaves you feeling a lift afterward," Pasternak said in *Easy the Hard Way*. "You come out saying to yourself, well, the world isn't such a bad place after all." On his return from Europe in 1936, he told an interviewer, "No one's going to get sick or die in my pictures. That's no sort of entertainment." He quotes the interview in his autobiography and, although Frenchy (Dietrich), Wash (Charles Winninger), and Kent (Brian Donlevy) all die in *Destry Rides Again*, he could still reiterate at the end of the book, "In my stories everybody is always around for another day." The line is factually inaccurate, but it is spiritually correct. *Destry Rides Again* may be a great deal more sophisticated than a Deanna Durbin comedy—and it has serious implications for 1939 that may not have been among its makers' overt intentions—but it is essentially an entertainment in the best uplifting Pasternak tradition. It came about, Felix Jackson once said, because "Pasternak wanted to do a Western with Jimmy Stewart" and set the writer to looking at the films Tom Mix had made for Universal early in the decade. In his monograph on Marlene Dietrich, Richard Griffith suggests something a touch more mercenary than a longing for Stewart and a new genre. The production heads at Universal, "to squeeze every dollar of value from the studio's assets," called for "a review of all the scripts of old Universal films with a view to remaking the best of them at no additional story cost." However Jackson got to Mix, he came up with *Destry Rides Again*.

Destry Rides Again began as a novel by Max Brand, the most celebrated pseudonym of Frederick Faust, that paragon of the pulps and the popular magazines who wrote "under at least nineteen names in addition to his own" and who in his heyday could turn out a full-length novel in ten days. It was published by Dodd, Mead in 1930, after having run earlier that year as a serial, "Twelve Peers," in *Western Story Magazine*. Robert Easton in his biography of Faust suggests that the novel is self-parody and calls it "almost farce" in which men "die as if shot down in musical comedy." It is possible that, after having read a sizable portion of the twenty-five million words Faust wrote, a critic might see *Destry* as a joke, but it seems to me a conventional enough Western despite the playfulness in the early chapters and overt comic scenes like the one in which Destry talks to the boy who does not recognize him. I doubt that Faust took it seriously—a man who measured out fiction as though it were yard goods hardly had time to develop artistic or intellectual pretensions—but that is not the same thing as writing parody. Ostensibly a revenge novel, in which Harry Destry comes back from prison to pay out the jurymen—the twelve peers of the magazine title—who convicted him of a robbery he did not commit, it is actually a purification tale in which Harry comes to understand that his own pride and his dependence on violence have created the animosities that led to the unfair verdict. The book becomes strongly didactic in the scene in which Harry faces the false friend, Brand's chief villain, and ponders his own weakness when he should be concentrating on the wicked shenanigans of Chester Bent. The novel ends when Destry, having killed Bent almost by accident, puts away his gun and marries the spunky girl who has loved him from the beginning.

One reason for doubting Easton's critical reading of *Destry* is that he seems to think that the Tom Mix version of the novel (1932), unlike the later ones (George Marshall directed it again in 1954 with Audie Murphy), is played straight. Not only is ZaSu Pitts introduced for a gratuitous comic bit as a temperance worker caught in a stagecoach robbery, but Stanley Fields plays the frightened crooked sheriff as a farce character who has a way of bobbing up alongside the election posters that proclaim him HONEST AND FEARLESS. The film retains some of the Brand plot, but cleans up Destry—a gambler, a drunk, and a no-good at the beginning of the novel—to fit the Tom Mix public image. It provides a ludicrous opening ("like a comic opera chorus paving the way for the prima donna's first entrance," said *Variety*) in which an eager bunch of kids in the schoolyard await the arrival of their hero, who does some fancy shooting for them while Tony, the wonder horse, goes through his feedbag of equine tricks. The film is even more predictable than the novel, working its way to the appropriate happy ending after Mix bests the villain (Earle Fox) in a marvelous fistfight that has much swinging but very little hitting. It is difficult to see how Felix Jackson ever saw it as the stepping-off place for a film as clever as the 1939 *Destry Rides Again*.

There is precious little of either Max Brand or Tom Mix left in the new film. It is possible that one of the many hands on the Pasternak ranch saw the last line of the book, "for Harrison Destry had put away his Colt," not as an ending but as a beginning, and came up with the idea of a lawman who refused to bear arms—"no-gun Destry," as one of the thugs calls him. Which hand would be hard to guess. Pasternak said that it was "my writers Bruce Manning and Felix Jackson." Manning *was* a Pasternak writer and frequently worked with Jackson, both before and after *Destry*, but his name does not appear in the credits for the Western. That does not mean that he did not work on the story any more than the absence of Grover Jones's name means that he did not do the screenplay that the *New York Times* reported his having prepared. Jones had written *The Under-pup* (1939), the film with which Pasternak—faced with the fact that Deanna Durbin was growing up—launched Gloria Jean in the hope that vocal lightning would strike twice. That sentimental script makes Jones no less likely a writer for *Destry Rides Again* than those whose names appear on it, but Jones did not have much luck with his initial screenplays for comedy Westerns; W. C. Fields, looking at a script Jones prepared for what would eventually become *My Little Chickadee* (1940), snarled in a letter to a Universal executive, "Now I ask you, Cliff, has he written this for Fields or Shirley Temple?"

When *Destry Rides Again* appeared, Felix Jackson was credited for the original story, "Suggested by" the Brand novel, and he, Gertrude Purcell, and Henry Myers are listed as authors of the screenplay.

Jackson, one of Pasternak's Berlin writers, "had a knack for charming tales about nice people," which perhaps explains why his four pre-*Destry* American credits consist of two Deanna Durbin scripts—*Mad about Music* (1938), *Three Smart Girls Grow Up* (1939)—and confections fashioned for two European lovelies—Danielle Darrieux (*Rage of Paris* [1938]) and Franciska Gaal (*The Girl Downstairs* [1939]). There is nothing there to suggest that he was ready to work on a Western, but the same could be said for his coauthors. Gertrude Purcell had created a mild stir back in 1922 when she and Leila Taylor wrote a play about Voltaire. Most of her other stage offerings were adaptations of European musicals and the best known of her film contributions were sentimental tales of "mother love and sacrifice"—*Stella Dallas* (1937) and *Mother Carey's Chickens* (1938). An anecdote in Kenneth L. Geist's *Pictures Will Talk* seems to put Purcell at Paramount in the early 1930s, but none of her writing credits suggest that she worked in that studio. Henry Myers certainly did. He was a Broadway press agent turned lyricist (mostly for Charles M. Schwab) and playwright, who found his way into films as early as 1930. Joseph L. Mankiewicz, his collaborator on *June Moon* (1931: uncredited), *Million Dollar Legs* (1932), and *Diplomaniacs* (1933), has described him as "a wonderful character, a marvelous daffy and very funny man." According to Richard Meryman, he was hired by Herman Mankiewicz to "think up jokes" for *Horse Feathers* (1932), but whether or not he ever wrote for the Marx Brothers, the credits above place him in the company of the nonsense writers who flourished in Hollywood in the early 1930s. Not that such associations were preparation for working on a mixed-genre film like *Destry Rides Again*. B. R. Crisler described *The Luckiest Girl in the World* (1936), on which Myers shared screenplay credit, as "a better-than-average contribution to the field of machine-made entertainment," which suggests that Myers—like Jackson, like Purcell—was more practitioner than artist, a worker used to adding his mite to group endeavor. Frederick Faust was apparently not one of the *Destry* group, although he was in Hollywood at the time. As Max Brand, he was churning out Dr. Kildare stories in time to get them placed in *Argosy* or *Cosmopolitan* before the latest installment of the popular young doctor's adventures hit the theaters. If Brand was unavailable for the transformation of his hero, there was always George Marshall as director; he was already doing cheap Westerns at Universal in 1917 when Faust/Brand was just beginning to find his way into the pages of *All-Story Weekly*.

"I was a contract player at M-G-M, and I did what I was told," James Stewart said in 1972. "They told me I was going to do a picture for George Marshall, a picture written by Felix Jackson and produced by Joe Pasternak. I couldn't think of anything to do but just jump up and cheer and wave my arms 'cause everybody knew the type of work George Marshall did." The occasion was a discussion on the making of *Destry* and since both Marshall and Jackson were members of the panel, Stewart's remembered joyful leap may be nothing more than a polite fiction; he somehow forgot to mention the cameraman although Hal Mohr was also one of the guests. Although some of the best things in *Destry* are clearly directorial touches, there was little in George Marshall's record to 1939—and not much after—to account for so enthusiastic a response from a young actor who had just come from doing *Mr. Smith Goes to Washington* for Frank Capra. Marshall had begun at Universal as an extra in 1913 and had quickly switched to directing, grinding out one Western after another; in a publicity biography prepared when the octagenarian director turned performer again for *Vrooder's Hooch* (released in 1974 as *The Crazy World of Julius Vrooder*), he is credited with almost five hundred films. He worked with Francis Ford on serials, directed Tom Mix at Fox, did Bobby Jones's "How I Play Golf" series for Warner's, did comedy shorts for Mack Sennett and Hal Roach (working with Laurel and Hardy and Thelma Todd and ZaSu Pitts among others). His not very distinguished list of feature films, a mixture of comedies and melodramas, suggests that he was a journeyman director willing to get on with any assignment that came his way. Aside from all those Westerns, which presumably taught the director to relax into the genre formula, the Marshall pictures that have the most direct bearing on *Destry* are those he did with Will Rogers—or one of them at least. *In Old Kentucky* (1935), the last Rogers film to be released, is so weak that it reflects badly on both the comedian and his director. On the other hand, *Life Begins at Forty* (1935) is vintage Rogers and one of the best pictures Marshall ever made. A director who had handled a performer like Rogers, whose character was at once garrulous and laconic, deceptively naive, a power figure who pretended not to be, was ready for Tom Destry, and the man who directed the grand shindy at the end of *Life* would have no trouble with the battle royal that provides the climax if not the ending of *Destry Rides Again*.

The film begins with a precredits shot of the sign "Welcome to Bottleneck." We hear the sound of gunfire, and bullets smash a bottle sitting on the sign and another which is tied to it for no reason except that Marshall apparently wants to leave us with a real bottleneck gently swaying in front of this unlikely avowal of cordiality. As Destry says later, after Frenchy has thrown at him everything movable in the saloon, "You sure have a knack of makin' a stranger feel right at home, ma'am." A neater variation of the original sign, no longer an ironic welcome, will introduce the last, long, summing-up sequence. His initial point made, Marshall elaborates by showing much cheerful violence beneath the credits—a fistfight outside the saloon, a horse riding through the swinging doors. To get from the noisy scene on the street to the poker game on the second floor, Marshall has the camera climb the front of the saloon, moving from the frenetic doings below to the peaceful balcony and the lighted window before he brings us inside to the game itself. A conventional but quite effective device, it takes the audience where the director wants them and establishes a necessary atmosphere, deceptive in this case because the violence in this room is more dangerous than the horseplay outside. Marshall uses a similar teaser later in the film when he first introduces us to the hero. Wash, the new sheriff, tells the saloon crowd that he is hiring the great Tom Destry's son as deputy and he ends his announcement with a fine Charles Winninger crow of challenge, "Destry will ride again!" We cut to the legs of running horses, which might for a second suggest a hard-riding hombre, but these are horses in harness; the camera moves up to their head, along their backs, to the coach itself and then—after a distant shot of the stage racing along the road—to the passengers inside and our first glimpse of the pacific Destry, who will be such an unhappy surprise to Wash.

The poker game appears at first to be a gathering of hats. Although we can see Bugs Watson (Warren Hymer) full face when the camera takes its initial look at the table as a whole (his is not a wide-brimmed hat), the general impression is of men obscured as they study their cards. When a head is lifted, it is as though the performer were being allowed a preliminary bow before the character gets on with the matter at hand—an artificial introduction set within a presumably realistic action, a counterpart to what follows in the saloon scene. There is nothing unusual about the face we see under the first raised hat. It belongs to Tom Fadden, cast to type as Lem Claggett, the farmer who is being set up to lose everything he owns in the crooked poker game. Whether Claggett is bragging about the run of luck that seems to make him invincible or turning accusatory as he realizes he has been cheated, Fadden plays him so that a whine can be heard beneath both exultation and anger. Anyone who knows Brand's novel might suspect that the character is derived from that boasting weakling, the father of Willie Thornton, the boy who figures so prominently in the book. After all, Claggett's son Eli (Dickie Jones), like Willie, is a Destry worshiper, although the film, unlike the novel, arranges things so that the boy's admiration can temporarily turn to disappointment. Although Claggett has courage (he tries to come back and shoot Kent, he defends his home against Kent's men), he is essentially an unattractive character and that, I think, is the point of Fadden's performance. Claggett is clearly a victim—certainly no match for the four professional thugs in the cardroom—but villainy in this film cannot be unambiguously nasty. The murder of Sheriff Keogh (Joe King) is similarly softened; it takes place offscreen and the character, however well-intentioned, is never more than a plot device. That becomes obvious in our response to the exchange between Frenchy and Mayor Slade (Samuel S. Hinds). "I think I'll have to buy an option on his curiosity," says Slade, and, after a shot is heard from upstairs, Frenchy adds, "I think you'll have to buy a whole new sheriff." We recognize the line as outrageous and its delivery helps to characterize Frenchy at this point, but it is still a comedy line to be appreciated for its neatness.

That the film plays with the idea that Kent and his cohorts are uncharacteristic villains is obvious in the second face we see. It belongs to Kent, the man who runs Bottleneck, the owner of the Last Chance Saloon, the town's "social and political center."[2] He lifts his head to drop out of the game, letting Claggett win to soften him for the kill, and the camera lingers on the face of Brian Donlevy, the most celebrated movie villain of that time. Donlevy made his stage debut as Corporal Gowdy, one of the kvetching soldiers who open the Laurence Stallings–Maxwell Anderson *What Price Glory?* (1924), and spent the next decade as a busy supporting player on Broadway. He made a few movies in the 1920s, but his film career really began when he came to Hollywood hoping to repeat the role of the champion in *The Milky Way* which he had played on Broadway in 1934; it went to William Gargan. By the time that film was released in 1936, Donlevy had already been seen in the role that was to shape his movie career—Knuckles, the henchman of Edward G. Robinson's underworld boss in *Barbary Coast* (1935). "P'-ying a killer was part of the fun," he told *Silver Screen*. "A change from the things I had been doing. I didn't know that I wasn't going to be able to keep on changing." B. R. Crisler, interviewing him in 1937, wrote that "Mr. Donlevy says his status in Hollywood is simple: he plays heavies in big productions and heroes in Class B's." Crisler reported that Donlevy was worried that "he has probably ruined himself with his fans by stepping in Don Ameche's face" in the not yet released *In Old Chicago* (1938). In *Jesse James* (1939) he played a character so despicable ("resemblance to any member of the human race was strictly coincidental") that he asked 20th Century-Fox to release him from his contract. Or so he told *Silver Screen*, but the new free-lance performer went into *Beau Geste* (1939) to play Sergeant Markoff, the most notorious of his villains. He had generally played comedy or farce on the stage—he did sketches with Bert Lahr in his last Broadway appearance, *Life Begins at 8:40* (1934)—but the few early attempts at comedy in Hollywood made use of his evil image. In *Strike Me Pink* (1936), he was the boss of the gangsters outsmarted by Eddie Cantor as the titular Pink. Donlevy presumably took part in the slapstick chase sequence, but, if so, he is simply one of a group of hurrying figures so unidentifiable that his role could have been played—as it may have been—by a stunt extra; that was certainly not Cantor on the trapeze. The menace lies in the casting of Donlevy, not in his playing the role.

Graham Greene complained that the marvelous comics in *Destry* "don't belong in the same world as Brian Donlevy." Not with the Donlevy of *Beau Geste* and *Jesse James* perhaps, although the melodrama world has never been as comic-free as Greene's remark suggests. George Marshall had directed *Battle of Broadway* (1938), the first of two films in which Donlevy was paired with Victor McLaglen in Fox's attempt to revive the Flagg-Quirt kind of buddy movie. It may have been Marshall's experience with Donlevy in this film that made him think that he could use the performer in two different ways—as a villain and as a comedian. That he was not completely successful in the second endeavor reflects the limitations of Donlevy as a performer. There was always something clumpy about Donlevy as an actor, a four-square heaviness that denied subtlety and flexibility. This quality helped make him effectively nasty when the role called for it, but it was not until Preston Sturges cast him in *The Great McGinty* (1940) that the full comic possibilities of the actor's apparent intractability were realized. In *Destry*, however, Marshall is already using that quality by juxtaposing Donlevy with other performers—most notably Samuel S. Hinds and James Stewart. Donlevy's Kent, so much more elegant than most of his henchmen, suggests the conventional Western gang boss, the banker or saloonkeeper who is the secret brains behind all the crime in the countryside. This character must be plausibly ingratiating (see Max Brand's Chester Bent) to sustain his mask, and Kent sometimes appears to be playing that game although there is nothing secret about his operation. The facade of conviviality that he sometimes tries on is a function not of his role but of his claim to a place in the world from which Graham Greene would exclude him; this is a villain who wears a gray hat, not a black one.

Kent knows who runs things around Bottleneck, however, and his bluntness—the performer's bluntness—keeps breaking through. He bristles in direct threat to Destry, after the deputy announces the arrest of Gyp Watson, but both Kent's outburst and Donlevy's playing of it are undercut by the obviously fake, oily correctness of Samuel S. Hinds's Slade. Much earlier, in Kent's first confrontation with Destry, Marshall sets the scene for the conventional Western showdown, only to have Destry refuse to give up his gun because he does not have one. This deflation of Kent is emphasized by the easiness of Stewart as a player and the rigidity of Donlevy; even when Donlevy breaks into that nice and nicely condescending smile of his, he gives the impression of a man standing his ground, not knowing that it has been cut from under him. In the one scene in which real lightness is necessary, Donlevy and his director fall short of what is required. Kent, growing jealous of Destry, goes to Frenchy's dressing room to warn and threaten her; as he leaves, she snatches a weapon off her dressing table and throws it after him. The joke is that her behavior is so predictable that Kent simply sidesteps the missile and goes on out the door. A well-conceived gag, it is somehow out of sync in the playing; the crash comes before Kent ducks it. The awkwardness here is the more obvious when one compares it to the well-timed exit of Destry after Frenchy's first flamboyant display of her temper; he makes his remark about appreciating her welcome, turns toward the door, and then neatly ducks as a chair comes flying over his head. The one scene aside, Donlevy is used effectively in *Destry* and never more so than in our first glimpse under the brim of that gray hat when we see in an instant the character, the performer, and an accompanying chorus of past Donlevy villains.

Aside from the dealer, more a function than a character, the other people at the poker table are Rockwell (Edmund MacDonald) and the Watson boys, Bugs and Gyp (Hymer and Allen Jenkins). There is nothing special about Rockwell, a big man, a presence, menacing scene decoration, but the Watson brothers are something else again. Jenkins and Hymer were specialists in the urban tough, the hanger-on, the petty gangster. Both were adept at the use of elegantly illiterate slang (see Hymer's role in *A Lady's Profession*, 1933, Jenkins's in *Ball of Fire*, 1941), and their familiar voices evoke other films, other settings even as we accept them as proper denizens of Bottleneck. Jenkins, whose parents were musical comedy performers, began as a chorus boy; after the closing of *What's the Odds?*, with which he toured in 1919, he went into *Pitter Patter* (1920), in which he tapped with James Cagney. After formal schooling at the American Academy of Dramatic Arts, Jenkins turned away from musicals to do character bits including a clutch of reporters for *The Front Page* (1928), *The Last Mile* (1930) and *Five Star Final* (1930). He went to Hollywood to repeat his role in *Blessed Event* (1932)—another newspaper play/film, but this time he was a gangster—and stayed to become one of the gang that Warner Brothers kept around to back up Edward G. Robinson and Cagney, who had come a long way from *Pitter Patter*. Hymer, like Jenkins a show-biz child, made a vaudeville appearance at eight, but that is a deceptive fact to report about him. He made his real entry into the theater by way of Yale and George Pierce Baker, and he must be the oddest advertisement ever turned out by that haven of medium-high art. "When they want a big dumb-looking mug they pick me," he said in a playful *New York Herald Tribune* piece in which he was identified as Yale, '27. His only Broadway appearance was in *The Grey Fox* (1928), a Lemist Esler play about Machiavelli which had come to Broadway by way of Yale; by 1929, he was in the movies. He was paired with Spencer Tracy in Tracy's first film, *Up the River* (1930), and in *Goldie* (1931), in which they played two sailors competing for Jean Harlow in the title role. Even though Hymer quickly slipped into supporting roles, reviewers continued to praise him, once when he was not even in the film; in the review of *If You Could Only Cook* (1935), the *New York Times* said, "Lionel Stander does nobly in a part which seemed to clamor for Warren Hymer." Sometimes his bits became so tiny that they were almost invisible, as in *Mr. Deeds Goes to Town* (1936), in which he plays one of the bodyguards that an impatient Deeds (Gary Cooper) locks in the closet, and *San Francisco* (1936), in which, as a paid heckler, he gets out only a single heckle before Blackie (Clark Gable) steps off the platform and knocks him cold. Still, he occasionally got substantial roles and Bugs Watson is one of his best.

Both Jenkins and Hymer are playing variations of their standard roles in *Destry*. Although Brooks Atkinson praised Jenkins for being "comically thick-witted" in *Blessed Event*, that really is Hymer's stereotype, and he developed a physical-verbal business, a second cousin to the double take, to express his habitual bewilderment. There is a good example of it in *Belle of the Nineties* (1934), in which he plays a fighter who is unwisely persuaded to pretend to be "your bunny boy" to Ruby (Mae West) in the hopes that Tiger Kid (Roger Pryor) will lose interest in her. At one point, he and Tiger pause outside the club where Ruby is performing to glance at her picture and when Tiger says, "Coming, Bunny Boy?" he goes into the hesitation routine—a partial turn, a "yeh," a return—that conveys the disorientation which besets him when an unexpected line from another character distracts him from the immediate purpose. There is such an occasion in *Destry*, but the exchange is so macabre that it becomes almost surrealistic. When Kent, rising to Destry's bait, sends Gyp to see if Keogh's body is still safely hidden, Bugs assumes Destry's involvement and offers to "personally slap him in the mouth with my pistol." Kent says—and Donlevy's delivery here is properly throwaway—"You wouldn't hit a dead man, would you?" Bugs reacts with a "Yeah—no—well, I don't know," and the camera contemplates him from a distance as he stands befuddled at the bar.

Jenkins's usual character was rather more capable, more obviously aware of the world around him. At times he was "a virtuoso of croaky compassion," as Wallace Markfield put it, but, comforting or demanding, he had a pushy delivery that made even his asides abrasive.[3] Although Marguerite Tazelaar's line is not the customary way to speak of Jenkins, she touched something central to his characterizations when, in describing a scene, in a Turkish bath in *The Case of the Lucky Legs* (1935), she called Jenkins one "whose natural savoir faire nothing could ever jolt." The abrasion is more visible than the savoir faire in *Destry*—particularly in the jail scene in which Gyp gives Wash so much trouble—but there is unflappability under Gyp's rough exterior, put there by the plot (he refuses to talk) and by the personality of the performer.

It is hardly apparent in our first glimpse of the Watsons, but as the film progresses we can see that Gyp is the stronger of the two brothers and Bugs, as his name suggests, the slightly wafty sibling. There is a brotherly concern between them which is a key to the comedy in these otherwise unsavory characters. It can best be seen when Boris (Mischa Auer) brings Bugs a message from his brother in jail: "No more cheese."

"Did he say that?"

"I'm quoting his every word."

"Gee, that's bad if he don't want no more cheese," Bugs says and, then, as though he dimly understands that something more dangerous than constipation might befall his brother, he adds, "Do you think they'll hang him?" The suggestion of affection here cannot hide the fact that the Watsons, like the Ogden brothers in Brand's novel, carry "a trail of the eternal slime upon them." They are a mindlessly vicious pair, this side of them shown in the neat, brutal way they disarm the angry Claggett. Jenkins is more effectively ugly than Hymer, but then he occasionally broke out of the comic mold for a dramatic variation on his usual character, as in his Hunk in *Dead End* (1937). Back in the summer of 1930, while Spencer Tracy was on leave from *The Last Mile* to make *Up the River* with Hymer, Allen Jenkins took over the role of Killer Mears in John Wexley's play; Dore Schary, then assistant stage manager on *Mile*, has testified to Jenkins's excellence in the role. This was a side of Jenkins's talent seldom tapped in the movies, and he preferred it that way if we can take his 1938 interview with Thornton Delehanty as anything more than a plug for *A Slight Case of Murder*. It is Jenkins, the comedian, who keeps Gyp from becoming reprehensible.

Having given us a first glimpse of the upstairs crowd, Marshall is ready to take us down to the saloon proper to meet most of the rest of the cast. Kent goes out on the interior balcony, ostensibly to signal

Frenchy that she is needed, actually to give him and us a chance to watch the first musical number. The character that we see first is Loupgerou, the bartender, presiding over the hubbub. He is played by Billy Gilbert, a veteran of burlesque and vaudeville, who, once he came to the movies in 1929, appeared in hundreds of roles in both feature pictures and two-reel comedies (George Marshall directed him in two 1932 Laurel and Hardy shorts, *Their First Mistake* and *Towed in the Hole*). He is remembered primarily as the sneezing comedian (*Million Dollar Legs* [1932]), who was so adept at his unusual calling that he persuaded Walt Disney to make one of Snow White's seven dwarfs (1937) a sneezer and played the part on the sound track. That, however, is an insufficient way of characterizing Gilbert. His main bit—played with or without an accent—is an agitated character, often disturbed by nothing perceptible, whose distress leads to verbal confusion, a fumble of sentences that stop and start, dwindle into nothing, or become transformed into puffs of outrage. Watch him trying to take a photograph in *Toast of New York* (1937) or attempting to deliver a reprieve in *His Girl Friday* (1940). Pushed far enough, he can become painstakingly articulate, oozing complaints around every syllable, as Loupgerou does in the scene in *Destry* when he protests the loss of his trousers. He lists his painful but acceptable grievances ("prunes every day"), savoring each one, but this last indignity is too much, and his landlady (Una Merkel), who has de-pantsed her henpecked husband to keep him at home, goes to reclaim the pants Boris has stolen.

For the most part, Loupgerou is seen behind the bar, where Gilbert is his sputtery self since the bartender, even when he is taking pleasure in the action around him (Frenchy's singing, the mocking of Destry), appears to be beset. One of his nicest moments comes when the house treats to celebrate Wash's appointment as sheriff. "I set 'em up, and you drink 'em down," he says, as he passes out the mugs of beer, and then repeats the phrase; after a cut away to Wash, we return for the line once again, echo and refrain, and even his "This is getting monotonous," accompanied as it is by the same movement, reinforces the rhythm of the scene. In the fight at the end of the film, the women back Bugs, then Gyp, then Slade against the bar, where each is knocked unconscious by a well-aimed rolling pin and then pushed up and over the bar. This is an old routine—consider the belt-cutting gag Frank Capra used in the "Hey, Rube" in *Rain or Shine* (1930)—and Marshall had already done it with Charles Sellon as the bottle-wielder in *Life Begins at Forty*. The scene has a special appeal—for me, at least—because as each of the villains is polished off I can hear, in my mind's ear, Gilbert's Loupgerou: "You set 'em up, and you knock 'em down. . . . This is getting monotonous." Although Gilbert's standard character could be disruptive, he was, even with his nervous manner-isms attached, an often beneficent figure—as in his counterman in *On the Avenue* (1937). That diners tended to be sanctuaries in 1930s movies may heighten that sense of Gilbert in *Avenue*, but there is a similar feel to his Loupgerou. Here, as with most of the characters in the film, there is a deceptive quality, for this amiable stumbletongue is a know-ing part of the Kent operation. He is the one who actually signals Frenchy that Kent wants her, but not until Kent catches his attention by hitting him in the back of the head with a half-eaten apple.

Loupgerou needs this call to alertness for he, like everyone else in the saloon, is listening to Frenchy sing. The film provides no elaborate lead-in to Frenchy—as it does for Destry—but one exists all the same. Or did in 1939, when the film was new. The popular audience—the "mob," as Josef von Sternberg liked to say—had presumably turned its back on Marlene Dietrich in the mid-1930s; she was one of the stars listed as box-office poison in the notorious 1938 advertisement of the motion-picture exhibitors. Now, moviegoers were being told and told again that Dietrich was back, completely transformed. The weight of the publicity (see the spread in *Life*) was placed on the famous battle between Frenchy and Mrs. Callahan in which Dietrich and Una Merkel did their own fighting and finished tattered, disheveled, soaking wet from the bucket of water Destry uses to part the two women. That the movie was making use of the extramural teaser is obvious in the fact that we first hear, rather than see, Frenchy. She is a familiar voice lost in a great cluster of men. Then, the camera elbows its way through the crowd and picks up the back of her head. Finally she turns into a close-up, looking a great deal lovelier than the sopping stills have led us to expect—and Dietrich still, despite the mass of curls that suggest no Dietrich hairdo since the one in *The Blue Angel* (1930), unless it is the blonde Afro fright wig she wore when she sang "Hot Voodoo" in *Blonde Venus* (1932).

So much has been written about Dietrich as an image, a desider-atum, an aphrodisiac—or, as Jean Cocteau put it, "a frigate, a figure-head, a Chinese fish, a lyre-bird, a legend, a wonder"—that there seems little need to reawaken that creature here. Yet Frenchy is not only a new Dietrich, she carries in her Lola-Lola from *The Blue Angel* and that string of glacial women that she embodied until, as *Life* put it, "the Age of Exotics . . . ended." Without attempting to track her myth through the male libido—or the female one—it might be useful to consider briefly the actress and the way she was received by the film audience and the press that both created and reflected that audience. Dietrich's professional apprenticeship, on stage and screen in Ger-many in the 1920s, was honorable if not triumphant. When Josef von

Sternberg chose her to play the cabaret Lorelei in *The Blue Angel*, she took the first step toward international stardom; as Heinrich Mann, whose novel *Professor Unrat* was the source of the movie, put it: "The success of the film will rely in a great measure on the naked thighs of Miss Dietrich!" It was an impressive thigh as Dietrich exposed it, standing, one foot up on a chair, in the pose that has been parodied by everyone from Madeline Kahn in *Blazing Saddles* to Helmut Berger in *The Damned* (1969). Her legs became a trademark, a label, an easy occasion for jokes, but the emphasis changed once she and Sternberg began working in the United States, as the first major publicity push ("She Threatens Garbo's Throne," trumpeted a *Photoplay* title) and the films themselves indicate. It was the face Sternberg concentrated on, the mask behind which, presumably, passion smoldered. In *Fun in a Chinese Laundry*, he speaks of Dietrich at their first interview as "a study in apathy" with a "bovine listlessness" waiting for him to reveal the "great deal of vitality" concealed beneath her surface. That vitality is apparent in *The Blue Angel*, even when Lola-Lola seems indifferent to the sexual turmoil surrounding her, but it pretty much disappears in the American films.

Sternberg saw actors as tools or material and, in *Fun in a Chinese Laundry*, listed "face" and "body" among the "lifeless surfaces" which "must be made responsive to light." In *Morocco* (1930), the first of the Dietrich-Sternberg American movies and the one that lifted her into the empyrean, she moves languidly and registers emotion only by opening her eyes widely. Sternberg poses her in static shots which have visual significance for him and which presumably suggest mystery to the hoi polloi. This film became the model for the ones to follow. The plots of the Sternberg films are so silly that Pare Lorentz, one of the director's early admirers, could say that "the Messrs. Wanger, Lasky, and their assistants, who furnish Mr. Sternberg with celluloid, should make every effort in the future to keep him away from a typewriter." This was in a review of *Dishonored* (1931), and since *Blonde Venus* and *The Devil Is a Woman* (1935) lay ahead, it is obvious that Lorentz went unheeded. These days, admirers of Sternberg and Dietrich are likely to take the films as jokes—ironic or camp, depending on one's orientation—and it is obvious that the stories were never more than a foolish frame in which the Dietrich image could be displayed. And, once displayed, could be admired, worshiped, invested with mythic significance. At first, reviewers, fan magazines, moviegoers embraced the image, found what they wanted in it, but after a few films the magic began to fade. To take a single example, Richard Watts, Jr., could speak of "her almost lyrically ironic air of detachment" in *Dishonored* and, three years later, say that she "has become a hapless sort of automaton" in *The Scarlet Empress* (1934). The actress's progress through the movie magazines is instructive. She was welcomed when she arrived in this country, as the stories comparing her to Garbo indicate. Freed of that cliché, she began to be discussed as the victim/ creation of Sternberg. He is generally assumed to have invented—or to have properly packaged—the actress,[4] and her acquiescence to his demands gave the movie magazines what they wanted, the Svengali-Trilby accusation. According to Homer Dickens, Sternberg was already being called Svengali Joe while *Morocco* was being made, but the earliest use of the analogy I have seen is in Cal York's gossip column in the October 1931 *Photoplay*; that was the year in which Archie Mayo's *Svengali* was released, and John Baxter has suggested that that John Barrymore movie provided the fan magazines with the easy reference. Sternberg, who never hesitated to show his contempt for Hollywood, was a predictable target (a *Cinema Digest* item began, "Jo(k)e Von Sternberg has returned . . . "), but Dietrich, who remained loyal to the director—and more significantly became difficult with the press—began to get the needle as well. By 1936, when *Silver Screen* published a piece by the uninominal Liza, the campaign had become almost xenophobic. The article passes from a bitchy rehash of the Sternberg-Dietrich decline to the presumed failure of Ernst Lubitsch, "a Continental like herself," to salvage the actress in *Desire* (1936) and the aborted *I Loved a Soldier*; Liza seems to take great pleasure in the discomfiture of Dietrich and the removal of Lubitsch from his post as production head at Paramount. It is a very ugly article at a time when refugees from the Nazis were beginning to stream into Hollywood.

I do not want to lay the dwindling popularity of Dietrich to the incipient isolationism on the American scene. After all, whatever Liza said, *Desire*—although certainly no *Morocco*—was hardly a failure. Frank S. Nugent, ignoring that Frank Borzage directed *Desire*, wrote, "Ernst Lubitsch, the Gay Emancipator, has freed Marlene Dietrich from Josef von Sternberg's artistic bondage, and has brought her vibrantly alive." *Desire* is one of Dietrich's most charming movies, and it does indicate a direction that she might have taken after her separation from Sternberg. Unhappily, in the films that followed—*The Garden of Allah* (1936), *Knight without Armour* (1937), *Angel* (1937)—she is as immobilized as ever and without the saving suggestion of eroticism which at first made her popular with the "mob." She was released/ fired by Paramount and was vegetating on the Riviera when Pasternak called to ask her to play in a Western. Sternberg, who was visiting her at the time, advised, "Make the film!"

Although audiences may not have wanted to see Dietrich in *The*

316 • Chapter Twelve

Garden of Allah and *Angel*, she was still a film personality with an iconographic significance with which the makers of *Destry* could play. The film cuts beneath any high-flown sense of the actress as the eternal feminine, and, harking back to the days when she was "Legs" Dietrich, turns its attention to the sexual significance of her past popularity. As she walks across the saloon singing "Little Joe the Wrangler," Boris slaps her on the fanny to show his appreciation. She throws a drink in his face, and Mischa Auer, in a wonderfully graphic bit, nibbles eagerly at the wetness on his lips—as though he were tasting Frenchy rather than the whiskey. He has an even more outrageous bit later, during the singing of "You've Got That Look." Here, as usual in Hollywood musicals, the director will not let the singer hold the screen; he cuts back and forth between Frenchy and her audience, but this time, for a change, the jokes are connected with the presumed appeal of the woman on stage. As Dietrich lets her voice glide sexily into a lower register, Auer's Boris rolls his eyes heavenward, exposing a great expanse of white. Beside himself, he embraces the post he is standing next to and, as he kisses it, he bends between thumb and fingers a deck of cards and sprays them like a fountain into the air. Then, nervous at what he has done, he pretends nonchalance toward the post as though it might have noticed. As if this ejaculation image were not clear enough, another of Frenchy's admirers fires off his pistol in his excitement—which carries to an extreme the idea of getting it off with Dietrich.

There are overtones of the indifferent Dietrich of old in the way she delivers her lines. Early in the film, Frenchy speaks with a kind of verbal shrug that dismisses illegality and immorality as trivial matters. Yet, her temper, her teasing sense of humor, her fight with Mrs. Callahan, even her singing suggest another woman altogether, or one who had been missing for ten years. Charles Silver, whose heart belongs to another Dietrich, has written correctly that "The key to Frenchy's character, like that of Lola-Lola, is vulgarity," and many of the contemporary reviewers agreed, welcoming the return of the girl from *The Blue Angel*. Yet Frenchy is not Lola-Lola. She is Hollywood's good-bad girl, the saloon singer with the heart of gold, ready to shed her vulgarity and switch allegiances from the villain who keeps her to the hero for whom she dies. The strength of the character, as written and as played by Dietrich, is that she never goes soft, never loses her sustaining irony. Even at her death, when the interrupted kiss of an earlier scene is once again unfinished as her head rolls away just as Destry's lips touch hers, there is nothing saccharine about so grandly sentimental a finish. It is almost a last, sad, lovely joke.

Although Frenchy is not quite Lola-Lola, she has the German girl's songwriter working for her. Frederick Hollander came to *The Blue Angel* with perfect credits. He had begun as a cabaret composer in 1919 in the Schall und Rauch, a club that was opened, with the blessings of Max Reinhardt, to provide parodies of the plays he put on in the Grosse Schauspielhaus. Hollander moved from the cabaret to what Lisa Appignanesi calls "the cabaretistic satirical revue," but continued to work in an idiom that was just right for the Sternberg film. The songs—particularly the one that became "Falling in Love Again" in English—were not only popular at the time but became part of Marlene Dietrich's permanent repertory. Later, in Hollywood, Dietrich sang "Jonny," a song that Hollander wrote in 1920, in *Song of Songs* (1933), and Hollander contributed both the score and (with Leo Robin) the songs for *Desire* and *Angel*. Although The Last Chance Saloon may seem rather far removed from The Blue Angel, Hollander wrote three songs for *Destry Rides Again* with words by Frank Loesser, a highly successful Hollywood lyricist who would later turn composer and write some of the best of the Broadway musicals—*Where's Charley?* (1948), *Guys and Dolls* (1950), and *How to Succeed in Business without Really Trying* (1961). Of the songs, "You've Got That Look" is the most characteristic Hollander-Dietrich number, but it was the raucous "The Boys in the Back Room" that became identified with Dietrich. "I'm making fun of myself," she told Rex Reed in 1967, commenting on her use of "Boys" in her cabaret show. ". . . I have a straight face and I say 'Here is a typical romantic song from one of my pictures.'" The overorchestrated glitter of her club act could not make fun of the Hollywood Dietrich more than *Destry* did of her provocative chanteuse when it put her into a cowgirl suit to sing "Boys" and had her create a corny quaver by grasping the loose flesh under her chin and jiggling it. There is nothing comparable in the Dietrich canon until *The Monte Carlo Story* (1957), in which she soulfully sings "Back Home in Indiana" to Arthur O'Connell's Hoosier millionaire. Despite the continued success of "Boys," the most important song in the film is "Little Joe," which Hollander adapted from N. Howard Thorp's 1898 ballad and for which Loesser provided new lyrics. "Little Joe" belongs not only to Frenchy but to Wash, who attacks it vigorously on his banjo, and at the end of the film, when Destry hears some children singing the song, Stewart's look invokes both characters and suggests a quality that helped make and is missing from the now peaceful Bottleneck.

As Frenchy moves across the saloon in the initial presentation of "Little Joe," we meet in quick succession Boris, Wash, and Slade, who is both mayor and judge in Bottleneck. Samuel S. Hinds's performance in this last role is as much a happy departure as Dietrich's Frenchy. Hinds, a successful lawyer with a passion for acting, helped found the Pasadena Playhouse in 1917 and played leading roles there for years. Wiped out by the 1929 crash, he became a professional, working first as an extra and then as a very successful supporting player. In her review of *The Raven* (1935), Regina Crewe wrote that "Mr. Hinds lends balance to the lurid proceedings." Since that charmingly ludicrous Poe pastiche has not only Bela Lugosi and Boris Karloff but a girl who does an interpretive dance to a recitation of "The Raven," it can use all the balance it can get, but Hinds brought the same sense of calm rectitude to movies that were not so desperate for it. He made a career of playing doctors, judges, lawyers, conservative businessmen—Hollywood's idea of society's surrogate father—and a string of understanding real fathers, most persistently old Dr. Kildare to Lew Ayers's young Dr. Kildare. As Slade, with his tiny, ill-fitting glasses, his habitual plug of tobacco, his partnerless checker game, Hinds travesties his conventional role. Slade's command of public rhetoric (his announcement of Wash's appointment as sheriff sounds like a nominating speech) and legalistic formulas are both a joke and a satirical comment on the criminal uses of governing officials and their obfuscating vocabularies.

We first see Wash as a hand trying to steal a bottle from a table, and, when he is detected, he jumps up and goes into his reprise of "Little Joe" as though he were as innocent as the cherubic face of Charles Winninger. (See chap. 10, pp. 262–63, 269). The frenetic mannerisms that Winninger brings to Wash, as both town drunk and reformed sheriff, serve the film well. Whether excited, determined, angry, or frustrated, he seems always about to explode, his volatility used against the placidity of James Stewart's Destry and as preparation for his death scene, in which his familiar responses are both present and transformed. For Boris, Mischa Auer uses his misunderstood Russian of *My Man Godfrey* (see chap. 8, pp. 209–10), by now a figure well known to moviegoers. The Boris in this scene and in the card-flipping sequence is misleading (the first is called simply "a miner" in the published script and the second not mentioned at all) because his character is defined in terms that have nothing to do with his momentary adoration of Frenchy.

Boris, whose name is Stavrogin (a Dostoyevsky joke?), is called Callahan through much of the film—even by his wife, the former Mrs. Callahan—and his work with Destry and Wash allows him to claim his rightful manhood, as Wash's appointment as sheriff—a joke to Kent and his crowd—becomes the means to his reclamation. During the celebration of Wash's investiture, he tastes the free whiskey and then spits it out—to signal that he will become the man he was when he was deputy to Tom Destry's father—and there is a shot of Boris, who half drops, half tosses away his whiskey glass. Although he shrugs as if in surprise at his own action, the gesture is an indication—unprepared for at this point—that he will become one of the unlikely trio of lawmen. There is a more extended presentation of the connection between Wash and Boris in the parallel sequences in which Boris loses his pants to Frenchy in a poker game and a Destry so unlike the one Wash is expecting is shown coming in on the stage. Marshall cuts back and forth between the scenes—extended passages, not quick shots—and he manages to bring Destry and the embarrassed Wash into the saloon just as the pantsless Boris makes an exit. These are comedy scenes, of course, but they do depict the simultaneous humiliation of two characters who will become the men they want to be in the course of the movie. Wash dies in the image of the older Tom Destry. Boris—like W. C. Fields's Elmer Finch in *Running Wild* (1927)—smashes the photograph of the first husband and commands the respect of his wife.

By the time we get to the end of the "Little Joe" scene, as Frenchy goes upstairs to play her coffee-spilling role in the cheating of Claggett, the audience has been introduced to all of the main characters except Mrs. Callahan, the irascible Jack Tyndall (Jack Carson), his sister Janice (Irene Hervey), the good girl who gets the hero, and Destry, of course. I have lingered over the characters and the performers who play them because the special quality of *Destry* lies in the confrontation of conventional Western stereotypes with familiar comic performers whose presence at once fulfills and alters them. The film's use of comedic devices for dramatic purposes is imaginative, as the sequence leading to Wash's death indicates. Boris, in his enthusiasm for his role as deputy, finds his own rhetoric ("I'll be a bloodhound, sniffing and silent" "I'm a mummy, I'm a sphinx—I don't answer questions") and a sense of importance that undermines his emphatic words. He answers Bugs's question about the likelihood of Gyp's hanging with a primly dismissive, "It's up to Judge Murtaugh," and after the usual Hymer incorrect response, "Oh, that's good," Bugs turns toward Slade with a "Say, who's Judge Murtaugh?" The histrionic dignity of Boris and the real confusion of Bugs—used comically through much of the film—combine to let Kent know that Destry is bringing in an outside judge, which forces him to rescue Gyp from jail and kill Wash in the process. The core of the Western melodrama remains comic in *Destry*, but the comedy can become dangerous.

Although the work of all the performers is necessary to the texture of *Destry*, the film depends most on James Stewart in the title tole. "He was good in anything," John Ford said. "Played himself but he played the character. . . . People just liked him." Ford did not get around to directing Stewart until the 1960s, long after Anthony Mann had broken him in on Westerns very different from *Destry Rides Again*, but Ford's remark will serve for Stewart in the late 1930s when, just moving into stardom, he played a group of roles that nicely balanced character and performer. He had begun to build a reputation for himself on Broadway in the early 1930s—notably as one of the soldiers in Sidney Howard's *Yellow Jack* (1934)—when he moved on to Hollywood and a small role in *The Murder Man* (1935). "I was all legs and arms," he said, "it was awful. I've never outlived the horror of it." There is less truth than humility in his confession, for his is a very respectable performance. He plays Shorty, a young newspaperman sent to track down the missing star reporter (Spencer Tracy), and when he unfolds his frame from the rumble seat in which he has been hiding, the discomfort he displays and the sheepish look he throws the other man belong to the character, not to the actor. The voice (he has to say *mebbe* several times) and the mannerisms are already taking clear shape in another tiny role, that of the sincere young man in *Wife vs. Secretary* (1936) who almost loses Whitey (Jean Harlow) to her boss (Clark Gable). Although there was some variety in his early roles—he was a murderer in *After the Thin Man* (1936)—he quickly developed a persona that informed the characters he played and was exploited in publicity pieces offscreen. "He is the kid from Elm Street who rents the tux to go to the Junior Prom," said Kyle Crichton in *Collier's*, and Alva Johnston in *Woman's Home Companion* became one of the first writers to invoke Booth Tarkington, although the Indiana where Stewart grew up is not the state but the town in Pennsylvania.

All this boy-next-door publicity was well intentioned, but the image is essentially reductive, suggesting ineptitude and callowness, a kind of fake innocence that does not begin to describe characters as different as his midshipman in *Navy Blue and Gold* (1937), his inhibited professor in *Vivacious Lady* (1938), his nice young man in *You Can't Take It with You* (1938), his self-pitying husband in the sudsy *Made for Each Other* (1939), his slightly disreputable detective in the slapstick *It's a Wonderful World* (1939), his embattled idealist in *Mr. Smith Goes to Washington* (1939), his Destry. These are all unmistakably James Stewart, but the impressive thing about the actor at this period is that he had learned to use his personality in the service of his characters and the differing demands of the genres in which he performed. This skill is crucial in *Destry Rides Again*, for it would be easy to make a simpleton out of the lawman who refuses to carry guns. Some of the other characters in the film may think him foolish or cowardly, but the audience cannot be allowed to doubt him for a moment. When the filmmakers named him Thomas Jefferson Destry[5] it was almost certainly a reference to Jefferson Smith, the protagonist of the film Stewart had just made, but the fact that both Destry and Mr. Smith are idealists should not obscure the differences between them. Unlike Smith, who begins his film as a genuine innocent, Destry is knowledgeable about violence and power. And about sex.

The kind of small-boy silliness that Frank Capra imposed on Stewart in Smith's hat-dropping nervousness at meeting the senator's daughter is completely absent from *Destry*. At their first meeting, Destry

---

Destry meets a recoiffed Frenchy. James Stewart, Marlene Dietrich. (*Destry Rides Again*, Universal, 1939. The Museum of Modern Art/Film Stills Archive.)

takes Frenchy's cliché ("How's the weather up there") out of her mouth and finishes it for her, adding, "You can do better than that." In that exchange Destry establishes a relationship with Frenchy in which, for once, she is not dominant. In *Marlene Dietrich's ABC*, the actress spoke sharply of "the school of acting which I call the 'Looking-for-the-other-shoe method,'" a kind of "naturalness" that allows the actor to look everywhere but at his partner in a love scene, and in her autobiography she enrolled Stewart in that school. An odd dismissal of one of her most effective costars, coming, as it does, from an actress who, in her waxen image days, often played her love scenes as though she and the man were in different rooms. The remark suggests that Dietrich has forgotten both the characters in *Destry* and the way they play together. The closest Destry and Frenchy come to a conventional love scene is their exchange outside the saloon in which he obliquely compliments her on her beauty and she expresses her concern (affection) by giving him her rabbit's foot. The first scene they play in her house shows Destry using his amiability and pretended naiveté to elicit from her information she does not want to give; the second presents a preoccupied Frenchy, trying to keep Destry there to protect him from the assault on the jail. Sex is central to both scenes, but the motivational line lies elsewhere. In every meeting with Frenchy, Stewart's Destry plays with quiet and amused authority, the same quality that he brings to his encounters with Kent, Tyndall, and that unlikely trio of roisterers to whom he gives a lesson in shooting.

One of the bromides of Stewart commentary is that would-be witty writers presenting the actor's screen image like to play on what would be his habitual way of talking if he actually spoke as impressionists pretend he does. Thus we get articles with cute titles like "Box Office Drawl" and "Th' Respawnsibility of Bein' J...Jimmy Stewart. Gosh!" His lovable stammer, like his presumed simplicity, has been done to death. Years ago, in his review of *The Shopworn Angel* (1938), Otis Ferguson pointed out the essential thing about Stewart's verbal mannerisms when he said that the actor was "rapidly perfecting a technique of saying the thing by planting it in the unsaid territory of false starts, half words, and general confusion." Watching Destry accidentally let slip something he wants Kent to know, one can understand Ferguson's admiration for Stewart's mastery of inarticulateness as an effective communication device. "What he has so wonderfully," Frank Capra once said, "is the ability to act what he's saying as though he'd just thought of it." For all that Stewart has a reputation for playing laconic characters, Destry is remarkably talkative. He speaks in parables. He regularly wraps his pedagogical points in anecdotes that begin "I had a friend once" or "I knew a man." This is an important characterizing mechanism because it allows him to speak at one remove from direct statement—as when he compliments Frenchy with a generalization that he pretends came from a book. Since the action of the film is going to force him to pick up his guns and do directly what he has intended to do by indirection, his storytelling has to be firmly established so that we can see it break down. When his probing into the death of Keogh begins to cause trouble, Frenchy quiets an incipient outburst from Kent by interrupting Destry as he begins one of his tales and warns him with one of her own about a man who found a pearl but died of the bad oyster. Gyp later cuts him off in the jail scene with "You know too many men." In Wash's death scene, Destry tries to tell a story about a man he knew once who fell asleep, but the hesitations here are the failure of invention, not the slow delivery that he customarily uses to let the meaning soak in; he finally abandons the story completely and compares Wash with his own father who was murdered by a shot in the back: "They didn't dare face him either." Finally, at the end of the film, there is one last, perhaps too cunning use of the device. Destry, sparking Janice Tyndall, begins, "I had a friend once . . . " only to be interrupted this time by THE END across the screen. The audience knows by now that Destry no longer finishes his stories, that he has moved from talk to action. It is as clearly a happy ending as a lovers' embrace.

The role of Janice is a small one in the film, but Marshall goes out of his way to make a connection between her and Frenchy. He cuts from Frenchy, looking in the mirror, wiping away the excessive makeup that Destry suggests may hide real loveliness, to Janice, looking in a mirror, applying the new chamois about which the good ladies of the town are eager to learn. Both Frenchy and Janice fall in love with Destry and he with them presumably, but the important developing relationship—the closest in the film—is between Destry and Wash. Destry may make Wash his father in the end, but the older man has been Destry's child for most of the film, a lovable creature who needs to be teased and tended and spoiled a little. Wash's initial distress at Destry's refusal to carry guns gives way to a fondness for and a trust in the younger man. In their first private scene together, as Destry unpacks after his noisy reception in the Last Chance, the film establishes a physical bit that will become both a running gag and an indication of the closeness of the two men. Whenever he is exasperated, Wash has a way of clawing at the front of his shirt which leaves the tail hanging out. Like an understanding parent, Destry soothes him and tucks the shirttail back in. Or starts to, usually, and a calmer Wash finishes the job. The film plays many variations on this routine. In another hotel scene, when Destry is washing up for dinner, he stuffs the edge of the towel into Wash's pants and the older man begins automatically to tuck it in until he realizes the joke. When Wash and Destry hurry out of the office to go to the beseiged Claggetts, Destry's refusal to arm brings Wash's gesture of anger, cleverly indicated by Winninger although Wash's hands are full of guns. As Boris and Wash wait outside the saloon to track Gyp to the hidden body, Boris starts to poke in the shirttail only to have his hands slapped away. Wash's "Take your hands off me" is an indication of his present uneasiness, but it is also a signal of which he is presumably not conscious; although he and Boris are friends, the shirt business is an intimacy shared only by him and Destry. Finally, inevitably, Destry tries to tuck in the shirt of the dying Wash.

I have touched several times on this death scene, but it deserves a few sentences of concentrated attention. The death of the comic side-kick is familiar enough in Westerns and in other melodramas (see Vincent Barnett's Angelo in *Scarface* [1932]), but its impressiveness here lies in the fact that it uses the comic mannerisms of both Wash and Destry, modulated into a new key, and lets their closeness, treated lightly in so much of the film, be seen in a context of pain, physical and emotional. Unabashedly sentimental, the effect is heightened by the use of "Little Joe" as background music, played very slowly, on strings, as though the jangle of Wash's banjo, like the man himself, were running down. Much of the strength of the scene comes from Marshall's inventive use of close-up. Destry enters through the crowd and stands silently, doing nothing. As he leans down to Wash, there is a third figure in the frame—an unidentified man who is presumably comforting Wash as Destry arrives. We go then to a two-shot as Wash tries to make a joke ("I bet you knew a fellow once . . . ") and stay with it as Destry begins the story he will not be able to tell. We go to Wash, and then we cut back and forth between the two men; except for one more two-shot, the scene is played in alternating close-ups. Destry speaks in his usual deliberate manner and Wash's rush of words is slowed by pain. There is, then, no verbal urgency in the scene, but the visuals deny the implicit gentleness of the unhurried rhythm. The cuts seem to grow more rapid as death approaches, an impression that is strengthened by the hugeness of the faces, filling the screen as no other of the film's few close-ups do. The beauty of the scene can best be understood by comparing it with the same scene in Marshall's remake of *Destry*. Although that film has some good character actors in it— Thomas Mitchell, Edgar Buchanan, Wallace Ford—and Marshall often seems to be trying for precisely the effects which worked well in 1939, it is a travesty of the original—leaden, awkward, vulgar. In the death scene, with only one real actor to work with, Marshall has to abandon the alternating close-ups; most of the scene is shot over Audie Murphy's shoulder, the camera on Mitchell's face. Since this is not simply Wash's death scene, but the moment of decision which will send Destry for his guns, the point is largely lost. In the original, the scene is the emotional climax of the film and the trigger for the remaining action; thanks to the presence of Stewart and Winninger it is also an extremely touching scene that carries in it the echoes of the shared comedy that the two performers brought with them from the earlier parts of the film.

Destry leaves the jail in silence and goes to his room for his father's guns. The film reverts to the kind of dispensation of justice that one traditionally expects in a Western, but there is still a difference. Although the good guys beat the bad guys, the good guys are really the women of the town, incited to action by Frenchy, led by Janice and Mrs. Callahan. They march between the opposing forces, into the saloon and there, in the final comic brawl, they punish the wicked without the shedding of blood. Except—and it is an important exception—Frenchy must die saving Destry from Kent's bullet, and the villain must be dispatched in turn. We go then to a peaceful Bottleneck patrolled by an unarmed Destry, his footsteps dogged by an adoring and imitative Eli Claggett. Happy ending, nice and tidy.

A Western that works out as a Western should and that still retains a solid comedic texture—why then should I have this vague uneasiness about the guns of Tom Destry? Popular drama has always had an impetus toward necessary violence. Movies as different as *Grandma's Boy* (1922), in which The Boy (Harold Lloyd) finally faces the villainous tramp, and *Straw Dogs* (1971), in which David (Dustin Hoffman) devises ingenious ways to murder the men harassing him and his wife, have been built on the assumption that peace, security, well-being can be earned only through a demonstration of force. *Destry Rides Again* is in that tradition.

Destry is special in that it goes to great lengths to show that its hero's rejection of guns is arrived at intellectually and to make his abandonment of his position an emotional rather than a rational decision. His pacifism has its roots not in morality ("Thou shalt not kill") but in practicality ("he that killeth with the sword must be killed with the sword"). Destry, his own parabolist, does not use biblical quotations, but he explains to Wash, in the scene in which he convinces the sheriff to give him the deputy's badge, that his father was wearing his weapons the day he was gunned down in Tombstone. The heart of Destry's argument is that men like Kent cannot be defeated by fighting them on their own terms. They become heroes if they are killed;

"they'll look little and cheap the way they ought to look" if they are sent to jail. Although the direct exposition of this scene may be necessary to the film, *Destry* is, as usual, more effective when it uses comedy to make a point. Wash takes Destry on a walk through Bottleneck and shows him a blood-soaked, bullet-ridden post which is one of the town's monuments. It is the site at which Sawtooth Magee shot it out with a neighbor in a quarrel over his wife's petticoat, and Sawtooth, neighbor, and "four innocent bystanders" were buried together. Wash, innocent of the implications of his tale, returns immediately to his attempt to persuade Destry to take up his guns with "You've got to listen to reason."

If Wash is the chief advocate of violence among the right-thinking people of Bottleneck, there are others. Mrs. Callahan, for instance. She calls for action in the scene in which the Claggetts come to town, having been dispossessed by Destry, who, unlike Wash, insists that the sheriff must accept as legal the paper in which Claggett signed away his property. The loudest voice in this scene—as elsewhere in the film—belongs to Jack Tyndall. Although he is one of the good guys, his contempt for law is as obvious as Kent's; he believes that right can be maintained only through the fist or the gun. Aggressive, loud-mouthed, self-righteous, unpleasant—played by Jack Carson in that outraged whine which would shortly carry him to leading comedy roles—Tyndall is a satirical figure. Every time he opens his mouth, he seems to prove the wisdom of Destry's position.

Tyndall is also the cause of Destry's first falling away from nonaggression. At the end of Destry's soft scene with Frenchy outside the saloon, Tyndall bulls in, full of insinuation, and Destry knocks him down. An audience-pleasing punch, it is also an indication of the kind of emotional response of which Destry is capable. When Wash's death sends him for his guns, he arms for vengeance, not for right. Judge Murtaugh is still on his way to Bottleneck; Kent and company could presumably still be trapped in the old Destry way. Audience sentiment may be with the change in Destry, but the film calls the process in doubt by making the now approving Tyndall his ally. It is even possible to see Frenchy's death as a direct result of Destry's need for revenge. He moves through the nonlethal brawl in the saloon, as determined to get Kent as Kent is to get him, and although the hero-villain confrontation is a standard denouement for the Western, this film has already violated so many conventions of the Western that the demands of the genre are hardly an excuse for his behavior. Destry, acting in anger, finally listens to unreason.

That Destry never really puts his pacific sentiments to a test, does not mean that the film does not do so. When the women march to the saloon, they go—as Frenchy says they should—to protect their men, replacing angry violence with necessary violence. There are occasions, the film seems to say, in which one must take up arms (even if the arms here are pitchforks, hoes, and fence pickets) in the cause of peace and civilization. The film opened in New York City on November 29, 1939, almost three months after the invasion of Poland and the beginning of the Second World War. It would be two more years before that war would officially become ours, but President Roosevelt had tried to warn us as early as October 5, 1937, when, in his "quarantine" speech in Chicago, he made specific what he had said, in a very different context, a year earlier: "This generation of Americans has a rendezvous with destiny."

There was a rather strange comedy called *Thanks for Everything* released late in 1938. It was about Henry Smith (Jack Haley), a man whose tastes so closely reflect what the surveys say the general public wants that J. B. Harcourt (Adolphe Menjou) uses him as a one-man market research tool. The movie takes an odd turn when an unnamed foreign power asks Harcourt to find out whether or not Americans will fight. Henry is isolated in a hotel room, plied with fake newspapers and radio broadcasts, but no insult to American honor, no danger to our presumed interests abroad can send him into the army. Finally, a simulated bombing and a reported invasion make him eager to defend his country. Harcourt's conclusion: "You can tell the world that if American democracy is seriously threatened, we will fight to the last man." Graham Greene, who found *Thanks for Everything* "the funniest film I can remember seeing for many months," particularly liked the war sequence: "It is a great deal in these days to be made to laugh at the sight of a man in a gas-mask." As Greene's comment suggests, the movie may not be taking its war game seriously, but it is significant that a joke so designed and with such a conclusion should find its way into an unpretentious comedy released on the eve of 1939.

Destry Rides Again may be innocent of social comment. Still, when you build a film on whether or not a man should take up the gun, you invite serious consideration of the pacifist impulse. Today, in the wake of an unwanted and divisive war, the movie, behind its Western facade, may seem to be about the failure of Destry, the defeat of nonaggression and rational law. In 1939, however, the final violence found its justification in a social and political context far more demanding than the claims of the screen. Interventionism was in the air; the pacifism of the 1930s—its idealism wrecked on the fact of the Nazis— was already beginning to disintegrate.

The march of the women in *Destry* not only brought to an end a movie but a decade. And, quite incidentally, the kind of comedy I have been talking about in this book.

Notes

1. Jackson and Hollander were among the many European refugees who settled in Hollywood during the 1930s. Hollander came over in 1933; Jackson somewhat later—between 1935, when he wrote *Maria Baschkirtzeff* for production in Austria, and 1938, when he got his first American credit for *Mad about Music*. In the interviews Hollander gave when he stopped in New York on his way to the West coast (Eileen Creelman, *New York Sun*, June 1, 1933, p. 33; Marguerite Tazelaar, *New York Herald Tribune*, June 4, 1933, sec. 5, p. 4), there was no mention of the Nazis or of Germany's new chancellor. Germany was still an American film market in those days and it is not likely that Hollander's new employer, Fox, whose New York office presumably arranged the meeting with journalists, would have wanted him to linger on his nonartistic reasons for leaving Germany. So we get routine protestations of his desire to be part of the American film industry. "It has always been a dream of mine to go to Hollywood," he told Creelman. In 1941, Hollander published a novel, *Those Torn from the Earth*, which Thomas Mann sweetly but wrongly praised for its "visible, vigilant and colorful English" (in unpaged preface, New York, Liveright, 1941). The book, which does have a number of effective scenes, is primarily interesting for its content, which voices the unspoken assumptions behind those discreet 1933 interviews. It tells the story of a group of German intellectuals, some Jewish, some not, who get out of Germany in 1933 and who either succeed or fail to cope with a new life first in Paris, then in Los Angeles. Incidentally interesting in the light of Hollander's work with both Dietrich and Pasternak are a glimpse of a "Swedish" actress and "her director," who is clearly Dietrich and Josef von Sternberg, and a central character, the unfortunate Jaques Mando who seems to have been modeled in part—his pleasure in the good things of life, his belief in movies simply as entertainment—on Pasternak. Mando even serves "Hungarian goulash" at his first big Hollywood party (pp. 268–69).

2. The phrase is from the condensed script as it appears in *The Best Pictures, 1939–1940*, but whether it comes from the screenplay or from the editors of the collection, I do not know. Following the practice Burns Mantle worked out for his *Best Plays*, Jerry Wald and Richard Macaulay, both screenwriters at the time, present the screenplay in fragments of dialogue bridged by summarizing accounts of the action. I assume that much of the actual wording of the latter comes from Wald and Macaulay. In any case, the descriptions are frequently, and the dialogue occasionally, incorrect reflections of the film as it finally appeared. A useful tool, the published screenplay should be

approached with suspicion. The name of Kent's saloon, The Last Chance, presumably derives from the novel, in which Brand has some fun with his saloon names, offering a First Chance and a Second Chance as well as a Last Chance. The name is obviously as old as thirst on the edge of the wilderness. In *John Ford*, Jean Mitry, discussing *Three Godfathers* (1948), which has a Last Chance Saloon in it, mentions a Western dating from around 1916 called *Le Cabaret de la dernière chance*, which is presumably *The Last Chance Saloon* when it is at home (Paris, Éditions Universitaires, 1954, bk. 2, p. 91).

3. His most celebrated aside in *Destry Rides Again* is not in it all. At the end of the poker game, Frenchy picks up a stack of coins and drops them down the front of her dress. Gyp mutters, "Thar's gold in them hills." When the film opened in New York at the end of November, some of the reviewers praised the sense of humor of the Hays office and by December 5 the line had been ordered deleted. A teapot tempest ensued. The Rivoli Theater refused to cut the line despite Universal's demand that they do so. Frank S. Nugent wrote a Sunday piece for the *New York Times* ("No Gold in Them Thar Hills," December 10, 1939, sec. 10, pt. 2, p. 7) condemning "Elder Hays and his unmerry men," and Kenneth Clark, a representative of the Motion Picture Producers and Distributors of America, wrote in (*New York Times*, December 24, 1939, sec. 9, p. 4) to explain that Joseph I. Breen, of the Hays office, had assured him that, contrary to the assumption in the press, the line had been cut before the film left Hollywood. The wrong print had been sent. The line eventually came out. Oh, those innocent days!

4. And correctly, I assume, although there are other claims. Ronald Schiller ("Miraculous Marlene Dietrich," pt. 2, *Woman's Home Companion*, 80 [August 1953], 41, 51) said that "Von Sternberg brought her to America . . . and delivered her into the hands of the Hollywood beauticians," and then described the making of Dietrich in terms of pounds lost, inches cut away. Wally Westmore, the make-up man, has said (to Bruce Davidson, "The Dietrich Legend," *McCall's*, 87 [March 1960], 166), "her face requires special treatment—or it photographs flat." Lee Garmes, who photographed *Morocco*, told Charles Higham and Joel Greenberg, ("North Light and Cigarette Bulb," *Sight and Sound*, 36 [Autumn 1967], 193), "I can honestly say the Dietrich face was my creation." Sternberg, for whom every aspect of filmmaking was an extension of the directorial authority, would presumably say, of course, they are all me. My favorite claim for the discovery of the Dietrich face can be found in a piece in *Liberty*. The author explained that Dietrich went one day into one of those coin-operated photo booths found in train stations and amusement parks and that the

overhead bulb "turned Marlene's plump and jovial face into a brooding thing of planes and shadows. . . . Photomaton had given her a soul!" (Frederick Lewis, "The Girls Who Came Back," 18 [May 31, 1941], 18).

5. Max Brand's Harry Destry had already become Tom in the Mix version of the story, presumably because Mix's fans liked his heroes to bear his name. It would not be well to look too closely at presidential names in *Destry* in any of its versions, for Wash Dimsdale's name is Washington and Harry Destry's name is really Harrison, and what are we to make of that?

Bibliographic Notes

NYPL-PARC is the New York Public Library Performing Arts Research Center at Lincoln Center. All references, unless otherwise designated, are to the Billy Rose Theatre Collection there.

The quotations from works listed in the original French or German should be blamed on me, although I had more than a little help from my friends in making the translations.

Introduction

p. 1, *l. 1*   William Wellman, "Why Teach Cinema?" *Cinema Progress*, 4 (June–July 1939), 3.

p. 1, *l. 23*   Josef von Sternberg, *Fun in a Chinese Laundry*, London, Secker & Warburg, 1956, p. 190.

p. 3, *l. 12*   Louis Bunuel, "Cinématographe," *Cahiers d'Art*, 2 (1927), *feuilles volantes*, p. 6.

p. 3, *l. 29*   Pare Lorentz, *Lorentz on Film*, New York, Hopkinson and Blake, 1975, p. 40.

p. 4, *l. 14*   Odysseus Elytis, *Selected Poems*, Harmondsworth, Penguin, 1981, p. 88.

p. 4, *l. 16*   Vincent Canby, "Captain Spaulding Is Now a Lion," *New York Times*, April 13, 1967, p. 45.

p. 4, *l. 39*   James Stewart, "James Stewart," Part I, *Saturday Evening Post*, 234 (February 11, 1961), 76.

p. 5, *l. 31*   Madalynne Reuter, "Doubleday Honors Ferris Mack," *Publishers Weekly*, 225 (June 15, 1984), 25.

Chapter One

p. 9, *l. 2*   H. M., *Spectator*, 146 (March 7, 1931), 345.

p. 9, *l. 9*   *Era*, July 18, 1903, p. 10.

p. 9, *l. 11*   Charles Chaplin, *My Autobiography*, New York, Pocket Books, 1966, pp. 73–77.

p. 9, *l. 15*   *Era*, July 11, 1903, p. 12; *Stage*, July 9, 1903, pp. 12–13; *Stage*, July 16, 1903, pp. 12–13.

p. 9, *l. 21*   Charles Chaplin, "We Have Come to Stay," *Ladies' Home Journal*, 39 (October, 1922), 58.

p. 10, *l. 12*   Vsevolod Meyerhold, "Chaplin and Chaplinism," *Tulane Drama Review*, 11 (Fall 1966), 189.

p. 10, *l. 23*   George Jean Nathan, *Passing Judgments*, Madison, N.J., Fairleigh Dickinson University Press, 1970, p. 212.

p. 10, *l. 34*   Alistair Cooke, *Six Men*, New York, Knopf, 1977, p. 33.

p. 11, *l. 13*   Donald W. McCaffrey, *Focus on Chaplin*, Englewood Cliffs, N.J., Prentice-Hall, 1971, p. 48.

p. 12, *l. 1*   Pierre Leprohon, *Charles Chaplin*, Paris, André Bonne, 1970, pp. 302–3.

p. 12, *l. 4*   Guy Perol, "Analyse de 'City Lights,'" *Institut des Hautes Études Cinématographique* (Pâques 1953), p. 101.

p. 12, *l. 18*   Carlyle R. Robinson, "The Private Life of Charlie Chaplin," pt. 1, *Liberty*, 10 (July 29, 1933), 9.

p. 12, *l. 31*   Gilbert Seldes, "The Theatre," *Dial*, 84 (March 1928), 258.

p. 12, *l. 33*   Chaplin, *My Autobiography*, p. 267.

p. 12, *l. 35*   Waldo Frank, "Charles Chaplin, A Portrait," *Scribner's*, 86 (September 1929), 240.

p. 12, *l. 39*   Parker Tyler, *Chaplin*, New York, Vanguard, 1948, p. 43; pp. 128–29.

p. 13, *l. 17*   Chaplin, *My Autobiography*, p. 150.

p. 13, *l. 20*   Mack Sennett, *King of Comedy*, Garden City, N.Y., Doubleday, 1954, pp. 158–59.

p. 13, *l. 29*   Theodore Huff, *Charlie Chaplin*, New York, Arno Press, 1972, pp. 48, 49, 50, 53.

p. 13, *l. 35*   Robert E. Sherwood, *New York Post*, January 14, 1928, sec. 3, p. 10.

p. 14, *l. 1*   Stark Young, *The Flower in the Drama*, New York, Scribner's, 1925, pp. 47–55.

p. 14, *l. 4*   Charlie Chaplin, "How I Made My Success," *Theatre*, 22

(September, 1915), 120–21, 142; Harry C. Carr, "Charlie Chaplin's Story," pt. 4, *Photoplay*, 8 (October 1915), 99.

p. 14, *l. 19*   McCaffrey, p. 74.

p. 14, *l. 24*   Jim Tully, *A Dozen and One*, Hollywood, Murray & Gee, 1943, p. 13.

p. 15, *l. 12*   H. M., *Spectator*, p. 345.

p. 15, *l. 27*   Jean Mitry, *Tout Chaplin*, Paris, Cinema Club–Seghers, 1972, p. 299.

p. 16, *l. 3*   Chaplin, *My Autobiography*, p. 160.

p. 16, *l. 19*   Ibid., p. 150.

p. 16, *l. 29*   Denis Gifford, *Chaplin*, Garden City, N.Y., Doubleday, 1974, pp. 14–15.

p. 18, *l. 14*   Siegfried Kracauer, *Theory of Film*, New York, Oxford, 1960, p. 281.

p. 18, *l. 17*   Chaplin, "We Have Come to Stay," p. 61.

p. 18, *l. 24*   Richard Dana Skinner, *Commonweal*, 13 (March 18, 1931), 553.

p. 18, *l. 31*   Mitry, p. 302.

p. 18, *l. 41*   *City Lights* pressbook, NYPL-PARC.

p. 20, *l. 17*   Huff, p. 220.

p. 21, *l. 4*   Gilbert Seldes, "A Chaplin Masterpiece," *New Republic*, 66 (February 25, 1931), 47.

p. 22, *l. 2*   Mitry, p. 304.

p. 22, *l. 25*   McCaffrey, p. 49.

p. 23, *l. 21*   Huff, p. 231.

p. 23, *l. 30*   *Sid., Variety*, February 11, 1931, p. 14.

p. 23, *l. 33*   Walter Kerr, *The Silent Clowns*, New York, Knopf, 1975, p. 345.

p. 23, *l. 42*   Charles Chaplin, "Does the Public Know What It Wants?" *Adelphi*, 1 (January 1924), 704.

p. 25, *l. 27*   Muriel Brenner, "A Study of the Structure of Dance Comedy with Specific Reference to the Choreography in Chaplin Films," Master's thesis, New York University, 1951. Typescript, pp. 40, 52, NYPL-PARC (Music).

p. 26, *l. 3*   Alexander Bakshy, "Charlie Chaplin Falters," *Nation*, 132 (March 4, 1931), 250.

p. 26, *l. 22*   Robert Lewis Taylor, *W. C. Fields*, Garden City, N.Y., Doubleday, 1949, p. 2.

p. 26, l. 34   Mitry, p. 303.

p. 26, l. 40   James Agee, *Agee on Film*, New York, McDowell, Obolensky, 1958, p. 10.

p. 27, l. 3   Charlie Chaplin, *My Trip Abroad*, New York, Harper, 1922, p. 54.

p. 27, l. 11   Paul Brewsher, "Mr. Chaplin Comes Home—on the Roof of a Motor Car," *London Daily Mail*, February 20, 1931, p. 9; Tyler, p. 31.

p. 27, l. 31   Tyler, p. 128.

p. 27, l. 33   Tyler, p. 32.

Chapter Two

p. 31, l. 23   Sam M'Kee, *Morning Telegraph*, July 11, 1922, p. 4.

p. 32, l. 3   *Los Angeles Times*, May 20, 1934, pt. 2, p. 3.

p. 32, l. 6   Ruth Biery, "The Private Life of Mae West," pt. 3, *Movie Classic*, 6 (March 1934), 33.

p. 32, l. 10   Stark Young, "Diamond Lil," *New Republic*, 55 (June 27, 1928), 145–46.

p. 32, l. 13   Stark Young, "Angels and Ministers of Grace," *New Republic*, 77 (November 29, 1933), 75.

p. 32, l. 22   Fitzroy Davis, "The Wildest West," *Diners Club Magazine*, 16 (November, 1965), 74.

p. 32, l. 32   Lucius Beebe, *New York Herald Tribune*, December 5, 1948, sec. 5, p. 2.

p. 32, l. 35   C. Robert Jennings, "Playboy Interview: Mae West," *Playboy*, 18 (January 1971), 82.

p. 33, l. 4   Helen Lawrenson, "Mirror, Mirror, on the Ceiling: How'm I Doin'?" *Esquire*, 68 (July 1967), 72–74, 113–14.

p. 33, l. 8   Richard Meryman, "Mae West," *Life*, 66 (April 18, 1969), 62.

p. 33, l. 18   Diane Arbus, "Mae West, Emotion in Motion," *Show*, 5 (January 1965), 42–44; see also, Lawrenson, p. 73.

p. 33, l. 21   Gladys Hall, "Mae West's Advice to Young Girls in Love," *Movie Classic*, 4 (August 1933), 17, 56–57; Helen Harrison, "The Man You Want, Mae West Gives You His Number," *Photoplay*, 46 (September 1934), 67, 110.

p. 33, l. 26   George Davis, "The Decline of the West," *Vanity Fair*, 42 (May 1934), 82.

p. 33, l. 34   Mae West, "Sex in the Theatre," *Parade*, 1 (September 1929), 12.

p. 34, l. 3   *Mae West, Original Radio Broadcasts*, Mark 56 Records, 1974.

p. 34, l. 12   *Los Angeles Times*, May 20, 1934, pt. 2, p. 3.

p. 34, l. 15   Andre Sennwald, "Lines from a Mae West Scrap-book," *New York Times*, September 30, 1934, sec. 9, p. 4.

p. 34, l. 21   Nellie Revell, *Morning Telegraph*, October 1, 1913, p. 8.

p. 34, l. 25   Meryman, *Life*, p. 62D.

p. 34, l. 29   George Jean Nathan, *Judge*, 94 (May 5, 1928), 18.

p. 34, l. 30   Charles Brackett, "Budding Season," *New Yorker*, 4 (April 21, 1928), 33.

p. 34, l. 33   Mae West, *Goodness Had Nothing to Do with It*, Englewood Cliffs, N.J., Prentice-Hall, 1959, p. 111.

p. 34, l. 37   Ashton Stevens, *Chicago Herald and Examiner*, January 27, 1929, sec. 4, p. [11]; West, *Goodness*, p. 131.

p. 34, l. 42   Jennings, p. 78.

p. 35, l. 6   Regina Crewe, *New York American*, February 11, 1933, p. 7.

p. 35, l. 15   Graham Greene, *The Pleasure-Dome*, London, Secker & Warburg, 1972, p. 75.

p. 35, l. 17   Lewis H. Lapham, "Let Me Tell You about Mae West . . .," *Saturday Evening Post*, 237 (November 14, 1964), 77, 78.

p. 35, l. 22   George Eells and Stanley Musgrove, *Mae West*, New York, Morrow, 1982, p. 116.

p. 35, l. 24   Davis, p. 82.

p. 35, l. 25   George Kent, "The Mammy and Daddy of Us All," *Photoplay*, 45 (May 1934), pp. 32, 33.

p. 35, l. 33   D. W. C. [Douglas W. Churchill], "Miss West Talks Shop," *New York Times*, February 3, 1935, sec. 8, p. 5.

p. 35, l. 34   Parker Tyler, *The Hollywood Hallucination*, New York, Creative Age Press, 1944, pp. 96–97.

p. 35, l. 38   Harold Clurman, *Lies Like Truth*, New York, Grove/Evergreen, 1960, p. 100.

p. 36, l. 17   Parker Tyler, *Sex Psyche Etcetera in the Film*, Baltimore, Penguin, 1971, p. 25.

p. 36, l. 23   Cecelia Ager, "Mae West Reveals the Foundation of the 1900 Mode," *Vogue*, 82 (September 1, 1933), 86. See also, Mae West, *New York World-Telegram*, September 1, 1933, p. 14.

p. 36, l. 31   Lowell Brentano, "Between Covers—II," *Forum*, 93 (February 1935), 98.

p. 36, l. 40   Sondra Lowell, *Los Angeles Times*, May 21, 1981, pt. 6, p. 7.

p. 37, l. 18   Jennings, p. 78.

p. 37, l. 24   Frank S. Nugent, "The Passing of the Golden West," *New York Times*, March 15, 1936, sec. 10, p. 3.

p. 37, l. 33   West, *Goodness*, p. 135.

p. 38, l. 2   Ibid, p. 46.

p. 38, l. 4   Mae West, *On Sex, Health and ESP*, London and New York, W. H. Allen, 1975, p. 8.

p. 38, l. 19   *New York Times*, March 1, 1936, sec. 9, p. 5.

p. 39, l. 13   West, *Goodness*, p. 160.

p. 39, l. 19   *Variety*, November 21, 1933, p. 3.

p. 39, l. 23   Pauline Kael, "The Man from Dream City," *New Yorker*, 51 (July 14, 1975), 42.

p. 40, l. 5   Cary Grant, "Archie Leach," pt. 2, *Ladies' Home Journal*, 80 (March 1963), 40.

p. 40, l. 12   Alfonso Pinto, "Gilbert Roland," *Films in Review*, 29 (November 1978), 532.

p. 40, l. 29   Mae West, *She Done Him Wrong (Diamond Lil)*, London, John Long [1934].

p. 40, l. 30   Mae West, *Diamond Lil*, New York, Macaulay, 1932, p. 91.

p. 41, l. 43   Jon Tuska, *The Films of Mae West*, Secaucus, N.J., Citadel, 1973, p. 89.

p. 42, l. 14   Young, "Angels and Ministers of Grace," p. 75.

p. 42, l. 27   West, *Diamond Lil*, p. 121.

p. 42, l. 41   Ashton Stevens, *Chicago Herald and Examiner*, January 22, 1929, unpaged.

p. 43, l. 3   Francis R. Bellamy, "Melodrama—Old and New," *Outlook*, 149 (May 16, 1928), 103.

p. 43, l. 10   Eileen Creelman, *New York Sun*, February 6, 1933, p. 25.

p. 44, l. 7   John Mason Brown, *New York Post*, March 25, 1933, sec. 3, p. 4.

p. 44, l. 20   John Bright, letter to me, July 30, 1980.

p. 44, l. 27   Davis, p. 82.

p. 44, l. 40   John S. Cohen, Jr., *New York Sun*, January 18, 1932, p. 18.

p. 45, l. 2   *Los Angeles Times*, August 21, 1932, pt. 3, p. 20.

p. 45, *l. 7*	Creelman, p. 25.
p. 45, *l. 12*	Bright, letter.
p. 45, *l. 17*	Faith Service, "The Man You Hate to Love," *Motion Picture Classic*, 32 (December 1930), 51.
p. 45, *l. 21*	West, *Goodness*, p. 152.
p. 45, *l. 25*	Ibid., p. 159.
p. 46, *l. 35*	Tuska, p. 45.
p. 47, *l. 4*	West, *Goodness*, p. 106.
p. 47, *l. 34*	John Mason Brown, "Valedictory to a Season," *Theatre Arts*, 12 (June 1928), 394.
p. 48, *l. 5*	West, *Diamond Lil*, p. 24.
p. 48, *l. 26*	Robert Garland, *New York World-Telegram*, February 7, 1933, p. 16.
p. 49, *l. 13*	J. C. M. [John Chapin Mosher], "Comic Relief," *New Yorker*, 9 (February 18, 1933), 54.
p. 49, *l. 22*	Richard Schickel, *Movies*, New York, Basic Books, 1964, p. 127.
p. 49, *l. 43*	Harnett T. Kane, *Louisiana Hayride*, New York, Morrow, 1941, photo caption, opp. p. 72.

Chapter Three

p. 55, *l. 13*	W. C. Fields, *W. C. Fields by Himself*, New York, Warner, 1974, p. 563.
p. 55, *l. 18*	Marian Spitzer, *The Palace*, New York, Atheneum, 1969, p. 41.
p. 56, *l. 6*	Antonin Artaud, "Les Frères Marx au Cinéma du Panthéon," *Nouvelle Revue Française*, 38 (January 1, 1932), 156–58.
p. 56, *l. 10*	Francis Birrell, "The Marx Brothers," *New Statesman and Nation*, n. s. 4 (October 1, 1932), 374.
p. 56, *l. 12*	Philippe Soupault, *L'Europe Nouvelle*, 15 (October 8, 1932), 1202.
p. 56, *l. 17*	Antonin Artaud, *The Theater and Its Double*, New York, Grove, 1958, p. 142.
p. 56, *l. 20*	Robert Altman, Jon Carroll, and Michael Goodwin, "Groucho Marx, Portrait of the Artist as an Old Man," *Take One*, 3 (September–October, 1970), 14.
p. 56, *l. 27*	Pierre Bost, "Duck Sup (Soupe Au Canard)," *Les Annales politiques et littéraires*, 102 (March 30, 1934), 357; Marie

Seton, "S. Dali + 3 Marxes =," *Theatre Arts*, 23 (October 1939), 734.

p. 56, *l. 32*   Birrell, pp. 374–75.

p. 56, *l. 37*   Sara Hamilton, "The Nuttiest Quartette in the World," *Photoplay*, 42 (July 1932), 27.

p. 56, *l. 41*   Altman, et al., p. 13.

p. 57, *l. 10*   William Troy, "The Invisible Man," *Nation*, 137 (December 13, 1933), 688.

p. 57, *l. 12*   Alva Johnston, "The Marx Brothers, the Scientific Side of Lunacy," *Woman's Home Companion*, 63 (September 1936), 12.

p. 57, *l. 17*   Donald Ogden Stewart, chap. 5, *Mr and Mrs Haddock Abroad*, Carbondale, Southern Illinois University Press, 1975, pp. 123–37.

p. 58, *l. 11*   Stewart, Afterword, *Mr and Mrs Haddock Abroad*, p. 271.

p. 58, *l. 28*   Birrell, p. 374.

p. 58, *l. 31*   Groucho Marx, *Groucho and Me*, New York, Bernard Geis, 1959, pp. 224–25.

p. 59, *l. 11*   Kenneth L. Geist, *Pictures Will Talk*, New York, Scribner's, 1978, pp. 48–49; Richard Meryman, *Mank*, New York, Morrow, 1978, p. 176.

p. 59, *l. 14*   Richard Corliss, *Talking Pictures*, New York, Penguin, 1975, p. 249.

p. 59, *l. 16*   Pauline Kael, "Raising Kane," *The Citizen Kane Book*, Boston, Atlantic–Little, Brown, 1971, p. 15.

p. 59, *l. 19*   Groucho Marx, *The Groucho Phile*, Indianapolis, Bobbs-Merrill, 1976, p. 88.

p. 59, *l. 25*   *Groucho and Me*, pp. 238–41.

p. 59, *l. 27*   Meryman, p. 148; see also, Groucho Marx and Richard J. Anobile, *The Marx Bros. Scrapbook*, New York, Star Books–W. H. Allen, 1976, p. 315.

p. 59, *l. 34*   Meryman, p. 148.

p. 60, *l. 24*   *Groucho and Me*, p. 87.

p. 60, *l. 27*   Dickson Hartwell, "The Man Who Startled Hollywood," *Saturday Evening Post*, 223 (May 26, 1951), 139.

p. 60, *l. 29*   *Groucho and Me*, p. 88.

p. 60, *l. 36*   Hector Arce, *Groucho*, New York, Putnam's, 1979, p. 112.

p. 60, *l. 40*   *The Groucho Phile*, illustrations 22, 23, 24, 32, 34, pp. 19–29.

p. 61, *l. 1*   Arthur Marx, *Life with Groucho*, New York, Simon and Schuster, 1954, p. 163.

p. 61, *l. 21*   *The Marx Bros. Scrapbook*, p. 314.

p. 62, *l. 15*   S. J. Perelman, "Week End with Groucho," *Holiday*, 11 (April 1952), 59.

p. 62, *l. 33*   *Sime.*, *Variety*, February 24, 1912, p. 17.

p. 62, *l. 34*   Arce, pp. 93–94.

p. 62, *l. 36*   *The Marx Bros. Scrapbook*, pp. 29, 42.

p. 63, *l. 21*   *Time*, 20 (August 15, 1932), 25.

p. 63, *l. 26*   Harpo Marx, *Harpo Speaks!* New York, Bernard Geis, 1961, pp. 52–54, 108, 122, 133, 191, 122–26, 121–22.

p. 63, *l. 36*   Walter Kerr, "The Marx Brothers and How They Grew," *New York Times*, June 7, 1976, p. 37.

p. 63, *l. 40*   *The Groucho Phile*, p. 18.

p. 63, *l. 43*   "Harpo in Toyland," *New York Times Magazine*, November 5, 1961, p. 82.

p. 64, *l. 2*   Percy Hammond, *New York Herald Tribune*, November 11, 1928, sec. 8, p. 1.

p. 64, *l. 16*   Sylvia B. Golden, "Confessions of the Marx Brothers," *Theatre*, 49 (January 1929), 48.

p. 64, *l. 21*   *New York Times*, August 21, 1931, p. 20.

p. 64, *l. 25*   *The Marx Bros. Scrapbook*, p. 133.

p. 64, *l. 33*   Joe Adamson, *Groucho, Harpo, Chico and Sometimes Zeppo*, New York, Pocket Books, 1976, p. 229.

p. 64, *l. 36*   Adamson, p. 31.

p. 64, *l. 37*   *The Marx Bros. Scrapbook*, p. 210.

p. 65, *l. 19*   Arce, pp. 201, 207.

p. 65, *l. 37*   Mordaunt Hall, *New York Times*, April 24, 1933, p. 11.

p. 66, *l. 29*   Gilbert Gabriel, *New York Sun*, January 21, 1928, p. 6.

p. 67, *l. 3*   Thornton Delehanty, *New York Post*, November 23, 1933, p. 33.

p. 68, *l. 17*   Harry Ruby, "The Face That Launched a Thousand Quips," *Variety*, January 7, 1959, p. 17.

p. 68, *l. 25*   *The Marx Bros. Scrapbook*, p. 307.

p. 69, *l. 26*   Ibid., p. 209.

p. 69, *l. 34*   Serge Daney and Jean-Louis Noames, "Taking Chances," *Cahiers du Cinéma in English*, no. 7 (January 1967), 53.

p. 70, *l. 9*   Charles Silver, "Leo McCarey from Marx to McCarthy," *Film Comment*, 9 (September–October, 1973), 8–9.

p. 73, *l. 18*   *The Marx Bros. Scrapbook*, p. 209.

p. 73, *l. 24*   Bige. [Joe Bigelow], *Variety*, November 28, 1933, p. 20.

p. 73, *l. 26*   Mark Forrest, "Sheer Lunacy," *Saturday Review*, 157 (February 17, 1934), 195; Bost, p. 357.

p. 74, *l. 32*   John Hollander, *Spectral Emanations*, New York, Atheneum, 1978, p. 182.

p. 74, *l. 36*   Gerald Weales, "Sean O'Casey, A Playwright in Decline," Master's thesis, Columbia University, 1950, p. 72.

p. 75, *l. 9*   André Hodeir, "The Marx Brothers," in *Cinema, A Critical Dictionary*, ed. Richard Roud, New York, Viking, 1980, vol. 2, p. 670.

p. 75, *l. 12*   Adamson, p. 216.

p. 75, *l. 17*   Altman, et al., p. 12.

p. 75, *l. 21*   *The Marx Bros. Scrapbook*, p. 215.

p. 75, *l. 24*   Adamson, p. 216; Daney and Noames, pp. 49–50.

p. 75, *l. 27*   Adamson, p. 216.

p. 75, *l. 35*   Laurence G. Avery, *Dramatist in America*, Chapel Hill, University of North Carolina Press, 1977, p. 307.

p. 75, *l. 38*   Malcolm Goldstein, *George S. Kaufman*, New York, Oxford, 1979, pp. 133–36, 194; Scott Meredith, *George S. Kaufman and His Friends*, Garden City, N.Y., Doubleday, 1974, pp. 403, 412–15, 418–21.

p. 76, *l. 7*   Howard Dietz, *Dancing in the Dark*, New York, Quadrangle, 1974, pp. 147–48.

p. 76, *l. 17*   *Bige.*, p. 20.

p. 76, *l. 22*   John S. Cohen, Jr., *New York Sun*, November 24, 1933, p. 32.

p. 76, *l. 23*   Philip K. Scheuer, *Los Angeles Times*, November 18, 1933, pt. 2, p. 7.

p. 76, *l. 27*   Bost, p. 357.

p. 76, *l. 38*   Richard Watts, Jr., *New York Herald Tribune*, November 24, 1933, p. 15.

p. 77, *l. 8*   *Groucho and Me*, p. 225.

p. 77, *l. 11*   Clipping, wrongly identified as from *Variety*, December 12, 1933, *Duck Soup* file, NYPL-PARC.

p. 77, *l. 18*   Troy, p. 688.

p. 78, *l. 14*   Hodeir, p. 675.

p. 78, *l. 27*   J. Brooks Atkinson, *New York Times*, October 24, 1928, p. 26.

p. 78, *l. 29*   Alistair Cooke, *Six Men*, New York, Knopf, 1977, p. 30.

p. 79, *l. 7*   Artaud, p. 144.

p. 80, *l. 12*   Jim Marshall, "The Marx Menace," *Collier's*, 117 (March 16, 1946), 71.

Chapter Four

p. 85, *l. 3*   W. C. Fields, *W. C. Fields by Himself*, New York, Warner, 1974, p. 562.

p. 85, *l. 11*   Ken Tynan, "Toby Jug and Bottle," *Sight and Sound*, 19 (February 1951), 397.

p. 85, *l. 14*   "Gentle Grifter," *Time*, 49 (January 6, 1947), 54.

p. 85, *l. 18*   Clifton Fadiman, "A New High in Low Comedy," *Stage*, 13 (January 1936), 36.

p. 86, *l. 36*   Carlotta Monti, *W. C. Fields & Me*, Englewood Cliffs, N.J., Prentice-Hall, 1971, p. 67.

p. 87, *l. 2*   J. P. McEvoy, "The Comic Supplement," typescript, NYPL-PARC.

p. 87, *l. 8*   Gene Fowler, *Minutes of the Last Meeting*, New York, Viking, 1954, p. 169.

p. 87, *l. 11*   Robert Lewis Taylor, *W. C. Fields*, Garden City, N.Y., Doubleday, 1949, p. 46.

p. 87, *l. 14*   *Variety*, May 4, 1912, p. 28.

p. 87, *l. 17*   *W. C. Fields by Himself*, p. 80.

p. 87, *l. 21*   Joe Laurie, Jr., *Vaudeville*, New York, Holt, 1953, p. 23.

p. 87, *l. 24*   Douglas Gilbert, *American Vaudeville*, New York, Dover, 1963, pp. 269, 271.

p. 87, *l. 30*   *W. C. Fields by Himself*, p. 41.

p. 87, *l. 32*   *Sime.*, *Variety*, June 21, 1918, p. 14; June 25, 1920, p. 15.

p. 87, *l. 38*   Taylor, p. 82.

p. 87, *l. 43*   Alexander Woollcott, *New York Times*, August 29, 1922, p. 10.

p. 88, *l. 25*   *New York Times*, August 3, 1927, p. 29.

p. 88, *l. 42*   J. P. McEvoy, *The Potters*, Chicago, Reilly & Lee, 1924, pp. viii-ix.

p. 89, *l. 12*   Argus, *Literary Digest*, 119 (January 19, 1935), 30.

p. 89, *l. 20*   *W. C. Fields by Himself*, p. 66.

p. 89, *l. 29*   Laurie, p. 23.

p. 90, *l. 2*   *W. C. Fields by Himself*, p. 469.

p. 90, *l. 15*   Andrew Sarris, *The American Cinema*, New York, Dutton, 1968, p. 238.

p. 90, *l. 20*   Robert Altman, Jon Carroll, and Michael Goodwin, "Groucho Marx, Portrait of the Artist as an Old Man," *Take One*, 3 (September–October, 1970), 12; Groucho Marx and Richard J. Anobile, *The Marx Bros. Scrapbook*, New York, Star Books–W. H. Allen, 1976, p. 176.

p. 90, *l. 24*   Charles Higham, *Charles Laughton*, Garden City, N.Y., Doubleday, 1976, p. 126.

p. 90, *l. 40*   *W. C. Fields by Himself*, p. 556.

p. 91, *l. 7*   Joe Adamson, *Groucho, Harpo, Chico and Sometimes Zeppo*, New York, Pocket Books, 1976, p. 137.

p. 91, *l. 31*   A. D. S., *New York Times*, July 24, 1933, p. 11.

p. 92, *l. 3*   Norman Z. McLeod, "Gamble with Music," *Collier's*, 117 (March 23, 1946), 22.

p. 92, *l. 38*   Andre Sennwald, *New York Times*, January 5, 1935, p. 20.

p. 93, *l. 38*   Chic. [Epes Sargent], *Variety*, January 8, 1935, p. 18.

p. 94, *l. 34*   *New York Times*, June 23, 1920, p. 14.

p. 95, *l. 25*   W. C. Fields, "Anything for a Laugh," *American*, 118 (September 1934), 130.

p. 97, *l. 27*   W. C. Fields, "Alcohol and Me," *Pic*, 12 (October 13, 1942), 34.

p. 97, *l. 36*   Mordaunt Hall, *New York Times*, April 20, 1933, p. 20.

p. 97, *l. 38*   A. D. S., *New York Times*, October 7, 1933, p. 18.

p. 98, *l. 24*   *New York Times*, July 22, 1934, sec. 9, p. 3.

p. 99, *l. 39*   William K. Everson, *The Art of W. C. Fields*, New York, Bonanza Books, 1967, p. 74.

p. 100, *l. 39*   Richard Watts, Jr., *New York Herald Tribune*, January 5, 1935, p. 16; Andre Sennwald, *New York Times*, January 5, 1935, p. 20.

p. 103, *l. 32*   Alva Johnston, "Who Knows What Is Funny?" *Saturday Evening Post*, 211 (August 6, 1938), 10.

p. 104, *l. 13*   Heywood Broun, "W. C. Fields and the Cosmos," *Nation*, 132 (January 7, 1931), 24.

p. 104, *l. 26*   Johnston, p. 11.

p. 104, *l. 35*   Ibid., p. 10.

p. 104, *l. 39*   J. B. Priestley, "W. C. Fields," *New Statesman and Nation*, n.s. 33 (January 4, 1947), 8.

p. 105, *l. 8*   Wilfrid Sheed, "Toward the Black Pussy Cafe," *New York Review of Books*, 21 (October 31, 1974), 26.

Chapter Five

p. 109, *l. 13*   "The Cowboy Philosopher," *New Republic*, 84 (August 28, 1934), 62.

p. 109, *l. 18*   Roger Butterfield, "The Legend of Will Rogers," *Life*, 27 (July 18, 1949), 81.

p. 110, *l. 14*   Ibid., p. 92.

p. 110, *l. 18*   William R. Brown, *Imagemaker*, Columbia, University of Missouri Press, 1970, p. 19.

p. 110, *l. 22*   Will Rogers, "Letters of a Self-Made Diplomat to His President," *Saturday Evening Post*, 199 (November 6, 1926), 230.

p. 110, *l. 31*   Homer Croy, *Our Will Rogers*, New York, Duell, Sloan and Pearce, and Boston, Little, Brown, 1953, p. 287; *Boston Globe*, June 16, 1930, p. 12.

p. 110, *l. 38*   W. C. Fields, *W. C. Fields by Himself*, New York, Warner, 1974, p. 561.

p. 110, *l. 41*   Irvin S. Cobb, *New York Times*, August 22, 1935, p. 18.

p. 111, *l. 1*   Irvin S. Cobb, *Exit Laughing*, Indianapolis, Bobbs-Merrill, 1941, p. 406.

p. 111, *l. 6*   Donald Day, *Will Rogers*, Indianapolis, Bobbs-Merrill, 1941.

p. 111, *l. 15*   Jack Lait, *Our Will Rogers*, New York, Greenberg, 1935, p. 64.

p. 111, *l. 24*   Butterfield, pp. 92, 94.

p. 111, *l. 36*   L. H. Robbins, "Portrait of an American Philosopher," *New York Times Magazine*, November 3, 1935, p. 4; Damon Runyon, in *Folks Say of Will Rogers*, ed. William Howard Payne and Jake G. Lyons, New York, Putnam's, 1936, p. 207.

p. 112, *l. 2*   Andrew Sinclair, *John Ford*, New York, Dial–James Wade, 1979, p. 59.

p. 112, *l. 7*   Jerome Beatty, "Betty Holds the Reins," *American*, 110 (October 1930), 62.

p. 112, *l. 12*   Betty Rogers, *Will Rogers*, Indianapolis, Bobbs-Merrill, 1941, p. 110.

p. 112, *l. 16*   Day, p. 68.

p. 112, *l. 31*   Will Rogers, *The Autobiography of Will Rogers*, Boston, Houghton Mifflin, 1949, pp. 97–98.

p. 112, *l. 39*   Croy, p. 107.

p. 113, *l. 4*   "The Cowboy Philosopher," p. 62.

p. 113, *l. 11*   Betty Rogers, p. 24.

p. 113, *l. 17*   Bryan B. Sterling, *The Will Rogers Scrapbook*, New York, Grosset & Dunlap, 1976, p. 137.

p. 113, *l. 25*   *New York Times*, September 23, 1918, p. 7.

p. 113, *l. 31*   Will Rogers, *Rogers-isms, the Cowboy Philosopher on the Peace Conference*, New York, Harper, 1919; *Rogers-isms, the Cowboy Philosopher on Prohibition*, New York, Harper, 1919.

p. 113, *l. 42*   *New Yorker*, 7 (February 13, 1932), 5.

p. 114, *l. 3*   "The Cowboy Philosopher," p. 62.

p. 114, *l. 17*   Will Rogers, *Autobiography*, p. 248.

p. 115, *l. 32*   Sterling, p. 171.

p. 116, *l. 20*   Day, p. 217.

p. 116, *l. 24*   Cobb, *Times*, pp. 17–18.

p. 116, *l. 35*   Cobb, *Exit Laughing*, pp. 404–5.

p. 116, *l. 39*   Sterling, p. 175.

p. 117, *l. 1*   Peter Bogdanovich, *John Ford*, Berkeley, University of California Press, 1968, p. 57.

p. 117, *l. 24*   Andrew Sarris, *The John Ford Movie Mystery*, Bloomington, Indiana University Press, 1975, p. 23.

p. 117, *l. 31*   Ward Greene, *Star Reporters and 34 of Their Stories*, New York, Random House, 1948, p. 95.

p. 117, *l. 38*   Sara Hamilton, "Paducah Was Never Like This," *Photoplay*, 46 (August 1934), 60.

p. 118, *l. 20*   Bogdanovich, p. 40.

p. 119, *l. 4*   Robin Brantley, "What Makes a Star?—Howard Hawks Knew Best of All," *New York Times*, January 22, 1978, sec. 2, p. 19.

p. 119, *l. 33*   *Time*, 64 (September 13, 1954), 104.

p. 120, *l. 34*   Mary B. Mullett, "The World Was His Oyster But It Took 35 Years to Open It!" *American*, 102 (November 1926), 174.

p. 121, *l. 1*   Ibid., p. 37.

p. 121, *l. 36*   *New York Times*, November 25, 1925, p. 14.

p. 122, *l. 39*   Sarris, pp. 58–59.

p. 122, *l.* 42   John E. O'Connor and Martin A. Jackson, *American History/ American Film*, New York, Ungar, 1979, p. 88.

p. 123, *l.* 3   Joseph McBride, "Stepin Fetchit Talks Back," *Film Quarterly*, 24 (Summer 1971), 22.

p. 123, *l.* 7   Donald Bogle, *Toms, Coons, Mulattoes, Mammies, & Bucks*, New York, Bantam, 1974, p. 56.

p. 123, *l.* 12   Ibid., p. 54.

p. 123, *l.* 19   Lindsay Patterson, *Black Films and Film-makers*, New York, Dodd, Mead, 1975, pp. 26–27.

p. 124, *l.* 10   Michael Dempsey, "John Ford: A Reassessment," *Film Quarterly*, 28 (Summer 1975), 6.

p. 124, *l.* 29   Andre Sennwald, *New York Times*, June 24, 1935, p. 12.

p. 124, *l.* 40   Dempsey, p. 6.

p. 125, *l.* 8   Ben Lucien Burman, *Steamboat Round the Bend*, New York, Ballantine, 1973, p. 15.

p. 125, *l.* 11   Eileen Creelman, *New York Sun*, September 18, 1935, p. 21; Beverly Hills, *Liberty*, 12 (September 7, 1935), 24.

p. 125, *l.* 21   Creelman, p. 21.

p. 125, *l.* 26   Dan Ford, *Pappy*, Englewood Cliffs, N.J., Prentice-Hall, 1979, p. 71.

p. 126, *l.* 1   Bogdanovich, p. 57.

p. 126, *l.* 3   Mel Gussow, *Don't Say Yes Until I Finish Talking*, Garden City, N.Y., Doubleday, 1971, pp. 88, 142, 156.

p. 126, *l.* 11   Will Rogers, *Autobiography*, p. 337.

p. 126, *l.* 31   Burman, p. 16.

p. 126, *l.* 41   Martin Rubin, "Mr. Ford & Mr. Rogers, The Will Rogers Trilogy," *Film Comment*, 10 (January–February, 1974), 54–57; Peter C. Rollins, "Will Rogers and the Relevance of Nostalgia: *Steamboat 'Round the Bend*," in O'Connor and Jackson, pp. 77–96.

p. 127, *l.* 31   Dempsey, p. 8.

p. 128, *l.* 17   Beverly Hills, p. 24.

p. 128, *l.* 43   Sinclair, p. 61.

p. 129, *l.* 5   John Reddington, *Brooklyn Eagle*, September 20, 1935, p. 12.

Chapter Six

p. 135, *l.* 1   Mordaunt Hall, *New York Times*, March 25, 1933, p. 13.

p. 135, *l. 7*   Harry Leon Wilson, *Ruggles of Red Gap*, Garden City, N.Y., Doubleday, Page, 1915, pp. 17–19.

p. 135, *l. 18*   Leo McCarey, "Mae West Can Play Anything," *Photoplay*, 48 (June 1935), 126.

p. 136, *l. 10*   Regina Crewe, *New York American*, March 7, 1935, p. 13.

p. 136, *l. 22*   Heywood Broun, *New York Tribune*, December 25, 1915, p. 7.

p. 136, *l. 34*   Grenville Vernon, *Commonweal*, 21 (March 29, 1935), 628.

p. 137, *l. 14*   Wilson, p. 156.

p. 137, *l. 39*   Pete Martin, "Going His Way," *Saturday Evening Post*, 219 (November 20, 1946), 68.

p. 138, *l. 2*   James Harvey, "Irene Dunne Interviewed," *Film Comment*, 16 (January–February, 1980), 68.

p. 138, *l. 3*   Scoop Conlon, "He Directs for Laughs—and Gets 'Em," *Motion Picture*, 50 (September 1935), 54.

p. 138, *l. 42*   Jonathan Rosenbaum, "Journals: Paris," *Film Comment*, 9 (November–December, 1973), 4.

p. 139, *l. 14*   Otis Ferguson, *The Film Criticism of Otis Ferguson*, Philadelphia, Temple University Press, 1971, p. 96.

p. 139, *l. 25*   Idwal Jones, "A Gentleman's Man," *New York Times*, March 3, 1935, sec. 8, pt. 1, p. 4.

p. 139, *l. 32*   Jack Cunningham clip file, NYPL-PARC; *Variety*, October 8, 1941, p. 54.

p. 139, *l. 37*   Elsa Lanchester, *Charles Laughton and I*, New York, Harcourt, Brace, 1938, p. 158.

p. 140, *l. 1*   Serge Daney and Jean-Louis Noames, "Taking Chances," *Cahiers du Cinéma in English*, no. 7 (January, 1967), 53.

p. 140, *l. 5*   Harvey, p. 29.

p. 140, *l. 9*   Leo McCarey, "Slant on 'Satan,'" *New York Times*, February 18, 1962, sec. 2, p. 10.

p. 140, *l. 18*   Scott Meredith, *George S. Kaufman and His Friends*, Garden City, N.Y., Doubleday, 1974, p. 111.

p. 140, *l. 22*   Ben Lucien Burman, *Steamboat Round the Bend*, New York, Ballantine, 1973, p. 16; Eileen Creelman, *New York Sun*, April 15, 1936, p. 32.

p. 140, *l. 32*   Wilson, p. 28.

p. 141, *l. 26*   Ibid., p. 229.

p. 141, *l. 29*   McCarey, *Times*, p. 10.

p. 142, *l. 9*   Marguerite Tazelaar, *New York Herald Tribune*, October 31, 1937, sec. 8, p. 3.

p. 142, *l. 22*   Lanchester, p. 117.

p. 142, *l. 36*   John Mason Brown, *New York Post*, October 1, 1931, p. 14.

p. 143, *l. 18*   Mark Van Doren, "When Acting Counts," *Nation*, 141 (December 4, 1935), 658.

p. 143, *l. 43*   J. P. McEvoy, "The Almost Incredible Laughton," *This Week, New York Herald Tribune*, October 11, 1942, p. 20.

p. 144, *l. 3*   Charles Higham, *Charles Laughton*, Garden City, N.Y., Doubleday, 1976.

p. 144, *l. 10*   Lanchester, p. 6.

p. 144, *l. 12*   Emlyn Williams, *Emlyn*, London, Bodley Head, 1973, pp. 113; 129–30.

p. 144, *l. 20*   *Brecht on Theatre*, ed. John Willett, New York, Hill and Wang, 1964, p. 166.

p. 144, *l. 28*   [C. A. Lejeune], "Charles Laughton's New Film," *Observer* (London), September 6, 1936, p. 10.

p. 144, *l. 32*   Quentin Reynolds, "Meet an Actor," *Collier's*, 95 (February 2, 1935), 53.

p. 145, *l. 15*   Lanchester, p. 121.

p. 146, *l. 24*   Basil Wright, *Spectator*, 159 (October 1, 1937), 547.

p. 146, *l. 34*   John Corbin, *New York Times*, April 24, 1923, p. 24.

p. 147, *l. 2*   Sara Hamilton, "We Want a Divorce," *Photoplay*, 47 (February 1935), 46–47, 97–98.

p. 147, *l. 40*   "Lighter Than Air," *Newsweek*, 57 (May 29, 1961), 100.

p. 148, *l. 43*   J. Brooks Atkinson, *New York Times*, November 20, 1930, p. 30.

p. 149, *l. 3*   John B. Kennedy, "Making Them Laugh," *Collier's*, 88 (August 22, 1931), 22.

p. 153, *l. 30*   William Boehnel, *New York World-Telegram*, November 3, 1937, p. 33.

p. 153, *l. 39*   Wilson, p. 371.

p. 156, *l. 3*   C. Gerald Fraser, Hyams obituary, *New York Times*, December 9, 1977, p. B2.

p. 156, *l. 15*   Ruth Biery, "Why Carole Changed Her Mind," *Photoplay*, 40 (September 1931), 104.

Chapter Seven

p. 161, *l. 3*   Mary Hamman, "Meet Frank Capra Making a Picture," *Good Housekeeping*, 112 (March 1941), 11.

p. 161, *l. 15*   Ibid., p. 74.

348 · Bibliographical Notes

p. 161, *l. 18*   Richard Glatzer and John Raeburn, *Frank Capra, the Man and His Films*, Ann Arbor, University of Michigan Press, 1975, p. 15.

p. 162, *l. 3*   Richard Schickel, *The Men Who Made the Movies*, New York, Atheneum, 1975, pp. 87–88.

p. 162, *l. 6*   Stephen Handzo, "Under Capracorn," in Glatzer and Raeburn, pp. 164–76.

p. 162, *l. 12*   Leland A. Poague, *The Cinema of Frank Capra*, South Brunswick, N.J., Barnes, 1975, p. 227.

p. 162, *l. 18*   Margaret Case Harriman, "Mr. and Mrs. Frank Capra," *Ladies' Home Journal*, 58 (April 1941), 35.

p. 162, *l. 25*   Glatzer and Raeburn, p. 5.

p. 162, *l. 33*   Graham Greene, *The Pleasure-Dome*, London, Secker & Warburg, 1972, pp. 203–4.

p. 162, *l. 40*   William S. Pechter, "American Madness," in Glatzer and Raeburn, pp. 177–85.

p. 162, *l. 41*   Otis Ferguson, *The Film Criticism of Otis Ferguson*, Philadelphia, Temple University Press, 1971, p. 58.

p. 163, *l. 1*   Frank Capra, "Sacred Cows to the Slaughter," *Stage*, 13 (July 1936), 40.

p. 163, *l. 5*   Frank Capra, *The Name above the Title*, New York, Macmillan, 1971, pp. 247–48.

p. 163, *l. 12*   Glatzer and Raeburn, p. 27; Joseph McBride, "Capra Conks Creepy Pic Heroes," *Variety*, April 23, 1975, p. 24.

p. 163, *l. 26*   Glatzer and Raeburn, p. 127.

p. 163, *l. 29*   Ferguson, p. 126.

p. 163, *l. 37*   Capra, *Stage*, p. 40.

p. 164, *l. 12*   Glatzer and Raeburn, p. 166.

p. 164, *l. 40*   Capra, *Name*, p. 182.

p. 165, *l. 9*   John Stuart, "Fine Italian Hand," *Collier's*, 96 (August 17, 1935), 48.

p. 165, *l. 10*   Capra, *Name*, p. 182.

p. 165, *l. 12*   Robert Stebbins, "Mr. Capra Goes to Town," in Glatzer and Raeburn, pp. 117–20; *New Statesman and Nation*, n.s. 12 (August 29, 1936), 289.

p. 165, *l. 23*   Capra, *Name*, pp. 426–30.

p. 165, *l. 30*   Oren Arnold, "One-Plot Kelland Best-Paid Author," *Baltimore Sun Sunday Magazine*, October 8, 1944, p. 1.

p. 165, *l. 39*   Clarence Budington Kelland, "Several Birds and One Stone," *Saturday Evening Post*, 204 (December 5, 1931), 81.

p. 166, *l. 13*   Clarence Budington Kelland, "Ex-Banker," *American*, 113 (April 1932), 90.

p. 166, *l. 24*   Capra, *Name*, p. 179.

p. 166, *l. 33*   Clarence Budington Kelland, "Opera Hat," pt. 2, *American*, 119 (May 1935), 21.

p. 167, *l. 25*   M. H., *New York Times*, August 4, 1934, p. 14.

p. 167, *l. 29*   Mordaunt Hall, *New York Times*, May 16, 1930, p. 20; May 7, 1932, p. 11; November 16, 1933, p. 30.

p. 167, *l. 36*   L. N., *New York Times*, July 16, 1932, p. 5; Mordaunt Hall, *New York Times*, November 27, 1931, p. 29.

p. 168, *l. 14*   Victor Scherle and William Turner Levy, *The Films of Frank Capra*, Secaucus, N.J., Citadel Press, 1977, p. 137.

p. 170, *l. 10*   A. P., "A Female David Warfield," *Theatre*, 21 (June 1915), 302.

p. 171, *l. 11*   Ferguson, p. 128.

p. 171, *l. 25*   Gary Cooper, "I Took a Good Look at Myself and This Is What I Saw," *McCall's*, 88 (January 1961), 138.

p. 172, *l. 18*   Jerome Beatty, "Super-duper Cooper," *American*, 134 (November 1942), 34.

p. 172, *l. 23*   [C. A. Lejeune], "Charles Laughton's New Film," *Observer* (London), September 6, 1936, p. 10.

p. 172, *l. 26*   Cooper, p. 138.

p. 172, *l. 29*   Brennan in Pete Martin, "That Man Cooper," *Saturday Evening Post*, 222 (January 14, 1950), 65; Tamiroff in Gary Cooper, "Well, It Was This Way," pt. 8, *Saturday Evening Post*, 228 (April 7, 1956), 121; Lilli Palmer, *Change Lobsters—and Dance*, New York, Macmillan, 1975, p. 140; Hawks in Frank S. Nugent, "The All-American Man," *New York Times Magazine*, July 5, 1942, p. 27; Wood in Larry Swindell, *The Last Hero*, Garden City, N.Y., Doubleday, 1980, p. 241; Gavin Lambert, *On Cukor*, New York, Capricorn Books, 1973, p. 70.

p. 172, *l. 33*   Martin, p. 65; Swindell, p. 221.

p. 172, *l. 44*   Cooper, pt. 7, *Saturday Evening Post*, 228 (March 31, 1956), 132.

p. 173, *l. 18*   Glatzer and Raeburn, p. 60.

p. 174, *l. 6*   Ibid., p. 5.

p. 174, *l. 16*   Poague, p. 89.

p. 174, *l. 20*   Glatzer and Raeburn, p. 19.

p. 179, *l. 19*   Richard Corliss, *Talking Pictures*, New York, Penguin, 1975, p. 222.

p. 181, *l. 11*   Ralph Borsodi, *The Flight from the City*, New York, Harper, 1933.

p. 182, *l. 5*   Ralph Borsodi, "Dayton, Ohio, Makes Social History," *Nation*, 136 (April 19, 1933), 448.

p. 182, *l. 15*   John Crowe Ransom, "Land! An Answer to the Unemployment Problem," *Harper's*, 165 (July 1932), 219.

p. 182, *l. 16*   *The Public Papers and Addresses of Franklin D. Roosevelt*, New York, Random House, 1938, 2: 291–95.

p. 182, *l. 23*   Schickel, p. 74.

p. 182, *l. 34*   Regina Crewe, *New York American*, April 17, 1936, p. 18.

p. 184, *l. 7*   Ben Ray Redman, "Pictures and Censorship," *Saturday Review of Literature*, 19 (December 31, 1938), 13.

p. 184, *l. 19*   Poague, pp. 29–32 and passim.

p. 184, *l. 34*   Redman, p. 13.

Chapter Eight

p. 189, *l. 1*   Quentin Reynolds, "Give Me Real People," *Collier's*, 101 (March 26, 1938), 18.

p. 189, *l. 10*   *Time*, 28 (September 14, 1936), 30.

p. 189, *l. 12*   Quentin Reynolds, "Smoothie," *Collier's*, 105 (May 11, 1940), 55.

p. 189, *l. 14*   Reynolds, "Give Me Real People," p. 53.

p. 190, *l. 28*   Frank S. Nugent, *New York Times*, September 18, 1936, p. 18; Regina Crewe, *New York American*, September 18, 1936, p. 16; Eileen Creelman, *New York Sun*, September 18, 1936, p. 35; Kate Cameron, *New York Daily News*, September 18, 1936, p. 56.

p. 192, *l. 28*   D. A. N., *Brooklyn Eagle*, September 18, 1936, p. 12.

p. 192, *l. 32*   *News-Week*, 8 (September 12, 1936), 42.

p. 193, *l. 2*   Eileen Creelman, *New York Sun*, September 21, 1936, p. 26.

p. 193, *l. 13*   Ibid.

p. 193, *l. 18*   Creelman, September 18, 1936.

p. 193, *l. 21*   Eric Hatch, *My Man Godfrey*, Boston, Little, Brown, 1935, p. 8.

p. 193, *l. 28*   *The Public Papers and Addresses of Franklin D. Roosevelt*, New York, Random House, 1938, 1: 625.

p. 193, *l. 32*   Ted Shane, "The Week's Work," *Collier's*, 121 (January 10, 1948), 8.

p. 194, *l. 8* Robert Altman, Jon Carroll, and Michael Goodwin, "Groucho Marx, Portrait of the Artist as an Old Man," *Take One*, 3 (September–October, 1970), 13.

p. 194, *l. 25* Morrie Ryskind, "Thou Art the Man," *Photo-play Journal*, 4 (May 1920), 23.

p. 195, *l. 18* Morrie Ryskind, "Explaining to Dmitri," *Nation*, 135 (August 10, 1932), 125; "Another Letter to Dmitri," 135 (November 16, 1932), 473.

p. 195, *l. 21* Morrie Ryskind, "Move Over, Mr. Frankenstein," *Nation*, 147 (September 10, 1938), 245.

p. 195, *l. 33* John Chapman, *New York Daily News*, August 6, 1940, p. 37.

p. 196, *l. 5* Walter Lippmann, *New York Herald Tribune*, April 4, 1933, p. 15.

p. 196, *l. 23* Reynolds, "Smoothie," p. 55.

p. 196, *l. 30* *Life*, 11 (September 15, 1941), 75; *Time*, 38 (September 15, 1941), 78–79; Frank Daugherty, "Director of 'My Man Godfrey' Prefers to 'Shoot from Cuff,'" *Christian Science Monitor*, March 21, 1941, p. 8.

p. 196, *l. 35* David O. Selznick, *Memo From: David O. Selznick*, New York, Avon, 1973, p. 147.

p. 196, *l. 40* Irene Thirer, *New York Post*, June 25, 1936, p. 12.

p. 196, *l. 42* Creelman, September 21, 1936.

p. 197, *l. 10* Richard Corliss, *The Hollywood Screenwriters*, New York, Discus–Avon, 1972, p. 281.

p. 197, *l. 15* Bosley Crowther, "A Gregorian Chat," *New York Times*, October 17, 1937, sec. 11, p. 4.

p. 198, *l. 29* Irene Thirer, *New York Post*, August 16, 1935, p. 6.

p. 198, *l. 32* Whitney Bolton, *New York Morning Telegraph*, March 6, 1952, p. 2.

p. 199, *l. 4* "Alice in Stageland," *Cosmopolitan*, 57 (October 1914), 702.

p. 199, *l. 6* Unidentified clipping, Alice Brady file, NYPL-PARC.

p. 199, *l. 10* Gregory La Cava, "The Fretting Frog," *Photoplay*, 48 (November 1935), 26–27, 99.

p. 199, *l. 25* Charles Higham, *Kate*, New York, Norton, 1975, p. 84.

p. 199, *l. 28* Edd Johnson, *New York World-Telegram*, November 5, 1938, p. 8.

p. 200, *l. 1* Reynolds, "Smoothie," p. 55.

p. 200, *l. 6* Crowther, p. 4.

p. 200, *l. 15* John Godfrey, "Powell—Practically in Person," *Screenland*, 32 (November 1930), 82.

p. 200, *l. 19* Elinor Hughes, *Famous Stars of Filmdom (Men)*, Boston, Page, 1932, p. 285.

p. 201, *l. 1* Joan Standish, "William Powell Weds Carole Lombard," *Movie Classic*, 1 (September 1931), 37.

p. 201, *l. 3* Reynolds, "Smoothie," p. 55.

p. 201, *l. 14* Morrie Ryskind and Eric Hatch, *My Man Godfrey*, in *Twenty Best Film Plays*, ed. John Gassner and Dudley Nichols, New York, Crown, 1943, p. 161.

p. 201, *l. 17* Ida Zeitlin, "Bill Powell Turns the Spotlight on Himself," *Motion Picture*, 50 (January 1936), 28.

p. 202, *l. 3* Reynolds, "Smoothie," p. 55.

p. 202, *l. 9* Ryskind and Hatch, p. 132.

p. 203, *l. 39* Ruth Biery, "The Girl Whom Hollywood Can't Understand," *Motion Picture*, 52 (August 1936), 85.

p. 203, *l. 42* Kyle Crichton, "Ex Leopard Lady," *Collier's*, 101 (May 7, 1938), 11.

p. 203, *l. 43* Carolyn Van Wyck, "Photoplay's Own Beauty Shop," *Photoplay*, 53 (August 1939), 59.

p. 204, *l. 3* Edwin Schallert, *Los Angeles Times*, September 9, 1932, pt. 1, p. 15.

p. 204, *l. 29* Leonard Maltin, *Carole Lombard*, New York, Pyramid, 1976, p. 35.

p. 204, *l. 34* William F. French, "Be Modern or Be a Wallflower . . Says Carole Lombard," *Motion Picture*, 50 (August 1935), 58.

p. 204, *l. 37* Richard Schickel, *The Men Who Made the Movies*, New York, Atheneum, 1975, pp. 110–11.

p. 205, *l. 30* Charles Reed Jones, *Breaking into the Movies*, New York, Unicorn Press, 1927, pp. 95–96.

p. 205, *l. 40* Crewe, p. 16.

p. 206, *l. 21* Maltin, p. 96.

p. 207, *l. 8* *New York Post*, September 12, 1936, p. 9.

p. 208, *l. 6* Ryskind and Hatch, p. 135.

p. 208, *l. 30* Arthur Pollock, *Brooklyn Eagle*, October 19, 1932, p. 8.

p. 208, *l. 32* DeWitt Bodeen, "Alice Brady," *Films in Review*, 17 (November 1966), 562.

p. 208, *l. 34* John Mason Brown, *New York Post*, October 19, 1932, p. 17.

p. 208, *l. 38*   Richard Watts, Jr., *New York Herald Tribune*, December 16, 1933, p. 10; John S. Cohen, Jr., *New York Sun*, December 16, 1933, p. 10.

p. 209, *l. 18*   *Brooklyn Eagle*, April 2, 1939, p. 10.

p. 209, *l. 27*   Hatch, p. 51.

p. 209, *l. 38*   Mischa Auer clip file, NYPL-PARC.

p. 210, *l. 16*   Carol Craig, "After the Powell Man," *Motion Picture*, 53 (February 1937), 45.

p. 212 *l. 1*   John Mason Brown, *New York Post*, September 16, 1933, p. 28.

p. 212, *l. 18*   Andre Sennwald, *New York Times*, March 30, 1935, p. 11.

p. 214, *l. 2*   Crewe, p. 16.

Chapter Nine

p. 217, *l. 1*   Theodore Dreiser, "Theodore Dreiser Picks the Six Worst Pictures of the Year," *New Movie*, 5 (January 1932), 27.

p. 217, *l. 18*   Nicholas von Hoffman, "Bring Back Whiskey, Turkeys and Loot," *More*, 6 (July–August, 1976), 43.

p. 218, *l. 10*   Ben Hecht, *A Child of the Century*, New York, Simon and Schuster, 1954, p. 118.

p. 218, *l. 14*   Archer Winsten, *New York Post*, October 31, 1936, p. 9.

p. 218, *l. 19*   Hecht, p. 120.

p. 218, *l. 31*   Ben Hecht, *Charlie*, New York, Harper, 1957, p. 69.

p. 219, *l. 15*   Frank Capra, *The Name above the Title*, New York, Macmillan, 1971, p. 134.

p. 219, *l. 28*   Hecht, *Charlie*, pp. 37, 135.

p. 220, *l. 11*   *New York Daily News*, February 22, 1936, p. 3.

p. 220, *l. 15*   *New York Mirror*, February 20, 1936, p. 3; *New York American*, February 20, 1936, p. 3.

p. 220, *l. 20*   *New York American*, February 21, 1936, p. 3.

p. 220, *l. 28*   *New York Mirror*, February 21, 1936, p. 4.

p. 220, *l. 29*   *New York Times*, February 21, 1936, p. 19.

p. 220, *l. 34*   *New York World-Telegram*, *New York Sun*, both February 20, 1936, p. 1.

p. 221, *l. 33*   J. Brooks Atkinson, *New York Times*, September 13, 1927, p. 37.

p. 221, *l. 36*   Peter Bogdanovich, *John Ford*, Berkeley, University of California Press, 1968, p. 52.

p. 222, *l. 22*   Groucho Marx and Richard J. Anobile, *The Marx Bros. Scrapbook*, New York, Star Books, 1976, p. 303.

p. 222, *l. 29*   Brooks Atkinson, *New York Times*, September 18, 1932, sec. 9, p. 1.

p. 222, *l. 32*   George Oppenheimer, *The View from the Sixties*, New York, McKay, 1966, p. 153.

p. 222, *l. 37*   M. S., *Film Dope*, no. 8, October 1975, p. 4.

p. 222, *l. 41*   Samuel Marx, *Mayer and Thalberg*, New York, Random House, 1975, p. 96.

p. 223, *l. 6*   Ben Hecht, "If Hollywood Is Dead or Dying as a Moviemaker Perhaps the Following Are Some of the Reasons," *Playboy*, 7 (November 1960), 133.

p. 223, *l. 11*   Anita Loos, *Kiss Hollywood Good-by*, New York, Viking, 1974, pp. 38, 40, 41.

p. 223, *l. 26*   Ronald Haver, *David O. Selznick's Hollywood*, New York, Knopf, 1980, p. 152; Peter Bogdanovich, *The Cinema of Howard Hawks*, New York, Museum of Modern Art, 1962, p. 13.

p. 223, *l. 31*   Bogdanovich, *The Cinema of Howard Hawks*, p. 13.

p. 223, *l. 41*   Joseph McBride, *Focus on Howard Hawks*, Englewood Cliffs, N.J., Prentice-Hall, 1972, p. 43.

p. 223, *l. 43*   The Academy Awards, television broadcast, NBC, April 8, 1975.

p. 224, *l. 18*   K. Owen, "Their Lieutenants," *Photoplay*, 9 (March 1916), 46.

p. 224, *l. 19*   *Brooklyn Eagle*, November 15, 1936, sec. C, p. 7.

p. 224, *l. 23*   Owen, p. 46.

p. 224, *l. 34*   Marguerite Tazelaar, *New York Herald Tribune*, December 20, 1936, sec. 7, p. 3.

p. 225, *l. 3*   Garson Kanin, *Tracy and Hepburn*, New York, Viking, 1971, p. 237.

p. 225, *l. 23*   *Standard School Broadcast Teacher's Manual, 1940–41*, Standard Oil of California, p. 48.

p. 227, *l. 14*   Loos, p. 168.

p. 227, *l. 21*   Larry Swindell, *Spencer Tracy*, New York and Cleveland, NAL–World, 1969, pp. 44, 55.

p. 227, *l. 34*   Bill Davidson, "Spencer Tracy," *Look*, 26 (January 30, 1962), 38.

p. 228, *l. 3*   Graham Greene, *The Pleasure-Dome*, London, Secker & Warburg, 1972, p. 10.

p. 228, *l. 9*   *New Statesman and Nation*, n.s. 12 (November 21, 1936), 811.

p. 228, *l. 12*   *Time*, 31 (April 25, 1938), 46; Ed Sullivan, "Actor's Actor," *Pictorial Review*, 39 (July 1938), 21.

p. 229, *l. 2*   Curtis F. Brown, *Jean Harlow*, New York, Pyramid, 1977, p. 67.

p. 229, *l. 22*   Richard Watts, Jr., *New York Herald Tribune*, November 7, 1932, p. 10; September 3, 1933, sec. 5, p. 1.

p. 230, *l. 35*   J. C. M., "Jean Harlow, Comédienne," *New Yorker*, 9 (October 28, 1933), 49.

p. 230, *l. 40*   Dwight Whitney, "They're Still Accepting That Invitation," *TV Guide*, 13 (February 27, 1965), 21.

p. 233, *l. 11*   Otis Ferguson, *The Film Criticism of Otis Ferguson*, Philadelphia, Temple University Press, 1971, p. 161.

p. 233, *l. 18*   Larry Swindell, *Screwball*, New York, Morrow, 1975, p. 224.

p. 233, *l. 23*   Harry T. Brundige, "The Bookkeeper Who 'Died' and Became an Actor," *Movie Classic*, 7 (January 1935), 56.

p. 233, *l. 32*   Brooks Atkinson, *New York Times*, November 1, 1932, p. 24.

p. 233, *l. 39*   "Charm Begins at Forty," *Literary Digest*, 12 (March 23, 1935), 19.

p. 234, *l. 7*   Swindell, *Screwball*, p. 148.

p. 235, *l. 5*   Bob Thomas, *Thalberg*, Garden City, N.Y., Doubleday, 1969, p. 198.

p. 235, *l. 11*   *Brooklyn Eagle*, March 15, 1936, sec. C, p. 5.

p. 235, *l. 15*   Pare Lorentz, *Lorentz on Film*, New York, Hopkinson and Blake, 1975, pp. 98, 86.

p. 235, *l. 29*   David Chierichetti, "Myrna Loy," *Film Fan Monthly*, no. 141, March 1973, p. 6.

p. 235, *l. 33*   Rob Edelman, "Myrna Loy's Star Still Shines Bright," *New York Times*, February 3, 1980, sec. 2, p. 23.

p. 236, *l. 12*   Alva Johnston, "Myrna Loy—From Asia to America in 100 Reels," *Woman's Home Companion*, 62 (May 1935), 13.

p. 238, *l. 2*   *New Statesman and Nation*, p. 811.

p. 238, *l. 22*   Karyn Kay, *Myrna Loy*, New York, Pyramid, 1977, p. 76.

p. 238, *l. 25*   Chierichetti, p. 9.

p. 239, *l. 9*   Ferguson, p. 161.

p. 240, *l. 1*   *New Statesman and Nation*, p. 811.

p. 240, *l. 16*   Vincent Canby, "How a 1936 Screwball Comedy Illumi-
                   nates Movie History," *New York Times*, February 1, 1981,
                   sec. 2, p. 15.

Chapter Ten

p. 245, *l. 2*   Richard Glatzer and John Raeburn, *Frank Capra*, Ann
                   Arbor, University of Michigan Press, 1975, p. 37.

p. 246, *l. 21*   *New York World-Telegram*, April 2, 1938, p. 10.

p. 247, *l. 15*   Robert Benchley, "Surprise!" *New Yorker*, 8 (May 7, 1932),
                   26.

p. 247 *l. 20*   Karl Kohrs, "I'm Glad I'm Homely," *Parade*, October 7,
                   1951, p. 23.

p. 248, *l. 10*   Scott Eyman, "'Wild Bill' William A. Wellman," *Focus on
                   Film*, no. 29, March, 1978, pp. 13–14.

p. 248, *l. 22*   Chris Chase, *New York Times*, July 31, 1981, p. C6.

p. 248, *l. 31*   Harpo Marx, *Harpo Speaks!* New York, Bernard Geis, 1961,
                   in unpaged gathering of photographs following p. 320.

p. 248, *l. 38*   Mark Van Doren, "Boy Bites Man," *Nation*, 145 (December
                   18, 1937), 696–97.

p. 249, *l. 26*   Marian Spitzer, *The Palace*, New York, Atheneum, 1969,
                   p. 104.

p. 250, *l. 4*   Jerry Stagg, *The Brothers Shubert*, New York, Ballantine,
                   1969, p. 227.

p. 250, *l. 11*   Burton Rascoe, *New York World-Telegram*, September 9,
                   1943, p. 22.

p. 250, *l. 30*   *A Code to Govern the Making of Motion Pictures*, Motion Pic-
                   ture Association of America, 1930–55, p. 4.

p. 251, *l. 9*   Richard Schickel, *The Men Who Made the Movies*, New York,
                   Atheneum, 1975, p. 218.

p. 251, *l. 10*   Ronald Haver, *David O. Selznick's Hollywood*, New York,
                   Knopf, 1980, p. 214.

p. 251, *l. 18*   Ben Hecht, *Charlie*, New York, Harper, 1957, p. 159.

p. 251, *l. 22*   Katharine Best, "Horseplay into Photoplay," *Stage*, 15
                   (November 1937), 63–66.

p. 251, *l. 25*   Otis Ferguson, *The Film Criticism of Otis Ferguson*, Phil-
                   adelphia, Temple University Press, 1971, p. 257.

p. 251, *l. 30*   David O. Selznick, *Memo From: David O. Selznick*, New
                   York, Avon, 1973, pp. 181–82.

p. 251, *l. 33*   Richard Corliss, *The Hollywood Screenwriters*, New York,
                   Discus–Avon, 1972, pp. 87–88.

p. 251, *l. 39*   Selznick, p. 104.

p. 251, *l. 42*   Ben Hecht, *A Child of the Century*, New York, Simon and Schuster, 1954, p. 488.

p. 252, *l. 1*   Haver, p. 217.

p. 252, *l. 12*   Carol Leh, *Raleigh News and Observer*, December 21, 1952, sec. 4, p. 8.

p. 252, *l. 15*   James H. Street, "Nothing Sacred," *Cosmopolitan*, 103 (October 1937), 165.

p. 252, *l. 19*   Ben Hecht, "Elegy for Wonderland," *Esquire*, 51 (March 1959), 60.

p. 252, *l. 20*   Hecht, *Charlie*, p. 3.

p. 252, *l. 22*   Bob Thomas, *Selznick*, Garden City, N.Y., Doubleday, 1970, pp. 118, 120.

p. 252, *l. 25*   Ring Lardner, Jr., *The Lardners*, New York, Harper & Row, 1976, p. 253; Kenneth Geist, "Trials and Traumas: Ring Lardner Jr.," in Corliss, pp. 134–135; Aaron Latham, "The Lardners: A Writing Dynasty," *New York Times Magazine*, August 22, 1971, p. 45.

p. 252, *l. 29*   Lardner, p. 253.

p. 252, *l. 33*   Curtis Lee Hanson, "William Wellman, A Memorable Visit with an Elder Statesman," *Cinema* (U.S.), 3 (July 1966), 24.

p. 252, *l. 36*   Julian Fox, "A Man's World," pt. 1, *Films and Filming*, 19 (March 1973), 35.

p. 253, *l. 4*   Schickel, p. 208; Zanuck, quoted in Mel Gussow, *Don't Say Yes Until I Finish Talking*, Garden City, N.Y., Doubleday, 1971, p. 49.

p. 253, *l. 20*   Eyman, p. 13.

p. 253, *l. 23*   William A. Wellman, *A Short Time for Insanity*, New York, Hawthorne, 1974, p. 107.

p. 253, *l. 35*   Haver, p. 206.

p. 254, *l. 2*   Selznick, p. 155.

p. 254, *l. 23*   Best, p. 63.

p. 254, *l. 38*   Ferguson, p. 78.

p. 254, *l. 40*   Selznick, p. 125.

p. 255, *l. 1, 3*   Alexander Woollcott, *New York World*, March 30, 1926, p. 13; Alan Dale, *New York American*, March 30, 1926, p. 8.

p. 255, *l. 7*   Elisabeth Goldbeck, "Tired of Being Himself," *Motion Picture Classic*, 33 (March 1931), 71.

p. 255, *l. 34*   John Paxton, "The Militant March," *Stage*, 16 (May 15, 1939), 23.

p. 255, *l. 35*   Donald Ogden Stewart, *By a Stroke of Luck!* New York, Paddington Press, 1975, p. 183.

p. 256, *l. 9*   *New York World-Telegram*, May 14, 1938, p. 3.

p. 256, *l. 17*   Richard Corliss, *Talking Pictures*, New York, Penguin, 1975, p. 17.

p. 256, *l. 40*   *Nothing Sacred* pressbook, NYPL-PARC.

p. 257, *l. 3*   Haver, pp. 218, 196.

p. 257, *l. 20*   Larry Swindell, *Screwball*, New York, Morrow, 1975, pp. 224, 148.

p. 258, *l. 11*   Hecht, *Charlie*, p. 83.

p. 259, *l. 11*   *Nothing Sacred* photographs, NYPL-PARC.

p. 259, *l. 36*   Street, p. 165.

p. 261, *l. 1*   Christopher Finch, *Norman Rockwell, 332 Magazine Covers*, New York, Abbeville–Random House, 1979, pp. 209, 58.

p. 261, *l. 30*   Dan Thomas, *New York World-Telegram*, December 12, 1934, p. 32.

p. 262, *l. 10*   Will Rogers, *The Autobiography of Will Rogers*, Boston, Houghton Mifflin, 1949, p. 367.

p. 262, *l. 18*   Charles Winninger, "Tripling in Brass Buttons," *Stage*, 12 (December 1934), 47.

p. 264, *l. 27*   Mike Steen, *Hollywood Speaks!* New York, Putnam's, 1974, p. 165.

p. 264, *l. 31*   Fox, pt. 1, pp. 40, 39.

p. 265, *l. 26*   Hecht, *A Child of the Century*, p. 4.

p. 266, *l. 33*   Katharine Best, "Ha! The Triumph of Evil," *Stage*, 15 (January 1938), 64, 66–67.

p. 266, *l. 38*   Basil Wright, *Spectator*, 160 (February 18, 1938), 271.

p. 266, *l. 42*   Peter Galway, *New Statesman and Nation*, n.s. 15 (February 12, 1938), 248.

p. 267, *l. 8*   Wright, p. 271.

p. 267, *l. 25*   Hecht, *A Child of the Century*, p. 67.

p. 268, *l. 18*   *Literary Digest*, 1 (December 18, 1937), 34.

p. 268, *l. 28*   Schickel, p. 228.

Chapter Eleven

p. 273, *l. 13*   Letters from Cowley (November 4, 1981), Blotner (December 4, 1981), and Meriwether (November 24, 1981).

p. 273, *l. 16*   James B. Meriwether and Michael Millgate, *Lion in the Garden*, New York, Random House, 1968, pp. 61–62.

p. 273, *l. 21*   Carlos Baker, *Hemingway and His Critics*, New York, Hill and Wang, 1961, p. 37.

p. 274, *l. 9*   Andrew Sarris, *The American Cinema*, New York, Dutton, 1968, p. 54.

p. 274, *l. 11*   Joseph McBride, *Focus on Howard Hawks*, Englewood Cliffs, N.J., Prentice-Hall, 1972, p. 24.

p. 274, *l. 20*   Andrew Sarris, *Interviews with Film Directors*, Indianapolis, Bobbs-Merrill, 1967, p. 190.

p. 274, *l. 23*   Peter Bogdanovich, *The Cinema of Howard Hawks*, New York, Museum of Modern Art, 1962, p. 5.

p. 274, *l. 26*   Baker, p. 29.

p. 274, *l. 33*   Richard Schickel, *The Men Who Made the Movies*, New York, Atheneum, 1975, p. 113.

p. 274, *l. 37*   Peter John Dyer, "Sling Low the Lamps," in McBride, p. 78.

p. 274, *l. 40*   Jacques Rivette, "The Genius of Howard Hawks," in McBride, pp. 70–77.

p. 274, *l. 41*   Olivier Eyquem, "Howard Hawks, Ingénieur," *Positif*, no. 195/196, July–August, 1977, pp. 6–7.

p. 275, *l. 5*   Andrew Sarris, "The World of Howard Hawks," in McBride, pp. 35–64; Henri Agel, *Les Grands Cinéastes Que Je Propose*, Paris, Éditions du Cerf, 1967; Jean-Claude Missiaen, *Howard Hawks*, Paris, Éditions Universitaires, 1966; Michel Ciment, "Hawks et l'écrit," *Positif*, no. 195/196, July–August, 1977, pp. 43–49.

p. 275, *l. 10*   McBride, p. 35; Bogdanovich, p. 5.

p. 275, *l. 13*   Peter Wollen, *Signs and Meaning in the Cinema*, Bloomington, Indiana University Press, 1972, p. 84.

p. 275, *l. 18*   Pauline Kael, *I Lost It at the Movies*, Boston, Atlantic–Little, Brown, 1965, pp. 304–5; Manny Farber, "Howard Hawks," in McBride, pp. 28–34.

p. 275, *l. 22*   John Belton, "Howard Hawks," in *The Hollywood Professionals*, London, Tantivy Press, and New York, Barnes, 1974, 3: 10.

p. 275, *l. 23*   "Homage à Hawks," *Cinéma*, no. 231, March 1978, p. 62.

p. 275, *l. 28*   McBride, p. 47.

p. 275, *l. 35*   Ibid., p. 71.

p. 275, *l. 43*   Robin Wood, *Howard Hawks*, Garden City, N.Y., Double-day, 1968, p. 82.

p. 276, *l. 2*   Sarris, *Interviews with Film Directors*, p. 191.

p. 276, *l. 27*   V. F. Perkins, "Comedies," *Movie*, no. 5, December 1962, p. 22.

p. 276, *l. 32*   Eric Bentley, *Let's Get a Divorce! and Other Plays*, New York, Hill and Wang, 1958, p. xvii.

p. 276, *l. 37*   Perkins, p. 22.

p. 276, *l. 41*   Wood, p. 58.

p. 277, *l. 24*   Jean-Louis Comolli, Jean Narboni, and Bertrand Tavernier, "Entretien avec Howard Hawks," *Cahiers du Cinéma*, no. 192, July–August, 1967, p. 21.

p. 277, *l. 32*   *Saturday Review of Literature*, 10 (December 2, 1933), 315.

p. 277, *l. 42*   Olga Celeste, "A Leopard on the Spot," *New York Times*, March 6, 1938, sec. 11, p. 4.

p. 278, *l. 6*   Hagar Wilde, "Bringing Up Baby," *Collier's*, 99 (April 10, 1937), 21.

p. 278, *l. 34*   Michel Ciment, "Entretien avec Howard Hawks," *Positif*, no. 195/196, July–August, 1977, p. 54.

p. 278, *l. 39*   Bogdanovich, p. 18.

p. 279, *l. 17*   Virginia T. Lane, "How Grant Took Hollywood," *Photoplay*, 52 (May 1938), 22.

p. 279, *l. 20*   Cary Grant, "What It Means to Be a Star," *Films and Filming*, 7 (July 1961), 13.

p. 279, *l. 26*   Charles Higham, *Kate*, New York, Norton, 1975, p. 75.

p. 279, *l. 41*   Ibid., p. 76.

p. 279, *l. 42*   *Variety*, November 21, 1933, p. 3; Higham, p. 90.

p. 280, *l. 6*   Cary Grant, "Archie Leach," pt. 1, *Ladies' Home Journal*, 80 (Winter 1963), 142.

p. 280, *l. 8*   Roy Newquist, *A Special Kind of Magic*, Chicago, Rand, McNally, 1967, p. 81.

p. 280, *l. 12*   Pauline Kael, "The Man from Dream City," *New Yorker*, 51 (July 14, 1975), 42.

p. 280, *l. 27*   Basil Wright, *Spectator*, 160 (April 8, 1938), 627.

p. 280, *l. 29*   Edith Winter McGinnis, *St. Nicholas*, 65 (April 1938), 42.

p. 280, *l. 38*   Joan Barthel, "Quartet of Queens," *Life*, 70 (February 19, 1971), 68.

p. 280, *l. 41*   Comolli et al., p. 68.

p. 280, *l. 43*   Higham, p. 87.

p. 281, *l. 31*   Bogdanovich, pp. 16–17.

p. 282, *l. 21*   James Harvey, "Irene Dunne Interviewed," *Film Comment*, 16 (January–February, 1980), 30.

p. 283, *l. 22*   *Life*, 4 (February 28, 1938), 22.

p. 283, *l. 33*   Lupton A. Wilkinson and J. Bryan III, "The Hepburn Story," pt. 2, *Saturday Evening Post*, 214 (December 6, 1941), 87.

p. 283, *l. 35*   Adela Rogers St. Johns, "The Private Life of Katharine Hepburn," *Liberty*, 11 (January 6, 1934), 20; Wilkinson and Bryan, pt. 3, 214 (December 13, 1941), 97.

p. 284, *l. 1*   Wilkinson and Bryan, pt. 3, p. 100.

p. 284, *l. 5*   Regina Crewe, *New York American*, March 10, 1933, p. 11.

p. 284, *l. 12*   George Jean Nathan, "Susan Minus God," *Newsweek*, 13 (April 10, 1939), 28.

p. 284, *l. 15*   Frank S. Nugent, "A Purely Personal Reaction," *New York Times*, April 18, 1937, sec. 11, p. 3.

p. 284, *l. 20*   Alan Jackson, "Hepburn from A to B," *Cinema Arts*, 1 (July 1937), 96.

p. 285, *l. 1*   J. C. Furnas, *New York Herald Tribune*, September 17, 1933, sec. 5, p. 3.

p. 285, *l. 5*   Ruth Suckow, "Hollywood Gods and Goddesses," *Harper's*, 173 (July 1936), 196.

p. 285, *l. 20*   Homer Dickens, *The Films of Katharine Hepburn*, New York, Citadel Press, 1971, p. 95.

p. 286, *l. 40*   Robert Hogan and Michael J. O'Neill, *Joseph Holloway's Abbey Theatre*, Carbondale, Southern Illinois University Press, 1967, p. 253.

p. 288, *l. 9*   Bogdanovich, pp. 17–18.

p. 288, *l. 31*   Vernon Scott, *San Francisco Examiner*, January 2, 1978, p. 25.

p. 288, *l. 40*   *Boston Herald*, November 15, 1925, sec. D, p. 5.

p. 289, *l. 2*   George E. Wellwarth and Alfred G. Brooks, *Max Reinhardt, 1873–1973*, Binghamton, N.Y., Max Reinhardt Archive, 1973, p. 47.

p. 294, *l. 5*   Michael Goodwin and Naomi Wise, "An Interview with Howard Hawks," *Take One*, 3 (November–December, 1971), 21.

p. 294, *l. 9*   John Kobal, "Howard Hawks," pt. 2, *Film* (London), ser. 2, no. 15, June 1974, p. 5.

p. 294, *l. 13*   McBride, p. 53.

p. 296, *l. 8*   Wood, pp. 68, 70–71, 103–4.

Chapter Twelve

p. 299, *l. 2*   *New York Times*, December 3, 1939, sec. 9, pt. 2, p. 8.

p. 300, *l. 2*   Anthony Bower, *New Statesman and Nation*, n.s. 19 (February 10, 1940), 172.

p. 300, *l. 3*   Graham Greene, *The Pleasure-Dome*, London, Secker & Warburg, 1972, p. 270.

p. 300, *l. 17*   Sheridan Morley, *Marlene Dietrich*, London, Elm Tree Books–Hamish Hamilton, 1976, p. 87.

p. 300, *l. 30*   Greene, p. 270.

p. 300, *l. 37*   William Boehnel, *New York World-Telegram*, November 30, 1939, p. 15.

p. 301, *l. 3*   Jerry Wald and Richard Macaulay, *The Best Pictures, 1939–1940*, New York, Dodd, Mead, 1940, p. 291.

p. 301, *l. 10*   Howard Barnes, *New York Herald Tribune*, November 30, 1939, p. 17.

p. 301, *l. 14*   Joe Pasternak, *Easy the Hard Way*, New York, Putnam's, 1956, pp. 140, 201.

p. 301, *l. 32*   Ibid., p. 6.

p. 301, *l. 35*   William A. H. Birnie, *New York World-Telegram*, February 25, 1936, p. 1; Pasternak, p. 157.

p. 301, *l. 40*   Pasternak, p. 301.

p. 302, *l. 4*   Charles Higham, *Marlene*, New York, Norton, 1977, p. 189.

p. 302, *l. 7*   Richard Griffith, *Marlene Dietrich, Image and Legend*, New York, Museum of Modern Art, 1959, p. 11.

p. 302, *l. 15*   Robert Easton, *Max Brand, the Big "Westerner,"* Norman, University of Oklahoma Press, 1970, pp. 265, 143.

p. 302, *l. 42*   Ibid., p. 144.

p. 303, *l. 9*   *Variety*, June 21, 1932, p. 14.

p. 303, *l. 21*   Max Brand, *Destry Rides Again*, New York, Dodd, Mead, 1930, p. 296.

p. 303, *l. 25*   Pasternak, p. 200.

p. 303, *l. 30*   *New York Times*, August 9, 1939, p. 15.

p. 303, *l. 39*   W. C. Fields, *W. C. Fields by Himself*, New York, Warner, 1974, p. 420.

p. 304, *l. 1*   Pasternak, p. 120.

p. 304, *l. 12*   Frank S. Nugent, *New York Times*, August 6, 1937, p. 21.

p. 304, *l. 13*   Kenneth L. Geist, *People Will Talk*, New York, Scribner's, 1978, p. 49.

p. 304, *l. 20*   Ibid., p. 45.

p. 304, *l. 22*   Richard Meryman, *Mank*, New York, Morrow, 1978, p. 146.

p. 304, *l. 28*   B. R. C., *New York Times*, December 5, 1936, p. 16.

p. 304, *l. 40*   "6 Pioneers," *Action*, 7 (November–December, 1972), 20–21.

p. 305, *l. 13*   Typed press release, George Marshall clip file, NYPL-PARC.

p. 307, *l. 16*   Wald and Macaulay, p. 292.

p. 307, *l. 29*   James Reid, "Shake Hands with an Ex-Villain," *Silver Screen*, 11 (July 1941), 94.

p. 307, *l. 32*   B. R. Crisler, *New York Times*, October 10, 1937, sec. 11, p. 6.

p. 307, *l. 37*   Donlevy, quoted Reid, p. 45.

p. 308, *l. 9*   Greene, pp. 270–71.

p. 310, *l. 3*   "Education Note," *New York Herald Tribune*, May 1, 1938, sec. 6, p. 4.

p. 310, *l. 14*   M. B., *New York Times*, December 26, 1935, p. 21.

p. 310, *l. 24*   J. Brooks Atkinson, *New York Times*, February 13, 1932, p. 23.

p. 311, *l. 2*   Wallace Markfield, "Somebody Should Have Put Their Names in Lights," *New York Times*, April 18, 1976, p. 15.

p. 311, *l. 8*   Marguerite Tazelaar, *New York Herald Tribune*, November 1, 1935, p. 15.

p. 311, *l. 28*   Brand, p. 51.

p. 311, *l. 36*   Dore Schary, *Heyday*, Boston, Little, Brown, 1979, p. 37.

p. 311, *l. 38*   Thornton Delehanty, *New York World-Telegram*, February 26, 1938, p. 10.

p. 312, *l. 9*   Billy Gilbert, letter, *Films in Review*, 20 (June–July, 1969), 385–86.

p. 313, *l. 14*   Josef von Sternberg, *Fun in a Chinese Laundry*, London, Secker & Warburg, 1966, pp. 171, 337.

p. 313, *l. 15*   Charles Silver, *Marlene Dietrich*, New York, Pyramid, 1974, p. 92.

p. 313, *l. 19*   *Life*, 7 (October 9, 1939), 12–15.

p. 313, *l. 33*   Griffith, p. 5.

p. 313, *l. 38*   "The Most Famous Legs in History Lose Their Job," *Life*, 4 (January 3, 1938), 18.

p. 314, *l. 3*   Herman G. Weinberg, *Josef von Sternberg*, New York, Dutton, 1967, p. 51.

p. 314, *l. 11*   Katherine Albert, "She Threatens Garbo's Throne," *Photoplay*, 39 (December 1930), 60, 140–41.

p. 314, *l. 14*   Sternberg, pp. 233–34.

p. 314, *l. 21*   Ibid., p. 324.

p. 314, *l. 29*   Pare Lorentz, *Lorentz on Film*, New York, Hopkinson and Blake, 1975, p. 67.

p. 314, *l. 42*   Richard Watts, Jr., *New York Herald Tribune*, March 6, 1931, p. 19; "Svengali and Trilby," *New York Herald Tribune*, September 23, 1934, sec. 5, p. 1.

p. 315, *l. 8*   Homer Dickens, *The Films of Marlene Dietrich*, New York, Citadel, 1968, p. 17; Cal York, "The Monthly Broadcast of Hollywood Goings-On!" *Photoplay*, 40 (October 1931), 42; John Baxter, *The Cinema of Josef von Sternberg*, London, Zwemmer, and New York, Barnes, 1971, p. 99.

p. 315, *l. 16*   Howard Hall, "Hall-Marks and Re-Marks," *Cinema Digest*, 3 (April 3, 1933), 3.

p. 315, *l. 22*   Liza, "Unlucky Lady," *Silver Screen*, 6 (June 1936), 64.

p. 315, *l. 32*   Frank S. Nugent, *New York Times*, April 13, 1936, p. 15.

p. 315, *l. 42*   Marlene Dietrich, *Nehmt nur mein Leben . . . Reflexionen*, Munich, C. Bertelsmann, 1979, p. 126.

p. 316, *l. 31*   Silver, p. 92.

p. 317, *l. 7*   Lisa Appignanesi, *The Cabaret*, London, Studio Vista, 1975, p. 145.

p. 317, *l. 23*   Rex Reed, "Dietrich: 'I Am the Queen of Ajax,'" *New York Times*, October 22, 1967, sec. 2, p. 11.

p. 318, *l. 6*   Regina Crewe, *New York American*, July 5, 1935, p. 8.

p. 318, *l. 33*   Wald and Macaulay, p. 293.

p. 319, *l. 42*   Peter Bogdanovich, "Th' Respawnsibility of Bein' J . . . Jimmy Stewart. Gosh!" *Esquire*, 66 (July 1966), 106.

p. 320, *l. 8*   Maude Cheatham, "Jimmy to You," *Silver Screen*, 6 (October 1936), 81.

p. 320, *l. 22*   Kyle Crichton, "Blade of Beverly Hills," *Collier's*, 100 (October 9, 1937), 26.

p. 320, *l. 24*   Alva Johnston, "The Quest for New Stars," *Woman's Home Companion*, 64 (October 1937), 32.

p. 322, *l. 5*   Marlene Dietrich, *Marlene Dietrich's ABC*, Garden City, N.Y., Doubleday, 1962, p. 21.

p. 322, *l. 8*   Dietrich, *Nehmt nur mein Leben*, p. 233.

p. 322, *l. 28*   Dennis John Hall, "Box Office Drawl," *Films and Filming*, 19 (December 1972), 24–25; Bogdanovich, p. 104.

p. 322, *l. 33*   Otis Ferguson, *The Film Criticism of Otis Ferguson*, Philadelphia, Temple University Press, 1971, p. 224.

p. 322, *l. 38*   Louise Sweeney, "Jimmy Stewart, Hollywood Didn't Invent Him," *Christian Science Monitor*, February 19, 1980, pp. B2–B3.

p. 327, *l. 10*   *The Public Papers and Addresses of Franklin D. Roosevelt*, New York, Macmillan, 1941, 6: 410–11; New York, Random House, 1938, 5: 235.

p. 327, *l. 24*   Greene, p. 218.

Published Screenplays
and Original Sources

Brand, Max, *Destry Rides Again*, New York, Dodd, Mead, 1930. Serialized as "Twelve Peers," *Western Story Magazine*, beginning February 1, 1930.

Burman, Ben Lucien, *Steamboat Round the Bend*, New York, Farrar & Rinehart, 1933. Serialized as "Steamboat 'Round the Bend," *Pictorial Review*, 34 (September 1933), 8–11, 26–27; 35 (October 1933), 10–12, 26–39; (November 1933), 14–15, 28–35; (December 1933), 20–21, 49–54, 62; (January 1934), 20–21, 37–38, 41–43; (February 1934), 20–21, 54–56.

Hatch, Eric, *My Man Godfrey*, Boston, Little, Brown, 1935. Serialized as "Irene, the Stubborn Girl," *Liberty*, 12 (May 11, 1935), 6–12; (May 18), 28–33, 36–37; (May 25), 30–35; (June 1), 50–57; (June 8), 52–58; (June 15), 56–59.

Jackson, Felix, Gertrude Purcell, and Henry Myers, *Destry Rides Again*, in *The Best Pictures, 1939–1940*, ed. Jerry Wald and Richard Macaulay, New York, Dodd, Mead, 1940, pp. 289–330; credits, p. 385. (This version is very different in its details from the finished film.)

Kalmar, Bert, Harry Ruby, Arthur Sheekman, and Nat Perrin, *Duck Soup*, in *The Four Marx Brothers in Monkey Business and Duck Soup*, New York, Simon and Schuster, 1972, pp. 94–183.

Kelland, Clarence Budington, "Opera Hat," *American Magazine*, 119 (April 1935), 12–15, 86–94; (May 1935), 18–21, 148–55; (June 1935), 64–67, 166–74; 120 (July 1935), 42–45, 114–20; (August 1935), 62–65, 148–51, 154; (September 1935), 60–63, 142–46.

Ryskind, Morrie, and Eric Hatch, *My Man Godfrey*, in *Twenty Best Film Plays*, ed. John Gassner and Dudley Nichols, New York, Crown, 1943, pp. 131–79.

Street, James H., "Nothing Sacred," *Cosmopolitan*, 103 (October 1937), 46–47, 161–65.

West, Mae, *Diamond Lil*, New York, Macaulay, 1932.

Wilde, Hagar, "Bringing Up Baby," *Collier's*, 99 (April 10, 1937), 20–22, 70.

Wilson, Harry Leon, *Ruggles of Red Gap*, Garden City, N.Y., Doubleday, Page, 1915. Serialized, *The Saturday Evening Post*, 187 (December 26, 1914), 3–5, 34–36; (January 2, 1915), 17–19, 49–50; (January 9, 1915), 16–19, 46; (January 16, 1915), 18–21, 35–38; (January 25, 1915), 16–18, 45–46; (January 30, 1915), 19–21, 37–38; (February 6, 1915), 18–21, 32–37; (February 13, 1915), 19–21, 51–54; (February 20, 1915), 17–20, 36–38; (February 27, 1915), 17–19, 25–27.

General Index

Adamson, Joe, 64, 75, 82, 91
Agee, James, 26, 64
Agel, Henri, 275
Ager, Cecelia, 36
Alberni, Luis, 63
Albertson, Frank, 286
Alias the Deacon, 120, 121
Allez-Oop, 88
Ameche, Don, 307
Ames, Adrienne, 93
Ames, Robert, 203
Anderson, Eddie, 124
Anderson, Maxwell, 75, 210, 278, 307
Andrews, Stanley, 185
Animal Crackers (play), 58, 60, 64, 65, 68, 78, 194
Anobile, Richard J., 64, 75
Appignanesi, Lisa, 317
Arbuckle, Fatty, 13, 25
Arbus, Diane, 33
Arce, Hector, 60, 65, 81
Armetta, Henry, 62–63
Armstrong, Robert, 204
Artaud, Antonin, 56, 60, 78, 79
Arthur, Jean, 164, 177–78, 180, 229, 246; *illus.*, 181
Asta, 295

Astor, Gertrude, 163
Astor, Mary, 203, 231
Atkinson, Brooks, 78, 148–49, 221, 222, 233, 310
Auer, Mischa, 209–10, 311, 316, 318
Axt, William, 225–26
Ayres, Lew, 113, 318

Bacall, Lauren, 274
Bacon, Irving, 290
Baker, George Pierce, 221, 310
Baker, Kenny, 64–65
Bakshy, Alexander, 26
Bancroft, George, 167
Banton, Travis, 206–7
Barbier, George, 117
Barnes, Howard, 301
Barnes, T. Roy, 102
Barnett, Vincent, 324
Barry, Philip, 185, 203
Barrymore, John, 200, 204–5, 223, 255, 284, 297, 315
Barrymore, Lionel, 223, 227
Barty, Billy, 248–49
Baxter, John, 315
Baxter, Warner, 164, 203, 235–36
Beatty, Jerome, 112, 172
Beavers, Louise, 41

Index of Films